THE
EXCEPTION

The Story of Ashland Oil
& Refining Company

by
Otto J. Scott

THE EXCEPTION

The Story of Ashland Oil & Refining Company

by
Otto J. Scott

McGraw-Hill Book Company

New York   Toronto   London   Sydney   Johannesburg

THE EXCEPTION
The Story of Ashland Oil & Refining Company

Library of Congress Catalog Card Number: 68–54938

First Edition

Acknowledgments

In particular, the author wishes to thank Georgia Monroe Blazer, Phyllis Geyer, Dr. Joseph Massie (who graciously provided much of the material on Swiss Oil and its management, as well as the loan of his taped interviews with Paul G. Blazer, Edward McDonald and J. Fred Miles); Floyd R. Newman and James Weeks; James Breuil, Earle M. Craig, Edward S. Dabney, J. Robert Fisher, William C. Freeman, Angus W. McDonald, Ross K. Shoolroy, Edward W. Seaton, James Vandeveer—members of the board of directors; Lillian Seale (whose skill at proofreading is unexcelled); John Hess, senior editor at McGraw-Hill, who patiently endured many vicissitudes and whose advice and suggestions were both astute and kindly; Ashland Oil officers Rexford S. Blazer, Orin Atkins, Robert Yancey, Everett Wells, Robert McCowan, William Seaton, Carlton D. Weaver and John Hall; Lucile Blazer, Katherine Agee Atkins, Mary Wells, Suzanne Seaton, Ann Hall and other wives of Ashland Oil men; members of the Ashland community itself including Janet Humphrey, Henrietta Hager, Henderson Dysard, and all others who contributed their recollections, and, of course, Ann Barney Scott, without whose assistance and encouragement this book could not have been created.

Dedicated to those whose unrecognized efforts contributed toward the triumphs and accomplishments celebrated here— without whom these successes would not have occurred.

Foreword

Centuries ago, generations of effort went into building great Cathedrals: monuments to the soaring thought and faith of men.

Today, men construct more subtle vehicles of progress that seem —to the unthinking—to have animation and power of their own. The greatest of these modern marvels of science and technology are huge international enterprises known as U.S. corporations.

Many of these are oil companies; most were built on successive discoveries of crude oil. How one survived and grew as an exception to this pattern is the theme of this book.

The inspiration came from the senior management, who wanted in particular to pay honor to one in their midst who gave the major part of his life and attention to this undertaking: Paul Garrett Blazer.

But Mr. Blazer wanted not a story of himself, but a description of the enterprise that would be at once human and constructive.

How well this task has been performed is not for the worker to assess. Let it suffice to say that all the persons engaged in the tasks described; the participants in the events; their wives, children and friends; the members of the petroleum industry and the men of Wall Street; acquaintances, employees and directors alike spoke with candor and kindness. The records of the company were made available. No facts have been withheld.

In this chronicle, 56 years are compressed and thousands of careers. All the persons described are seen mainly at their work. Their individual kindnesses and warmth are seldom mentioned. It should be borne in mind, therefore, that this is essentially a story of effort long sustained, and challenge overcome.

Any deficiency or inadequacy in this description is mine alone.

Otto J. Scott

Contents

Illustrations

(Continued)

Illustrations (continued)

Section One—Origins

1910–1924

There is a tendency in some quarters today to assume that mystery has departed from the world, and that all men can be explained. Nothing could be more erroneous. The mystery of personality: of why some men can overcome all challenges while others are invariably defeated, remains, as ever, inexplicable.

Concatenation—the links between a chain of events—[1] is still a conundrum. For instance, no observer, no matter how astute, could possibly have foreseen how the destinies of the Swiss Oil Company and its energetic promoter, J. Fred Miles, would be affected by a chance meeting of two young college friends at a nightclub in Chicago in 1917—but they were. Not only was the course of the Swiss Oil Company and the destiny of J. Fred Miles changed by that chance meeting, but one of those young men proceeded, from that point in time, to so alter and influence the lives of thousands of persons, through methods both visible and invisible, that the results continue today.

Such is the mystery of genius in the world.

John Fred Miles, a stocky, square-faced young man, was born in Missouri and raised in Oklahoma; inhaled the scent of oil during his childhood and never lost the feeling of pleasure and excitement it evoked in him. He grew up to work in the oil fields; drilled

[1] According to the definition in the Second International Edition of the Webster Merriam Dictionary (unabridged).

1

his first independent well on Bird Creek, Oklahoma, in 1907, the year the territory was admitted as a new state in the union. In later years, the names of the Indian lands where Miles worked and sought his fortune would roll off his tongue like so many bells: ". . . the Cherokee, the Creek and the Seminole *nations*," he would say. It was rumored he had Indian blood; perhaps this gave him his ability to make these names sing.[2]

By 1910, Miles advanced to the stage where two other men joined forces with him to create an Oklahoma corporation: the Swiss Drilling Company. This was a considerable distance from where he started, an independent operator, gambling his resources all the way down to his shoelaces.

That same year, 1910, young Paul Blazer received a wire from the Curtis Publishing Company, saying they had a possible opening and inviting him to Philadelphia, all expenses paid, to discuss it. Blazer was then finishing his second year at William & Vashti College, a new school his family helped found at Aledo, Illinois.[3] From the time he had been a high school student, Blazer, in com-

[2] Many other Oklahomans shared Miles' warmth toward Indians. In fact, the citizens of the territory originally voted to have the new state named Sequoya, after the inventor of the Cherokee syllabary, but Congress, for reasons forgotten, ruled otherwise.

[3] Jacob Blazer, his wife and 11 children arrived in the U. S. from Baden, Germany in the 1780s. Their descendants are now numerous enough to hold a several hundred person reunion every August at Gallipolis, Ohio. The family settled first in Virginia; moved to western Pennsylvania; some moved again to southeastern Ohio. In 1832 James Blazer, given $600 by his father, located a suitable property in McDonough County, Illinois, where his parents, brothers and sisters, moving by covered wagons, joined him. Among his sons was David N. Blazer, Paul's father. A onetime schoolmaster, David Blazer bought the *New Boston Times* at New Boston, Ill. (where Paul was born); he merged it with the *Aledo Record* at the county seat of Mercer, to make the *Aledo Times Record,* still published there weekly. David was succeeded as editor-publisher by son Fred who died in 1921; Fred was succeeded by youngest son Herschel who died in 1967. The newspaper made the Blazers important politically, in a quiet way, in Illinois.

William & Vashti College was launched in 1908; Paul Blazer was in the first class. The school did not survive the exodus of young men in World War I. The site is now a military academy.

mon with many other boys of the period, sold magazine subscriptions. In pre-World War I America, boys all over the country actually helped pay their school expenses through such sales. In time, it became a national joke. But magazines, in the reading days before movies, radio or television, were in their glory. Muckrakers stalked across the mental landscape of the nation, arousing indignation, creating issues and building images of villainy or heroism (mainly villainy) for the nation. The publishers who employed these movers and shakers operated in an equivalent aura of influence and importance.

Blazer, a football star in high school and a track star in both high school and college, was precocious in many respects. His father, confronted with a six-footer who graduated from high school at the age of sixteen, insisted he attend business school for a year until the new college opened. Once in William & Vashti, Paul shot up another inch and a half; discovered he had such an aptitude for mathematics he could race through his trigonometry texts as though they were novels. He found most other physical sciences easy to grasp also, but shied from chemistry because of its fearsome terminology. "I didn't think I could memorize or even get through such a conglomeration," he said later. "They were still naming chemicals after people and things then; there was

Paul Blazer clearing the pole at 5′ 3½″ at the Mercer County, Illinois' High School Meet. (May 1906)

Paul Blazer with athletic medals.
(May 1907)

no logic to its terms. Later, when the chemists began to use built-up words that were self-explanatory, I found it much easier."

In addition to his physical and mental attainments, Blazer was the most successful magazine salesman in the area. While still in high school, which means sometime between the ages of twelve and sixteen, his business became so large he hired a full-time adult secretary, and paid her wages himself.[4] Eventually, while still attending William & Vashti, he wrote Curtis a letter outlining some of his innovations: a youthful exhibition of pride, but understandable under the circumstances. Curtis, after checking on the author of the letter, decided it would be smarter to adopt *him*. Hence the wire and the free trip to Philadelphia—an unusual gesture.

The train that carried young Blazer to Philadelphia in 1910 was crowded and had a whistle that Casey Jones himself could have played; it paused at and passed stations crowded with peo-

[4] Young Blazer was, in fact, completely self-supporting from this time forward. He paid for his own clothes, books and expenses, his own school tuition. His family, spartan, strict and high-minded, was remarkable for its rigorous attention to duty, and somewhat cold, impersonal attitude.

ple; the conductor was a man of presence and the passengers were proud in the knowledge that they were traveling as fast as man's ingenuity could contrive.

Jack Johnson defeated Jim Jeffries under a broiling sun at Reno in 15 rounds that year, bringing joy to the hearts of Negroes and gloom to many whites. Johnson's mother made a notable contribution to the American language on this occasion[5] when she remarked, "He said he'd bring home the bacon, and the honey boy done did."

The Los Angeles *Times* plant was shattered by a union bomb in 1910, witty signs being still a weapon of the future; Caruso appeared in the *Girl of the Golden West* and so overshadowed the heroine her name has been misplaced; John Barrymore and Douglas Fairbanks appeared on Broadway, but not together; foul rumor said Mrs. Alice Longworth smoked cigarettes and she did not deny it; s-x was a forbidden word but most towns and all cities had red light districts; most intelligent persons thought the world, at least *their* world, was too civilized to ever again have a war; the Standard Oil empire was starting to sag under its own bureaucratic weight, but was nevertheless being pummeled almost daily by the press and the magazines. The oil industry, in fact, had been joined to the railroads in the nation's demon-group, and though some of the criticism seemed well founded, the naked face of jealousy toward the wealthy obtruded unpleasantly in many of the arguments.

But these events were headline material. The majority of persons lived then, as now, in quiet obscurity. Men worked or sought work; families expanded and bickered; industry and commerce forged ahead and in directions and at a pace the world had never before witnessed. Some truly remarkable developments had taken place: the Wright brothers, self-taught printers and mathematicians, had already exploded many of the theories of higher mathematics and discovered the truth of principles that enabled them to fly machines through the sky: machines they personally built. This was such an incredible accomplishment, performed so modestly, that they had to demonstrate it for several years, before

[5] Appreciatively recorded by Mark Sullivan in *Our Times*.

eyewitnesses, let alone the rest of the world, would believe it. When the world did believe, it elbowed them out of the limelight hastily, unwilling to long credit such unlearned audacity.

But audacity was in the air, and it was unselfconscious. Mr. Ford, although over forty years old, was pioneering as casually as any stripling; Edison was in his prime and still finding marvels in his bag of magic; Luther Burbank was working horticultural miracles without a research grant; horses of every description from Percherons to trotters were beginning to shy and rear at goggled, giggling society motorists; telephones, still a social luxury, had become business necessities.

We know now that 1910 was in many ways a wonderful time, but then it was just the way things were, as is the present always: a time to live and work, and to hope, and to get through, and for some, a time to die. Count Leo Tolstoy, Mary Baker Eddy and Mark Twain died that year.

For Paul Blazer 1910 was a shell-breaking time—a time to get out into the world beyond tiny Aledo, with its few hundred souls. He impressed the men at Curtis with his sparkling blue eyes, his straight black hair, his lucidity, his height, and his smile. The company in turn persuaded him to forget college and accept the post of manager of all their school subscriptions in the United States in their Educational division. The salary and commission brought him, within a few months, to the level of $10,000 a year. At a time when workingmen supported their families on $10 a week, this was a princely sum; it is illustrative of Blazer's inherent practicality that it did not unhinge him.

Once immersed in the atmosphere at the *Saturday Evening Post,* where the air was heavy with discussions of political, cultural and social events, Blazer's interest in mathematics and the physical sciences began to fade, and his interest in the social sciences began to flower. More and more he began to consider that problems of society were paramount in importance, and he became intellectually engaged in the issues that Theodore Roosevelt and his followers began to press against such men as Woodrow Wilson. One particularly violent storm swirled around the Supreme Court of the United States and the anti-trust laws. Originally designed to break apart only trusts that were against the public interest, these laws were being extended into instruments against all large businesses. Roosevelt was against this trend, and with his remarkable charisma, managed to oppose the popular direction in such a manner that his conservatism seemed not only bold but innovational.

Meanwhile, Blazer's tasks at Curtis were absorbing. One of his responsibilities was to devise ads that ran in the *Saturday Evening Post* to attract fresh recruits willing to sell subscriptions. He created a blind-teaser ad that said "We'll pay your way through any College in the U. S." The responses ran as heavy as 15,000 to 20,000 letters a week. He learned to dictate to batteries of secretaries and to use an Ediphone, one of Edison's early machines; soon devised form letters with appropriate blanks for the secretaries to plug. Sifting the curiosity seekers and the clearly unsuited from those the company sought was a considerable task; Blazer found his own correspondence running 1,000 letters a day.

This led Blazer to a place on Curtis' "Correspondence Committee," whose members would select incoming letters and analyze the replies from various departments within the company for clarity, succinctness and effectiveness. The work of the committee and the tremendous influence of the *Saturday Evening Post* and its writers fascinated Blazer, and gave him a lasting insight into the effectiveness of skillful writing as a means not only of reaching the minds of people, but of enlisting their support. Years later, he was to put these perceptions and skills to excellent use as the chief executive officer of an enterprise physically separated from its board of directors and financial backers.

In 1911, the Supreme Court ordered the Standard Oil empire to fragment within six months. The decision was greeted by much of the nation with jubilation, but arguments broke out in intellectual and legal circles. The Court's ruling did not clarify the central issue, but left the whole question of what constitutes an illegal trust up in the air. Businessmen remained as much in the dark regarding what was legal and what was not, as before; it was clear the Court had left itself free to rule either way when new circumstances arose. Theodore Roosevelt, with a prescience that seems uncanny today, argued that the absence of clear law would place the Court in a virtually dictatorial position, and he began to plump for an amendment to the Constitution which he termed the "right to recall," in which the people would decide, by popular vote, whether a Supreme Court decision on a Constitutional issue (where an interpretation of the Constitution is invoked), would be allowed to stand or not.

The newspapers fell on the proposal with fury, stretching the point to such extraordinary lengths as to make it appear that Roosevelt wanted the public to ratify or negate every court decision in every case: criminal, constitutional or merely civil. The great trust buster was painted into a corner where he appeared to be defending trusts. Ruefully, he concluded he had failed to make himself clear. Actually, he was the casualty of a propaganda technique that was to become increasingly common. But in 1911, the net result was to make the Supreme Court even more supreme, and to leave business open to further attacks on the basis of size, and not behavior.

Meanwhile, Standard Oil obediently broke up into eleven separate companies. Some of these firms, cast adrift without the navigational guidance of their former staff officers, were left in peculiar positions. The Standard Oil Company of Ohio (the *original* Standard Oil) for instance, was bereft of its own sources of crude oil; it remained primarily a refining and marketing organization.

Immersed in his own activities as only a young man can be, it is doubtful that Paul Blazer felt the dissolution of Standard Oil had any great personal meaning for him. But throughout the reaches of the oil industry, the dismembering of the octopus left openings for smaller companies and independents, as well as entrepreneurs attracted by the growth of oil both as a transportation fuel and as a replacement for coal in the new technology.

In Oklahoma, J. Fred Miles and his partners were among the numerous groups searching for oil. The passing of the great market regulator, Standard, meant that crude oil producers no longer had to chafe at fixed prices; they could bargain and haggle more freely—a circumstance many found a mixed blessing.

By 1912, Blazer was sufficiently sociologized to find himself on a platform with the man himself at a Theodore Roosevelt rally; he became so ardently involved in the Rough Rider's campaign on a third party ticket that he toured Philadelphia in an open touring car, haranguing street corner crowds.

The result of that campaign, however, was a split Republican vote and the election of Woodrow Wilson—a man whose ideas and methods were antithetical to both Roosevelt's and Taft's. Paul Blazer not only watched his hero fall in the field during this conflict, but later saw him reduced to impotence by the chilly Princeton idealist. He turned, sobered, away from the spectacle; for the balance of his life he was to be a political pragmatist.

Late in 1913, the year after the Bull Moose campaign, Blazer's enthusiasm for the climate at Curtis Publishing Co. waned. He decided to complete his education, and gave his employers notice. The rival Crowell Publishing Co., publishers of the *Woman's Home Companion* and the *American,* promptly offered him the post of national subscription manager at a starting salary of $100 a week and commission, but he turned it down.

During the entire period he was away from Aledo, young Blazer had retained his own magazine subscription business; a secretary maintained the routine chores during most of the year. When he left Curtis, this enterprise remained his only source of income. He decided to go to the University of Chicago (students then being able to choose their schools), largely because it was possible to attend on a quarterly—instead of an annual—basis. He could attend school three quarters of the year, he reasoned, and skip the fall semester, when pre-Christmas subscription sales were heavy.

In addition, the school was near Aledo, and he could visit his home often. Many of his friends studied at Chicago and their School of Social Studies was highly regarded. Still under the socially conscious ambience of Curtis, he entered that school. ATO (Alpha Tau Omega) bid him, and he not only joined, but chose the Chapter House as a residence. Years later, he recalled telling one of the boys there that he had turned down a job at $100 a week to return to school. The boy stared at him, and then said earnestly, "I just think you're a damned liar." Blazer laughed.

Meanwhile, J. Fred Miles, several years older and completely unaware of Blazer's existence, was discovering that finding oil in Oklahoma was getting more difficult and more expensive all the time. Holes had to be drilled ever deeper; new fields were harder to find. The entire oil industry was thrown into a new situation by September 1914, however, when war started in Europe. To most Americans, the sequence of events which led to the tragedy seemed, at first, pure opera bouffe. They were to learn it was not.

Henry Ford introduced his $5-a-day wage that year; mass production methods and "scientific" management emerged. The war was to alter the transportation industry almost totally; horses would be swept off the landscape for effective military purposes; the airplane was to be catapulted into the sky and fleets would darken the air; American industry became a fulcrum upon which swung the destiny of nations. Propaganda, for and against the Allies or the Entente, began to appear, oddly, in our free press. Slowly and then with increasing intensity, the nation became emotionally involved in the war.

But in 1914 there was time to spare. The injections of war orders into the economy and changes in the politics of the situation came slowly, though inexorably. Some commodities began to rise in value, oil among them. J. Fred Miles by this time discovered—one is tempted to say the hard way—that the oil producer is in a farmer's position within the industry: everyone wants his crop, but he is dependent upon prices set by others. The more he reflected about the situation, the more clearly Miles could see that the oil business is really four great industries rolled into one.

The first industry involves exploration and production: oil is located under the surface of the earth, and is extracted. The second industry consists of transportation: crude oil is moved by pipelines, barges, ships, railroad cars, to the refineries, and moved out again in the form of refined products. The third industry is refining: in any other industry this would be called manufacturing, but since the oil industry started by refining crude oil, all the manufacturing processes are still called refining. The fourth industry is known as marketing: every buying and selling transaction at any stage in any of the other industries—whether it is buying and selling crude oil, or refined products sold in bulk and moved via water, highway, railroad or air, or the sale of gasoline to a man in an automobile at the corner service station.

The rise of the industry during the years 1911 to 1916 was rapid. Not only did new major oil companies come into being— companies that enveloped all four sectors of the industry within their operations and are known as "majors"—but a host of independent companies specializing in or restricted to one facet or another came to life. Filling stations appeared, and men have been arguing ever since their inception about who thought of them first. Let it suffice to say that by 1916 they were commonplace. Also, bulk stations where large amounts of gasoline were stored began to appear all over the landscape. Pipelines stretched; refineries sprouted like mushrooms.

To J. Fred Miles, this great industrial vista stretched, beckoning and receding. He began to cultivate men who might be able to help him realize his dream of organizing a larger, more comprehensive company to such good effect that years later Paul Blazer was to say wryly that Miles's greatest talent was "an uncanny ability to attract men of substance to his schemes."

The observation was accurate, but it was not all of the truth. Miles's greatest ability was a talent for seeing the whole sweep of the oil industry, and a capacity to put these pieces together. His was the true vision of the born empire builder, but like many such men, circumstances were not to permit him the realization of his conceptions. Nevertheless, he was to lay the groundwork for their realization, and it was on the foundations of his observations and the contacts he made and the company he promoted that Paul Blazer and his associates later built a real empire.

In 1916, an election year, J. Fred Miles read that a man named Charles Dulin had struck oil in the shallow Weir sands on Tick Ford in Cow Creek, near Irvine, Kentucky. Kentucky had experienced an oil boom before: in the 1880s and in 1900, and again in 1912. But Dulin was to spark the largest. Miles was interested for several reasons. Foremost, of course, was his dream. Hard on its heels was the knowledge that Kentucky was close to the great industrial markets of Ohio, Pennsylvania and Illinois, and constituted a closer base to the industrial heartland of America than did remote Oklahoma. Also—and this was important —Miles had had a friend since childhood named J. I. Lamprecht, who was head of a large national company: the National Refining Co., with headquarters in Cleveland, Ohio. Should Miles find crude oil in Kentucky, National Refining, operating in twenty-seven states, could buy whatever he could produce. And the Kentucky discovery, was made in shallow sands, which meant that Miles, with his limited capital, could gamble on at least an equal well basis with larger and better-financed competitors.

Miles set out for Kentucky in mid-summer 1916, with high hopes.

At the University of Chicago, at about the same time in the fall of 1916 when J. Fred Miles was traveling around Kentucky by buckboard, shrewdly assessing possible oil sites and bargaining for lease rights with farmers and property owners, Paul Blazer became business manager for the *Cap & Gown,* one of the University of Chicago's two student magazines.

The *Cap & Gown* was managed and written by students in their junior year. That year one of the two student editors on the publication, Joe Levin,[6] took notice of Blazer, and years later repeated his impression.

"He was older than the average student," Levin recalled, "and he seemed a lot *surer* than the rest of us. He had a lot of money, of course, and he talked and carried himself like a man of a different generation. But," and Levin paused, savoring the recollection, "he did a fantastic job for the magazine." Blazer's sales and business ability led the magazine that year to all-time money-making heights.

"I wasn't particularly aware of him before then," said Levin, "but he certainly impressed me as a business manager. Especially," he added, "because in those days the student staff benefited personally when the magazine made money."

On the last day of October 1915, Blazer had met Miss Georgia Monroe. In all Chicago they had only one mutual acquaintance

[6] Biographical footnote on page 206.

before they met; from their meeting forward, their lives were never again to be separate.

"I thought Paul was the most sophisticated man I had ever met," she said later. "The only man over whom my father couldn't take command. They got along *tremendously* together; they played tennis and swapped sales stories . . . My father was a salesman and so was Paul—even though he was a student."

Watching the two men, Miss Monroe thought they were like two boys together. And she was delighted to see that, beneath the jokes and the banter, they developed a strong liking and respect for one another.

But with all his gifts and poise, Blazer was still boyish enough to own and operate a motorcycle. Once he was thrown over the handlebars, and landed on a grassy knoll. His back, already weakened by football injuries, was not benefited.

Meanwhile, Woodrow Wilson campaigned for reelection in 1916. His eloquent addresses, glistening with intelligence, swept the opposition virtually off the boards. His phrase "too proud to fight," carried the sentimental and the humanitarian-minded in a great tide. Paradoxically, when the phrase rang hollow against a backdrop of dreadful events, Wilson as President became chief strategist of the hawks; a switch that neatly sidestepped the old guard.

By early 1917 it was clear America would be drawn into the vortex. Roosevelt organized a volunteer division and asked to be placed in command. The old warrior was crushed when told by intermediary Newton D. Baker that President Wilson was cool to his efforts. "This war," the President said coldly, "will be conducted along methods that will be undramatic, practical and of great scientific definiteness and precision." In fact, for the first time in American history, vast armies of conscripts were planned.

The nation would have been puzzled by these plans had they been announced in such terms. In early April 1917, when Congress, in session around the clock, voted to give President Wilson power to declare war against Imperial Germany, the decision was greeted by soaring patriotic fervor and enthusiasm. Throughout the nation the marriage rate went up sharply, as young men took this traditional step before rushing to the enlistment office.

Among these was Paul Blazer; he and Miss Georgia Monroe were married on April 10, 1917, at the very moment the nation cast its lot. Blazer's name was on a list the University gave the Army of suitable and recommended officer-candidates; he had every reason to expect to be accepted. He and his bride, therefore, did not waste time apartment-hunting; he moved—for what was expected to be a brief period—in with the Monroes.

It was a shock to the athlete, therefore, to fail his physical. Anxious to do his part nevertheless, his next step was to enroll in the 123rd U.S. Army Hospital Unit, then being organized at the University. The Unit was certain to be shipped overseas.

During the summer of 1917, however, before the 123rd Hospital Unit was sufficiently organized to be sent anywhere, while bending over his motorcycle one afternoon, Blazer felt his sacroiliac give way. He was carted off to the St. Luke's Hospital in Chicago, where he spent two months in traction, and emerged on crutches.

The accident had several consequences. One was that it effectively ended his school days, and cost him his degree—although it need not have. He did not finish the semester because he was in the hospital. It did not occur to him that he would have received the degree, had he applied, by virtue of being in the Army; he learned that bit of esoterica much later.

The second consequence was that his military career ended practically before it began. He was carried on the rolls of the U.S. Army, but his honorable discharge was on its way, and eventually reached him.

The third consequence of the other two was that Paul Blazer's mind turned toward the practical matter of earning a living, as befitted a newly married young man. He had turned, in other words, onto a new road.

He obtained the post of advertising service manager for the Chittenden Press, in Chicago. Persons outside the printing, advertising and allied trades usually have difficulty in understanding the multi-faceted activities that thrive in these industries; Blazer's duties sound more mixed than, in all likelihood, they seemed to him. He wrote circulars and leaflets, assisted customers with their advertising themes and campaigns, sold space and solicited printing. Among other accounts he landed the large red directory of the oil industry for Chittenden: a major coup that landed him a fat commission.

Then one night Georgia and Paul Blazer decided to go dancing at the College Inn, a popular nightspot in the Sherman House. On the dance floor they met an old college chum of Paul's from William & Vashti: Eric Shatford, and his wife Ruth.[7]

Eric Shatford's father was an oil refiner who had worked for the old Standard Oil Co. in Nova Scotia, left its employ, emigrated to the U.S., and established himself as a petroleum refiner with a plant at Blue Island in Chicago. Young Eric, who graduated from William & Vashti, worked briefly for his father—with whom he did not always agree—and had become an associate in a marketing company called The Great Northern that handled, among others, products his father's firm produced. The Great Northern also had a refinery at Joliet, Illinois.

All of this came out when the two friends, in the nightclub, compared notes on their respective progress. When Shatford asked Paul what he was doing, Paul said simply, "I sell printing."

Shatford, an enthusiastic and friendly man, said, "We use printing. Why don't you come and sell us some?"

A few days later, Paul went to see his friend, and the conversation became discursive. Paul admitted he was slightly bored and drifting, and Eric Shatford offered him a job "on excellent terms." Paul accepted, and joined The Great Northern as advertising manager.

The oil industry, with its reputation for large and significant negotiations, its famous successes and attendant publicity, intrigued and attracted him.

"I soon discovered that Eric's firm didn't really have any need for an advertising manager," Paul said later. "I could handle his few trade publication ads by working a day or two a month. So after watching the operation for a little while, I suggested that I join the sales department and try to do a little selling in my spare time."

[7] Ruth Shatford was an Aledo girl; her father was, for many years, the Blazer family physician.

That was how Paul G. Blazer entered the oil industry in 1917: as the result of a chance meeting on a dance floor.

MILES IN KENTUCKY

In Kentucky, at the same time, J. Fred Miles received a hard kick from Fate. He had traveled about the eastern part of the state since mid-summer 1916, and succeeded in obtaining oil leases on 183,000 acres of promising sites extending all the way from Estill County to the West Virginia line. He had financial backing lined up in Cleveland through his friends the Lamprechts. Then he added to his untested locations an option to buy forty-nine producing wells from the United Oil Company. But title searches are necessary in the oil industry, and when Louisville attorney E. L. McDonald had completed his investigation, the titles of the United Oil leases proved to be worthless. Dismayed, Miles's Cleveland backers backed right out of the situation.

Many men faced with such a savage turn of the wheel at the end of a year's hard work would have thrown in their chips, but Miles was not a man to acknowledge defeat, even when it grinned in his face. As far as he was concerned, there was oil in eastern Kentucky; there was a market for this oil through his friends in the National Refining Company and there was money in Lexington. The fact that he did not put all these elements together on his first try did not change these essential realities.

Accordingly, he went back to Oklahoma and dissolved his Swiss Drilling Company, realizing all he could from his share of its assets, and held the drilling equipment in readiness to ship to Kentucky. With more leases in Kentucky on his hands than he could himself handle, he sold them to various friends of his in the oil industry: Frank Cullinan, head of the Texas Company's Houston-based production department; Murray Dohm, general manager of the Gypsy Oil Company, Frank Phillips, head of a small bank in Bartlesville, Oklahoma (and founder of Phillips Petroleum) ; Jim Chapman and Bob McFarland of the Macman Oil Company. Each of these groups agreed to drill from eight to ten wells each. Miles not only refurbished his bank balance, but helped swell the number of participants in the Kentucky oil boom.

Eastern Kentucky oil field boom. (1918)

He then returned to Kentucky, which, in common with the rest of the nation, was experiencing a tremendous war-inspired boom. In later years there were persons who would point to this phenomenon and declare the war was fought in order to bring it into being; a *reductio ad absurdum*. The fact was that the war had drawn into its orbit the entire resources of nations; these nations used money. Hence, money cascaded throughout the business community. Among the many commodities and industries that were lifted by this stream into great heights of prosperity was the oil industry. The businessmen of Kentucky, particularly in the Lexington and Louisville areas, were well aware that oil was essential to the conduct of the war and was bringing a high price in the marketplace. They were not anxious to see this harvest gathered by entrepreneurs who rushed into the state: Miles appeared at the exact moment when they were most anxious to have an expert lead them into good investments in the boom.

Nevertheless, it took Miles until mid-summer 1918 to recreate all the pieces essential for organization. By that time, his sights had risen, and his dream company was in view.

While Miles was assembling his forces in Kentucky in 1917–1918, Paul Blazer had been learning the inner pathways of the industry

Camp Martha; early location of the Swiss Oil Company.

in Chicago. Great Northern not only handled the output from its own refinery in Joliet, but the output from the Blue Island refinery owned by the senior Shatford as well. Because the relationship between Eric and his father was uneasy, Paul became their go-between. He not only sold with smoothly polished skill, but he applied his mathematically-oriented mind toward the balancing of freight rates, refinery costs and a fluctuating market to strike the best bargain. These were the sorts of calculations in which he excelled and that he enjoyed. He developed the habit of poring over the oil trade press to spot clues, trends and directions; read the technical literature that explained refinery shortcuts and new processes and equipment; spent a great deal of time visiting and learning from men on various levels in the industry. In modern terms, one would be tempted to call Blazer a market researcher at a time when even the term was unknown. He would not make a move without attempting to discover all the facts. This sounds as banal as virtue; it is as rare. Within the year he had replaced the Great Northern sales manager and by mid-winter 1918, he was a vice president.

In mid-summer 1918, J. Fred Miles had reason to feel good. Together with a number of Lexington and Louisville associates, he had signed the papers incorporating the Swiss Oil Company.

His old friend and valuable customer J. I. Lamprecht, head of National Refining, was named president. J. Fred Miles himself was treasurer and general manager at a salary of $12,000 a year, and received $500,000 in stock for the assets of his Swiss Drilling Company. Louisville attorney E. L. McDonald would soon join the firm as secretary. The firm began with a capital stock of 500,000 shares with a par value of $100; was soon to expand the shares to 1,000,000 and reduce their value to $5. Some appreciation of Miles's sales ability can be gleaned from the fact that soon after the company started he made a trip to Chicago, interested some more men in the venture, and returned with an additional $1 million: big money then.

These negotiations were far above the level upon which Blazer and Shatford operated but they too were busy. In mid-summer 1918, the Allies were cracking the Germans in Europe and the Prohibitionists were drying up the United States in the sympathetically idealistic and authoritarian climate created by the Wilson government. Business was extraordinarily good. Blazer and Shatford couldn't get enough oil to meet their orders.

Having read about the oil boom in Kentucky and realizing that the crude oil freight rate was lower from there than it was from Oklahoma, Blazer decided to go down and look over the region. He lined up a pipeline deal in western Kentucky that fell through. Then the Big Sinking field came in in eastern Kentucky and aroused much attention, including Blazer's. He and Shatford (who had joined him) went hotfooting to eastern Kentucky, where J. Fred Miles was settling in as a big operator. Blazer and Shatford met Desha Breckenridge, owner of the *Lexington Herald*, Leonard Cox Sr., George Graves, Charley Manning, Frank Justice, Jim Justice and other Kentucky businessmen. Dabbling in the boom, these men owned producing wells in the Big Sinking district, but were faced with the problem of getting oil to market and finding customers. Being unversed in the oil industry, they had problems similar to those of gentlemen farmers. They blamed at least part of their troubles on the management of the Cumberland Pipeline. Cumberland, a relic of the old Standard Oil Company had, oddly, remained under the control of Standard executives in New York, who were relatively indifferent to the enterprise.

To Blazer and Shatford, this spelled opportunity in capital letters. They raced around Chicago looking for capital, and found backers through Shatford Sr. in the form of two Buffalo business-men named Hockstetter and Forman. Then they organized a new venture they called the Great Northern Pipeline Company, and began construction of a pipeline that paralleled the Cumberland line in many areas, to extend from the Big Sinking field to Beattyville, Kentucky. Eric Shatford was president of this venture, Paul Blazer, vice president.

But in the fall of 1919 change reached the Chicago apartment of the Monroe family. Georgia's father was critically injured in an automobile accident on August 27; Paul Blazer Jr. was born on August 31, and three days later, Mr. Monroe tragically died. He was only 45.

Paul Blazer suddenly found himself head of the family: he met this circumstance in a welcoming manner. Mrs. Monroe, well pro-vided for but psychologically lost without her husband, remained with Paul and Georgia; young Dorothy (Dotty) was to have Paul as her surrogate father until she grew, finished school and married. But the young family head, although his father-in-law had been killed and his son newly born, had to leave Chicago to see the new pipeline completed.

Beattyville, Kentucky was, in 1919, a holdover from the nine-teenth century.[8] Years later, reminiscing in the cool elegance of his home in Ashland, Kentucky, Blazer was graphic.

"Beattyville," he said, "was a place with no roads at all. The streets were just mud wallows. Even the pigs preferred the side-walks; there were plenty of pigs. There were only two telephones in the whole town; one of these was in the hotel." He looked at his wife. "I would call you at midnight, when the hotel phone was free," he reminded, and she nodded. "Paul Jr. was awake at midnight to be fed," she said, "so I was up at that time every night. But you came home on Christmas. Christmas, 1919. I re-member that date very well."

"As a matter of fact," Blazer continued, "that hotel was so bad

[8] Today it is a far different town, of course—and this is an advance the entire nation has made.

that although they had stoves in each room, you had to go downstairs and out back to get your own coal. The hotel did supply kindling, though. And the hotel was so filthy that some of the men—including me—went to the home of a Negro woman who served meals. It was the cleanest place in town, but we didn't advertise the fact."

One day, he recalled, he met a drunk in the middle of a bridge. Large, unruly, truculent and unwilling to allow a chance for violence to escape him, the drunk pulled a gun. With a sweep of his arm, Paul knocked him off the bridge into the sobering waters. He was strong, even though the results of his motorcycle accident and football injuries had truncated his athletic period. He had to wear a brace for his back, and as a consequence moved stiffly, his torso canted forward. It was a posture the passing years would not improve.

By the time the pipeline was complete, Blazer and Shatford had many good business friends in Kentucky. Then their business problems changed: they now had too much crude oil on their hands. Paul began to travel around as a salesman to unload their surplus. He ranged far: through southwestern Pennsylvania and southern Ohio as well as throughout Kentucky.

At the same time, in 1919, J. Fred Miles began drilling in Lee County. Miles bought forty acres of virgin pineland twenty-two miles from Torrent, Kentucky—a railroad point—and, using a small sawmill located on the tract, obtained his own lumber and built fifteen three-room houses for his supervisors, a main bunkhouse for the roughnecks, a commissary, a schoolhouse, a headquarters building, a church and a ball diamond. With one of his brothers in immediate charge, he hired mountain boys—skilled labor being then, as always, in short supply.

In order to transport his drilling rigs from the railroad to the camp, Miles, with characteristic ingenuity, went to Cincinnati and Columbus and bought Percherons, their heavy harnesses and wagons, from breweries that were being legislated out of existence by the Volstead Act.

While taking these practical steps, Miles persuaded important and powerful men in Chicago to invest in his venture: Hiram J.

Men of the Swiss Oil Company moving drilling tools toward a site near
White Oak Creek.

Halle, who became president of Universal Oil Products, never became a director, but attended board meetings, received reports,
and was treated as a director; Martin Insull, the younger brother
of the utility magnate, himself manager of the Kentucky utilities
owned by the Insull empire; Arthur and George Reynolds of the
Continental and Commercial National Bank of Chicago; J. L.
Washburn and J. Ogden Armour of Chicago. Locally, the most
potent figure attracted was Senator Tom Combs, of Lexington,
Kentucky. Senator Combs, one-time Speaker of the Kentucky
House of Representatives and an ex-Lieutenant Governor, was
also owner of the Combs Lumber Company and the Fayette
County Home Telephone Company, a director of the Federal
Reserve Bank in Cleveland, Ohio, and a political boss in the
Lexington area. It is almost impossible to exaggerate the influence
of Senator Combs at this time, although it is pleasant to relate
that he bore himself with considerable grace: his courtly manners
and dapper presence were a sharp contrast to the uncouth bosses
of the great northern cities.

Since, in Lexington, virtually every door opened at a wave of the Senator's hand, J. Fred Miles was starting at the top. With a million dollars and the presence of the men from Chicago, in addition to the assets realized from the sale of Swiss Oil stock ($2.7 million in all), Miles bought the Quaker Oil Company in 1919 for $240,000, half in stock and half in cash. One of the largest stockholders in Quaker, C. S. Evans, a close friend of Senator Combs and Louisville manager of the Clinton Corn Syrup Refining Company, a subsidiary of the National Candy Company, joined the board. He was to remain, through all the various incarnations of the venture afterward, a director down to 1967, missing only one annual and two regular meetings in all these 48 years.[9]

In addition to buying Quaker Oil in 1919, J. Fred Miles also bought a well known as the Big Moulder, considered then one of the greatest producers in the area, as well as some pipelines and other properties; he began construction of a gasoline plant at Big Sinking Creek. Big Moulder cost $500,000; the gasoline plant cost $150,000: Miles was pouring money as though it would melt if left unspent. But crude oil was selling for $3.25 a bbl.—a high price. The year 1919 was, all in all, a great year for Miles. In true promoter's fashion he put out heavy dividends and extended his drilling operations into Warren County (200 miles southwest of the Lee County operations).

Lunching one day in the Phoenix Hotel in Lexington, Blazer recalled that someone pointed out J. Fred Miles to him, as the head of Swiss Oil, and the "man who bought the Big Moulder." Blazer stared at the stocky promoter with interest.

He and Shatford, however, were busy as could be themselves, though not on so grand a scale as Miles. One prospect in particular was interesting: Messrs. Breckenridge, Graves, Cox Sr., Manning, Justice, et al., had approached the young men and invited them to join in the formation of a new refining company. This was, of course, a big decision for Blazer and Shatford to make. In order to make it possible, Blazer offered to find a purchaser for The Great Northern—and he did. The buyer was the Warren Oil Company, whose western Pennsylvania branch had purchased crude oil from Paul on many occasions.

[9] Mr. Evans died, age eighty-nine, in October 1967.

Thus equipped, the two young entrepreneurs joined forces with their Kentucky associates, and the great Southern Refining Company was formed. Shortly afterward, it was decided to build a refinery in Lexington itself, and the name of the venture was stretched to The Great Southern Oil & Refining Company. Names with 'great' in them were as popular then as names without human connotations are popular now.

Blazer was vice president of sales, with a salary of $10,000 a year and 3 per cent ownership; Shatford was president. By mid-year 1920, all maneuvers were complete, and it was time to relocate Georgia, her mother and sister and the infant Paul Jr. from Chicago. From then on, their destinies were joined to Kentucky.

Georgia came down from Chicago by train, carrying six-month-old Paul Jr. and the family canary. Paul was waiting, and together they found a house at High Street and Ashland Avenue. There, life took on a totally different hue.

Lexington was then, as now, a number of light years removed from Chicago, but Paul had thought ahead, as usual. The day before Georgia arrived, he visited the Lexington Chapter of ATO. A tall, slender young man had greeted him: his name was Ed Dabney. Later he was to become a director of the Ashland Oil & Refining Company, and president of the Security Bank & Trust Co. in Lexington. But in 1920, Dabney and his fraternity brothers had more immediate reasons to welcome the Blazers: they needed chaperones for the fraternity dances and picnics. They were delighted when the young couple, so close to their own ages, agreed.

Wheeling her baby around, Georgia Blazer found Lexington a far more personal world than bustling, anonymous Chicago. Most families employed nurses for their babies, she noticed. But she was warmed by the friendliness and the courtesy of her neighbors. "It was all very Southern," she said years later, "or so it seemed to me then. I can still see my next door neighbor, Miss Amelia Hamilton, whose brother was a United States Representative, coming to visit me with a great handful of lilies-of-the-valley." To Georgia Blazer, whose ideas of the South were entirely nebulous and based on little more than her childhood reading of the Little Colonel stories, it seemed wonderful.

With the refinery of The Great Southern complete and in operation, Blazer spent a great deal of his time between sales efforts delving into the mysteries of processing, and asking questions of Joe Downey, the superintendent. Downey, who had been brought from the Blue Island refinery at Joliet when it was sold to the Warren Oil Co., was a man with a short fuse and a stubborn streak. Like most refinery superintendents at that time, he was sketchily educated and operated in an empirical, totally unscientific manner. Blazer would make suggestions and Downey would resist them profanely; Blazer would become persuasive and Downey would accede reluctantly and with open misgivings; the experiment would succeed. Blazer began to be known as a refinery expert, which amused him. "There was no mystery about it," he said. "I would read about developments in the trade literature that Joe Downey didn't read. I would spend time talking to men in other refineries; they would tell me what they had tried, and what had worked. My suggestions were based on this sort of information and my own observations. But I had to be tactful in making them, for I had no real authority at the refinery; I was only in charge of sales, although of course I was a vice president. Since sales and refining are linked, my interest was entirely practical."

While Miles and Blazer were, in their separate ways, absorbed in the oil industry, the world around them was transformed as though some celestial magician had passed his hand over the globe, making the familiar suddenly alien and unfamiliar.

At the other end of the earth, in Russia, Lenin and his followers had forcibly introduced a system of government based on the theory that the individual has no rights whatever, either to property or to his own destiny. His behavior, status, morality and circumstances became policy matters of the state. The individual concept of good and evil was denied; the extent of his obedience to what was ordered by the state became the measure of man.

There were signs that this reasoning was part of a world-wide desire to have done with the old order, whatever it was. Kings and emperors were toppled; President Wilson, who disapproved of the world on many scores, refused to accept German peace overtures until that nation deposed its Kaiser and established a social structure Wilson considered more equitable. At home, in a similar mood of authoritarian exaltation, the nation voted the eighteenth amendment into existence.

When peace negotiations began in late 1918, Wilson seemed to epitomize a world attitude he had helped shape; when they ended, the world mood had changed. He was never to understand he had helped to create the disillusionment by insisting on redrawing the map of a Europe he did not know, and by attempting to create a supranational world order: the League of Nations.

He returned to a nation seething with resentment, convinced Wilsonian rhetoric had led it into believing, for a time, in a fool's paradise. Prohibition, which went into effect in mid-summer 1918, did not assist matters: many people admired virtue, but few liked it to be compulsory.

Perhaps persons in other parts of the world, including Russia, had similar second thoughts. They were not fortunate enough to have a voice with which to state them. In the United States, a strong pull back to the pre-war world gained momentum. It was another illusion; time does not reverse. But the people tried; Mr. Harding was elected as part of that reaction. He seemed a magnified version of a small town American. He spoke of restoring "normalcy"—a word since used as a symbol of ridicule. At the time the people forgave his error of syntax: they knew what he meant.

But change had progressed too far to be stopped; the tide of change, in fact, was in flood. Women received the vote in 1920 and confounded prophets both benign and baleful; their inclusion among the voters seemed to make no particular difference. The Ku Klux Klan was reborn in travesty; eight Chicago White Sox players were indicted for throwing the previous year's World Series and baseball was hurt for a while; Sinclair Lewis' *Main Street* appeared and the prestige of small businessmen all over the country seemed damaged permanently; John Barrymore appeared on Broadway in *Richard III;* the theater season brought 150 new plays to Broadway and none were openly obscene; Mary Pickford and Douglas Fairbanks were married in real life, to the delight of movie-goers; William Jennings Bryan suggested that lame duck president Wilson resign to allow Mr. Harding to move into the White House at once.

In the year 1920 the fortunes of the Paul Blazers took a definite upward turn, and the fortunes of J. Fred Miles, at least as far as the Swiss Oil Company was concerned, began to show some soft spots.

Miles suffered a personal as well as a business loss when J. I. Lamprecht died. Mr. Lamprecht, head of National Refining, had been content to let Miles manage Swiss as he willed. Lamprecht's place as president of Swiss Oil was taken by John Gund, owner of a Lexington brewery. Mr. Gund was not an oil man; he showed no signs of interfering, or wanting to interfere, with Miles—but he was not Mr. Lamprecht.

Early in 1920 Miles's salary was increased from $12,000 a year to $20,000, and he was given a bonus of $50,000 in stock. He continued his acquisitions on behalf of Swiss Oil: the Jewel Oil Company for $280,000; the Crown Oil Company for $130,000; the George Booth Company for a sum that seems to have been forgotten.

Then the Big Moulder, that fabulous gusher in which Miles had enough confidence to have paid half the million dollars he and James Martin had obtained in Chicago, unaccountably fell off; its great flow slowed to a trickle. In time, this development undermined Miles's prestige as an oil expert, and changed into a spectre that would arise, gibbering, at every board meeting for years thereafter, causing the directors to shake their heads and to grumble.

And, toward the end of the year 1920, the economy of the nation began to tremble. The impact of demobilized soldiers and the curtailment of war orders had made itself felt briefly in 1919. Late in 1920 there came, heavily, what we today call a Depression, and what men then—perhaps more honestly and certainly more graphically—called a Panic.

Miles, possibly feeling premonitions, arranged to receive a five year contract at a salary of $25,000 a year, ensuring his position as general manager.

In January 1921, the price of Somerset crude oil, which Swiss produced and that had soared throughout 1920 to a high of $4.50 a barrel, plummeted straight down until it reached $1 a barrel. Swiss was in trouble; so was J. Fred Miles.

The shrewd financial brains on the board had no intention of seeing their money disappear into smoke. They devised, late in the year 1921, a public offering which could only have been conceived—let alone produced—in the hard-sell Twenties. It was a first mortgage, 7 per cent sinking fund issue of gold bonds to mature in 1927. It is doubtful if any additional lure could have been added to this glittering array.

Certainly it attracted the attention of Robert D. Gordon, partner in the Chicago investment firm of Gordon and Bartlett. Mr. Gordon was related, through marriage, to Swiss president John Gund. But the Swiss public offering attracted also by its own glitter. "Do you realize what a first mortgage amounts to?" he asked later. "It was like buying the company."

Gordon undertook to sell a large quantity of the issue. He found —despite its combination of blue sky and clouds as well—that many others could resist a bargain. He received a large bloc of common stock as a commission. Years later, he was to be grateful for this but that was *years* later.

Then John Gund died, and his place as president of the Swiss Oil Company was taken by none other than the redoubtable Senator Tom Combs himself. If any single development can be said to mark the pivot upon which J. Fred Miles's fortunes turned in the Swiss Oil Company, this was probably it. Senator Combs, a practical businessman with a politician's insight into men, was not a figurehead.

Despite the dike-plugging bond issue and the accession of the Senator, the fortunes of the Swiss Oil Company continued to decline through 1922. In 1923, these shadows became even darker. It was not that the oil industry had gone to wrack; on the contrary, with the automobile business booming and the consumption of gasoline increasing, oil was prosperous: it was that Swiss had been poorly managed. No new wells were being drilled and the wells Swiss owned were ebbing. Large expenditures had been made to little purpose; the company's credit was turning sour. J. Fred Miles, who had made many short-term loans, found his relations with creditors going beyond courtesy and reaching the edge of invective and threat.

Meanwhile, Paul G. Blazer had extended his knowledge of the regional market to razor-sharp keenness. His travels had brought him into contact with the Craigs of the Freedom Oil Works in Freedom, Pennsylvania; with F. R. Newman and W. W. Vande-veer in Cleveland; oil men throughout Pennsylvania, Ohio, Ken-tucky and other areas; with the businessmen of Lexington and many in Louisville. His acquaintances ranged from the unedu-cated operators in the refineries to the heads of companies.

In the fall of 1923, Stalin, a colorless eminence affecting the drab clothes of a workingman, had assumed the dictatorship of Russia from the nearly invisible post of secretary of the Commu-nist Party; Luis Firpo knocked Jack Dempsey clear out of the ring; Mussolini had become dictator of Italy; Adolph Hitler failed on his first putsch and Germany was filled with dissension, confu-sion and inflation; war lords ruled in China; Einstein's theories created discussion throughout the United States (many people said they disagreed with them); Chaplin, Keaton, Turpin and Rin-Tin-Tin reigned in Hollywood; business was spotty, but a three-million-car year was realized by Detroit.

The year 1923 was also when the speakeasy had become common-place, women's dresses rose higher than any elderly man had ever expected to see in public, music began to syncopate, illegal stills became a secondary industry, marathon dances became popular, and gangsters began to kill one another in broad daylight in city streets.

Prices on the stock market began to reach new highs, business was frenetic and erratic; mergers, acquisitions, new ventures and joint ventures joined in midair. Many became convinced of the nearness of riches: a conviction which lent a certain aura of un-reality and instability to a nation in ferment. Yet there were large pockets of the population unaltered by the spirit of the times: there was urban agitation to change such areas, forthwith. In self-defense, rural America began to defend propositions that might, left alone, have withered naturally; William Jennings Bryan spear-headed a movement to retain the barriers in public schools against teaching the theory of evolution, offensive to fundamentalists. Then in August, President Harding took sick of ptomaine poison-ing and pneumonia, and died. His mind was heavy with the knowledge that his administration was tainted by the corruption of his friends. The public would learn of this later; meanwhile, Calvin Coolidge, the epitome of rectitude, entered the White House.

Despite growing trends toward regulation, business remained essentially free. The oil markets were capable of great dips, soarings and dives. "You must remember," said Paul Blazer later, "that the fluctuations were extremely wide in a free market." His eyes sharpened and his ability to calculate mentally improved; he soon discovered a key invisible to most men then: that changes in the price of crude oil were invariably *preceded* by changes in the prices of refined products. He became so adept at anticipating the drops or the rises in the crude oil market that many men came to rely upon him as an oracle. On one occasion, watching the market with his usual acuity, and knowing that a friend of his, Dick Childs, of Mt. Sterling, was holding a large quantity of crude oil, he called Childs on the phone and advised him to sell.

"Thanks for warning me," Childs said. "I'll get my man next week."

"Better get him today," Blazer warned.

"You mean it's going to drop that soon?" Childs asked, shocked. "I'll call right away."

Childs finally located his buyer playing cards in the Lexington Club. Childs pressed him for an immediate order asking only the current market price, and the customer gave him one. On Monday the price dropped, but the sale held. Childs was eternally grateful; when the Blazers' daughter, Doris, was born, in March 1923, Mrs. Blazer was agreeably surprised to receive a great mass of beautiful long-stemmed roses from Dick Childs.

But at The Great Southern, Blazer's reputation for omniscience was not always accepted. Aetna Oil, a company in trouble, had managed to run up a large debt with Great Southern, and ordered an additional $300,000 worth of crude oil shipped to it by barge. Blazer watching both the market and the uncertain fortunes of Aetna Oil, had grave misgivings. He and Eric Shatford discussed the situation and Blazer expressed his objections, but Shatford waved them aside. The shipment was made, and while it was still en route to the Aetna refinery, Blazer decided the market price of crude oil would drop. He went to Shatford, and asked him to stop and return the shipment on the grounds that Aetna would not pay the original price contracted, but the price on arrival: if there was to be a loss, he would prefer to have the oil back in hand, take a temporary inventory devaluation, and wait for the market to come back. Again Shatford disagreed. The shipment proceeded; the price fell. It was received, and Aetna promptly went bankrupt. The loss was total.

This caused a chill in the relationship between the two men. Although they remained cordial, and even—years afterward—had later business dealings with one another, it was the virtual end of their partnership at the time. Blazer, unhappy at Great Southern, began to consider a move. Such desires usually become known: a phenomenon with which most persons are familiar, and Blazer's case followed the pattern.

In the fall of 1923, he was approached by Mr. Kimball, secretary of the Petroleum Exploration Company of Sistersville, West Virginia. The Petroleum Exploration Company was a producing firm that wanted to extend its operations into refining. Blazer was, by this time, considered an expert on refining, and Mr. Kimball wanted Blazer to become general manager of refining for Petroleum Exploration. Blazer was interested, and Kimball outlined the situation. Petroleum Exploration had no refinery of its own, but Mr. Kimball thought that Blazer could advise them on a proper course in this respect. The company might consider buying an existing refinery, or constructing a new one, dependent on Paul Blazer's estimate of the situation and recommendation. Also, of course, they would hire Blazer to manage the property, once acquired. There was only one hitch.

The Petroleum Exploration Company had eleven directors, and it was a rule of the firm that it undertook only actions which received the unanimous approval of all eleven. In addition, Mr. Kimball thought the Petroleum Exploration Company could not honorably offer Blazer a job unless he was a free agent. That meant that he would have to resign from The Great Southern.

Paul resigned from The Great Southern, and undertook a survey of the existing refineries and possibilities of the region. He looked over a refinery at Louisville and one at Latonia, and an-

other at a railroad stop called Leach, at Catlettsburg, a few miles
from Ashland, Kentucky, near the confluence of the Big Sandy
and the Ohio rivers.

While Blazer's destiny was at its crossroad, the management of
the Swiss Oil Company was thrashing, in meeting after meeting,
with its difficulties. The company was facing ruin; its stock had
dropped down to 10 per cent of its par value with no takers. Swiss
seemed to have exhausted its possibilities of raising money from
the public with its gold bond issue the year before. At this time,
they learned that a strong, stable and profitable competitor, the
Union Oil and Gas Company, with many productive wells and
leases throughout Kentucky, was for sale.

Ordinarily, one would expect that such information would
evoke ironic laughter from the board of the Swiss Oil Company,
but that would be to underestimate the agility of men seeking to
save their money, especially the quick-witted men from Chicago.

The Union Oil and Gas Company had been incorporated in
Indiana by three experienced and successful gas men: A. B. Ayres
of Fortville, Indiana, Frank A. Millikan of Indianapolis, and
A. C. Albin of Newman, Illinois, in 1917—the year that Miles first
attempted to form Swiss. By 1923, Union had accumulated 440
oil and gas leases and 3,200 producing oil wells—most of which
were small—in the Bowling Green district of western Kentucky.
They had also attracted a number of lawsuits. The lawsuits
stemmed from the fact that the three co-owners of Union quar-
reled incessantly among themselves. All three were gas men; none
could seem to grasp the intricacies of the oil business, and they
couldn't get along with each other. Through inexperience, they
allowed many of their leases to go undrilled beyond the time
promised at purchase, and not only left themselves open to the
charge that they were unreliable, but opened the way for other
oil companies and lease speculators to move in on these rights.[10]
This practice led them into many vexatious lawsuits.

[10] An oil lease is not a purchase of land, but often the purchase of the
right to drill and extract oil from someone else's land. Usually, the
lease is granted on the basis that drilling will take place within a
specified time or the oil rights revert to the landowner, who may sell
them again. Leases may also be sold before they expire, by one oilman
to another; or obtained by speculators who swap leases with oilmen.

Mainly because they couldn't get along with each other, however, Ayres, Albin and Millikan began to look for someone to whom they could sell. Their first firm offer came from a Philadelphia company, which offered $4.25 million. The offer, far below the estimates universally held of the Union properties, was refused as too low. J. I. Lamprecht II, son of Miles's old friend and a staunch friend of Miles himself (he was also successor to his father as head of the National Refining Company), estimated Union's worth at somewhere between $8 and $10 million. The worth of anything, however, is determined by the market situation. In other words, properties are worth only what one can actually persuade someone else to pay. The Philadelphia offer seemed to effectively set the range of what Union could expect to receive. Even at this price buyers were scarce.

The board of directors at Swiss Oil, considering the situation, moved as boldly as though the company were solvent: they negotiated an option to buy the Union Oil and Gas Company for $5 million. The terms were $1.5 million in cash; Ayres, Albin and Millikan to retain operating control until another $1 million was accumulated out of earnings, and the remaining $2.5 million to be paid in quarterly installments of $200,000.

All that remained was to raise the purchase money. In view of their financial circumstances, this did not look easy.

One would suppose that during 1923, with Swiss Oil in such a precarious position, that J. Fred Miles would have had too much on his mind to continue his efforts to expand. But Miles had created a large, though leaky vessel, and was determined to carry it into deeper waters, even though men were desperately manning the pumps to keep it afloat.

Miles wanted to integrate forward into refining. A crude oil producer could extend into the market. That had been Miles's vision for years; it was his dream; he would not relinquish it. Other worries existed, it was true, and these would probably have delayed his expansion toward refining had he not heard that Paul Blazer had resigned from The Great Southern and was dickering with the Petroleum Exploration Company. This meant that his plans would be anticipated by a competitor and this could hurt the fu-

ture position of the Swiss Oil Company—assuming it survived its
crisis.

In October 1923, at home, Paul Blazer was surprised to receive
a telephone call from Mr. Miles. Miles asked Blazer if he could
come over to the Swiss Oil offices that evening. Blazer said he was
engaged; he had an appointment that night with Petroleum Exploration, and the talks were too far along to be dropped.

"Come see me on your way over there," Miles urged, "I may
offer you a better proposition," and Blazer agreed to see him. Miles
offered the younger man a glittering proposition. He said he
would buy or build a refinery that Blazer could select, which was
the same offer, essentially, that Petroleum Exploration held out.
But Miles went further, saying that Blazer would not only be in
charge, but that a new company would be formed; Blazer would
become president and be given 10 per cent ownership. Blazer
listened, and left impressed.

During the following weeks Blazer received more telephone calls
and urgings from the persuasive Mr. Miles. In the interim, he
received little encouragement from Petroleum Exploration. By
one of those curious turns of the wheel that so often torment human beings, Mr. Kimball fell ill, and was unable to attend board
meetings. Furthermore, though the remaining ten members of the
board agreed, one by one, that the company should hire Paul
Blazer, Mr. Kimball's opinion began to reverse. Eventually, he
changed his mind entirely and the vote on Blazer became ten
against one. The one holdout was Mr. Kimball, the man who had
first approached and recommended him.

At this point, in December, Blazer called Petroleum Exploration
and asked to be released from his commitment. The directors in
his favor reluctantly agreed. Then Blazer called Miles, and said he
could accept his offer.

Miles immediately reduced his terms. Instead of giving Blazer
10 per cent of the stock of a new company formed by Swiss Oil
to operate a refinery, he offered to *lend Paul the money* to buy
10 per cent of the stock of such a company. Instead of being president of such a company, he said he could make Paul general manager.

By this time, Paul's bargaining position was greatly weakened, and he gave way to Miles's new terms. Miles left the selection and recommendation of a new refinery entirely up to Blazer; on that point he agreed with Petroleum Exploration. Blazer's first choice was the Latonia refinery owned by Mr. Edwards, of the Edwards Manufacturing Company. Mr. Edwards named a figure, and said, "If you can raise the money, I'll sell you the refinery."

Blazer went to Miles, who agreed to the sum, and then went back to Mr. Edwards. Edwards, when he heard the money was available, grinned craftily and said, "Now that I know what it's worth, I think I'll keep this refinery."

But Blazer had taken a good look around and the Catlettsburg refinery offered, in his opinion, as many advantages as the refinery at Latonia. He said later, "I don't think the history of the company would have been any different if the Latonia deal had gone through." By the first of January 1924, he had organized his observations and conclusions, and turned them over to Miles for presentation to the board of Swiss. To this day, the memorandum constitutes an almost classic analysis; for many years it served as a blueprint.

On January 26, 1924, the board of directors of Swiss Oil decided to pay the Union Oil and Gas management $91,000 for an option to buy their company for $5 million. Almost as a by-the-way, they agreed to the organization of a subsidiary corporation to be named the Ashland Refining Company, with Paul G. Blazer as general manager, and to purchase the Catlettsburg refinery for $212,000 ($50,000 in cash and the balance in five installments), from the Great Eastern Refinery Company.

Paul G. Blazer had no way of knowing, in early 1924, of the dreadful extent of the Swiss Oil Company's difficulties. To him, his new position as general manager of the Ashland Refining Company was a heaven-sent opportunity both to prove himself and to improve his circumstances.

And the board of directors of the Swiss Oil Company had no way of knowing that this young man, not yet thirty-four years old, would lead them out of the woods.

Section Two—Ashland Refining and Swiss Oil

1924–1929

In their youths, the towns of Catlettsburg and Ashland, Kentucky, presented a study in contrasts. Catlettsburg, called the Gate City in its prime because it is located just west of the confluence of the Big Sandy and Ohio rivers, was a lusty, brawling port whose saloons echoed to the caterwauling of river rats and lumberjacks; where the sound of sawmills made the air shrill; where rafts formed a "solid carpet of logs from the mouth of the Sandy to Keyes Creek," [1] whose fancy women (as different as could be from plain women) were renowned.

A few miles above the bend, past the merging of the rivers, Ashland enjoyed a contrary reputation: it was known as "the place where they have seven Sundays a week." It was a town of many virtues, few vices. In addition to iron works and furnaces, it had thriving churches, watchful clergymen and faithful congregations; tidy, well-tended farms; quiet shops and citizens; and seemed outstripped by its rowdy neighbor.

But years passed and the lumbermen moved on to other areas, and the destinies of the two towns shifted in a manner to warm the heart of any moralist. The river trade slowed to a trickle and the sawmills stilled, the saloons and their habitués disappeared, Catlettsburg began to reminisce and drift into the peace of the sedate. Ashland,[2] however, began to reap the rewards of virtue

[1] *A History of Ashland, Kentucky, Centennial Souvenir;* p. 6.
[2] Situated 147 miles upriver from Cincinnati, O., 320 miles downriver

The Ashland Refining Company. (1924)

and diligence. The American Rolling Mill Company, predecessor of today's Armco Steel, arrived at Ashland in 1920 to build the world's first continuous sheet rolling mill; by 1922 had purchased the Ashland Steel Company and the Norton Iron Works as well as the Ironton[3] furnaces; and was the major reason the population of Ashland jumped from less than 15,000 to 29,000 in five years.

At the crest of this boom, the Swiss Oil Company organized the Ashland Refining Company and placed Paul Blazer in charge. Blazer moved his wife Georgia, infant children Paul Jr. and Doris from Lexington.[4]

Senator Tom Combs, president of Swiss Oil, was impressed with

---

from Pittsburgh, Pa., 203 rail miles from Louisville, Ky. Ashland was originally settled by the Poage family, Scots Presbyterians, who came to America in 1738 and played a large part in the Revolution. They were landowners and slaveowners in Virginia who moved into Kentucky in the 1790s. The new community was called Poage's Settlement until it was incorporated in 1856; the name Ashland was taken from the name of Henry Clay's estate near Lexington, Kentucky.

[3] Situated on the opposite bank of the Ohio River from Ashland, Ky.

[4] Dottie Monroe and Mrs. Monroe accompanied them, but only briefly. Soon, Dottie went elsewhere to teach school, and her mother accompanied her. Eventually Dottie returned to Ashland as a teacher, and with her mother had an apartment in town.

young Blazer and visited his home. Georgia Blazer was never to
forget the stocky, ruddy-faced Senator standing before the mantle
in their new home, telling anecdotes packed with colorful detail
about Kentucky life, personalities, and politics. Paul briefed her on
the foibles of the Swiss Oil directors generally. She recalls his saying, "Charley Evans is a demon for hot coffee. I've seen him send
steaming cups back to the kitchen on the basis they were *too cold*."

The activities of the American Rolling Mill Company in Ashland helped the atmosphere for the newcomers. The town was
breaking out of its insular Kentucky mold; its streets were filled
with persons from Illinois, Indiana, Ohio and other states, as

Senator Tom Combs,
president of the Swiss Oil Company.

well as job seekers from Appalachia. Its old established families watched the influx warily.

J. Fred Miles, general manager of Swiss Oil, proved a prickly sponsor for Blazer. Paul agreed to the appointment of Charley Jouett, an experienced refinery superintendent who had managed The Great Southern's refinery at Pryse, Kentucky. But Blazer was not pleased to be told that Jouett would receive 4 per cent of the Ashland stock—and that this inducement would come from Paul's 10 per cent share. Paul had to sell Jouett the 4 per cent at cost and reduce his own equity to 6 per cent—although the lure of a 10 per cent share had been dangled before Paul as an inducement in the beginning.

Paul's organization was modest: three rooms on the seventh floor of the Second National Bank building on Ashland's main Winchester Avenue. There a small staff consisting of Roy Grossenbach who handled the books, Bill Waples in charge of purchasing, S. D. Rion, an expert on freight rates, and Paul's faithful secretary, Margaret Hallnan, worked.[5]

The core of Paul Blazer's new domain was a tiny refinery at Catlettsburg, that town now settling sedately into gentility. The works were extremely simple, being, in the words of one observer, "a skimming plant consisting of three batch stills hooked together with steam lines." Its capacity was 1,000 bbls. a day—when it was working. Altogether, counting superintendent Charley Jouett and the watchman's dog, it had a staff of twenty-five.

The history of the refinery was not designed to reassure the faint-hearted. Originally constructed by oil men from Pennsylvania, it had produced red lubricating stock during World War I, and had passed through a series of owners. All, apparently, had lost money; the men who sold it to Swiss Oil had succeeded in losing $96,325 in the two years 1922–1924. These men, who operated under the then fashionably grandiose name of the Great East-

---

[5] Miss Hallnan was Paul Blazer's secretary in Lexington; when he moved to Ashland, she decided to come along. She remained with him until her death in 1946, and after a brief interval, was replaced by Mrs. Phyllis Geyer. In his entire career—one of the most illustrious in the oil industry—Mr. Blazer had only two secretaries.

ern Refining Company, consisted of two coal experts: J. A. Dalton
and John Kelly. They had been persuaded to enter the refining
business by a chemist, D. H. Gilman. Mr. Gilman, who was later
described by Paul Blazer as "a good chemist but a poor businessman," had—Paul thought—listened attentively when Paul and
Eric Shatford discussed the possibilities of the Catlettsburg plant
at the time that all three were working in The Great Southern.

Mr. Gilman also, it seems, convinced young John C. C. Mayo
Jr.[6] to set up an oil marketing venture in the Ashland area. Both
ventures were worthy in the abstract—as Paul Blazer was later to
prove—but neither succeeded at the time.

Both ventures were launched while Blazer was still working
very hard at The Great Southern, and were of mostly passing interest to him then.[7] But when he became general manager of the
Ashland Refining Company, and the problems of the refinery and
the marketing possibilities of the Ashland area became matters of
intense interest to him, the experiences of his predecessors became
matters worthy of closer study.

Most refineries in the region received their crude oil either from
the eastern seaboard, the Southwest, or the Gulf. The Catlettsburg
plant was located, as exactly as an "x" on a treasure map, at the
point of maximum transportation costs from all these quarters.
This meant that the Catlettsburg plant, assured of its own crude
supply from local sources, could not only meet but go below the
prices of such competitors as Standard Oil (Ohio). Not only would
the Ashland Refining Company be able to meet prices set by its
competitors; it could underprice them and still be able to exceed

[6] John C. C. Mayo is still a resident of Ashland, and has had an extensive and highly interesting business career; he has served for many
years as Chairman of the Board of the Second National Bank in Ashland.
The Mayo family, once prominent in the coal business, has been one of
the most outstanding in eastern Kentucky for many years.

[7] Paul Blazer, when he was sales vice president for Great Southern,
sold gasoline in the Ashland area and became fairly well acquainted
with the Catlettsburg refinery, although as an observer only. During his
survey, when he was in actuality looking for a job, he was conducted
around the area by John Buckingham, a local banker. This circumstance
later gave rise to the legend that the tour was responsible for his later
arrival in the area.

their per barrel profit. In effect, it could create its own market while benefiting from its regional position.

The inherent advantages of the Catlettsburg-Ashland location existed before Blazer arrived on the scene. It was his clear perception and ability to use these advantages, and to create from them levers to expand the operation, that later made them seem self-evident. Their obviousness, however, only became generally evident after he exhibited their value—like a safety-pin, whose utility is clear—after its invention.

Nevertheless, the first four months of the Catlettsburg operation, from February to June 1924, showed a steady loss. Blazer, going through the plant with a microscope, saw that it had been allowed to deteriorate. For safety reasons alone, repairs and replacements had to be immediately instituted. He spent $25,000 almost at once on repairs; another $10,000 on new equipment. He and Charley Jouett examined the staff with the searching eyes of men anxious to reduce slackness; they dismissed some whose performances had become indifferent, and told the rest they were associated with a property that had cost all previous owners dearly. But Paul Blazer, to whom the refinery represented opportunity, gave each of the men his personal assurance that their own long-range interests were the same as his: sensible men would pull together to retain a mutual livelihood.

The following month, July, Paul made a trip to Columbus, Ohio to meet a burly, shock-haired young University of Michigan graduate named Ben Heath.[8] Heath, who had received his degree

---

[8] Heath was a considerably young man himself. He was born in Warren, Pa. in 1900; his mother was from Denmark, his father from Newfoundland. His grandfather had, in Newfoundland, been a manufacturer of fish barrels. Hearing about the oil business in Pennsylvania, Heath's grandfather had emigrated to the U. S. where he made barrels; eventually went to work for Valvoline in 1885. When lube oils were developed, Ben's father became an oil blender, a highly prized skill. Ben himself went to work at an early age; decided to go back to school after working in machine shops and drafting offices. He bullied his way into the University of Michigan without a high school diploma, took straight A's the first year, graduated in 1923. He was recommended to Paul Blazer by one of his teachers, Dr. Leslie, his own letter of application being a coincidence. Blazer, who knew Dr. Leslie to be an authority,

The refinery personnel. (Spring, 1924)

in chemical engineering the year before, had read in one of the
trade publications that Paul Blazer was in charge of the Catlettsburg plant, and had written asking for a job. Not receiving an immediate reply, he had almost forgotten the matter when Paul sent
him a letter.

Blazer made a tremendous impression on Ben Heath. Still athletic and vigorous, his questions were shrewd and his comments
to the point. As they were seated in Paul's Maxwell roadster waiting for a light to change, Paul—as soon as the light changed—
moved up against the car ahead and helped it to move by a
mighty shove. "Whew," Heath thought, "this is a real go-getter."
Actually, Blazer had probably been looking at a filling station—
it was his only bad driving habit—but Heath, slightly bemused
by the interview and the energy of his prospective employer—
thought the incident deliberate.

Heath arrived in Catlettsburg toward the end of the month and

had asked for the name of a promising young graduate. Heath was ten
years younger than Blazer, whose personality never ceased to amaze and
mystify him.

began his duties as assistant superintendent under Charley Jouett. "I was chief chemist and engineer as well," he recalls. Jouett, a Texan who had learned refining on the job with the Texas Oil Company and The Great Southern, was glad to get the help: Blazer's questions, suggestions and directives were more than he could comfortably handle himself.

In July and August 1924, the improvement in the plant's efficiency and in general conditions in the industry combined to lift profits to $5,000 a month; by September they were up to $10,000 a month. Heath considered his new boss a phenomenon of nature who seemed able to go without sleep or rest, and who was constantly on the other end of the telephone. Heath thought Blazer slept surrounded by telephones.[9] This was an exaggeration, but a revealing one.

Heath had, at the time, a large family; his absence from home and his absorption in the plant were not always understood. He would allude to this, but Blazer—a product of a stern home where work was paramount—seemed oblivious.

The refinery men generally considered themselves the focus of Paul Blazer's attention. But Blazer was also star salesman of the Ashland Refining Company, as well as its office manager, planner, and director. During the day, he was most often in its offices in the Second National Bank building talking either personally or on the phone with customers and the many persons who kept him abreast of the market. Often, he was on the road. Equally often he dictated letters, examined the accounts and gave instructions regarding the books.

While Blazer was immersed in these details, the directors of the Swiss Oil Company were fending off their creditors with one hand, and searching the bushes for money with the other. J. Fred Miles and Senator Combs, accompanied at times by the corporation secretary and legal counsel E. L. McDonald and at other times by other men whose presence they thought might be helpful, visited men in Cleveland, Chicago, New York City, Baltimore and Philadelphia in search of financing. At one time it appeared Blair & Co. might come to their assistance; at another, Cyrus Eaton of Otis & Com-

⁹ He had only the usual number: one upstairs and one down.

pany seemed encouraging. Between times, Swiss Oil underwent the humiliation of requesting repeated extensions of their option to buy from the three owners of the Union Oil Company. Finally these gentlemen granted a last extension to January 25, 1925. After that date, they warned, the doors of this opportunity would be closed.

Shortly after the year 1924 ended, in January 1925, Blazer reported quietly that the Ashland Refining Company had made a profit of $20,000 in the month of December alone and $60,000 in the preceding six months. Its throughput for the year was in the neighborhood of a half-million barrels—more than at any time in the history of the plant. Its refined products sales amounted to 18 million gallons for a total revenue of $1.2 million, plus $100,000 in products resold from other refiners.

The Colonel, a small boat captained by Charley Lewis, and a barge had been included in the original purchase of the Catlettsburg property of Great Eastern. In his annual report to the directors, Paul Blazer mentioned that the boat made a profit of $6,000. He went on to outline the advantages that expansion of river transportation would bring in its wake . . . and concluded with a description of his credit policies—which were rigorous—and with the dry comment that bad debts in his first ten and a half months as general manager amounted to $53.

His report ran to seven pages on legal size paper and was remarkable because it was written as a straight narrative in which the explanations were accompanied by figures, and both light and shadow were presented. This evidence of Blazer's literary talent, no surprise to those who knew him from his days at Curtis, was nevertheless unusual in business. Many businessmen were apt to talk to their directors only in numbers; Blazer did not make this mistake.

His report was also prophetic: he discussed both immediate and long range market tactics and possibilities and laid the groundwork for fairly large expenditures to come.

But despite this gratifying report from their small subsidiary, the directors of the Swiss Oil Company received it with relative inattention: their eyes were riveted upon the Union Oil and Gas purchase.

At the eleventh hour, Mr. James Martin of Pynchon & Company, a member of the board almost from the inception of the company, and a man whose recommendations originally persuaded Mr. Halle, Mr. Insull and a number of other Chicago financiers to invest in the company, came to the rescue of Swiss Oil. One can see his reasons: the failure of Swiss at this moment would not only cost him money, but would seriously embarrass him in front of some very important persons whom he had persuaded into the situation.

Mr. Martin was one of eleven partners in Pynchon & Company; he proposed to his partners that Pynchon & Company advance Swiss Oil $1.75 million in cash, in return for a $2 million note from Swiss Oil. This amounted to a discount of 12½ per cent. Also that Pynchon receive $2 million in Swiss Oil common stock as a bonus; plus three more seats—excluding Mr. Martin's—on the Swiss Oil board of directors.

This meant that the Swiss Oil Company would not only be saved from immediate ruin, but that the investments already made in the company would be buttressed and strengthened by the addition of the Union Oil and Gas properties. These consisted, in the main, of 486 producing oil wells and 70 producing gas wells on 13,000 acres in Lawrence and Johnson counties, Kentucky. Their aggregate value, as rated by observers, was in the neighborhood of $8 million.

Faced with this tremendously loaded choice, the Swiss Oil board of directors gratefully voted for their own rescue, and delivered their down payment to the three owners of the Union Oil company on the very last day of their option.

Jonah had swallowed the whale.

One result of this last-minute rescue was the virtual eclipse of J. Fred Miles within the Swiss Oil Company. For the first time the annual report for 1924, issued in March 1925, was signed by Senator Tom Combs instead of Miles. Miles would never again be *de facto* chief executive of Swiss Oil. But Paul Blazer's star, although still fairly low on the horizon, was rising.

In Chicago, young Joe Levin caught sight of that star out of the corner of his eye when he was called into the office of Robert C.

Schaffner,[10] president of A. G. Becker & Co., the investment firm
where Levin had gone to work in 1922.

"You went to the University of Chicago," Mr. Schaffner said to
Levin. "D'you remember a student named Paul G. Blazer?"

Levin had no need to cudgel his memory; he and Blazer had
worked together on the *Cap & Gown* in their junior year, and he
vividly recalled the stellar performance Blazer put on as business
manager of the annual. Naturally, after explaining this, he asked
why the question had been put, and Schaffner said, "Halle thinks
he's smart; a good man to keep an eye on."

The year that Swiss Oil obtained the Union Oil properties and
that Blazer started on the road to success with the Ashland Refining Company, 1925, was also the year that the long, drawn-out,
sensational developments regarding the Teapot Dome scandal
were finally beginning to draw to a close. Indictments of Harry F.
Sinclair, ex-Secretary of the Interior Albert B. Fall and Edward L.
Doheny Sr. were handed down. An investigation had revealed the
skeleton of this disgraceful affair: that oil man Doheny had given
Mr. Fall $100,000 for a government lease of an oil field in Cali-
fornia, and collusion regarding the allotment of oil leases to gov-
ernment-owned land in Wyoming. Even from this distance, one
can still feel the shock waves that went through the nation as
these matters were disclosed. Technically, the issues became hope-
lessly entangled in court; eventually Mr. Fall was sent to the
penitentiary, Mr. Sinclair was sent to the Washington, D.C., jail
for three months for contempt of the Senate, and Mr. Doheny, on
a variety of technicalities, escaped.

A great injury was done the oil industry. The resentment of
the public against the industry, so virulent before World War I,
had been somewhat assuaged by the Supreme Court ruling that
broke up the Standard Oil Company; now the oil industry had to
struggle against the weight of a new onus. To Blazer, toiling
diligently in the least glamorous, most competitive and exacting

[10] Mr. Schaffner's brother was a partner in Hart, Schaffner & Marx.
A. G. Becker & Co., founded in 1893, is one of the largest commercial
paper (short-term notes, etc.) handlers in the U.S., includes investment
banking among its services, is a very well-known midwest brokerage firm
and frequent underwriter of large issues.

end of the industry, the issue seemed far away. To the nation it was traumatic because the men involved had been friendly at one time with President Harding. Although President Harding's records and accounts were examined later and proved that despite his personal failings, he was rigidly honest, the mystique of the White House was tarnished—and the press did not make any effort to restore its gloss. The period between 1922 and 1925, when the Teapot Dome was in the presslight, gave rise to such thunderous editorial clamor that one wonders how the industry survived at all.

Also, in 1925, Floyd Collins was trapped in a cave in Cave City, Kentucky, on January 31. A national press vigil swelled by the morbidly curious lasted two weeks (Mr. Collins was not extricated in time, and died in the cave). Wine bricks were popular; Dillon, Read & Company bought the Dodge Motor Car Company for $146 million, the largest cash transaction in the nation's history until then; later, Dillon, Read headed a banking syndicate that issued stock and converted Dodge into a public company. The Scopes trial—used ever since as a symbol of American imbecility by those who dote on such examples—began in Tennessee. Crossword puzzles became the rage, the Florida land boom began; Trinity in North Carolina changed its name to Duke University in order to benefit from a trust established by the tobacco magnate; Christopher Wren's *Beau Geste* was a best seller; *Desire Under the Elms* opened on Broadway; Lon Chaney scared movie-goers in *Phantom of the Opera*; writers of biographies, traditionally saccharine, dipped their pens in vitriol; three major poets, Sandburg, Eliot, and Lindsay, appeared. People boasted of having made "whoopee" together; Texas Guinan glittered like a rhinestone; Jimmy Durante became popular and so did the Twenty-One Club; H. L. Mencken became the leading national scold of the decade. Later, Georgia Blazer said, "They write about the Roaring Twenties, but we certainly didn't see them. I was too busy with my home and children, and Paul with the company."

It was a period of work for others also. Most of the widely publicized events and personalities of the time amounted only to spume on the ocean of events, worthy only of the quicksilver attention of newspapermen. Beneath the surface, mighty changes were

at work in the deeps of science, psychology and technology. It was
a year when a large section of the economy began to revolve like
a wheel around the hub of the automobile industry. Discoveries
came cracking: carbon black, a byproduct of natural gas and later
of oil, previously useful only to printers and a few other trades,
was discovered to have miraculous abilities to strengthen and
extend the life of rubber and hence of tires; the steel industry
boomed under the need for car bodies and construction; highways
began to thread their way across the nation; garages mushroomed
everywhere; filling stations began to compete on all four corners
of busy intersections; the oil industry argued over patent rights
and new methods of refining new products—including gasoline.

In the spring of 1925, "Flood" Newman and "Van" Vandeveer,
two young men with whom Paul Blazer had various business dealings and who worked for the American Petroleum Products Company, a firm of Cleveland oil resellers, made a mysterious appointment to meet Paul in the Cleveland Public Library.

Paul kept the appointment, and with many glances over their
shoulders and suspicious glances at other library patrons, the two
men confided they would soon go into business on their own.
Blazer assured them of his cooperation; it was a period when men
generally sought their own ventures. Shortly afterward, in July
1925, they established the Allied Oil Company, to specialize in
fuel oil; motored down to Ashland during the summer and spent
the day with the Blazers. It was a period for young men and young
businesses.

Among other young men in the city of Ashland was Dr. Leslie
Winans, whose offices were directly across the hall on the seventh
floor of the Second National Bank building from those of Ashland
Refining Company. Dr. Winans became aware, after a time, that
someone in the Ashland Refining offices worked at all hours of
the night. He discovered that it was Paul Blazer when he was
summoned by Mrs. Blazer to attend one of the children. In conversation, he learned that the Blazers and the Winanses had, without knowing one another, once lived only a few blocks from each
other in Chicago; had even attended the University of Chicago
at the same time, and had mutual friends at the University. The
coincidences delighted all four, and they became close friends.

After these discoveries, Paul Blazer would often drop in to chat with Dr. Winans; Winans thought Blazer was a tremendous talker and an even harder worker. His sharp physician's eye took note of the fact that Blazer drove himself hard. "He probably didn't pay enough attention to his diet," Winans said. "He rarely ate breakfast, lunched when he remembered, missed many dinners at home. He would work all day, drive to Columbus or Cincinnati and get a train for Chicago; return, drive back. . . . If he was exhausted, he would pull up in the car somewhere and take a nap. He seemed to work hardest, then and later, from 10 o'clock at night to 3 or 4 in the morning . . ."

Dr. Winans was drawn into the Blazer vortex. "He was a brilliant guy," he said of Paul, "I never met a more brilliant." It was a revelation to Winans—as it would be to many professional men today—to realize that business can be a dedication.

Meanwhile the Ashland Refining Company was manufacturing gasoline. Blazer explained to the Swiss Oil directors that gasoline could be marketed all year round. The plant also produced fuel oils, a residual refinery product that Blazer considered an excellent item mainly in the winter. Other products included naphthas, rubber solvent, manufacturer's kerosene, petroleum coke and furnace distillates.

In his second year as general manager of Ashland Refining, according to the distilled version of his performance printed (for the first time) in a separate section of the Swiss Oil annual report for 1926, the refinery racked up a clear profit of $78,000. In his report to the directors of Swiss Oil, Blazer explained, in his usual expository manner, that the refinery had been improved by the addition of "bubble towers" to two of the stills, thus allowing continuous distillation, at a cost of $100,000. The towers made it possible to fractionate various products at different stages of introduced heat; the products were then piped off. This extended the product range and the performance of the refinery, and also allowed the production of high test premium gasoline. This premium gasoline was sold under the name Pepper, sold through a number of service stations J. Fred Miles had earlier acquired for Swiss Oil. In addition to these changes, Blazer knew that other important but expensive improvements should be introduced into the plant, but because a number of different systems of thermal cracking methods had appeared on the market, truly difficult and crucial questions of selection arose.

Blazer was spared some agonies of choice by the fact that J. Ogden Armour, prime mover and owner of 40 per cent of the stock of Universal Oil Products, was also an investor in Swiss Oil. So was Mr. Halle. On his trips to Chicago, Blazer met with both men a number of times, and described the condition of his refinery, its equipment, and its prospects. They arranged in turn for Universal Oil Products engineers to survey the Catlettsburg plant and estimate the cost of installing a Dubbs cracking unit. Blazer was the third refiner in the nation to obtain such a unit, a circumstance that gave him a substantial lead over many of his competitors, and put him near the head of the line in terms of modern equipment.

The step was important for other reasons as well, because it meant that the Ashland Refining Company was judged, by these senior men, worthy of heavier investment. A preferred stock issue of Ashland Refining was put out, amounting to $125,000— the actual cost of the Dubbs unit.

By the end of 1926, with three years of Paul Blazer's management on record, gross figures ran to $1.2 million in 1924, $2.3 million in 1925, and $3 million in 1926. In all that time only $53 in bad debts were charged off, and $325 in disputed accounts: remarkable evidence of careful management. Blazer, whose reactions were invariably creative, himself remarked that this indicated his restrictions were too narrow, and announced he would relax some of his earlier rules.

At this ingenuous note, doubts suddenly seize us, and we begin to read the record more carefully. One remarkable aspect of Blazer's refinery improvements was in the selections he made. The first, which consisted of adding fractionating towers, was a direct result of his trade reading. Seeing in a publication that a small young group of modernizers called the Southwest Engineers had successfully made such an installation at a refinery in California that had shell stills, he called them to Catlettsburg; the result was the first such installation east of the Rockies.

In the same manner, despite the happy propinquity of Mr.

Armour, Mr. Halle and their connection with UOP, it seems obvious that Blazer did not select the Dubbs unit on their recommendation, but because The Great Southern had, in 1923, ordered and installed a Dubbs Unit, and Blazer *knew it worked.*

Neither in 1925 nor later did Blazer ever seem to be imbued with a desire to be first in any experiment; on the contrary. His was a very hard head; he operated on the soundest of business principles: try only what you know—and have proof—will work. In his late thirties, Blazer had learned the basics of business; later he was to learn more intricate maneuvers, but one lesson he seemed to have mastered ahead of all others: the art of persuasion.

In retrospect, it appears that Paul Blazer began his operations at Catlettsburg with a grand strategy in mind, but he himself always denied this. He met the problems of each day as they rose before him, and sought to solve them in the most practical manner. The increase in the use of waterways to carry the refinery products, and the improvements in the functioning of the refinery added up, as they accumulated, to extensive and ambitious movements.

But in his lengthy letters to the directors, Paul Blazer did not present either the use of the waterways or the expansion of the refinery as grand objectives. The waterways became alluring because the railroad rates were high. New refinery units, additions and improvements were suggested only after the possibilities of repairs became exhausted. Blazer examined and re-examined the number of his accounts and the geographical distribution of his market, and added a new customer here and there only after he had met and talked with the man, had considered his probity and means, and how he could provide the services needed.

His accounts of operations are highly detailed, and one can only speculate about the awe with which they must have filled his readers, for they impress—even years later—with his grasp of every particular aspect of the Ashland Refining Co. operations. Throughout, they exude a practicality of approach, and a carefulness, that at first convey a sense of great caution. It is a shock to realize, reading the record a second time, that in his first nine months as general manager, Blazer spent $35,000 for new equipment; in his second year, 1925, he spent $100,000 for fractionating towers (or

ordered them); in 1926 invested another $150,000. He managed to
spend more in improvements than the refinery originally cost,
within his first two years of operation. But this breakneck speed
was accompanied by rhetoric—and habits—of extreme caution.
Oddly enough, the combination was an accurate reflection of his
methods. He was keenly aware that a business is a living organism,
vulnerable both to outside attack and to internal illness. It was
necessary not only to overcome internal problems, but to exert
effort and move forward. But he was chary of glowing promises;
he avoided the discussion of glittering opportunities. In his pragmatic view, the dark shadows of possible failure fell across the
greenest pastures, even as he galloped toward them. He knew the
world, and the frailty of its glitter.

While he strengthened Ashland Refining and extended its markets, he made fairly frequent trips to Aledo to see his friends of
childhood, and to keep his stern but far-seeing father, David
Blazer, apprised of his progress. While there on a visit in the
spring of 1926, he listened while his brother Herschel praised
young Everett Wells,[11] who was then a student at the University
of Illinois at Urbana.

Young Wells happened to be home at the time, recovering from
scarlet fever (in those days of quarantine, ailing students were

[11] Everett F. Wells, born 1905 in Aledo, Ill., where his father owned a
hardware store and was president of the First National Bank and a
State Representative.

A close friend of Herschel Blazer, Everett knew Paul Blazer—mostly
casually and by hearsay—from childhood.

Wells entered the University of Illinois at Urbana, was sponsored
into the Psi Upsilon fraternity by another Aledo boy two years older
named Emrick; became president of the Illinois Chapter of Psi Upsilon,
and was student manager of the famous Red Grange football team that
made headlines during this period.

A better than average student, Wells was a member of "practically all
the honorary societies," majored in economics and law—the same subjects that interested Paul Blazer in a corresponding period—was slim,
quietly friendly and well-known to Paul Blazer.

Over the years, Everett Wells was to rise to the top reaches of the
corporation: he was president of the Company (1957–1964), remains a
potent policy maker and is today chairman of the executive committee
and a senior member of management.

sent home); he was due to graduate shortly and had no particular plans. Paul talked to young Wells about the exciting prospects at Ashland Refining, a forerunner of dozens of such talks he was to have with other young men in later years. Such prospects sound terribly convincing when they come from the man in charge.

Wells agreed to a trial, and after a slight delay reported to work in Ashland on June 10, 1926. He was the second college man to be hired and was soon spending long days at the Catlettsburg refinery, helping to load and unload cars; cleaning tanks; working in the product laboratory; doing whatever he was told. He also absorbed the meaning of the activities around him and learned the basics of refining. He seldom saw Paul Blazer, but learned that Blazer was always on the other end of the phone.

Ben Heath was one of the busiest men in the refinery. Once during this period Heath said to Blazer, "I've worked 18 straight hours today, *and I'm going home.*" His angry tone left no room to mistake his humor; he was amazed the next day to learn that Blazer had decided to raise his salary.

Newman and Vandeveer, in Cleveland, placed their first fuel oil order with Ashland; in the next few months they began to place a number of such orders for their new venture, Allied Oil. One day Blazer told Heath that Allied would buy a number of cars of fuel oil, provided it would resist twenty-degree-below-zero temperatures. Heath assured him Ashland could meet these specifications. The order was placed and the fuel oil sent on its way. Then Heath got a call from Blazer in Cleveland, who said the oil was frozen in the cars: come at once.

Heath—to whom an emergency trip was routine—went to Cleveland to the railroad siding where the shipment sat. He clambered atop one of the cars, inserted a stick and discovered the oil had the consistency of wet cement. He took away a sample, melted it, put it through the standard ASTM [12] test, and according to the book, discovered that the oil met the twenty below zero specifications. The test, in other words, was no good. Searching for a solution, Heath went to the Cosmo Laboratories in Cleveland—with

[12] American Society of Testing Materials.

whom Allied had a contract—and devised a better test for the future.

"What happened to the oil in those tank cars?" someone asked, unwilling to allow that part of the anecdote to dangle forgotten.

"Oh, I ordered some steam coils and had that melted," Heath said quickly. Obviously, that had presented no particular problem; he could only recall his exasperation that the test had proven him wrong, and the fact that within a day or so he had devised a new and better test for the future.

Newman and Vandeveer, delighted and impressed with the outcome, especially since they had followed the sequence with the rapt attention that only men struggling in their first few months on a venture can appreciate, insisted on taking Heath out on the town at this conclusion, and smilingly watched as he hugely ate and drank . . .

In the interim, the Dubbs unit was being installed by men from the Universal Oil Products Company; slowly grew into position with Paul Blazer watching it between his other activities. Among the men hired to work on the Dubbs unit once it was installed was a 27-year-old named Palmer Talbutt,[13] at that time the Dubbs operator at the Pryse refinery of Great Southern—Paul's old company.

Although they worked for the same company, Palmer Talbutt hadn't met Paul Blazer; he recalls that someone pointed Blazer out to him in a bowling alley in Lexington a few summers before.

[13] Palmer Cummins Talbutt, born 1899, was raised in Lexington, Ky. His grandfather operated a hotel in Blue Lick Springs, where the discovery of a cache of dinosaur bones and scenic attractions combined to create one of America's first fashionable resorts of the region, circa the early 1800s. Talbutt's family emigrated to the U.S. from England in the late 1700s.

Palmer himself graduated from high school in Lexington, cut his education short to join the U.S. Navy during World War I and was sent overseas, returned to briefly attend the University of Kentucky, held a variety of jobs. He joined the Great Southern's Pryse refinery where he became a Dubbs operator, joined the Ashland Refining Company in 1926 as a Dubbs operator. Paul Blazer came to realize his potential and Talbutt moved upward in the organization; eventually became a vice president and director, and is now a consultant to the corporation; remains a director.

He noticed then that Blazer moved stiffly, discovered later that he wore a brace for his back. Once Talbutt went to work for the Ashland Refining Company, he was to revise his estimate of Blazer many times—always upward.

Talbutt soon became aware that the Catlettsburg refinery was an experimental laboratory for Paul Blazer. "He spent hours, days, weeks and months poring over its details," Talbutt said. "He got so he knew the location of every valve."

While Palmer Talbutt was discovering the unusual personality of his new boss and Ben Heath was struggling against manifold problems, Everett Wells was moved, after four probationary months, from the refinery in Catlettsburg to the Ashland offices in the bank building. He found himself elevated, without further ado, from helper and apprentice to full-fledged sales partner with Paul Blazer.

"We each did whatever arose," Wells said. His conversations with Paul became extensive and instructive. "He was mature," Wells recalls, looking back. "He had matured in the magazine business."

They had plenty to discuss. The price of crude was high in 1926, which meant that refined products did well also; Somerset (Kentucky) crude sold for $2.60 a barrel. But problems that Blazer, Wells, Waples and Rion had to bear in mind centered around crude oil inventories and purchases, refinery runs, possible sales and new distributors, and rail costs. The rail costs were crucial: "There were more independent companies then," Wells says, "and more independent refineries. Ashland competed with majors as well as minors—with Standard, Shell, Pure (now a major itself)—all selling fast with an emphasis on price. Competition from the West and Southwest also existed, but their rates were high and their deliveries slower. Within the office, work was freely and openly conducted; there was no secrecy regarding accounts. Everything was based on mutual effort." He paused, and then added, "But the days were long, and they added up to a long year."

The year 1926 was a long year that added up to net earnings ("after liberal charges for depreciation and all contingencies," said

Senator Combs in the annual report) of $160,850 for Ashland
Refining. The following year, prices began to fall and a great
many refineries began to undergo hard, extremely hard, times.

Difficulties arrived at Catlettsburg, not through any of these
normal avenues, however—Blazer had prepared against those—
but through the great persuasive skill of J. Fred Miles himself.
Shortly after the Ides of March 1927, Miles abandoned his at-
tempts to regain his control of Swiss Oil,[14] and resigned. Simultaneously upon his resignation, he announced he had formed
(with the help of the Texas Company), the Louisville Refining
Company, and would reactivate a shutdown refinery in Louisville,
Kentucky.

News that Miles would become a competitor could not have
been pleasing to Paul Blazer; Miles was, after all, a powerful and
gifted man. But even worse was the fact that Miles had, apparently, been lining up men throughout the company to leave with
him. Among them was Charley Jouett, the superintendent at the
Catlettsburg refinery. In turn, Jouett convinced all the number
one and two operators (the most highly rated men) that their
future would be better with Miles than remaining with Blazer,
and when he left, these men left with him. So did Bill Waples,
the purchasing agent in the office in Ashland, who became Miles's
purchasing agent.

Not only did Blazer have to take personal charge of the refinery
during this emergency; he had to find replacements. The first task
was a mankiller: he met it with his usual head-on approach. For
three days and nights, Blazer went with catnaps instead of sleep,
to see that the production at the refinery was not interrupted or
stopped. Boldly, he promoted all his number three and four operators into the two top grades; discovered—as have so many managers before and since—that seniority sometimes makes distinctions less tangible than impressive—and that his new top operators
worked well.

He learned a hard lesson though, that he was not to forget.
He had always paid close attention to the performance of the

[14] Several of the directors, and in particular a Louisville attorney
named Eli Brown, thought Miles had not been well treated, and agitated
over this and other issues for several years.

men; he was the sort of supervisor who learned each man's name, and the names of his wife and children; who knew and liked his men. He also trusted them, and it was a great shock when so many departed in the wake of Charley Jouett. Miles and Jouett seemed to prove the fragility of labor relationships, but Blazer did not—either then or later—turn against the men in the refinery. On the contrary, he went to extraordinary lengths to establish and maintain his friendships among the operators; years later these friendships were still firm, and extended to their sons. Long after the company had grown beyond the stage where one might have expected such contacts to continue, the chairman of the board and operators in the plant were still on a first name, personal basis.

Before Charley Jouett left, however, he added injury to insult by selling back to Blazer—at a price 2½ times greater—the 4 per cent share in Ashland Refining stock that Blazer had originally sold to him at par. Blazer swallowed hard, and paid the price. He did not forget, but evidence that he did forgive came years later, when Jouett fell upon evil times and could not find even modest employment. Blazer, apprised of this, saw to it that Jouett was given a job.

Through a close friendship with a vice president of the Ethyl Corporation, Blazer managed to obtain bulk shipments of this valuable additive at the refinery; was, in fact, one of the first refiners to do so. Ben Heath recalls this coup vividly; it was a period when Ethyl fluid was delivered to filling stations in tanks, and added to regular gasoline with hand pumps. At the refinery, Heath would don a rubber hat, jacket, gloves, boots and a gas mask, ascend a special platform created for the purpose, and pour the mixture . . .

One result of the addition of Ethyl fluid to the refinery gasoline output was that Ashland could supply both white and red gasoline to its customers, including their own distributors who sold gasoline under the Ashland brand name, Pepper.

Blazer decided that Green Pepper, as well as Red Pepper, would be great for sales, and urged Heath to develop some green-colored gasoline. Heath made a number of tries, but couldn't seem to solve this particular problem: Blazer, more insistent by the hour, kept after him. "Get a dye," he ordered, but Heath discovered that no green dye existed in the industry. Blazer scoffed at this, and stepped up his pressure.

The problem, minor in the beginning, began to loom in Heath's mind; he couldn't sleep nights. One night, as he tossed and turned restlessly, the solution appeared, so obvious he felt foolish not to have found it sooner. He arose, dressed and rushed down to the refinery, where he mixed yellow and blue gasoline to get green . . . Hours later, he had vials of every shade of green from pastel to kelly strewn around his office. In triumph, he called Paul Blazer who said instantly, "I'll be right down."

When Blazer arrived, he had with him a vice president from the Ethyl Corporation.

"Where are they?" Blazer asked Heath as soon as he arrived. Heath proudly led the two men to his green vials. Then, turning to the Ethyl executive, Paul said, "D'you see? Had to mix yellow and blue gasoline, but I got the green."

Heath was outraged. Blazer, conscious only of the pride of a manager whose pressure had finally achieved a desired result, didn't realize how his calm acceptance of this particular accomplishment would unforgettably sting Ben Heath.

By 1927, Heath openly began to find his job too exacting; the hours were too long and the region, although interesting, was in many ways too primitive for his liking. Seated in a barber chair in a shop on Front Street in Catlettsburg one day (the town still retained, in the twenties, some of its earlier robust flavor), Heath was informed by the barber in a whisper that the man in the next chair was out on bail, on suspicion of having killed a revenue agent. "His third," the barber said huskily.

Devil Anse Hatfield's[15] sister lived not far from the Catlettsburg refinery at the time, Heath recalls. Her house was surrounded by small trees, of the type used at Christmas. One day a man stopped his car, got out and started to chop one down. Devil Anse's sister emerged from her house and told him, "Those are my trees. I'll sell you that one for two dollars." "Okay," the man said, and chopped it down. Once the tree was in his car he started to drive away, only to find Devil Anse's sister blocking his exit. "I want my money," she said, and the driver handed her a twenty-dollar

[15] Of Hatfield and McCoy fame.

bill. She took it, produced a revolver and pointed it at him and said, "Get going!" He drove away.

All in all, a hard country. Heath thought he himself was leading a hard life despite several increases in salary; a harder life than necessary.

But as far as the Ashland Refining Company was concerned, Paul Blazer was building fast. By year's end, 1927, with his cracking plant almost fully operational and other improvements well settled, the refinery was producing enough for him to drop his resale business on behalf of other refiners in the area. His annual report to the directors of Swiss showed a net profit, after liberal allowances, of $205,942. Earnings were $77 a share on the Ashland common stock—an increase of $42.76 a share after paying out $35 a share in dividends.

Paul Blazer's attention now turned toward creating a marketing organization. This included a plan to hire more salesmen; the disclosure that his nearest competitor, the Tri-State Refinery, had stopped making kerosene and was buying this product from Ashland; a recommendation that Ashland enter, more vigorously, into retail and tank car distribution. He fortified his recommendations, as usual, with comments about the general direction of the industry that supplied a background context without being didactic. He pointed out that most purchasers of crude oil had marketing arms and that Ashland was the only refiner in the region making profits in manufacturing *per se*. As usual, he managed to narrow the options for his auditors, warning that 1928 might be a much harder year in terms of refinery profits. All these comments cast many shadows on the path. One can easily follow Blazer's turn in the road and his reasoning: now that he had lifted the capacity of his refinery at Catlettsburg from 47,000 barrels a month to what would become 120,000 barrels a month by the end of 1928, he was going to add another leg in his structure. On the two, refining and marketing, he expected to be able to walk farther and faster toward the mountain peaks that appeared in his mind's eye.

On November 25, 1927, when Paul Blazer was developing, on paper, arguments toward expansion, the directors and shareholders of Swiss Oil found their continuing dispute with J. Fred Miles virtually ended. A decision handed down in the eastern Kentucky district of the Federal Court by Judge A. M. J. Cochran, dismissed a suit brought by J. I. Lamprecht II against the Swiss board of directors, for having issued $2 million worth of common stock to Pynchon & Co. without proper authorization. Judge Cochran reviewed the predicament of Swiss when Mr. Martin of Pynchon had rescued it, and found that the board had not only acted properly, but that it could have acted in no other sensible way.

That cleared the air, finally, and the difficulties of the Swiss Oil Company from then on began to recede; the efforts of Ashland Refining and Paul Blazer began to emerge.

The difference in management approach between Miles and Blazer, already apparent in the unique reports to the directors that Paul Blazer submitted, became accentuated as time passed. Early in 1928, when Blazer's 1927 report was submitted, he began to increase the rate of his epistles. Monthly, weekly and at some periods even daily letters began to pour from him, in which various activities, situations, problems and plans were discussed in elaborate detail. The result was a combination diary, ship's log, persuasion, exhortation, and the equivalent of a business stream-of-consciousness. The total impact was of intimacy, coherence and clarity, especially because his readers, like himself, were men whose minds could best be reached through print; all had been educated and learned through the written word.

J. Fred Miles had been a *talking* manager: he excelled in personal contacts with men. His written reports were sparse and did not fully reflect all his abilities and contributions. One notices, with the clarity of hindsight and the advantage of comparisons at hand, that his reports did not project, did not romance his performance. On the basis of Miles's written reports alone, one would not realize that Swiss Oil was his creation from the inception. His methods were the rough and ready; the intuitive; the rainbow-chasing wildcatter who saw a larger vision. He operated, day by day, in the casual fashion of a man who had always been his own boss—unused to answering pointed or challenging questions from the calculating moneymen of the big city. At one point he borrowed over $30,000 from the Swiss Oil Company, an action he had probably taken with his own enterprises a number of times. He put his personal note down for the amount. It was legal, but it did not sit well with the directors when it was discovered. The action stands: a clear symbol of the difference between the Miles and the Blazer styles of management.

Blazer was not too many years younger, but was of a different generation than Miles. He was closer, in fact, to the modern corporation executive than one would expect of a young man whose business experience began in 1910. He thought in organized ways. He was accustomed to the idea of a large audience peering over his shoulder, so to speak, watching whatever he did, curious about what he planned to do. From his first days at the refinery he would remind the Ashland employees of the shareholders; repeatedly told them that the shareholders deserved a profit on their investment; he would discuss the employees with the shareholders in turn. He did not move, nor did he seem to move, without having the board of Swiss Oil and its president in psychological step with him.

His application of his Curtis letter-writing skills in his corporation post at Ashland Refining was clear: he applied his direct mail and advertising experience to the board of directors of Swiss Oil. His letters and reports were prepared as cannily as an advertising campaign. He wrote and rewrote many times, but brief messages were often dictated to Miss Hallnan, sometimes over the phone. Every sentence was calculated to evoke a response, as carefully as a professional writer seeks to convey a mood, a continuity and a set of three-dimensional characters.

Where Miles depended on face to face contacts, personal comments, immediate persuasion and the creation of a man-among-men atmosphere, Blazer carefully created a backlog of paper reportage, records and a flattering record of deference. With each message he reached all the directors—or at least all that would read—directly and without interruption. Many messages were written to forestall questions.

One result was that Miles left a smaller-than-life record of his own efforts. His failure to give full explanations made it seem as though he operated in a hit or miss fashion, was poorly organized, and had no particular or overall plan. Blazer, on the other hand, gave a larger-than-life impression of a man with great capacity for detail who could include overall circumstances in his

area of observation, and who had plans. The difference was between mystery and revelation; the style of each man accentuated
the difference.

The same contrast emerged in a number of companies during
the twenties. On a grand scale, it occurred between founder and
promoter Durant and organization man Alfred P. Sloane Jr., at
General Motors. It occurred at Goodyear, between founder and
promoter F. A. Sieberling and his successor Paul Litchfield.

On an infinitely large and grand scale, the same change was to
overtake the great national promoters: men like the Insulls and
the Van Sweringens—but not, in 1927, quite yet. The portents
were looming, the clouds were still only tiny tendrils. In the meantime, there was more than enough activity to engross the public
attention.

In the Blazer home, young Stuart was born, the third and last
of Paul and Georgia's children.[16]

In May 1927, Paul Blazer was with Roscoe Turner[17] at Texas
Guinan's nightclub in New York City; on impulse the two men
took a taxi to Roosevelt Field, Long Island. At a few minutes
before 8 A.M., they watched Lindbergh trundle his monoplane
down the runway and disappear into the horizon, headed for
Paris, $25,000 in prize money, worldwide fame and a hero's in-
evitable fate in this century.

That year the stock market took off on a similar flight into the
blue, and unlike Lindbergh, it sought to ascend eternally. For an
incredible period, it looked as though it would succeed. By December 1927, new highs both in prices and volumes of trade were
being reached; throughout 1928 the indexes rose. Standard Statistics was 100 in 1926; 114 by June 1927; by June 1928 it reached
148; by September 1929, it was to reach 216.

A large part of this movement was created by holding company
manipulations in which insiders created companies that sold one

[16] Altogether: Paul Jr., in 1919, in Chicago; Doris, in 1924, in Lexington; Stuart, in 1927, in Ashland.

[17] Roscoe Turner, a famous barnstormer, at one time traveled with a
pet lion. He knew Lindbergh well, and was keenly interested in his
flight.

another's shares back and forth to create a demand and a rise in value. Small investors, unsophisticated in these intricacies, followed the corporate shills as they built each pot. One result was a debasement of actual economic values throughout the economy: a pyramiding of credit, an increasingly unrealistic amount of commercial paper let loose through the nation.

In other areas of national life, similar dichotomies between fantasy and reality began to appear. While Hemingway and Fitzgerald and their coteries were painting decadent pictures of expatriate life, the workingmen in the United States lost interest in unions and the membership in these organizations declined precipitately. Cultural fads became increasingly bizarre; some of the worst dances in history began to appear and become popular: the Charleston, for instance. Women began to behave hoydenishly, music became nervous and lyrics cynical; the schism between the rural and urban areas became deeply embittered. The election campaign during the summer of 1928 was between Catholic Al Smith from the Big City and the "great engineer" Herbert Hoover from more traditional levels among candidates. The wonder was not that Smith did not win but that the country had progressed to such a nominee: the United States intellectual's curious habit of looking upon his own country with scorn had reached such an apogee that this demonstration of democracy was scorned because it was contentious.

Internationally, fantasies about universal and eternal peace became increasingly popular, although a visible totalitarian drift overtook many parts of the world. Russia and Italy were joined as countries under dictatorship by Turkey; China remained torn; Marxism emerged as the new religion of the disfranchised intellectuals of Asia; India began its agitation for freedom, as did many other areas of the British Empire.

In July 1928, for the first time, one begins to read letters from Paul Blazer to Robert Gordon of Bartlett & Gordon, in Chicago. Blazer has added directors to his list of men who will receive his reports, in addition to Senator Combs. Many of the letters are sent on by Senator Combs, in fact. It is interesting to note that Blazer is meticulous in his salutations: he always begins Dear

Senator, and Combs always replies, My Dear Paul. The correspondence is notably more courteous and more formal than business
correspondence today; the language is clearer.

Another change has overtaken the situation: the directors of
the Swiss Oil Company, having escaped disaster by the Union Oil
purchase, now found themselves with a profitable refining operation, and began to hope they could get out altogether. Apparently, conversations took place between Paul Blazer and the directors and they called on his sales ability, for we find him reporting
on trips and conversations he had with various highly-placed corporation officials throughout the oil industry. He sought to sell
the Swiss Oil Company to them.

Among these new contacts was a new, young president of the
Standard Oil Company (Ohio), W. T. (Bill) Holliday. Mr. Holliday was interested in acquiring Swiss Oil (Standard of Ohio at the
time was short of its own sources of crude oil; was left, by the dis-
memberment of the Standard Oil octopus, mainly with a refining
and marketing organization), and even went so far as to suggest a
talking figure: par value for the Swiss stock.

The board of directors of Swiss, however, assured that they could
get their money back if necessary, proved how human they were
by turning the offer down: they wanted a profit. Then Holliday
made another offer, highly significant: to buy the Ashland Refining Company for $1 million, and to make a long term contract
regarding the Swiss Oil crude properties. For the first time, we
have an independent valuation of what Paul Blazer had accomplished in four years, with a refinery that cost $212,000; it was
rated in 1928 as a million-dollar property. But the Swiss directors,
highly gratified one hopes, turned this offer down, too.

In 1928, Dr. Leslie, Heath's old college mentor, was hired by
the Badger Engineering Company of Boston to advise on the installation of a new fractionating tower at the Freedom refinery in
Pennsylvania. After looking the situation over, Dr. Leslie decided
that Freedom needed, in addition, a good man to operate the installation, and thought of Ben. Heath, informed that he had a
chance for this opening at a higher salary than he was receiving
at Catlettsburg, told Dr. Leslie he was willing to make a move.

"At Catlettsburg we were handling dark crudes and black fuel oil," he said later; "the Freedom refinery was larger and more complex."

When Heath told Paul Blazer about the opening, Blazer was encouraging; he didn't want to stand in the way of Heath advancing himself, he said, and gave him the warmest recommendation to Earle M. Craig, the owner of Freedom.

But when Heath landed the job and was ready to leave, Blazer was not anxious to see him go. "How much will they pay you?" he asked Heath.

"That doesn't matter," Heath said sharply. *"I've agreed."*

"How much?" Paul insisted, but Heath shook his head silently. Then Paul said, "I'll pay you $50 a month more than whatever they've offered." Heath still shook his head, and Paul raised his offer to $100 a month more; the Freedom offer was, actually, only $100 a month more than Paul had been paying Ben originally, but Heath was adamant.

Finally Blazer said simply, "I don't want you to go."

Heath was astonished. The two men agreed, somewhat emotionally, that they had a high regard for one another, but Heath stuck to his decision, and left. Later, Blazer would get him back —but that was years in the future.

Dubbs crew—after breaking the world's record for clean-out time.

By the time Heath departed, in 1928, the Dubbs unit was not only working, but the ordinarily frequent delays to clean accumulated coke had been reduced, under Blazer's incessant care, from a day to a day and a half every three days, to thirty hours, then to twenty hours and finally to eleven hours: at the time a world's record for the equipment.

That same summer in 1928, Rex Blazer, 6′ 1¾″ tall, florid and slender, graduated from the University of Illinois, hitchhiked to Columbus, Ohio, and phoned Paul Blazer. He was invited to Ashland where he became a house guest of Paul and Georgia for a couple of weeks. In the interim, the subject of his future was examined.

"I've been asked by your grandfather and your Uncle Herschel to give you a job," Paul told the young man, "but I think this company is too small to afford a relative of mine. If you succeed, it will be said you did so because of your relationship. If you fail, I would have to fire you, and that would cause problems in the family. Recently, two friends of mine in the oil business in Cleveland told me they are looking for a young man. I'll be glad to call them and see if they'll talk to you."

"Fine," said Rex, feeling somewhat chilled by this austere analysis of his situation.

Paul lent Rex the train fare, and a day or two later he found himself talking with Vandeveer and Newman, who were doing quite well as the Allied Oil Company. Both men were well impressed; Newman coined a witticism. "If you're half as smart as your uncle, you'll do very well," he said.

To his surprise, they hired him and then sent him back to Ashland Refining to learn the business from the ground up at the Catlettsburg plant: a high compliment to Paul Blazer. In accordance with the system then almost universally followed, he loaded tank cars, worked in the product laboratory, and made himself generally useful for the balance of the year.[18]

18 Rexford S. Blazer, born in Aledo, Ill. in 1907, was the son of Fred B. Blazer, Paul Blazer's older brother. The year Rex was born, his father took the helm of the Aledo *Times-Record*. David Blazer, Rex's grandfather, had established the paper; was at one time a

By mid- 1928, Blazer had begun to use his long-range telescope again, and on one of his frequent trips to New York City met and became friendly with a Mr. Forrest M. Towl, president of the Cumberland, Eureka and affiliated pipelines. Mr. Towl, an elderly man, had begun his career in the oil industry with John D. Rockefeller himself in 1885; over the years rose in the Standard Oil organization to the post of chief engineer of the entire corporation.

When Standard Oil was broken into fragments by court order in 1911, Mr. Towl found himself, among other responsibilities, continuing as president of the Cumberland, Eureka and other pipeline companies. The Cumberland line consisted of a 750-mile system in eastern Kentucky, which served more than 5,000 small wells. When Paul Blazer and Eric Shatford first went to Kentucky in 1918, their first venture was the creation of a competitive pipeline to the Cumberland system. It is doubtful if anyone had examined, pored over and ruminated on the Cumberland Pipeline more than Paul Blazer over the years; there is every reason to believe he thought about it at greater length than did Mr. Towl.

In a letter to Mr. W. T. Holliday of the Standard Oil of Ohio, during the period in 1928 when Blazer was attempting to negotiate

---

partner in an Iowa newspaper with the father of Henry Wallace (U. S. vice president under Franklin D. Roosevelt 1940–1944); entertained Adlai Stevenson's grandfather when *he* was U. S. vice president (under Grover Cleveland, 1893–1897). Fred Blazer became politically potent as publisher and editor in his turn; entertained the governors of Illinois, sparked various local and state improvements during his tenure from 1907 to 1921. In 1921 he died of influenza.

Rexford and his brother Fred Jr. went to Kemper Military School at Boonville, Mo. At Kemper, Rex mastered four academic years in three with the assistance of his grandfather, David Blazer (who had once been a schoolteacher). He entered the University of Illinois in 1924 with $2,500 borrowed from his grandfather and aunt; joined the Psi Upsilon fraternity two years after Everett Wells and became, in his turn, president of the Chapter. In the fraternity house, he washed dishes for his meals, worked summers; majored in what is today called business administration.

Like most of the Blazers, his boyhood was filled with chores, his grandfather was only a generation removed from a pioneer family. Rex early received instruction in responsibility; learned habits of diligence which helped him move far in the world. His career, still in progress, has been eminent, and will reenter this chronicle later.

a sale of the Swiss Oil Company and its affiliate the Ashland Refining Company to Holliday, we read:

"While in the East I discussed with Mr. Forrest M. Towl . . . the question of obtaining for our refinery a supply of Mid-Continent crude oil *should we desire to enlarge the capacity of our plant to a point exceeding the available supply of Kentucky crude oil*. He expressed the opinion the matter could be very easily handled . . . If Mid-Continent crude can be delivered into our plant at approximately the same cost as to Northern Ohio, it should be possible for us to refine that oil profitably, under normal conditions, and move it by barge into the Cincinnati district . . . If we were assured of a permanent market at Cincinnati for a substantial quantity of gasoline, I believe that our company would be willing to make the large investment necessary for barge movement . . ."

Paul Blazer was considering a combination of river transportation and pipelines and had estimated the extension necessary to the Cumberland systems to not only gain some degree of control over eastern Kentucky crude oil but also to obtain crude inexpensively from Mid-Continent; and to sell the refined products in the Standard of Ohio marketing area in southern Ohio. The advantages to Standard of Ohio in acquiring the Swiss Oil Company and the Ashland Refining Company are spelled out in the most attractive and reasonable colors; Blazer exhibits clearly that his efforts to find a purchaser for Swiss were by no means perfunctory but of a very high level and expertly conducted. He also gives us a preview of his own course of action when the Standard offer was not high enough to induce the directors of Swiss to sell.

By autumn 1928, the Catlettsburg refinery lost a competitor: the Waverly Oil Works. Paul Blazer was beginning to feel restive over the fact that the posted price of Somerset (Kentucky) crude oil was still set by the New Domain and the Seep Purchasing[19] Agencies, although Ashland had become a larger purchaser. Furthermore, the refinery needs, by this time, exceeded Swiss Oil's

[19]Representing the South Penn Oil Co., originally part of Standard Oil trust; for years official poster of crude prices in Kentucky.

crude properties output by some 25 per cent. Looking ahead, Blazer recommended that more crude producing wells be purchased. The child was beginning to outstrip the parent.

As though to demonstrate the reality of Lewis Carroll's moving landscape, the nation in 1929 moved, together with England, France, Italy, Germany, The Netherlands and most of what we know as Western civilization, inexorably toward a new meridian.

Early in the year, most serious financiers were worried, for the bull market in Wall Street had gone so high that it was frightening; talking pictures were being introduced and Al Jolson's *Mammy* rang from every radio; *The Bridge of San Luis Rey* was a bestseller; inflation had set in so deeply that the banks had not only caught the fever, they were feeding it with loans; *All Quiet on the Western Front* was playing on Broadway to crowds so heavy the management in the movie house produced camp chairs for overflows; Rudy Vallee was crooning.

It was a pleasant summer. Among the men who joined the company that season was D. Hugh Jenks Jr.[20] Interviewed by Paul Blazer, who was impressed, young Jenks was intended for the sales department, but was sent first to the refinery laboratory for grounding in the specifics. He soon proved to be so valuable —mainly due to his college background in chemistry—that he found himself stuck; a circumstance that was to prove an opportunity in disguise.

In September the market cracked and in October it fell apart, carrying millions down with it. Yet—and this is an indication of how memory fools humans—records of the period show that the news of the stock market crash did not seem any clap of thunder to everyone, although in fairness it must be mentioned that the market broke toward the end of the year. The early part of the year, at least as far as the press was concerned, was devoted to such events as the St. Valentine's Day massacre of gangsters by

[20] David Hugh Jenks Jr. was born 1907, in Raleigh, N. C., where his forebears settled in the early 1800s. He attended, after two years of high school, the Staunton Military Academy; then entered pre-medical studies at the University of Cincinnati; dropped his plans to become a physician in favor of an early marriage which led him to business and Ashland Refining.

gangsters in Chicago; a soft story written in hard style called
A Farewell To Arms; the exiling of Trotsky by Stalin; clashes in
the Middle East and elsewhere. In all, 1929 has been one of the
years most often written about in modern times. Almost everyone
who has attempted to recreate it has managed to make it seem
worse than memory recalls. To those who were then adult, it was,
as a whole, like most other years: mixed, varied, not particularly
significant.

Paul Blazer, persuading the board of directors of Swiss Oil to
allow Ashland Refining to extend into marketing, had—for most
of 1929—40 per cent of equity earnings of the combined companies
in 1928 as a cincher. The result was a series of purchases, not of
machinery and equipment this time, but of marketing companies
and some more producing wells: the Highland Oil Company of
Hillsboro, Ohio, was purchased for $25,000; the Home Oil Com-
pany of Maysville, Kentucky, for $85,000; the Southern Oil Serv-
ice Company of Pomeroy, Ohio, for $15,000; the Dawson-Pepper
Oil Company for $27,000; the Keaton Oil & Gas Company for
$250,000. Altogether, $402,000 worth of marketing organizations
with their men, properties, customers and contacts. In his fifth
year as general manager of Ashland Refining, Blazer had spent,
in purchases of other companies alone (including some too small
to deserve mention), over twice as much as the amount of the
original capitalization of the company in 1924.

Ashland Refining ended 1929 with a net profit of $206,000, after
adding $106,000 to its reserves for depreciation and obsolescence,
and some $25,000 for income taxes. "After our preferred stock
dividend requirement of $18,956, our earnings available to com-
mon shareholders were approximately $188,000, or slightly over
$75 per share of common stock outstanding . . ." he wrote to the
directors of Swiss. "It will be recalled," he continued, "that during
the year (1929) we paid off a 20 per cent cash dividend on our
common stock, which leaves only 5 per cent of our original investment that has not been retired, disregarding interest charges. I
anticipate we will be able to pay 20 per cent again this year . . .
At the close of the year, our common stock had a book value of
slightly over $406 per share, and I believe the actual value is sub-
stantially in excess."

Furthermore, he had, through a friend, Mr. A. M. Maxwell of Standard Oil of Ohio, made an excellent deal in which that firm agreed to purchase a number of grades of naphtha and solvents— in quantities Blazer estimated might total one million gallons a month—from Ashland Refining. In addition to this plum, Standard of Ohio agreed to buy its gasoline for the Ironton, Portsmouth, Ohio and Ashland, Kentucky area from Ashland. This meant he would have the advantage afforded by Standard of Ohio's excellent marketing organization in Ohio with Standard itself as a major customer.

Then in conclusion, he said, "I feel reasonably optimistic concerning the future operation of our company . . . thus, I plan to take advantage of present conditions to the extent of taking a thirty-day vacation in Florida . . . I intend to set an example to our department heads . . . of not working so hard this year . . ."

While Blazer was ending 1929 in glory, Commander G. C. Davison, owner of the Tri-State Refinery across the Big Sandy River in Kenova, West Virginia, close enough to see, was having enormous difficulties. Originally, Davison had planned to invest a total of $100,000 in his relatively new, modern refinery. Instead, by 1929 he was in the hole for $500,000, and sinking deeper every month.

This naturally made Davison most unhappy, but he found in Blazer a sympathetic and understanding listener; Blazer watched the Tri-State Refinery with unwinking attention. In a letter to the Swiss directorate, Blazer described Davison as "temperamental," and gravely reported the various stages of that gentleman's despair as his refinery's business went from worse to awful.

Finally, Davison began to make specific proposals. He suggested that Blazer lease the Tri-State Refinery for $2,500 a month for ten years, and then buy the refinery outright for $1. Blazer, recognizing this offer as an expression of pain rather than thought, did it the honor of walking around it. He discovered that Tri-State employed Jenkins Process Equipment. The proprietors of this equipment did not believe that Ashland Refining, employers of a Dubbs unit, could use theirs too. It would confuse an already murky patent fight.

But Blazer, burning with repressed eagerness to get his hands on Tri-State, had no intention of allowing such extraneous considerations to block his direction. He applied his formidable powers of concentration to this complication.

In a letter to Senator Tom Combs, to whom he explained all these ramifications at considerable length, Blazer pointed out what an advantage the ownership of the Tri-State Refinery could be to Messrs. J. Fred Miles and Charley Jouett, in Louisville. The Senator, responding with his usual old-world courtesy, agreed this was a possible menace.

The condition of the two refineries, Tri-State and Ashland, so markedly disparate as to verge on the incredible, supplies—better than any series of adjectives—the necessary answer to any who might have conceived that Blazer's success in his location was fortuitous.

The price of Kentucky crude had dropped somewhat during the year; an event that was not good for Swiss Oil, but not bad for Ashland Refining. The year had introduced other changes invisible to the majority of men, but all too clear to some. Many men found dismissal notices in their envelope for Christmas that year, but none were at Ashland Refining. In brokerage offices, in the walnut suites of corporate executives, in governmental offices, the size of the October debacle was being measured: in all, *$30 billion worth of assets had vanished into the air,* and the winter had hardly begun.

Among other effects, the crash would halt, at some 29,000 souls, the population boom at Ashland, freeze Catlettsburg into its smaller size for years to come; thwart, twist, maim or destroy hopes, plans, expansions, dreams and directions whose details we shall never know.

Since the average man did not yet realize what had happened or would happen, Christmas 1929 seemed much as usual. But some of the investors in Swiss Oil knew better: men like Robert D. Gordon, James Martin, Mr. Halle, J. Ogden Armour and others; they were men of the market, the market that had just fallen. In their respective offices, they were deep in recovery efforts. So, in the White House, was President Herbert Hoover. No historian has recorded Mr. Hoover's stockholdings at the time, or whether he had any at all. Yet he lost as much as any man in the debacle, although he had little to do with the circumstances that led to it, or its immediate results.

For Paul Blazer, 1929 had been a good year; he was past his thirty-ninth birthday and as the Europeans say, was in his fortieth year; it was the end of his youth and the beginning of his middle age: the time of the prime.

Section Three—Swimming Upstream

1930–1935

When times go sour, men seek scapegoats. Modern man is no exception: he believes depressions are caused by sin. As a consequence, the great depression that began in the fall of 1929 and swept around the world was laid at the doorstep of all the men in charge everywhere. Real pundits—always a minuscule minority—confessed at the time that they were unable to explain the phenomenon. Since then, those who have felt capable of explaining its causes have been numerous—but their explanations have been almost as excruciating as the experience.

The best that can be done is to repeat random observations that, in their totality, add up to a modern version of Dante's great allegory—especially in *The Inferno*. Men walked down paths they had never known existed, onto levels formerly unimaginable, where demons attacked them.

Like every great event of mankind, individual experiences ranged the gamut. Not every company went bankrupt by any stretch of the imagination; not every man lost his job. Some men even became wealthy and prosperous—but they were swimming against the tide of general circumstances.

At Ashland, the deflation and the steady decline of crude oil and refined product prices forced Blazer to make a series of inventory markdowns. Nevertheless, each month showed an overall profit averaging between $30,000 and $40,000. In the spring of

74

1930 much of Ashland's business seemed unchanged, but Blazer was in a good humor because, among other reasons, he had solved the problem of the purchase of the Tri-State Refinery in Kenova, West Virginia, just across the river.

The solution seemed, as usual, fairly obvious once reached. Blazer agreed to pay advance royalties to the owners of the patents on the Jenkins process equipment being used at Tri-State. That left only the question of the overall refinery price and terms of payment. Later, Blazer described this as $300,000—a figure that is correct as far as the purchase was concerned. The total expenditure, however, including monies to operate the refinery, inventory and allied equipment, ran the sum up to $550,000.

The acquisition was important: it increased the 4,000-barrel-a-day capacity the Ashland refinery had attained, by some 1,500 additional barrels a day. Of equal, perhaps greater importance was the acquisition of an added marketing network that included new brand names of gasoline, terminals, bulk plants, distributors and service stations.

When both operations were combined, the aggregate, within a 150-mile radius of Ashland, was impressive. Blazer was now able to sell gasoline through several hundred service stations and more than fifty bulk stations. He could operate a fleet of motor trucks that carried refined products to warehouses, river terminals and railroad sidings, and oil barges that carried refined products to river terminals for sales to major oil companies lacking their own refining facilities in the area. The brands Blazer now controlled included such recondite but regionally well-known names as Red Pepper Ethyl, Green Pepper Anti-Knock, White Pepper, Tri-State Ethyl, Tri-State Super-Motor, Tri-State Aviation Gasoline.

Meanwhile the engineering firm of Dunn & Lewis had improved, through repressuring, the declining curves of the oil wells owned by Swiss Oil. At Blazer's suggestion, the parent company had purchased more producing wells in Johnson and Lawrence Counties (Kentucky) at a cost of $440,000.

By April, 1930, the arrangements for the purchase and capitalization of the Tri-State Refining Company were complete. Ashland Refining, as a result, seemed secure in its regional niche—at least for the nonce.

Mr. Olcott Payne, of New York City, relayed an offer to Blazer of a job for a "gulf coast refining company" that was looking for a new president. Blazer politely declined; the addition of Tri-State (in which he had a 10 per cent interest) and his own emoluments were sufficient, he explained, to keep him happy. He sent copies of the correspondence to Senator Combs, who made a graceful acknowledgment.

Plants and businesses in the area in the spring of 1930 were beginning to lay off men; Ashland Refining, busily building, was still hiring. The new employees, though, were mainly young men with little experience, who came in at modest beginning salaries. One was Lew Ware,[1] a liberal arts major, whom Blazer placed, as usual, in the refinery laboratory until he could find a better place. "Blazer hired the person," Ware said later, "and not a function."

Blazer kept a constant vigil over his force, for whom shifts from one job to another and changes of duty were constants. Then and later, Blazer made special efforts to avoid freezing men into niches. He expected a man to know what was going on around him, as well as within his own special area. This practice, relatively rare then, enabled him to get more out of fewer men than his competitors. Perhaps because it was not widespread, the practice required constant persuasion and explanation; Blazer had to wheedle as well as needle.

One day in the spring of 1930, Blazer called Palmer Talbutt into his office. Talbutt had by then attained the position of assistant superintendent of the refinery, and was proud both of that and the fact that he was receiving the second highest salary in the plant: $275 a month. Blazer told Talbutt, in effect, that he was being transferred to sales with a salary cut of $100 a month.

Talbutt was thunderstruck. Naturally, he wanted to know why he was being transferred; why his hard-won skill was being dis-

---

[1] Lewis Ware was born in 1905 at Brannon Station, a hamlet near Lexington. The family emigrated from England to Virginia before the Revolution; Ware is a well-known name in Virginia and Kentucky; one, Ora Ware, was a U.S. Senator from Kentucky. Lew Ware attended Transylvania College, oldest school west of the Alleghenies, founded in 1780. He is now a board member of his alma mater; he is travel coordinator at Ashland Oil & Refining, where he was one of the architects of its personnel and labor relations programs.

carded. Blazer began to discuss long-range matters. "The oil industry," he said, "is undergoing profound changes. We will need different types of men in refineries; men with a scientific background, men who are graduates of colleges and universities." He discussed his future plans for Ashland Refining in considerable detail. Talbutt was greatly impressed with how much thought Blazer had devoted to the subject; how extensive his reading had been, and how great a grasp he had of the conditions and trends in the industry. Blazer was careful to stress that he was not the innovator; "I would rather not be the first man to introduce a technical change; let some other man be first; let *him* struggle to get the bugs out."

He drew parallels between the position of Ashland Refining and that of the larger oil companies. He was careful to remind Talbutt that these changes were already well underway in the major companies, and made the point that they would, inevitably, reach the smaller refiners as well.

But, Talbutt protested, he didn't know anything about sales. He had never done any selling. "We'll teach you," Blazer said calmly, knowing that with the addition of the Tri-State Refinery he needed more men. He knew also that when Charley Jouett had taken away all his skilled men to J. Fred Miles in Louisville, Talbutt had remained loyal.

Persuaded against his will, Talbutt said, finally, "All right. But I still think I'm worth more than $175 a month."

"Perhaps you are," said Blazer, smiling slightly. "I'll give you $200 a month."

A few days later, Talbutt found himself in the office as understudy to Everett Wells. "Everett," said Talbutt, "was a man of few words. You had to learn under Everett by observation; *close* observation."

Talbutt became familiar with records associated with sales work: shipment invoices and bills of lading, railroad freight rates, discounts, price lists, market reports. Watching Everett Wells, Talbutt began to discover what kept him so busy.

"Once," says Talbutt, "Everett sold the Standard Oil of Ohio thirty carloads of kerosene. Then I watched him pacing the floor, scowling over the problem of where he himself could get that much kerosene at a lower price. I began to realize we were like the man who was so poor he had to wear whatever clothes came his way. It was said of him that *he fit all sizes.* We operated that way: we fit whatever the situation required."

Talbutt began to make sales calls, and was reassured to discover that, everywhere he went, Paul Blazer had preceded him. "How's Paul?" the customers would ask. "Say hello to him for me."

Palmer Talbutt's world began to expand. It would never be the same again.

In the great world outside the valley, cold winds began to blow. At first, they affected only the most fragile, but one out of every four factory workers lost his job. There was a perceptible increase in drunkenness, wild parties, and crime. Dutch Schultz and Vincent Coll engaged in bloody shoot-outs in the streets of New York. By common consent, citizens became more concerned over the increase in general lawlessness than they were in the depressed business conditions. Everyone was confident the slump would soon end.

There were indications that Ashland Refining's situation was good: Blazer reported, confidentially, to Senator Combs that Mr. Grant, the Ohio manager of Gulf Oil, had told him Gulf was planning a major expansion in Ohio. Because Gulf had no desire to compete in West Virginia or Kentucky, Mr. Grant thought the Ashland refining plant would be especially valuable to his company. He wondered whether Blazer and Swiss Oil might not be willing to sell the Ashland Refinery and its distribution in southern Ohio. Blazer, thinking fast, decided this might be possible: Everett Wells could handle sales, and Fred Irwin, the plant superintendent, could handle the refinery for Gulf. He himself could retain the Kenova, West Virginia, Tri-State plant, and the Kentucky and West Virginia sales territories. The price, Blazer said to Senator Combs, would be somewhere between $9 and $10 million.

This proposition interested Senator Combs, as indeed it might —since it would practically return the Swiss Oil investors' equity and still leave them with good money-making properties. Blazer cannily prevented such enthusiasm from getting out of hand by adding, calmly, "Better offers will come from other major companies, without such exceptions." In our mind's eye, we can see Senator Tom Combs settling back with a smile.

The offer did make the managements of Swiss Oil and Ashland Refining feel good, though. Blazer, adding his assets at this point, realized he had achieved financial independence. He and his wife and children would never again have that particular worry. The goal had been reached twelve years after, by unlikely chance, he first entered the oil industry.

"In that case," he was asked years later, "why did you keep working?"

"It wasn't for money," he answered. "I really think," he added, "that it would have broken my heart if the venture had failed, if Ashland had ever gone bankrupt or gone into receivership. I wanted to build a success. Not necessarily the largest, but certainly the soundest company possible."

By August 1930, Ashland Refining was buying 5,000 barrels of crude oil a day from the eastern Kentucky fields. The official price posting agency, Seep Purchasing Company, was buying only five hundred barrels a day. For the first time, Ashland Refining began to post prices for these fields. The first price it listed was $1.30 a barrel.

By spending three quarters of his time at Tri-State, Blazer succeeded in bringing the operating loss at that plant down from $25,000 a month to $3,000. Business at the Ashland refinery continued to be excellent. Standard of New Jersey established a new subsidiary called Standard of Pennsylvania (to compete in that state with Atlantic Refining); Blazer made a deal to sell the new firm its fuel oil at a profit of $20,000. As a result, profits for Ashland Refining in September 1930, reached $30,000 in spite of more inventory markdowns. By the end of September, Blazer predicted he would equal, in 1930, his profits in 1929.

In other reaches of the Swiss Oil Company, however, matters were not pleasant. Many of the directors, who had business interests elsewhere, were feeling the pinch. Their anxiety to get their money back and get out of the oil business grew with each passing day. Blazer found himself under strong pressure to find someone who would buy the company. On a trip to New York City, he found himself staying at the same hotel as W. T. Holliday, the president of Standard Oil of Ohio. The two men resumed an old topic: the purchase of Ashland Refining by Holliday's company. Mr. Holliday, usually very frank with Blazer, seemed somewhat reluctant to get into specifics on this occasion, and Blazer realized the rumors might have had some foundation: Standard of Ohio, that fall of 1930, was short of money.

The directors, however, continued to press. Obediently, Blazer paid calls on Cities Service and Sinclair. With gravity, he reported back that he did not receive any particular encouragement, but that he had "paved the way" for future discussions: salesman's jargon for "no sale."

Writing to Senator Combs, Blazer told him that crude oil prices were tumbling all over the landscape. "I cannot believe that anyone would be interested in buying a producing company today," he said. "Our marketing and refining groups seem to attract the most attention," he added. From this period onward, in fact, Blazer's own opinion began to swing in the same direction. Throughout most of the thirties, oil was to be cheap and plentiful: too plentiful. Proration (production allowables) was just around the corner.

In New York City again, this time at the arrangement of Mr. Halle, president of the Universal Oil Products Company and an investor in Swiss Oil, Blazer had an appointment with Mr. Van Eck, president of Shell Oil. Mr. Van Eck was candid about the situation of his company, and admitted they did not have the cash in hand to buy any new important properties. Furthermore, he said, the price of Shell common stock had fallen so far in the market that any trade based on its present position would turn out "when proper values are restored," to be far more costly than might appear in 1930.

Meanwhile, the Dubbs cracking unit, originally Blazer's pride and joy, had begun to irk him. The plant built up deposits of coke in operation, which necessitated frequent shutdowns and cleanouts. Blazer had pressed, urged and pushed until these were reduced to record minimums, but he was still dissatisfied. One day, reading the trade press, he saw where some small refiners in the west had produced a grade of asphalt from residuum runs in their cracking units. Ashland Refining, making these runs, was producing a low grade fuel oil, worth less than a cent a gallon. Blazer decided that if others could produce asphalt from their cracking units, his men could do the same. He assigned Commander Davison, the engineer who at one time had been operating superintendent at the Tri-State Refinery, and Hugh Jenks Jr., by this time the chief chemist at Ashland, to go to work on a program to develop asphalt. They had considerable barriers to overcome.

Specifications for asphalt in those days were based on the product in existence, made mainly by the major companies, and obtained from heavy crude oil from Mexico, Venezuela, Colombia and California. As so often happens, the specifications worked backward from the best available product. Therefore only asphalt made from these oils was eligible for consideration in state highway use, the largest area of application. Blazer ignored this entirely. "Produce asphalt," he told Jenks and Davison, and then adjusted his internal needle to jab them at frequent intervals.

That Christmas was sad and hard for many. Georgia Blazer and Mrs. Winans, aware of this, decided the families of the Ashland employees should attend the company parties. They bought, wrapped and labeled presents and decorated a tree. The result was cheering, warm and a great success. Blazer was delighted, and the Christmas parties became an institution that was to wax mightily with the years.

By year's end, 1930, Blazer had reason to feel times were not as bad as the newspapers said. Ashland Refining profits were $167,955, "a return of a little over 10 per cent on total investment." Common stock earnings were slightly over $50 a share. Blazer said the figures would have been larger had the continued decline in crude oil prices throughout the year not forced him to make successive inventory markdowns.

The figures did not give all the story. The addition of the Tri-State Refinery had not only increased the gasoline volume of the Ashland Refining Company by forty per cent, it added lower grades of gasoline and other modest-priced items to Ashland's high-priced, quality products. Furthermore, Ashland lent Tri-State money to make improvements: the interest on these loans alone came to $30,000 a year. In arranging for this financing, Blazer had made deals with the Ashland National Bank, the National Bank of Kentucky and the Chicago Bank of Commerce (where Bob Gordon was a director). He had borrowed $150,000 and established an open credit for another $100,000. Ostensibly, this financing was started to help Tri-State and his expansion, but Blazer shrewdly used his excellent credit to get more money than he needed. This was to allow him to take advantage of bargains beginning to appear.

The year 1930 ended with the symptoms of calamity beginning to emerge publicly. Moved by a constructive impulse, the International Apple Shippers' Association decided to let unemployed men have its oversupply of apples on credit, so they could sell them and make some money. The results were more shocking than helpful: the nation saw men standing on virtually every street corner, patient in the cold, trying to sell apples for a nickel apiece. Desperation was given form, and Want made visible.

Other ephemera, of a different nature, appeared. Miniature golf, a most unlikely pastime, became the rage throughout the nation and crowds appeared to play; Amos 'n' Andy broadcasts actually stopped traffic; Louisiana reelected Huey Long; Bobby Jones dominated regular golf; tree sitting became a passion among young boys; Jean Harlow made her debut; President Hoover's Farm Bureau bought great amounts of wheat and cotton in a Canute-like attempt to stop the erosion of prices; the number of unemployed soared to between 5 and 6 million.

A great series of arguments about people in distress began to engross the nation. Demands arose that *something* be done, preferably by the government, to alleviate their circumstances. Conservatives, headed by the President, objected that such an undertaking would enlarge the American concept of government; undermine the fabric of liberty and the independence of the people alike. Ironically, the name of the man associated with relief in Europe would become associated with anti-relief in the United States. The fall elections resulted in a landslide for the Democrats; a mixed blessing for the nation, for this ensured a divided government during the next two years. At a time when action was urgently needed, a stalemate existed.

Prices were not all that eroded; values of all descriptions began to shift. Bankers and businessmen, the upper middle class, the professions, figures of authority and position generally began to suffer an incalculable loss of prestige and influence. Men who worked on Wall Street began to conceal the fact from strangers, lest the admission bring unpleasant comments and expressions of indignation. Demonologists became respectable; soothsayers and prophets began to appear; fanatics found fuel and ordinary citizens began to feel the earth shifting beneath their feet, as in an earthquake.

The winter of 1931 found Paul Blazer staring fixedly at another object of intense desire: the Cumberland Pipeline Company. The very fact that he was able to consider such a purchase illustrated how far the wheel had turned since he arrived in Kentucky. Then, the lack of attention the management of the Cumberland line had paid to new business had constituted an opportunity for Paul Blazer and Eric Shatford to enter the pipeline business in eastern Kentucky in 1918. Through this venture the young men met the organizers of the Great Southern Oil & Refining Company, where Blazer learned about refining and the regional market. Now, as principal customer of the Cumberland line in his capacity as general manager of Ashland Refining, Blazer wondered how he could acquire the company itself. He could be forgiven if he felt an affinity for Cumberland: it was inextricably intertwined in his destiny.

He had excellent practical reasons for his objective. The Cumberland system consisted of thousands of miles of gathering and trunk lines extending from the oil fields of Kentucky, West Virginia and western Delaware, to the large refineries located along the Delaware River. It served, in addition to the Louisville refinery owned by Standard Oil of Kentucky, the Parkersburg, West Virginia, plant of Standard of New Jersey; three refineries of Atlantic Refining at Philadelphia, Pittsburgh and Franklin, Pennsylvania, Ashland Refining and the Tri-State refinery at Kenova,

West Virginia. Blazer could buy only part of the system, but it was an important part.

Blazer had long ago acquainted himself with the management of the line in Kentucky, and had on a number of occasions held conversations with Mr. Forrest Towl, president of the Cumberland system. Mr. Towl, an elderly man with the formal manners of a bygone generation, had started his career in Standard Oil in 1885. Once chief engineer of the immense Standard Oil trust, he did not regard the Cumberland system as the largest single item on the horizon. Blazer made a trip to New York to see Mr. Towl, and it is revealing that Mr. Towl put him up as his house guest in his Brooklyn Heights home. Thirty-five years later, Blazer would recall the surroundings so distinctly that he wondered whether the Old Dutch Reformed Presbyterian Church was still there.[2] In their conversations, Blazer, as a principal customer of the line, thought that he could apply a little pressure. He told Mr. Towl that he obtained half his total requirements through Cumberland. Towl looked at him and smiled, and said gently, "Then, Mr. Blazer, I can raise the price *on my half.*" Blazer was, for once, left without a ready reply.

The Rockefeller Foundation owned 25 per cent of Cumberland; the balance was traded on the New York Curb (The American Stock Exchange). The depreciated value of the line, Blazer explained later, was close to a million dollars; Ashland Refining at the time only had a net worth of $1.25 million. Furthermore, the Cumberland was losing $15,000 a month, a circumstance that would not ordinarily attract purchasers.

But Blazer had been prowling around this property for years. He had hired men who had worked on it; he had held long conversations with its operators; he flanked it by his refinery at one end and the Swiss Oil properties along its length; he had the markets and the customers for the crude oil that flowed through its mains. To him, it was an essential link; no other firm needed it as badly.

During this busy period, while leaving the Second National Bank building in Ashland one afternoon, Blazer found himself

[2] It was.

The fleet. (June 1931)

stopped by a young, slender man whom he recognized as one of the tellers in the bank: Arthur Points. Points, who had been watching Ashland Refining's progress from his desk at the bank, wanted to change jobs.

Blazer immediately brought him into his office and had a long talk with him. At its conclusion, Points found himself hired at $150 a month: less money than he had been making at the bank. He went home with mixed emotions, unsure whether he had improved his circumstances or not. But Blazer, ever-persuasive, had been most impressive. "In the long run," he had said, "you will do a great deal better. If you do a good job, it will be recognized, *and you won't be sorry.*" [3]

Shortly after this conversation, Points reported for work and

[3] Nor was he. Arthur Jones Points was born in 1904, in Salt Lick, Ky. His father's family were early settlers in Grant County, Ky.; his mother's maiden name was Jones. Her grandfather and father were contractors and builders; moved to Salt Lick in the early 1900s when the hamlet was a manufacturing center for barrel staves. Arthur's father founded a bank in Salt Lick, in 1901.

The Points family moved to Ashland in 1923, where Arthur's father went to work for the Second National Bank; left it to enter the electric refrigeration business; then went into real estate; wound up with a service station at the age of 70, which he operated for 14 years; at one time served in the Kentucky House of Representatives and the State Senate.

Art Points himself went to Georgetown College, received a B.A. in 1925; proceeded from this initial meeting with Blazer to high position in the company. He will reenter this chronicle.

was placed in charge of bookkeeping for Ashland Refining and Tri-State. Ben Vinson, a cousin of United States Representative Fred Vinson (later the Chief Justice of the United States Supreme Court) was then the company auditor; Vinson kept the balance sheets and Points kept track of operations.

The atmosphere, Points recalls, was "saturated" with work. His day began at 7:30, when he picked up and distributed the mail. By 8:00 A.M. the entire staff was present and at work. There was no conception of overtime; everyone worked straight through, excepting a break at lunch, until six in the evening. On many occasions, the men returned after dinner to resume their labors. The man who left finally at ten o'clock at night felt he was leaving early. That was the schedule five days a week. Friday was a short day, they knocked off at 5:30. Saturday was like Friday, a short day. Sundays were a breeze: they worked only until about three in the afternoon. And, lest the listener think his starting salary of $150 a month was terribly small, Points is careful to remind that until well along in the 1930s, bookkeepers were still applying, *en masse,* for jobs at $75 a month.

In June, Blazer added another quiet, diligent young man to his group in the person of Ed Emrick.[4] Emrick, who was placed in the credit department, was astounded at the length of the work week. He was even more astounded when Blazer asked him one Thanksgiving if he visited the refinery often. Emrick objected that he was tied up all day and most of the night in the office;

---

[4] Edward E. Emrick Jr. was born in 1909 in Aledo, Illinois. His family lived near the Blazers; knew them well. As a child, Emrick received $1 a month from David Blazer, Paul's father, to bring in the cow every night. His father was once a schoolteacher; became president of the Aledo Bank and owner of a drygoods (department) store. In 1925, Emrick Sr. opened another drygoods store in nearby Ottawa, Illinois. He was appointed guardian for young Rex Blazer in 1922. In 1925, Ed Emrick's oldest sister, Kathryn, married Herschel Blazer. Emrick attended the University of Illinois and joined Psi Upsilon fraternity three years after Rex Blazer, five years after Everett Wells. Emrick received a B.S. in economics and accounting. He applied at Ashland and although he was hired for a sales job, was placed temporarily in accounting where he remained for years. He became a top executive in the firm, and will reappear at frequent intervals in this chronicle.

Sunday was the only possible time he could even consider seeing the refinery. Blazer was astonished in his turn.

"A youngster like you should be able to work sixteen hours a day easily," he said.

In September, Art Points received a telephone call from a fellow graduate of tiny Georgetown College (Kentucky) named C. J. Bolton.[5] Bolton had recently arrived in Ashland with his bride, who had a job as a schoolteacher. Bolton was looking for a job, and Points suggested he see Blazer.

Bolton went down to the Second National Bank building to Ashland's seventh floor offices. Blazer emerged and told him, "See Irwin if you want a job at the refinery; see Grossenbach for a job in accounting," turned to leave, then wheeled around in astonishment when Bolton said, "Art Points told me if I want a job as a stenographer to see *you*."

"Are you good?" Blazer asked, after the briefest of pauses.

"Think I am," Bolton replied.

Blazer called him in, dictated some letters between telephone calls; Bolton typed them from his notes; Blazer read them carefully, then signed them and threw them into the outgoing mail box.

[5] Charles J. Bolton was born and raised in West Point, Ky., where the Salt River joins the Ohio. He is a direct descendant of one of three brothers named Bolton who were allies of Oliver Cromwell and who fled from England to Virginia when the Stuarts returned to power. Bolton's father was a Baptist minister who became pastor of the Knob Creek Baptist Church in Kentucky. Charley completed a business course, learned stenography to earn his way through college; worked through Georgetown in Georgetown, Ky., a Baptist school; became faculty secretary and secretary to the president; worked a 40-hour week *between* classes; took shorthand notes in class; became so adept he could read them without transcribing first. He still takes shorthand notes of his phone conversations and keeps the results in neat bundles in his desk. After a B.A. from Georgetown and some interim jobs, he received a fellowship in agricultural economics from the University of Florida. He studied business administration as a minor, wound up with an M.S. in agriculture and a B.S. in administration—a combination, he says, so unlikely no suitable slot existed; was adrift with this educational hodgepodge in 1931 when jobs were non-existent. Short, round-faced and cheerful, Mr. Bolton is today manager of the Ashland Division Marketing Department.

Bolton, aware that few people can resist giving trumped-up tests, was impressed at this lack of waste motion.

"Grossenbach will be in town Saturday, and he'll call you," Blazer said. On Saturday, Grossenbach *did* call, and offered him a job, which Bolton accepted immediately.

Told to report to work immediately, Bolton went to the office and was put to work cutting a stencil: the message was to the oil producers of eastern Kentucky; its import was that the Ashland Refining Company had become the new owner of the Cumberland Pipeline Company.

Few purchases have been so fortuitous. The terms were $60,000 cash and four $90,000 payments at six-month intervals, for a total of $420,000. When the line had been constructed in 1902, it had cost $3,600,000. And that had been when dollars were really hard.

As if the overall figures were not bargain enough, there was more to come. At the time of the purchase, oil pipelines were allowed (and had been allowed for many years) a bottom sediment and water allowance of 3 per cent of their inventories. Over the years, this 3 per cent allowance had been duly deducted from inventory by the bookkeepers, but the physical accumulation had been somehow overlooked. As a consequence, when Blazer's men began to check the physical dimensions and condition of the new property, they found more than $100,000 worth of unreported crude oil in the system: larger than the down payment for the entire system.

In addition to this windfall (or inventory-fall), the Cumberland brought another formidable asset to Ashland: Bill (W. H.) Keffer. Keffer was one of two pipeline engineers of considerable talent who had been employed by Cumberland: Mr. Towl had offered Blazer a choice between them. Mr. Wolf, the second man, was recognized as an excellent engineer, but Blazer considered him temperamentally too cold. Keffer, on the other hand, had few equals in charm. "He could beguile property owners into granting rights-of-way as though by magic," Blazer said later. "He carried the details of his job in his hat; his men loved him, and so did everyone else. So did I." Blazer chose Keffer, and Keffer became his strong right arm in matters concerning pipeline.

On a grander and more impersonal scale, the purchase of the Cumberland line filled in the last link for the Swiss Oil companies. The combined enterprise now stretched from oil wells in eastern and western Kentucky, through its own gathering and trunk lines into the largest refinery in the region, and out again as refined products through regional marketing arms.

Paul Blazer came into possession, therefore, of all the elements of J. Fred Miles's dream. In later years, he was to harken back to this purchase time and again, until younger men would shift in their chairs in silent dissent, thinking that larger and more obviously impressive acquisitions were surely more important. But Blazer was right; the Cumberland pipeline purchase was the

Paul G. Blazer (early 1930s)

bridge across which the firm moved from a venture operating in parts of the oil industry, to a firm operating in every phase.

At the time, Blazer talked about it to everyone in earshot. Dr. Winans recalls that Paul came into his office and said, "I have a chance to buy a pipeline; I think I can talk the board into it," and wandered out again smiling. Georgia Blazer recalls Paul walking with her around Central Park in Ashland in the evening, explaining the importance of the acquisition, at great length, every step of the way.

While Blazer was building his empire, the skies over the United States and much of the rest of the world were darkening, although the newspapers had enough ephemera to report to give the impression that much of life was as it had always been: Katherine Cornell was portraying Elizabeth Barrett on Broadway; *Green Pastures* was a hit; Pearl Buck made the best-seller list with *The Good Earth*. The short skirts of the twenties lengthened drastically; Starr Faithful's mysterious death inspired John O'Hara to write a novel woven from headlines, a practice that would eventually spread throughout literature; panic struck in Germany; England went off the gold standard. In September, when Bolton was cutting his stencil and Blazer making his announcement regarding Cumberland, 305 banks closed their doors in the United States; by October, the list had swollen to 522; U.S. Steel announced a 10 per cent wage cut throughout its vast reaches and all autumn smaller firms followed suit. In millions of homes, people sat down to figure how to cut corners, scrimp, do without, pinch and scratch: the nation went from tenderloin to hash.

Some darkness appeared in the skies over Ashland Refining as well: Mr. Rion, the traffic manager with a miraculous memory for freight rates, died unexpectedly of a heart attack, leaving a wife and two young daughters. Blazer, writing to Senator Combs in his usual detail, said the oldest Rion girl, only eight, had been "in school only two years and is already in the fourth grade," an item of information that may have come through Mrs. Blazer, although both Blazers knew all the people in the company. Mr. Rion, Blazer explained to Combs, had not left an estate in the proper sense, so much as debts: his insurance amounted to only

$8,500; he still owed $3,000 on his home (the figures look strangely small over the gulf of years; to understand them they should be multiplied several times). Blazer suggested the company create a fund to ensure the little girls' education, which was done. A strong family man himself, his thoughts were to increasingly turn toward the long-range security of the families of men who worked with Ashland. It was a time when the entire nation, made shockingly aware of the insecurity of life, became security-minded.

In the meantime, Swiss Oil itself was in serious trouble. The common stock, traded on the New York Curb, had fallen to a dollar a share, and there were no buyers. The directors began to fear that the price would drop even lower or perhaps dwindle away to practically nothing. This would mean an utter loss of confidence in the company, and that would be the beginning of the end. It was not an idle fear; many larger and better-known firms with fewer problems were dying. Rumors that Swiss was in trouble became fairly common. Many persons kept hearing that Ashland Refining was being sold to one or another of the larger companies.

"We are swamped with visitors these days," Blazer wrote Combs. "They are probably coming in to see for themselves how we are weathering the storm."

In addition, analysts knew that Swiss Oil itself was confronted with the task of making good $778,000 due in January, 1931. Because the market collapsed, a new issue of bonds found no purchasers. The Swiss Oil companies as a group had borrowed a total of $845,000 from the banks, and reached the outer limits of the firm's debt limit. In this extremity, Senator Combs pledged $100,000 personally, and the full assets of the Combs Lumber Company to assist Swiss; he was joined by another large shareholder who also pledged large sums the day before the bank notes were due. Thus, the firm was held together, but barely.

None of Blazer's young men had any idea of the size of the clouds that loomed over them, but Paul Blazer, whose radar by this time swung in great swoops without ceasing, was keenly knowledgeable about the force and the size of the storm. He asked attorney E. L. McDonald for an opinion on the legality of Ashland Refining buying Swiss common stock; in other words, supporting it in the market. When McDonald appeared dubious, Blazer looked up the law himself and could see no restrictions. He moved quickly. He began with the purchase of 9,000 shares of Swiss bonds in June, then shortly afterward purchased, as general manager of Ashland Refining, some $50,000 more. He then bought 10,000 shares of Swiss common stock at $1 a share and steadied the price at that figure. The child was beginning to support the parent.

At the end of 1931, the Ashland National Bank, unable to hold out against the crumbling tide, closed its doors. Blazer, working diligently behind the scenes, joined local businessmen in a plan to merge the healthy Second National Bank of Ashland with the invalid. He took part in a stock subscription for the new bank (Ashland Refining had $60,000 involved) and became a director of the merger result, as well as a shareholder in the reorganized firm.

The year 1931 ended, incredibly, with Ashland Refining in possession of another profitable statement: its after-taxes earnings amounted to $175,000.

The year 1932, like 1929, is one that has been exhaustively described. Generally speaking, it was a replay of 1931, with the dialogue more hackneyed, the arguments more emotional, the protagonists less hopeful, their rhetoric looser. Ashland Refining fought hard for business. It reduced the postings on crude oil again, built more bulk plants and worked closely with all its accounts.

In Chicago, the debacle caught—among others—the Insulls. Insull himself had borrowed very substantial sums from a number of banks in an attempt to bolster the market value of his securities—believing, until the very end, that they could be saved from collapse.

But in the spring of 1932, with the approach of large maturing obligations held by the public and various financial institutions, the strong downward pressures of the time resulted in Middle West Utilities and other holding companies managed by the Insulls being placed in receivership.

That was the beginning of an international *cause célèbre* during which Samuel Insull fled the country to escape a criminal indictment and trial. His brother Martin Insull, an early investor in Swiss Oil, fled to Canada. Both were eventually returned by the authorities; Samuel was taken off a ship en route, on the high seas, from Greece to Egypt; Martin returned from Canada.

Meanwhile, heroic efforts to unravel the awesomely complex affairs of the Insull holding companies were launched. One of the men engaged in this task was William C. Freeman, a banker, of Chicago. Mr. Freeman examined the securities that Samuel and Martin Insull [6] had turned over for the benefit of their creditors, and discovered among these Martin Insull's shares in Swiss Oil. Knowing that Bob Gordon's firm traded these issues, he contacted Gordon, who in turn called Paul Blazer. Paul lost no time in getting to Chicago.

Once together, Freeman and Blazer presented a study in contrasts. Blazer, unusually tall and eloquent in a polished, highly grammatical and wordy way; Freeman, unusually short with a craggy face and a conversational style that is, though colorful, blunt and monosyllabic. Freeman accepted an invitation to visit Ashland, Kentucky, and was conducted through Blazer's refinery at Catlettsburg.

The banker, accustomed to evaluating large enterprises, looked around with steely blue eyes, and considered it "rust and baling wire." To him, Swiss Oil had "some production and no capital." He was more impressed with Paul Blazer and he returned to Chicago with the opinion the man was worth supporting. Freeman retained, on behalf of the powerful interests he represented, the Swiss Oil stock. Blazer had enlisted a major asset at a crucial time.

In the efforts of the period, Bob Gordon played a major role and, at Senator Combs' invitation, joined the board of directors. He did more: on one of Paul Blazer's trips to Chicago, Gordon

[6] The Insulls were brought to trial and acquitted; the indictments had little more to them than general hysteria and the widespread need for scapegoats. But like much of the history of this period, the dismissal of the charges has never seemed to catch up with the accusation. Samuel Insull is still used as an example of business nefariousness, although the specifics are always left cloudy; U.S. historians are still strangely reluctant to drop the devil theory of the Depression.

had him give a talk about Ashland and Tri-State Refining to the
Gordon & Bartlett securities salesmen.

Blazer extended his efforts to bolster the Swiss stock position.
Combining several objectives, he bought 2,000 shares of Swiss
common at $1.05 a share and turned 1,000 shares each over to
Everett Wells and A. A. Hines, manager of the distribution department. Each man paid $500 down and agreed to pay off the
balance over a six-month period, during which Blazer held their
notes and the stock as collateral. A short time later, Blazer went
through the same routine with Pat Leonard of the pipeline department. Meanwhile he bought some shares of Swiss common
back from Roy Grossenbach, who wanted to cash his holdings. By
mid-summer, Ashland Refining held 11,200 shares of Swiss common stock, and the downward slide in its price was checked.

In October 1932, after holding back longer than many another company, Blazer cut salaries and wages 10 per cent across
the board for all the employees of Ashland. An interesting exchange of letters between him and Bob Gordon resulted. Gordon,
pleased at the economy move, wrote Blazer and congratulated
him. Blazer, writing back, gave a glimpse of the internal rigors
under which he managed the company, and some sense of the
dedication of his young men, saying, in part: ". . . our organization has been built up principally by men who were employed
originally at salaries of $125 a month or less . . . responsibilities
have been forced upon those who were capable. For example, we
have one very capable young man who is in charge of all of our
bulk plants, tank truck and filling station sales, has approximately
75 people under him and is drawing only $270 a month . . . An-
other young man[7] is drawing $360 a month; he has the title of
sales manager and is in direct charge of all our tank car sales, the
volume of which totals approximately three million dollars per
year . . . in most organizations, a man of his ability and responsibility would draw a salary of $10,000. I was drawing that
much ten or twelve years ago in another organization and my job
wasn't nearly so difficult as the one he holds with us . . ."

Art Points said the "foundations of this company were laid

[7] Our friend Everett Wells: the quiet man.

during the thirties by hard work." In this, Blazer was a pace-setter, but he was matched, step for step, by his men. Points would often walk from the office to Blazer's home for dinner; the two men would then both walk back to their offices and work till midnight; neither man was alone in the practice.

Gordon, however, was a stout man, whom no other man, not even Paul Blazer, could intimidate. In response to Blazer's implied rebuke, he wrote back that, with the price of everything going down, the man whose salary was not cut received, in effect, a raise. "I know of no man making a salary of $10,000 a year today," he said—understandably exaggerating somewhat—and added that when investors and stockholders were neither receiving dividends nor retaining the value of their holdings, he saw no reason why wage-earners should not share the sufferings of investors. Gordon's arguments appear, on reflection, to have considerable point; the exchange was typical of the relationship between the two men: ever contentious, never serene, but basically amicable and mutually stimulating.

During these days, however, all was not darkness: Blazer went to Europe for a month together with Mr. Maxwell of Standard Oil of Ohio; both Arch Maxwell and Blazer enjoyed themselves thoroughly. And while they were gone, a short, bright-eyed, smiling man at the Ashland National Bank added up the factors that separated Blazer from the other businessmen in the area.

Ned Seaton had been particularly interested in watching Blazer compete with Tri-State when that competitive refinery was independent. "Tri-State was managed by Commander Davison," Seaton said, "and the Commander was a chemical engineer. He prided himself on buying the best, the latest, and the most modern equipment—but he was often stung. At Ashland, Blazer installed old equipment, but he knew how to improve it and to make it function as well as the latest and the best." Seaton, intrigued at this ability, learned that Universal Oil Products (through Mr. Halle and others) would often tell Blazer about technological developments; Seaton was equally impressed by the fact that Blazer *understood what he was told.*

Seaton decided, "Blazer was going places . . . places I wanted to go, too." At the bank, where Seaton was a vice president and a director, he had just been offered the post of Trust Officer. His decision must have amazed his fellow directors: he applied to Ashland for a job, and accepted when Roy Grossenbach, the Ashland Refining treasurer, offered him half the salary he was getting at the bank.

The day Seaton reported to work, he recalls, Grossenbach kept him "sitting on his hands" all morning, without telling him what to do. In the afternoon, Grossenbach assigned him to the audit department, then came to him an hour later and said, "I just canned the credit manager: take that over."

Seaton[8] was not impressed with the Ashland treasurer after that first day, and the situation looked to him as promising as could be.

[8] Edward William Seaton was born in Ashland, Ky., in 1894. His mother's maiden name was Means. Both the Seatons and the Meanses are Old Ashland; their backgrounds encompass the development of the iron, steel, coal and railroad industries in the region, and the development of the city. The Means family moved to Ashland from South Carolina, "because other slave-owners objected to the Meanses teaching their slaves how to read and write," in 1818; built a charcoal iron furnace in 1847; David Seaton, a paternal ancestor, married later into the Means family, after *his* forebear, Sam Seaton, had built a charcoal furnace in Ashland in 1848 (the Seatons are an offshoot of the Scots Seton family). Through the years the names of Seaton, Means, Briggs, Russell, Humphrey, representative of the Ashland early elite, reappear in chronicles constantly.

The Seatons are related to the Taft family of Ohio; there is still a Seaton Hotel in Cincinnati; ex-U.S. President William Howard Taft was David Seaton's nephew. Ned went to Yale University from 1912 to 1916 (where his forebear John Means graduated in 1842), and was an undergraduate when William Howard Taft was Dean of the Law School. Ned recalls that Taft would "squeeze his great bulk into a small Tudor automobile in order to trundle around the campus," while Mrs. Taft rode in comfortable luxury in a limousine; heard Theodore Roosevelt announce that he would "throw his hat in the ring" in a speech at Seaton's prep in Havre-de-Grace, Maryland . . . a phrase Roosevelt said he heard "in the little mountain town of Ashland, Kentucky," a reference that tickled Ned immensely, then and now.

Seaton's family created the Russell Iron Company and the Ashland Iron & Mining Company; purchased the Norton Iron Works; built blast furnaces; owned one-third of the Ashland Steel Company; formed the Ashland Iron Mining Company and built a rolling mill during 1921–

The year 1932 was, of course, an election year. In retrospect, even realizing that the mood of the nation had swung so drastically against Hoover and the business traditions he represented, one wonders at the bitterness of the campaign. Some historians, even today, seem to echo the strident sentiment that existed then, especially in their acid description of those who sought to stand in the victorious way of the new voting blocs from the great cities, labor, and the universities, who combined in unlikely alliance against the older America. The election did more than swing one Administration out of power and another in: it changed the composition of American leadership. It is a reflection of the people's allegiance to the democratic method that this tremendous shift, that in many nations would have been accompanied by force, was here quietly accomplished in the voting booth, even though the fervor and the bitterness had a new depth for the nation.

Against this turbulent backdrop, it is a relief to turn back to arenas where men were quietly engaged in work. At Ashland, by the spring of 1932, Hugh Jenks and his group had produced several cars of asphalt for experimental work. These were rejected by the State Highway Department of Kentucky as being too low in viscosity; again, the laboratory tests had not been fulfilled by field results. Here, Senator Combs's enormous prestige with the state government became helpful, and at least Ashland asphalt was retained for experiments. The results, surprising to some, were highly promising.

Blazer, struck by the continuing need to economize, and aware that he himself had pushed everyone as close to the brink as he dared, decided to bring in outside experts. He chose the Emerson

---

1922; sold most of these properties to the American Rolling Mill Company (now Armco Steel) when it came to Ashland and owned large tracts of real estate in the area including the present site of the Bellefonte Country Club.

After graduation from Yale and service in the army during World War I, Ned Seaton joined the Ashland Iron & Mining Co. from 1916 to 1922; became a director and a vice president of the Ashland National Bank until 1932, a vantage spot from which he observed Blazer and Ashland Refining; became treasurer of Ashland Refining and its successor, Ashland Oil & Refining, from 1932 until his retirement in 1959, and remains a director.

Engineers to make a survey and suggest improvements or economies. The man from Emerson turned out to be partner Alexander S. Chamberlain, who had married young Dotty Monroe,
Mrs. Blazer's sister, in 1927. Chamberlain proved both bright and
efficient. The project lasted until well into 1933; Ashland benefited
and Chamberlain was attracted by what he learned of the company.

As the year drew toward its close, Blazer's prestige had risen
to the point where he was invited to make a speech before the
Ohio Marketers Association at Columbus. He chose as his title:
Current Marketing Evils. It was a bold topic upon which to em-
bark; the industry was in a state of internecine war, in which
discounts, rebates, special privileges and collapsing prices had
almost everyone at his competitor's throat. Blazer himself was
the victor of a thousand such struggles, and everyone in the
audience knew it. Nevertheless, the objectivity of his remarks
was refreshing; there was an absence of rancor and a vivifying
amount of candor in what he had to say. He made the observation
that executives in the major companies were moving in the direction of abstract reasoning in which policies had become more
important than profits, an example of misplaced academia that was
to astonish him with increasing frequency as the years passed.

"These gentlemen," Blazer said, ". . . prefer an orderly, uniform, easily visualized price and discount system, though at an
unprofitable level, to an unsystematic structure at a profitable
level. They have big, difficult jobs and they are forced to make
quick, sweeping decisions which cover too much territory. It becomes too easy for them to say, 'we can't afford to let them take
our business, go ahead and drop the market.' Their personal
salaries remain the same the day after the market drops. It might
be different if the cut meant thousands of dollars out of their
own pockets, as is the case with many of the smaller operators."

This is the tone of an owner talking about bureaucrats in
business; it was a tone Blazer was to retain.

Then, switching emphasis, Blazer discussed the cash-price operator, making decisions on the basis of profits. "He is destructive
as far as retail prices are concerned," Blazer said, "but constructive
as far as marketing costs are concerned. He forces the rest of the

industry down to his retail prices, but he also forces them to stop their expensive expansion programs, and eventually they will have to abandon their dealers' wide margins which support five times as many outlets as are desirable."

One wonders whether the line of reasoning was appreciated by an audience composed of sufferers: Blazer was talking about the tendency of business enterprises to turn into bureaucracies: he saw in this a peril not only to the small businessman and the public, but to business itself. He credited much of industry's difficulties to this development. The distinction was popular during the early thirties, but usually for the wrong reasons. Like Justice Brandeis, many people thought a smaller business was more moral, somehow, than a large business. Blazer saw, more clearly, that a threat to business was equally sinister whether the enterprise was small or large. He regarded many of the managers of very large corporations as little better than theorists: he had faith that smart little businessmen, working freely, would maintain the democratic balance in the marketplace—if left alone.

In any event, the distinction was too fine for the times. The general public was turning against business; the new Administration was to enter office in the spring with a layman's opinion very similar to that of the general public.

The year 1932 ended with Ashland Refining showing earnings of $304,051.47 on sales of $4.1 million, a showing Blazer was quick to ascribe to the acquisition and favorable earnings of the Cumberland pipeline. That venture was now making $15,000 a month where it had, under the old Standard Oil men, been losing $15,000 a month. Other charges and revenues of the line had helped swell the corporate coffers.

But the explanation did not dim the lustre of the accomplishment. Whether the profits were made from refining or transportation seemed of little consequence to the Swiss Oil board of directors; they were well aware that very few persons in the oil industry were making a profit from anything that year, while Blazer was making a profit all along the line.

Thus, when Bob Gordon sent Blazer a pleasant letter of congratulations, we are at first surprised to read that Blazer again took issue. As his letter to Gordon progresses though, we taste again that bitter flavor of that dark winter, one of the darkest winters this nation has ever endured.

"Dear Bob" Blazer wrote: "Due to the fact that in the past when the Ashland Refining Company has apparently been in a 'tight' place we have usually been able to get out without being hurt seriously, probably it will be difficult for me to convince you of the seriousness of our present market situation . . ." and then he goes on to detail widespread deterioration that has "reached the point where the price of gasoline to the customer is less than the freight and handling expenses, leaving nothing for the cost of crude oil, refinery operations or general overhead . . ."

Then he comments on a phenomenon which illustrates the imminence of the national disaster: "everybody in the oil business seems to be getting in an ugly mood. Executives and sales managers who ordinarily are level headed seem to be more interested in retaliation than in making profits. Competitors who formerly have gotten along together very nicely are now scarcely on speaking terms . . ."

This was true on even higher levels. President-elect Roosevelt, sweepingly victorious in the election, refused to meet with lame-duck President Hoover to discuss either his own plans or some cooperative measures out of the crisis: an attitude that seems strangely subjective in view of the dimensions of the catastrophe. This attitude existed also in an intransigent Congress that appeared intent on destroying Hoover before he left an office he had lost, without particular regard for the plight of the nation, and by an ugly, almost jeering note that began to recur in the national dialogue.

Blazer, in his turn, was contemplating a loss operation at Ashland Refining, a prospect he found almost unbearable. No matter where he looked, during that spring of 1933, it did not seem he could profitably function. Seated in his aerie, surveying the scene, his eyes fell on the royalty payments of the Dubbs cracking unit that were sent, as regularly as the ticking of a clock, to the Universal Oil Products Company (UOP). In 1932, they had mounted to the sum of $80,000. This struck Blazer as monstrous, and he fired a letter toward the UOP, saying that at a time when every other price was dropping, its charges remained constant. He asked whether they would not consider, in the light of their comfortable position, making some adjustment in their royalty demands.

His letter was relayed from the man to whom he wrote, to Mr. Halle, the president of UOP. Mr. Halle had been, over the years, a strong dose for Blazer. In the early days, when Blazer was stretching his wings as general manager of Ashland Refining, Mr. Halle, as an important stockholder in Swiss Oil, had opposed refining operations altogether. As the years passed, however, and Blazer's operation began to make money while Swiss Oil revenues declined, Halle's attitude had reflected the shift with almost comic consistency: in the last few years he had been particularly fulsome in his compliments. In addition, of course, the UOP had been most helpful to Ashland Refining in the transmission of valuable technical information, and the Dubbs cracking unit had been Blazer's pride and joy—when he first received it.

When Mr. Halle answered Blazer's letter on royalties, however, he was cool to the point of insouciance. Of Blazer's letter, he said, "It is very interesting reading, but we hardly know our old friend Blazer (although) I can well understand in the present demoralized state of the industry that no man should be expected to be normal." The balance of the letter repeated the virtues of the Dubbs cracking unit, and emphasized that no royalty reduction would be considered.

Mr. Halle, however, underestimated Blazer, and overestimated the strength of his own position. Blazer had been in constant touch with the Ethyl Corporation, and behind the scenes, had long been urging them toward a step that would seriously reduce the handicap that paying UOP royalties represented to small refiners like Ashland.[9]

Behind the scenes, Blazer had been working closely with his

[9] The major oil companies were all in possession of their own systems for cracking. Only small refiners like Ashland had to avail themselves of these systems and pay royalties to one group or another. The situation provided an advantage for the majors, therefore, since they could manufacture at low cost themselves and obtain an income from their smaller competitors, who then had to meet competitive prices in the marketplace. There were few men less temperamentally equipped to endure this situation indefinitely than Paul Blazer.

friends at the Ethyl Corporation. Early in April, these efforts bore fruit, and Ethyl sent him a letter announcing its intention to supply tetraethyl lead to refiners to add to their regular gasoline, instead of restricting it to Ethyl gasoline, at an extremely reasonable price. Ashland was the first small refiner to receive the offer, and this was no accident. Blazer had actually talked to the directors of the Ethyl Corporation, explaining the advantages and virtues of such a step; he was, therefore, a prime mover in the development. Most of the major companies, understandably, objected strenuously to Ethyl's decision, which helped the small independent refiner to become more competitive in the gasoline market.

It meant that, with the addition of the tetraethyl lead, any refiner could convert his ordinary gasoline into premium gasoline, and bypass the royalty-expensive process equipment. The importance of the Dubbs unit was reduced with a stroke of the pen. Blazer lost no time in breaking the good news to the board of Swiss Oil, and to Mr. Halle.

Mr. Halle's response was quite different in tone than his previous response: he was most anxious to see copies of the Ethyl agreements, and this time his letter was markedly absent of persiflage. Whether Blazer had intimations that Ethyl would take their step or not (he said he did not), the timing of the exchange could hardly have suited his situation better: Mr. Halle and the UOP became markedly more respectful.

That was in April 1933. In January, the Swiss Oil Company had taken sufficient cognizance of the generally devalued state of the nation to decrease the par value of its capital stock from $5 to $1. By this step the assets of the company were written down by $2.25 million, and a capital surplus created which made dividends possible.

Blazer busied himself tightening up his organization. He switched the post of treasurer from Roy Grossenbach to Ned Seaton, placed young Ed Emrick in charge of monies up to $500. Other duties were divided between Emrick and Art Points. Everett Wells became Sales Manager and, as knowledgeable about the marketplace by this time as Paul himself, became his virtual *alter ego*. The refinery was running economically and well. In Chicago, Bob Gordon was working hard to assist the company in the Exchange, and Bill Freeman, that astute citizen, was being enormously helpful behind the scenes.

In effect, Ashland Refining had taken a series of giant steps toward being independent; the directors of the Swiss Oil Company, although still important, were no longer the only important men with whom Blazer dealt: the child was making its own friends, had gathered its own supporters, and was growing rapidly. Throughout the oil industry, the name of the Swiss Oil Company had receded into the background; the name of the Ashland Refining Company had become far better known; the name of Paul Blazer began to carry weight.

In March 1933, the New Deal entered Washington through the rubble of the nation's collapsing banking system; the population was caught, by the oddly-named Bank Holiday, with only its spare change on hand.

The new Administration had the entire nation behind it; Congress was anxious to comply with whatever salvage signals were flashed from the White House. The Hundred Days are difficult to describe even after the passage of almost thirty-five years; it's doubtful if Washington itself retains either a clear recollection or even the records of all the activities that took place.

It seemed, during that period, as though all the reins of power in the nation were gathered from their scattered centers ranging from Wall Street to the Farm Belt, into the hands of one central group whose personae were largely unknown to the nation: the New Dealers. The impression was, of course, exaggerated, but that was the impression.

The Administration undertook a great many steps at once. The farm situation came under the Agricultural Adjustment Agency (AAA); banking received reorganization acts; industry and labor were placed under a sweeping mandate entitled the National Industrial Recovery Act (NIRA). The title alone was an indication of a rhetoric that would first efface and then replace the old language; the bill itself a sweeping mandate that established regulations governing virtually every aspect of business and industry, leaving the owning class in technical possession of its properties, but with its powers drastically reduced.

During the crisis, there was considerable sentiment for cooperative effort. Cut-throat competition, under the circumstances, simply seemed to add to the general distress. This sentiment helped create an atmosphere of anxious compliance to whatever was suggested; Washington was as crowded with businessmen seeking to be assisted as it was with bright young men anxious to assist.

The oil industry, which had long been a target of the nation's reformers (thanks in part to a bad press for decades, which had emphasized its scandals and defects at the expense of its accomplishments), was among the first to be honored by the special attention of the Roosevelt Administration.

At first, oil came under the administrator of the NIRA, General Hugh S. "Ironpants" Johnson, the Blue Eagle himself. But this situation did not please Harold Ickes, the Secretary of the Interior, the self-styled "old curmudgeon." [10]

Mr. Ickes began to read up on the oil industry situation, and among the articles which attracted his attention was one that appeared in the *Yale Law Review* entitled "Legal Planning in Petroleum Production (Two Years Later)," by an assistant professor of law and an assistant dean of the Yale Law School.

Mr. Ickes told his secretary to place a telephone call to New Haven, and get J. Howard Marshall [11] on the line. When Mr.

[10] According to Webster's *Collegiate Dictionary* at the time, curmudgeon is defined as "an avaricious, grasping fellow; niggard; churl; also a cross, ill-natured, cantankerous man." Ickes had an individual, prickly, but very real sense of humor.

[11] J. Howard Marshall, born 1905, in Germantown, Pa., is a direct descendant of a brother of John Marshall, Chief Justice of the U.S. Supreme Court (1801–1835), who is credited with having established the awesome powers of the Court; of the Marshall family of Virginia, notable for their contributions to the nation.

J. Howard Marshall's immediate paternal grandfather and two great uncles moved from Virginia to Philadelphia, Pa., entered the steel business, sold out to Andrew Carnegie when he was buying everything in sight to create U.S. Steel. The sale resulted in a quantity of U.S. Steel bonds, and preferred stock, and common stock. Mr. Marshall had little faith in the common stock, declared it "full of water," advised its

Marshall answered, Ickes invited him to come to Washington as an assistant solicitor to work on the hot oil situation in the Department of the Interior. It was one of the best moves Ickes ever made: similarly, it was to be an open sesame for Marshall.

J. Howard Marshall and his friend Norman L. Meyers[12] became part of Ickes' brain trust in the Department of the Interior; worked so well for Ickes that he was able to shift the administration of the oil industry away from General Johnson and have it placed in Interior. During that summer of 1933, work was well launched on an oil Code of Fair Practices; a body of regulations that encompassed all aspects of the industry from production and

---

disposal. J. Howard, years later, checked the rise in its value, settled at a figure of $28 million.

J. Howard Marshall received a B.A. from Haverford College, "a good Quaker school," where he was editor of the school paper; put in a stint at the Philadelphia *Ledger;* realized he had no special skills; taught history, English and economics on a student around-the-world cruise for 9 months, earned enough money to enter Yale Law School for a year, took a year's leave to take another such cruise, this time as director, for $5,000 and expenses, "a fortune then,"—was warned by Robert Hutchins, then Dean of Yale Law School, that he would not "make it back"; the prediction almost came true the summer of 1929 when Marshall was offered a $20,000-a-year job by Thomas Cook & Sons; thought it through and realized he would still be without a special skill. Back at Yale Law, he soared to the top of the class, was Case Editor of the *Yale Review,* a prestigious plum. In 1931, in his last year, was attracted to the details of the Oil Prorationing situation and case; together with Norman Meyers, an economist from the Brookings Institution also studying law at Yale, decided to write a lead article on the subject; with $500 collected from the Yale School of Economics and the Yale Law School, spent with Meyers two months in the oil fields of Oklahoma; wrote with Meyers an article entitled "Legal Planning in Petroleum Production" which discussed the interrelationships and interdependencies of price, control of production, supply, etc., in the oil industry. He graduated from Yale Law that same year (1931), was appointed assistant professor of law; in 1933, wrote a follow-up article with the same title with the addition "Two Years Later" which attracted the attention of Mr. Ickes; was by then also an assistant Dean of the Yale Law School. His subsequent career, including his term as president of the Ashland Oil & Refining Company, is carried in the main body of this chronology.

[12] Mr. Meyers, after graduating from Yale Law, had gone to work for the Federal Power Commission; Marshall had Ickes request his transfer.

attendant controls through to marketing practices, and that included prices. Similar efforts, under the NIRA charter, were taking place regarding other industries. Wages and hours came under
another section of the NIRA; these matters were not neglected in
the oil industry.

New Deal economics were based upon several assumptions. Foremost among them were the beliefs that the nation's economic frontiers had disappeared, that national industrial growth had reached
maximum levels, that the population was at virtual saturation (a
falling birth rate had convinced the experts of this), that economic
problems were traceable to inequities in the distribution of wealth.
The solutions were as various as the Administration's composition. Many different and even conflicting solutions were applied
at once, but through most of these efforts ran a broad common
denominator consisting of a desire to elevate the masses. The
obvious appeal of this objective clouded judgment on the means.

Moving boldly and with great speed, the Administration created
sweeping public works programs and instituted measures to relieve the distressed of the nation, who made an enormous group.
Estimates of the unemployed (who did not, by any means, constitute all the distressed but merely the most distressed) in early
1933 ranged from 9 to 20 million; there were hundreds of thousands (some say one million) absolutely homeless persons wandering the countryside. President Roosevelt, in a famous speech, declared "one third of the nation" was inadequately fed, clothed or
housed, and there was no reason to dispute the accuracy of the
statement.

The Administration also drastically devalued the dollar. The
combination of devaluation and spending combined to make
powerful medicine. Despite a host of other nostrums, these two
alone are credited by some with getting the patient out of bed.[13]

[13] Frederick Lewis Allen, in *Since Yesterday, 1929–1939*, says, ". . .
there would seem to be room for the somewhat cynical comment that
of all the economic medicines applied to the United States as a whole
during the nineteen thirties, only two have proved to be of general
effectiveness, and both of these have a habit-forming tendency and
may be lethal if too often repeated: these two medicines are devaluation
and spending."

The oil industry sent representatives to Washington to assist
in drawing up its Code. Blazer, who would not have missed all the
excitement for the world, managed tó have himself designated as
a representative from West Virginia (through the Tri-State properties), and arrived in Washington, like almost everyone else, filled
with curiosity.

He was to discover the world had changed. For one thing, the
theories of the early New Deal revolved around the need to fix
prices. Obviously, no economy can be planned that allows free
prices. Yet the consistency of this view was overshadowed by the
larger inconsistency of idealists who had decried price-fixing for
decades. To many of the businessmen, and especially to men like
Paul Blazer who sincerely believed in a free market, price-fixing
did not become moral simply because the machinery forbidden to
private hands was assumed by the government.

To some of the men of the New Deal, such distinctions amounted
to hairsplitting. But they attempted to straddle the issue, at least
publicly, by having industry *voluntarily* establish fair prices. The

Old streetcar converted into a service station selling Pepper gasoline.
(1933)

camouflage was thin, but by tacit consent most of the parties engaged agreed not to strip the rhetorical covering from the issue and expose it naked to the world. The nation was, after all, in an emergency.

Not all the men were in disagreement with the New Deal by any means. Many of the major oil companies were delighted with the chance to have the government fix prices for them. They could envision a freeze of the industry pecking order, with themselves in front. Therefore, they assured the economists of the New Deal— some of whom were not so much sophisticated as educated, and who did not realize the terms were not synonymous—that their reasoning was, indeed, excellent. It was the lowly independents, whose only chance for long-range survival was in competition with the majors, who mounted the strongest opposition. They could not survive a price freeze.[14] Blazer was, of course, busy in their ranks.

Despite this, Blazer did not push to the fore officially. He had long ago abandoned such practices: he preferred to work quietly, particularly when strong emotions existed in situations. He and Mr. Holliday[15] shared a suite together in Washington; Blazer

[14] To the surprise of some New Dealers, this reaction prevailed on a national scale as well. The greatest opposition to the new Administration came not from big business generally, but from small business. The minimum wage, the shorter work week, the rise of unions were vehemently opposed by small business. Small business seemed also more committed to free enterprise as an ideology; big business was more receptive to the planned economy. Perhaps the difference in reaction could be traced to circumstances: small business wanted to keep the avenues of growth open; big business wanted to retain its position. One unexpected side result, however, was that intellectuals became disillusioned with the lower middle class in contrast with their love affair with labor; today the intellectuals have switched much of their affection to minorities but still retain a disdain of the lower middle class.

[15] W. Trevor Holliday, six years older than Paul Blazer, was born in Newburg, a suburb of Cleveland; attended Western Reserve and Cornell, graduated from Harvard Law School in 1908. After graduation, he became acquainted with Ohio Standard, looking after production leases, pipeline rights of way and other legal matters. In 1928 he became the fourth president of Sohio and in April 1949 was elected chairman of the board.

The firm was the original Standard Oil Company, incorporated in

worked to have the independents elect Holliday as their representative on the most important committees, to represent their
common interests. Mr. Holliday was, of course, highly gratified;
he redoubled his efforts.

That summer, Mr. Holliday introduced Paul Blazer to young
J. Howard Marshall, who was favorably impressed: Mr. Marshall
was finding the oil industry men a colorful and interesting group.
Another young man in Washington at the time was Robert G. Dunlop, an assistant to J. Howard Pew and his brother, J. N. Pew,[16]
who operated the Sun Oil Company—another independent, although a large one. Years later, Dunlop recalled his impression of
Blazer, tall and well-groomed, "standing before a group of men

---

1870. For the first twelve years it was the parent of an organization
that spread around the world. As it acquired properties, separate companies were organized to own and operate them. Doubt existed, in
those days when corporate structures and laws were primitive, that a
corporation could own the stock of another. The stocks in these various
enterprises were held by trustees of Standard Oil. In 1882, the Standard
Oil trust was formed, and the trustees transferred their stock to it; thus
the term "trusts" came into being. In 1899 because New Jersey liberalized
its corporation laws, the Standard Oil trust was dissolved and its assets
transferred to Standard Oil of New Jersey; Standard of Ohio then became a subsidiary of Standard of New Jersey. In 1911, when the U.S.
Supreme Court ordered the dissolution of the Standard Oil of New
Jersey, the stockholders of each subsidiary received proportionate shares
of independent enterprises thus created. Standard of Ohio was returned
to its independent position, was left with only a 5,000-barrel-a-day
refinery, a string of bulk stations and tank wagons—all in Ohio state
marketing business. Its stock was traded on the N.Y. Curb. By 1950,
none of the original stockholders remained as owners. In the early
1930s, at the period of the Codes, Blazer had purchased shares in
Standard of Ohio; Standard of Ohio was a good customer of Ashland
Refining. Both companies were independents, although Standard of
Ohio, mainly by virtue of its name, retained the aura of a major.

[16] Robert G. Dunlop is president and chief executive officer of Sun Oil
today and a close friend of Rex Blazer, chairman of the board of Ashland
Oil & Refining. The Pews became aware of Blazer during the New Deal
days. They shared his general outlook; both the Pews and Blazer had
great admiration and sympathy for one another. Dunlop saw great
affinities between them; describes them as men of stern independence,
believers in free and open markets, strong and outspoken in their
opinions.

that were seated around the table, making a plea for one of his positions. I don't recall the subject today, but I can still see him, in my mind's eye, speaking with great clarity and power. I recall how I admired his lucidity, even though I don't remember the issue. I am sure he was successful; he was usually successful."

It was a great stage. Many highly important shifts in direction, not all of them visible on the surface, were taking place. Blazer's reputation was enhanced during this period; he came to the attention of many top men. It was the first time the oil industry had to cooperate; and the industry was getting acquainted with itself generally. The experience was salutary, and in later years was to be of great benefit to the nation.

Blazer took a highly pragmatic view of these developments, however. He did not—or at least tried not to—get into any heated personal exchanges. Later, he said it was clear the independents held a minority position and could not possibly win all their points; he was content that the points were considered.

He took much the same view regarding the union movement. In April 1933, just before the new Administration came into office in Washington, he had raised the wages of men in the refinery, an action which took some steam out of the organizers' appeal. But being a realist, he assumed some sort of union would arise in Ashland. He contented himself with trying to swing the men first into a company union, and when that failed, working toward an AFL union.

Meanwhile, as soon as the government issued its regulations regarding wages and hours and classifications, he pored over these to see how he could blend the rules with his objectives. He created no less than ten classifications in the refinery (the lowest man in each classification could be hired or fired without machinery), and took what he considered reasonable precautions to try to hold the close-knit nature of his men together. But, ever since Charley Jouett had decamped with all the highly skilled men some years before, swinging them to J. Fred Miles in Louisville, Blazer made special and particular efforts to be friendly with the men at the refinery. He spent days, hours, weeks and months talking to his refinery operators. They served as his eyes regarding the functioning of equipment, as his hands in increasing production runs. Over the years he had learned their names and their foibles; the names of their wives and children. He had long chats with them over the phone in the early hours of the morning; he would spend, literally, hours talking to them about operations. Walter Maynard, Harold Scott, Barney Brooks, Don Fuller, Clarence Scott, Herb Czeskleba and others were so used to having Blazer call and ask, "What's the gravity in the bottom? What's the temperature?" that they used to refer to these questions as the beginning of "the lecture on bottoms."

Few refinery operators in other companies could say they had been chatting the night before with the top man in the company. Blazer's intensity and meticulous attention to the details of their work convinced his men their work was important to the company, that they themselves were equally important.

His methods, classically democratic, cut across the usual divisions of rank, for to this concern for work Blazer added a personal interest that was real and unfeigned. He worked an arrangement with Mr. Donald Putnam, the firm's insurance broker, whereby men continued to receive their full pay when sick. He was keenly aware of the importance of wives and families. At gatherings he would talk seriously to wives; tell them about their husbands' progress, enlist their sympathy for company goals.

The result was a very close, almost familial organization. The closeness was accentuated by the relative isolation of the refinery and the usual intimacy of relationships in a small town. Blazer's home was not a place where only senior men were invited; foremen and operators from the refinery were just as apt to find themselves invited in for a drink, and a long chat about conditions, the trends in the industry, the value of education. When men said they wanted their sons to continue in school, Blazer was more than conventionally interested: he wanted to help.

All this added up to a formidable barrier for the union organizers. The international officers of the union that finally appeared on the scene (an AFL union) chafed against the reluctance of the Ashland employees to assume that their own interests and the company's were contrary. The first union contract was signed in an amicable and friendly atmosphere; the only complaint was over an impulsive firing of a refinery worker by Roy Grossenbach. Grossenbach himself regretted the incident and Blazer established review machinery to prevent a repetition. In line with the NIRA doctrine of shorter work weeks (to spread the jobs) a schedule of working nine days and five days off was established.

An international officer of the union, arriving too late to delay the pact, was highly incensed. "We had," Blazer wrote Senator Combs, "a stormy session in my office." It gave him great pleasure.

The year 1933 ended with Ashland Refining earning $416,205 on net sales of $2 million; a record for the company, and a boon to Swiss Oil. Once again, the genie beside the Big Sandy had produced wealth from his operation.

Early in 1934, Swiss Oil, taking advantage of the widespread devaluation that had occurred, reduced the par value of its stock from $5 to $1, which made possible the transfer of $4 million from capital to surplus funds. Blazer thought some self-congratulations in order, noted their absence, and wrote Senator Combs a soft criticism, saying that ". . . you took over a company that owned little more than 256 producing wells (and small ones, at that), that has now expanded to a completely integrated oil company having more than 1,000 small wells, 800 miles of pipelines, 5,000 barrels daily of modern, efficient refining capacity, river transportation equipment and terminals, bulk distributing plants in a dozen or more cities with tank trucks and service stations, and other valuable properties necessary for the marketing of more than 50 million gallons annually of petroleum products."

Nowhere in his letter did Blazer hint that this growth and expansion, which before the end of 1934 would result in the complete liquidation of all Swiss Oil's indebtedness, was his accomplishment: he laid it at the doorstep of Senator Combs. In truth, it was a dual accomplishment. At one point, Senator Combs had pledged his own personal fortune to ensure that Swiss Oil would survive. He had encouraged and assisted Blazer in all the immeasurable ways an intelligent and influential older man can protect a younger. His influence assisted in getting the Kentucky highway department to consider Ashland Refining's asphalt; his position in the state brought many customers and businesses into

Ashland Refining's orbit. At the same time, Senator Combs was not an oil man; his knowledge of the technical aspects of the industry was scant; in this area he relied on Blazer's judgment.

There would never have been an entity known as Swiss Oil had it not been for J. Fred Miles, but Swiss would not have endured had it not been for Senator Combs. The Senator could not have succeeded had it not been for Paul Blazer; Blazer himself could not have performed so well without the intelligent, dedicated and hard working young men with whom he surrounded himself.

In June 1934, six months after Blazer had written his tribute to Senator Combs, the Senator issued a jubilant broadside to the stockholders, telling them the company was issuing its first dividend (ten cents a share) since July 1, 1930. He added that the Swiss Oil Company was, at long last, completely out of debt.

The impact of this wonderful news was diluted, however, by the information that the government had both assessed additional taxes against the company of some $200,000 for the years 1926 to 1930 inclusive, and disputed rates used by Swiss Oil in calculating depreciation and depletion.

Blazer's unceasing mind was, meanwhile, scanning the horizon for omens. Even the offer by Mr. Halle of Universal Oil Products to reduce their royalty demands by one-third did not seem to stir him; he passed the information on to Senator Combs flatly. One detects, for the first time, a note of *ennui* in his letters. At one point, in March 1934, he wondered aloud if perhaps the Ashland Refining Company should not be liquidated and the money thus received invested in something else. This comes as a considerable shock. We have become so accustomed to his dedication that we have taken his stamina for granted; now he is talking about folding up.

Perhaps the times had something to do with his mood. The euphoria induced in the nation by the entry of the New Deal had begun to dissipate; had faded considerably, in fact, and the voice of the demagogue was raised throughout the land.

Huey Long, Dr. Townsend, Father Coughlin, Upton Sinclair and lesser lights preached their panaceas. Lawyers of every stripe argued over the issues created by the NIRA, the AAA and other governmental steps and programs; Moley, Tugwell, Joe Kennedy, Harry Hopkins, Ickes, Morgenthau, Eccles and others fought for position in the inner circle; experts from abroad like Harold Laski, Internationale-minded Communists, domestic and foreign Socialists added their voices; traditionalists of every description protested, denied, complained and criticized. Businessmen began to wonder whether order could result from such confusion, whether the nation would survive its mixed diet of remedies and discontent.

Blazer found himself knee-deep in the details of the marketing agreement drawn up as part of the Petroleum Code, and was not happy over arguments in Washington between himself and various spokesmen for the large companies.

However, in neither Washington nor in Kentucky was life altering quite as rapidly as the New Deal blueprints demanded: society is an iceberg difficult to move. In the Swiss Oil lease lands in eastern Kentucky, for instance, one Buck Williams, leader of a formidable clan, had finally become so unruly and troublesome he had been discharged from his job. As a result, he launched a campaign of retaliation against the company; when Mr. Mingus, an engineer working for Dunn & Lewis on the Ashland Refining's repressuring program, ventured onto some of the leases, Williams, brandishing a gun, drove him away.

Roy Grossenbach, who had been shifted from the post of Ashland Refining treasurer and made a sort of floating vice-president, volunteered to go and straighten out the situation. Blazer, worried, warned him of the personal risk, but Grossenbach was confident. Blazer, still reluctant, had his insurance increased and gave him his blessing.

Meantime, Ashland Refining's competitors became incensed by the fact that the firm was selling the state large quantities of asphalt for its road building program. As a result, an investigation was launched in Frankfort, the state capital.

Altogether, it was a period of arguments and bickerings; conflict seemed to arise from the earth itself.

By the end of the year, Ashland Refining had earnings of $146,-000 on net sales of $4 million, a considerable drop in percentage from the previous year. One senses an unusual drift for Blazer.

Then, on April 7, 1935, Senator Tom Combs died; he was sixty-seven. The Senator had been one of the great influences in Paul Blazer's life; almost a surrogate father, never to be replaced. Their correspondence reflected the relationship. From the beginning until the end, Blazer always wrote: "Dear Senator." The Senator always replied: "Dear Paul." At no time did Blazer ever falter in his deference; the Senator never withheld his support.

The Senator's death revived, as always, anecdotes; the scroll of his long and useful life was unfurled and examined with admiration and respect. He had, originally, come from the hills; with his brothers he had settled and entered business in Lexington. He had been mayor of Lexington from 1903 to 1907 and served three terms in the State Senate, where he obtained the title that pleased him most; on one occasion he had been Acting Governor.

Palmer Talbutt, attending Senator Combs' funeral, rode in the same car with A. B. Rausche, head of the Twin City Distributing Company and Democratic whip in Congress. Rausche regaled Talbutt with Combs stories all the way to the cemetery: Senator Combs had shared with Blazer both an unusual flair for words and a love for precise language.

One day, it was recalled, a fellow passenger in an automobile said, "Look at the bird in that tree."

Senator Combs replied, "Never be content to say 'a bird in a tree,' say,"—and he looked, then settled back, "say the *robin* in the *maple* tree."

Senator Combs' death brought Paul Blazer to the fore: he was 45 years old, well-known throughout the oil industry; had virtually saved the Swiss investment and paid off all its debts; was seething with plans and programs.

Section Four—Blazer in Charge

1936–1941

Organic changes in life come gradually; the dawn begins with a barely perceptible lightening in the sky, then with a dispersion of darkness so gentle it is below the threshold of our senses; by the time we see the tip of the glowing sun, a new day is already around us.

Senator Tom Combs's death left Blazer as the logical man to head Swiss Oil in the opinion of most of the directors. Most, but not all. Senator Combs had, after all, taken the baton from J. Fred Miles, and Mr. Miles retained some very strong friends and a green memory in the company—particularly with Louisville attorney Eli H. Brown, who also enjoyed the distinction of being the president of the Louisville Refining Company, an enterprise of which J. Fred Miles was operating manager. Another important director who shared this opinion was Mr. J. I. Lamprecht, whose family still owned one-third of the National Refining Company of Cleveland, Ohio, and who was himself chairman of the board of that firm.

Mr. Brown got in touch with Bob Gordon, of Gordon & Bartlett, and made strong representations in favor of making Jim Martin, formerly of Pynchon, president of Swiss Oil. Blazer, Brown said, would not do his best without supervision (!). Gordon handled the situation diplomatically, but being an extremely shrewd man in matters financial, began to wonder whether Mr. Brown might not be willing to sell his stock, one of these days.

Jim Martin himself recognized Brown's proposition as unrealistic, but he would not have been human had he not felt flattered. Brown and Lamprecht, in fact, might have prevailed and kept Blazer in a subsidiary position as president of Ashland Refining, had they prepared a better plan. Dudley Cates, vice president of the Commercial Investment Trust of New York and a large investor, and Charles Y. Freeman, an attorney and financier from Chicago, both showed signs that they were open to persuasion.

On the other hand, strong pro-Blazer sentiment existed among the late Senator Combs's closest associates: Charles S. Evans, the indefatigable director who came in with Quaker Oil; James Combs, the Senator's brother, and Edward L. McDonald, the notably cool and brainy chief counsel and secretary of the firm. Mr. McDonald was considered to have competitive feelings, but he always put the fate of the enterprise ahead of sentiment, and he recognized ability. Thus, Blazer had three men of whom he was absolutely sure, the opposition had at least two and possibly four, plus two neutrals.

Blazer had a plan, of course, and he swung into action. First he produced the formidably astute William C. Freeman, the reorganizer of the Insull interests and a man with widespread connections, as a new candidate for the board. It was a shrewd proposition, for no board could reasonably turn away such a potentially useful man. Then Blazer persuaded James Combs to resign as Swiss Oil treasurer in favor of Ned Seaton, who was not only treasurer of Ashland Refining, but a man with deep Kentucky roots and strong connections of his own—with the proviso that Mr. Combs remain a director. That gave Blazer two new votes.

Then he proposed that the post of chairman of the board be created, and that Jim Martin occupy this watchdog perch: a move that blunted Brown's proposal while appearing to agree with it. Then, as a last step, he proposed that Bob Gordon join Jim Martin and himself to compose an executive committee. These steps swung Martin and Gordon.

The upshot was that when the board of directors met, Messrs. Brown, Lamprecht, Cates and Charles Y. Freeman were confronted with a plan whose reasonableness seemed unassailable. Paul Garrett Blazer, eleven years after he was hired by Swiss Oil and eighteen years after he first entered the oil industry, was elected president and chief executive officer of the Swiss Oil Company as well as the Ashland Refining Company. On the surface, the vote was unanimous; below the surface, the sentiment (excepting Blazer, who of course could not vote in a decision regarding himself), was five to four. On such slender linchpins do the pendulums of life swing.

With this shift in the center of power, the headquarters of the Swiss Oil Company were transferred to Ashland from Lexington. Mr. McDonald preferred not to move. Blazer had further plans; he wanted to consolidate the operations of Swiss Oil and Ashland Refining. He also wanted listing on the New York Curb, where Swiss had only trading privileges.

The New Deal, through the creation of the Securities Exchange Commission, had changed the ground rules of the nation's exchanges; considerable confusion regarding the new rules existed in 1935. W. C. Freeman was well acquainted with the new rules through his manifold reorganization activities; Blazer was confident the firm could meet the new qualifications.

While these complex matters were under consideration, the Board of Tax Appeals handed down a ruling against Swiss Oil, and a back-tax bill amounting to more than $500,000, due immediately.

McDonald and the Washington law firm of Miller & Chevalier, who represented Swiss, advised an appeal to the federal courts; they were confident of eventual victory.

A great many companies and lawyers felt that way in 1935; fight was in the air. The New Deal, with its sweeping assumptions of authority, had aroused considerable resentment; by far the greatest resistance came from the federal courts. This was not unexpected. President Roosevelt himself had his qualms about the constitutionality of many of his programs, although the bright young men the New Deal had attracted to Washington were certain the NIRA and the AAA, the industrial and agricultural mandates of the planned economy, were cornerstones of a new order.

To FDR, the nine million persons still unemployed, and the countless millions more in circumstances of distress, seemed far more pressing problems. He had a compliant Congress; he had the majority of the people behind him; he was surrounded by men whose ideas appealed to him. The Supreme Court did not seem an insurmountable obstacle.

New days do not, however, arrive so abruptly. The Supreme Court ruled against Section 9c of the NIRA, that portion which prohibited interstate shipments of crude oil in excess of state production quotas. The oil industry was thrown into a near-anarchic condition again.

In Washington, Senator Tom Connelly of Texas, one of the last of the lion-maned solons in the nation, called J. Howard Marshall to his office.

"Do you think you could write a law that would be Constitutional and still stop this racket?" the Senator asked.

Marshall said he could.

"How quick?"

"Two days." Connelly told him to go ahead; Marshall summoned his friend Meyers and the two young men drafted the Connelly Act[1] that is still on the books.

By that time, J. Howard Marshall was on a first-name basis with almost every top man in the oil industry, and had become expert in the ways of Washington. He liked Paul Blazer—a feeling that was reciprocated. When a committee was appointed to examine the impact of the Petroleum Code on the small refiners, Marshall persuaded Ickes to appoint Blazer, together with Sidney Swensrud, assistant to the president of Standard of Ohio, and Mason Hoagland, at the time a leading independent marketer.

Blazer himself had become well known in Washington and throughout the oil industry. Harry Sinclair, by then getting older, used to send his limousine and chauffeur downtown to pick up Blazer and bring him to the Sinclair Oil Company executive suite. Once there, Blazer would find Sinclair waiting; the older man would pull his chair close, and say confidentially, *"Tell me the gossip."*

On the twenty-seventh of May, 1935, when Blazer was still considering the details of his own reorganization, the Administration's

[1] Passed February 22, 1935.

bright young men were horrified by a Supreme Court decision that, in effect, ruled the NIRA out of existence. Known to lawyers as the "sick chicken" [2] case, the ruling came in response to an appeal against NIRA regulations on the part of poultry shippers. In effect, because the poultry in question were slaughtered at their point of destination, the Court ruled that shipping them to the final store was not "interstate commerce." With comments and refinements too subtle to repeat, the justices limited the interpretation of "interstate commerce" severely. The effect of the ruling was to limit the powers of Congress and the Executive below what they had blithely assumed to exist.

If the reasoning on the definition of interstate commerce seemed somewhat sophistical, the Court's position on the larger issue of "delegated" powers had more substance. According to the New Deal, its codes and agencies, authorizations and administrators were operating on the basis of powers "delegated" by the Executive. Since the time of John Locke the whole theory of delegated powers had been considered settled by the lawyers, who agreed that while authority might be invested in a single office, this office could not, in effect, multiply itself by fission, or by delegation.

Some observers felt the Court was aghast at the extent of the powers delegated. The Justices believed there was a looseness about the alphabetical agencies created by the New Deal that was both unreasonable and unsound. The "sick chicken" decision was well received by at least 50 per cent of the people, opposed by the other 50 per cent, according to the pollsters. One suspects this was another exaggeration, that most persons understood neither the ruling nor the reasoning.

Franklin Roosevelt, recalling his cousin Theodore Roosevelt's issue of the "right of judicial recall" might well have wished that his cousin had won years before. In that case, it would have been relatively easy for FDR with his popularity in 1935, to have overturned the ruling.

However, in his discussions of the effect of the outlawing of the NIRA, FDR avoided the issue Theodore Roosevelt had once espoused. He used, instead, the reasoning of Woodrow Wilson,

[2] One of the innumerable colorful phrases of General Hugh S. Johnson.

under whom Franklin Roosevelt had served as Assistant Secretary of the Navy. Wilson had said, "The Constitution was not meant to hold the government back to the time of horses and wagons." "Horse and buggy," said FDR, enjoying himself hugely, and made jokes about old men.

In the light of more recent events, it is both amusing and instructive to read the unbridled attacks by the left wing and liberals against the Supreme Court, and to look at their sources. But there is reason to believe the White House was slightly relieved; the NIRA was an administrative nightmare, based on a mandate too hastily drawn. The Department of Justice had repeatedly warned the economic planners they could not plan the anti-trust laws out of existence. The NIRA was well-intentioned, but it was not law.

At the time, the issue was clouded with emotionalism. Some persons prematurely celebrated the death of the New Deal; some New Dealers wanted to eliminate the Justices of the Supreme Court. In the end, the issue became campaign fodder and the newspapers stretched its points into absurdity, as is their wont. But the Administration began to tackle its problems in a more organized and better formulated manner; many academically oriented young men, thinking the issues through, began to find their faith in total planning diminished, their sophistication sharpened. J. Howard Marshall was among these.

In immediate terms, it meant that some of the personae of the early New Deal departed from Washington and their places were taken by more pragmatic types who went to work on legislation based on the various Codes that had been devised with the cooperation of industry. Section 7a of the NIRA became, for instance, the basis for the Wagner Labor Relations Act with its provisions on wages, hours, union representation, bargaining rights and NLRB. The Code for the coal industry was transformed into the Guffey Bill; Marriner Eccles drew up the Banking Reorganization Act; Messrs. Cohen and Corcoran drew up the Public Utilities Holding Act; Harry Hopkins and his minions drew up the Relief Bill and the WPA. The net result was that, in an orderly and constitutional manner, control of the nation's economic life passed from Wall Street and the bankers to Washington, D. C.

Taxation, an instrument of life and death power in the hands of every government, came in for special attention. The New Dealers as a group were addicted to talking too much, and as a consequence, made the mistake of publicly announcing their plans to use taxation as a means of forcing social change. All governments do this to some extent, but seldom to the accompaniment of such alarming rhetoric; in this instance, it provoked piercing outcries in reaction. One effect was that the "undistributed profits" tax was softened, in words, to the "excess profits tax." The result, however, was the same: corporate taxes became more painful, and firms like Ashland Oil that had large earnings in proportion to their invested capital were confronted with the alternative of either paying considerably higher taxes or plowing back a larger percentage of earnings. In either event, the shareholders were not to receive undistributed profits in the form of large dividends.

But at the time of the tax board ruling against Swiss Oil, much of this legislation was still in the future; the atmosphere in the ruins of the NIRA indicated that business had lost its former influence everywhere but in the federal courts.

In Ashland, Kentucky, Paul Blazer might well have assumed the attitude of most industrialists of the time—adamant and bitter opposition to the tides of change—had it not been for the fact that his next-door neighbor was the highly intelligent and influential New Deal figure Fred M. Vinson.

A first cousin of Representative Vinson's, Ben Vinson, had worked for the Tri-State Refinery when Ashland Refining took over that enterprise in 1931; Ben Vinson became the Ashland Refining auditor, assistant secretary, insurance expert, and one of Paul Blazer's strong right arms. But Representative and Mrs. Vinson and the Blazers were even more: they were close personal friends and next-door neighbors. Representative Vinson was brilliant, dedicated and sincere; it was natural that he and Paul Blazer should become warm friends. Furthermore, Representative Vinson was one of the more influential men in the House; steered many of FDR's most favored measures through the legislative mill; was warmly regarded in the White House. The conversations between the Blazers and the Vinsons ranged over a wide field; they continued for years, and included—later on—young Stuart Blazer and Paul Blazer Jr., as well.

Blazer listened to Vinson's explanations on the direction of the New Deal; years later he said that without Fred Vinson to clarify matters, he might well have fallen into the pitfall of blind reaction, a trap into which many of the men of his generation fell. In Vinson, he found a mentality to equal his own. He translated Vinson's comments into the realization that Ashland Refining would have to avoid the charge of being socially obstructive by moving, as a corporate citizen, creatively into the community.

Because he could not square his obligation toward the stockholders with such a commitment on the part of the company, Blazer began to work in this direction personally. He sat down and wrote letters to churches with congregations both Caucasian and Negro, and began to make small donations from his own funds; he added schools and colleges, again for both races, to his lists; he began to press his assistants and managers to become active in the community; he pressed them to play leading roles in the charitable drives, in voter registration campaigns, in giving speeches before community and business groups. And he set an example himself.

More clearly than most executives of his time, Blazer worked to bridge the gap between the corporation and the balance of the society within which he lived; he saw that public relations could not be delegated to drum-beaters. "We all represent the company," he began to say; "all of us must work at public relations; we are all responsible."

In the meantime, the nation's employed were, proportionately, heavily taxed to support the millions of persons on relief. Counting the more than 3.5 million directly on WPA, some experts estimated as many as 25 million persons were being supported through relief payments. Prohibition was repealed (in 1933), and the nation's drinking did not increase but showed every sign of becoming markedly more civilized. The five-day week became a permanent feature in a large part of the country, although not in the offices of the Ashland Refining Company. College leaders became notably more intellectual; football heroes were overshadowed by tweedy, brainy types; bridge became more popular than ever; Huey Long was assassinated; Will Rogers and Wiley Post were killed in an airplane crash in Alaska; the Hauptmann trial was held; the Social Security Act was passed; G-men gunned down public enemies. In Germany, ugly scenes of violence against Jews were perpetrated; Mussolini called the Mediterranean Mare Nostrum; Thomas E. Dewey began his investigation of noisome New York and Okies began to drift away from their state as cruel winds began to blow their farms away.

In his refinery, Blazer, a tireless industrial housekeeper, swept through, peering at equipment, cross-examining his operators, pushing for more production at less cost. He engaged Everett Wells in long talks about sales and possible new accounts, pored over credit requests and made trips to the offices of ship's architects, barge companies, marine engineers' offices and the like, as preparation for his long-desired purchase of a river towboat, designed and built especially for the Ashland Refining Company.

Roland Whealy,[3] newly hired in 1935, was working in the refinery laboratory one afternoon when the door opened and Paul Blazer, accompanied by his younger brother, Herschel, entered. While Paul was examining the place, Herschel drew near Whealy and asked, in a whisper, "Do you know my brother well?"

Whealy admitted he did not, and Herschel, growing more confidential, said, "You'll find he's a very *strange* man. He asks questions all the time; many questions, *very* many questions." Looking

[3] Roland Whealy was born in Orient, So. Dakota, in 1907. His grandfather and several great uncles had emigrated to the area from upstate New York when it was still the Dakota Territory in the 1870s, and staked a group of contiguous Tree Claims, a local type of homestead. The Whealys originally came from England. Roland graduated from a Teacher's College in Madison, So. Dakota, in 1929; taught at a Sioux Indian reservation for two years; received an M.S. in chemical engineering from Iowa State University in 1935; worked as research fellow and completed Ph.D. requirements except language; went to work for Ashland Refining in 1935. He was subsequently in almost every phase of the company operations; was made a board member in 1949. In 1957 he was on loan to the Department of the Interior. Today he is a vice president stationed in New York City and a valued member of management.

intently at the younger man, he said, "Don't let it bother you if you can't answer all of them; nobody can."

The two brothers left, leaving Whealy staring after them.

Blazer had developed a close-knit management team: Everett Wells, Bill Keffer, Ned Seaton, Art Points, Ed Emrick, Mike Dupree, Percy Banks, Fred Irwin, Ben Vinson, Palmer Talbutt, Hugh Jenks, A. A. Hinds, and others. His refinery operators were dedicated and grateful to be employed by a firm that was moving ahead, while terrible tides were tearing other men loose from their moorings.

By the end of the year 1935, earnings after taxes amounted to $327,233 on net sales of $4 million; a considerable improvement in earnings over the year before, although the gross remained largely unchanged. This accomplishment had been achieved, though, at considerable internal pressure and economies.

SHIFTS IN THE SCENERY

In March 1936, the *Senator Combs,* a new towboat, came down the ways. Blazer was aboard her, peering into every cranny, asking for minute-by-minute reports on the specifics of its engines, its speed in the water with and without tow. He wrote lengthy letters to Jim Martin, with copies to Bob Gordon and others, about his new pride.

Shortly afterward, he took a brief vacation in Bermuda; Blazer took vacations in those days. Returning revitalized, he suggested electrical dehydration for the removal of salt from crude oil—a suggestion that resulted in contacting Ralph St. Hill of the Petroleum Rectifying Company of California, and the establishment of a unit at Catlettsburg that improved the quality of the Ashland asphalt, which the state of Kentucky was purchasing in large, and profitable, quantities. In addition, the collaboration with St. Hill resulted in Ashland participating in royalty payments when other units were established elsewhere.

Then, in May 1936, in a letter to Jim Martin, Blazer said, ". . . the entire oil industry is being investigated by a federal Grand Jury which is now in session in Madison, Wisconsin. Apparently, almost everyone has been subpoenaed. I am to appear on June 15, and must bring with me what I imagine may be literally a truck load of company records. Although I do not understand that I am one of those the government is attempting to indict, I notice that the names of the Ashland Refining Company and myself, personally, are included along with the names of all the major companies and those who were active in the NIRA. It is significant that the investigation calls for sales records since November 10, 1934, and for other records for the past five years . . . I anticipate that it will take the entire time of one or two members of our organization between now and June 15 to go through our files and search for the records, orders, letters, etc., that I am to take to Madison. It's just one more thing to worry about."

The case had a profound impact upon the industry, but was of no particular importance to Blazer excepting for the inconvenience at the moment. Basically, it consisted of a charge by the Department of Justice that various oil companies had maintained a gasoline price pool in contravention of the anti-trust laws. The defense was curious: in effect, the companies said that Secretary of the Interior Ickes, on behalf of the Administration, had encouraged them to continue the cooperative arrangements originally —though briefly—set up by the NIRA. Secretary Ickes refused to comment on this, and also refused to appear at the trial and take the stand.

Men like Paul Blazer and the Pews of Sun Oil, against such arrangements at all times, were not included in the indictment. The major companies indicted, despite their somewhat naive defense, attracted considerable sympathy throughout the oil industry and business generally; but were found guilty and fined, both personally and as corporations. The penalties were relatively minor. The important point was that competitive enterprise would continue despite the early enthusiasms of the New Deal.

One of the defense lawyers was J. Howard Marshall, who had left the employ of the government, when the Oil Code was translated into specific legislation and the NIRA was no more, to join Standard Oil of California. He said of the Madison case, "the defense tried, but had a poor case."

In the meantime, Blazer found on his return that the Kentucky

State Legislature had proposed to tax gasoline when used in diesel engines, or kerosene in internal combustion engines, and certain in-plant transfers. He traced the genesis of these ideas to a professor, talked to the professor and the legislators, and had this drastic and hindering measure emasculated. He learned that new and heavier taxes were pending against the industry in the federal House of Representatives and wrote a protesting letter to Kentucky Senator Barkley. Blazer listened while Miller & Chevalier, the Washington attorneys, suggested that Swiss Oil hire the eminent John W. Davis[4] to represent the firm in their appearance before the Court of Appeals on their tax case. He turned from that to discover that Ashland Refining was the target of accusations that it was polluting the waters of the Big Sandy and Ohio Rivers. Altogether, it was a month when the government began to seem hydra-headed; the new day had not only dawned, but moved well up into the sky.

Nevertheless, by June 1936, Blazer was able to report an excellent year in progress, and suggested that Swiss Oil and Ashland Refining be combined into one firm.

Despite his various troubles—which were essentially no different than anyone else's in the industry, what with Congress cudgeling its collective brains to anticipate the Administration's direction—Blazer had some advantages peculiarly his own. For one thing, 1936 was a year of strikes; labor, having discovered it had a franchise and rights, moved beyond them to invent the sit-down. Reading about the tribulations of other refiners, Blazer decided he would give his refinery workers a raise when contract time drew nearer.

The asphalt department, under Hugh Jenks, had worked hard and was making considerable progress; competitors began to search for means of slowing this momentum. A test was devised, by G. L. Oliensis, which was intended to eliminate cracked, or inferior asphalt from the market; in fact, however, the test determined whether asphalt was made by a straight reduction of crude oil or by cracking residuum. This was, no doubt, interesting, but it missed the mark: the test of asphalt lay in its application. Roads in the late 1920s were made mostly of concrete; spur

[4] Democratic candidate for President against Calvin Coolidge in 1924.

roads or cutbacks were made of a mixture of asphalt and aggregates. Initially, many areas made their aggregate beds too thin; under heavy traffic the whole road cracked up and competitors charged the failure was due to bad asphalt.

The Standard Oil of Ohio, which produced its asphalt from heavy crude oil, persuaded that state to adopt the Oliensis test as a standard, in effect ruling Ashland asphalt off the state highway program. (Only heavy crude from Mexico, California, Colombia or Venezuela could be used to make asphalt that would pass the Oliensis test.) In addition, taking a leaf from Blazer's book, Standard of Ohio decided to acquire a river terminal on the Ohio, to connect by pipeline with their refinery at Latonia. That would enable them to move gasoline into Kentucky and West Virginia by barge, and give Blazer a taste of his own medicine.

Asphalt troubles also loomed in Kentucky itself. Judge Robert W. Bingham, owner of the *Courier-Journal* in Louisville and a former Ambassador to the Court of St. James, had sold his Swiss Oil holdings when Senator Combs died and Paul Blazer had ascended to the head of the firm. Judge Bingham's reporters had been pumping the state highway department on the subject of asphalt; the newspapers had been photographing various cracked roads; the Judge himself had offered to pay a supplemental $4,000 a year out of his own pocket to induce a new head of the state highway department, a Major Thomas H. Cutler, to accept the post (Kentucky had a state salary limitation of $5,000); Major Cutler was known to be against large use of asphalt in road construction. Adding up these factors in Kentucky, and keenly aware that the death of Senator Combs left a vacuum of influence with the state, Blazer feared the worst. He did not, however, content himself with such premonitions, but began to make trips in and out of Frankfort, the state capital, to see what he personally could accomplish. He had Jenks and his men make searching investigations to ascertain whether road cracking was indeed traceable to asphalt. It was not, but they had a sales problem on their hands.

Meanwhile oil began to flow in the western Kentucky fields again; wildcatters had made new strikes. Blazer found that the press of other events had blinded him to this development. J.

Fred Miles, operating the Louisville Refining Company, had already made arrangements for a prospective pipeline; Standard of Ohio had combined with Hupp on a Pipeline in the area: competition was getting keener by the minute. Blazer, in his turn, joined with a promoter named L. S. Robbins to build a pipeline, and looked for producing property for Ashland Oil.

With one eye cocked in the direction of western Kentucky crude, Blazer hired a geologist, H. R. Pierce, to work with Bill Keffer, and advanced them a small sum for wildcatting. This was mainly a diversion: he was looking for property that was already producing.

Then, moving as usual on several fronts at once, he made an arrangement with the Continental Illinois Bank & Trust Company in Chicago to borrow $600,000 (at 1.5 per cent) so that he could fend off the encroachments that were pressing him; held long discussions with the directors about the future consolidated company, and with them, came to some understandings.

From the point of view of the enterprise itself, the most important agreement he made with the board was that the firm would maintain its existence, even after Kentucky crude oil was exhausted. Thus, he took a great step beyond J. Fred Miles's dream; in Blazer's own words, the company was "to be perpetuated."

Then, as though to assure the directors that his interest in the company was not a selfish one, he agreed to sell his 10 per cent minority interest (already split among his wife and children, his sister Jessie Blazer and his mother-in-law) back to the company at par value. This was a remarkable step; no more convincing proof that men in business are attracted by more than money could possibly exist. In exchange for selling his stock back to the firm, he accepted a regular employment contract, accepting a salary of $25,000 and a 1 per cent bonus based on consolidated net profit.

Blazer had consistently shown, by his lack of action in personally buying large amounts of Swiss Oil stock when it was available at bargain basement prices, that he was not greedy. Years later, he said he had invested in the common stocks of a number of companies when the prices were obviously unrealistically low and held them for years. Of course, he benefited proportionately. But he was not particularly interested in how much money he could amass; he *was* interested in how sound a company he could build: to enjoy the pleasure of such an effort, he passed up a much larger fortune.

After that, his conversations with the directors took on a new tone: Blazer had established his moral authority in the only manner in which this is possible—putting principles above gain. Nevertheless, the consolidation of the two companies and the matter of Curb listing were not exactly five-minute details. Many vexing particulars had to be thrashed out. At one point, a bank in Lexington couldn't find ten missing shares of Swiss Oil stock; when they were eventually located in some pigeonhole or another, everyone grinned with relief. Eli H. Brown disclosed that J. Fred Miles claimed ownership of 330 Swiss Oil shares, as the result of collateral someone had given him on an unpaid note he had settled; Blazer nodded his assent absently. The SEC then said it would not allow the new company to come onto the Curb with a new issue under the trading privileges formerly enjoyed by Swiss Oil, because it *was* a new company: as such it would have to supply voluminous information and fill out the formidable forms newly created for the purpose.

Director Charles Y. Freeman, who was himself knowledgeable in matters financial, was fearful the firm would find itself out in the cold in the period of reorganization while trying to get on the official list. This belief caused him to argue over many details and, finding himself invariably on the losing side in these bickerings, one day turned red, announced he had had enough, was through, and walked out.

Nonplussed for a change, Blazer turned toward Ned Seaton and asked, "What do you think we should do?"

"He said he quit, didn't he?" Seaton asked drily.

It was agreed the preferred stock of the Ashland Refining Company would be called in and the new company capitalized for $2 million. This would consist of 1 million shares of common stock exchanged share for share with the Swiss Oil stock, and 100,000 shares of 5 per cent preferred stock to be sold to the public at the time of consolidation. The final step was taken on October 31,

1936; by coincidence the twenty-first anniversary of the day that Georgia Monroe and Paul Blazer first met in Chicago.[5]

For a long time after the consolidation Blazer typically continued to use the old stationery and letterhead; simply had his secretary type, beneath the large name of the Swiss Oil Company, the legend: Ashland Oil & Refining Co., successor. Frugality had become ingrained, his attention to the penny-saving detail automatic.

The following month, November, FDR swept into office with the most overwhelming electoral victory in the history of the country. Every state except Maine and Vermont gave him their votes. In December, Ashland Oil & Refining had grown to the extent that a single Christmas Party no longer sufficed; simultaneous parties were held in Lawrence and Johnson Counties as well as in Ashland's Boyd County. At the celebration in Ashland, Blazer announced that every employee with more than six months' seniority would receive a week's pay as a bonus. The gesture was sufficiently unusual in those stark times to elicit a favorable editorial in the *Ashland Independent*. Despite the fact that Armco Steel and some other firms were larger employers, Ashland Oil & Refining had achieved significant stature in the community.

By year's end 1936, the net profits of the new company reached $677,583 on net sales of $4.8 million.

THE FLOOD

The new year, 1937, had hardly begun when Blazer informed the directors Ashland had purchased $350,000 worth of producing properties in western Kentucky; wildcatting was all very well, but it was preferable to have crude oil in hand. Furthermore, he kept the purchase a secret from his competitors: Standard of Ohio and J. Fred Miles would not steal any more marches on Blazer. He had exceeded his quota.

[5] Georgia Blazer had become emotionally attached to the Ashland Refining Company emblem, and was amazed to discover herself upset when the name was altered by the addition of "Oil &."

The change seemed to mark the end of a long effort. When she told Paul how she felt, he was surprised in his turn.

Then on January 26, he sent Jim Martin a telegram:

REFINERY UNDER SIX TO TWELVE FEET WATER
LOSS GASOLINE AND OIL NOT SERIOUS YET
BUT THREE MORE FEET EXPECTED SITUATION
LOOKS BAD ADVISE OTHER CHICAGO DIREC-
TORS

The Ohio produced its worst flood in generations, and so did
other rivers. Rain had fallen intermittently throughout much of
the country for weeks; the melting of heavy snows added to the
inundation; the waters were 7.9 feet higher than man had ever
before seen at Cincinnati, 6.8 feet higher at Louisville. The Mer-
rimac, the Connecticut, the Hudson, Delaware, Susquehanna,
Potomac, Allegheny and the Big Sandy flooded as well. In Washington, sandbags were piled to protect government buildings,
Pittsburgh was ten to twenty feet underwater and the whole great
metropolis was without water, lights or transport; millions were
marooned as power failed. Along the Ohio, the worst of the flooded
area, an estimated 900 people drowned; 500,000 were driven from
their homes; railroad tracks were washed away; whole towns
went dark. Hunger and disease stalked the landscape.

At Ashland, which was fortunate enough to be situated on one
of the highest points of the riverbank, industry stopped. Armco
and Semet-Solvay as well as Ashland Oil & Refining had to sus-
pend operations. Schools and churches were used as sheltering
places; men traversed the downtown business district in rowboats
and motorboats; the refinery at Catlettsburg was marooned;
92 per cent of the homes in Catlettsburg were temporarily
abandoned or partially flooded. The Ashland refinery superintendent Fred Irwin collapsed from exhaustion and worry; his
family stayed with the Blazers, who set up a second kitchen in
their basement. There the women cooked huge kettles of stew,
soup, dried fruits and other meals. Lewis Ware brought in great
quantities of supplies as the seriousness of the situation became
evident; many of the wives of refinery men joined in the effort.
Emergency commissary and sleeping quarters were arranged at the
refinery and approximately 30 men, working in 6-hour shifts, re-

mained; hot food was sent to them by motorboat. The town of Greenup, a few miles down the river, was completely cut off and without lights or food; Ashland Oil assumed responsibility for keeping its 1,000 persons supplied.

Everyone in town was involved in around-the-clock efforts during the emergency. Dr. Winans, by this time the company physician, gave more than 200 shots against typhus. Blazer was the center of the company command post and issued communiqués by the score, between trips up and down the river to survey the damage. Before the emergency ended, he contracted influenza, and telephoned from his sickbed, but he had been able to see most of the area for himself before he was felled.

"I was in Huntington Tuesday," he wrote Jim Martin. "It is a desolate place. Most of the city, including the best part of the business district, was under from five to twenty feet of water. Our Huntington manager lost all his furniture and suffered considerable damage to his brick bungalow. He worked so long endeavoring to protect company property (pumping out gasoline and filling the tanks with water, etc.) that he was not even able to save his personal car from the garage. His situation was no different from that of scores of other employees. We will have to help many of them . . ."

To Blazer's further dismay, two whole acres of embankment alongside the refinery slid into the river. "Presumably," he wrote with an undercurrent of complaint that was uncharacteristic, "that bank has been there for a thousand years, and with the exception of a big slide that occurred in 1933, there has been no trouble in the fifteen years we have been operating." He went out and looked at it time and again; at some points the new bank was within ten to fifteen feet of the tanks and equipment.

Altogether, the refinery was completely shut down for fifteen days; this alone made a great dent in earnings. But by far the greatest damage resulted from the regional dislocation; to the damage done to distributors and independent filling stations for the 250-mile length of the firm's operations up and down the river, the loss of business involved in the interruption of normal life, the disruption of credit and the dislocation of people. In direct, traceable terms, the damage at the refinery and its immediate environs was only between $5,000 and $10,000; in larger, overall terms, the loss ran ten times as high—$50,000 to $100,000.

Nevertheless, Ashland Oil's losses were so reasonable against the backdrop of staggering insurance claims put in by other firms and the actual and valid losses of other companies (including oil and oil marketing firms) that the insurance underwriters, some time later, sent a team to Ashland to discover the reasons for the discrepancy. After learning about the company's safety program, the specific and precise instructions with which the men were indoctrinated and prepared against such eventualities, they went away signally impressed and issued a memorandum to other firms based on their discoveries. But the real reasons for Ashland's relatively minor losses were intangible: the firm was loaded with sincere and dedicated men; the employees and the distributors were men who clearly knew their circumstances were dependent upon their labors and this contributed to the enterprise as a whole.

The floods had many results beyond the catastrophic; in classic fashion they led to improvements in the long run. In addition to Pare Lorenz's brilliant movie *The River*,[6] they sparked a sweeping program of flood controls and river improvements to prevent repetition, and provided examples of individual heroism in many places that served to remind the thoughtless that the people of America were still strong, healthy, valuable and capable of sustaining a forward-moving nation.

The floods provided a contrast to a problem arising from opposite origins—the droughts of the Great Plains. The winds that accompanied these droughts, during the summer of 1933 and stretching far into falls and springs as well during 1934, 1935, 1936, and even later, had literally blown away farms in an area that stretched from Texas to the Dakotas. With thousands of square miles laid waste, the small farmers scattered throughout these vast regions were blown like their topsoil before the wind. Their caravansaries trundled across the nation's trunk highways heading toward California, the golden land whose publicists regretted their own success, provoking border guards, restrictive

---

[6] Lorenz made two documentaries that sparked improvements: one was *The River,* the other was *The Plow That Broke The Plains.*

state citizenship laws; transient camps, shacktowns; books, articles; eventually songs, plays and social movements.

The combination of these results of deforestation and over-farming, together with the floods, gave birth to the great conservation programs of the New Deal; to flood protection measures; to reforestations and the building of levees alike; to power projects and irrigation programs. The plight of rural America became of prime concern to intellectuals for the first time; the disparity in living standards became visible and hence insupportable.

Results ranged from the TVA to the Civilian Conservation Corps, from *Tobacco Road* to the amalgamation of hillbilly music in the substratum of America, to an almost mystical belief in the brotherhood of trade unions and intellectuals.

In the late winter of 1937, Blazer learned that director Eli H. Brown, long one of his principal opponents, had sold his stock to Bob Gordon. Blazer canvassed the board and obtained majority agreement not to reelect Brown to the board. Accordingly, he wrote Brown a handsomely crafted letter, couched in the friendliest possible terms, informing the Louisville attorney that the board had decided not to recommend reelection, citing as the reasons the fact that he was no longer an investor in the enterprise; and that as president of Louisville Refining he would be privy to information of great value to a competitor. Blazer said, in effect, that there was no good reason to subject him to such a strain, and cordially invited Brown to visit Ashland whenever he liked.

Mr. Brown wrote back at length. He denied he would be embarrassed by confidential information, or that he experienced any difficulty in keeping it, intact, in a separate compartment of his mind; he protested he had sold the stock only to assist its market position, saying he planned to buy some more soon and protested he had not solicited proxies (he had once, in an effort to save J. Fred Miles) for *years,* by agreement. Brown also wrote Jim Martin, reminding the chairman that he, Brown, had tried to line up the presidency for him. Martin, unimpressed, sent the letter on to Blazer. Brown, protesting, faded from the scene.

Coupled with the voluntary departure of Mr. Charles Y. Freeman, the severance of Mr. Brown left Blazer with a clear majority of the board: his tenterhook days with the directors were over— for the nonce.

The correspondence with Mr. Brown contrasted with a letter from Mr. Halle, of Universal Oil Products, who said kind things about Ashland's splendid record of continued earnings, and asked specifically for more details on how the refinery was producing its newly-announced 80 octane gasoline. Since this was a clear reversal from the years during which the refinery gratefully subsisted on crumbs from the heaping technical table of UOP, Blazer was only too happy to oblige. The upshot was that, some months later, UOP sent three visiting Russians, Velikanov, Poliakoff and Tindo,[7] to visit Ashland and view for themselves, in Halle's words, "a 1926-style Dubbs cracking unit operating in 1937 style."

On a business trip, Blazer encountered a Mr. Waxman, the asphalt sales manager of Shell Oil, who was incredulous that asphalt could be produced from residuum of the Dubbs unit; Shell scientists, he said, had declared it impossible. Blazer told Mr. Waxman his firm had solved the problem, sent him samples later to prove his statement. As a consequence, Shell sent their leading asphalt scientist, Dr. Pfeiffer, all the way from Amsterdam, Holland, to Ashland; Pfeiffer arrived accompanied by Mr. Culbertson, the new Shell asphalt sales manager from their plant in St. Louis, Missouri. The visit did more than enhance Ashland Oil's prestige; it helped the climate for asphalt so produced, and was an important factor in swinging the tide against the Oliensis test. Getting Shell into the act made the Ashland case that much stronger.

At the same time, Eric Shatford, Blazer's old partner, living these many years in El Dorado, Arkansas, wrote Blazer about new oil fields opening up in the vicinity. Blazer made Shatford an Ashland agent, and advanced him money to obtain leases and

---

[7] During the early to middle thirties, a steady trickle of U.S. firms and engineers went to Russia to acquaint the Soviets with technical advances and to install equipment, erect factories, and help that nation to catch up with the west; Russian counterparts visited the U.S. to learn what was new and made such exchanges possible. UOP, at this time, was installing some iso-octane units in Russia. That nation was then considered very remote—almost on another planet.

help the company take part in this activity. "Eric is an old friend of mine," he explained in a letter to Jim Martin. "In his dealings with me in the past, he was not only equitable, but liberal." Typically, he digressed to explain that Shatford now operated a string of tank cars in the El Dorado area. He agreed to give Shatford a 10 per cent participation in any deal he made on behalf of Ashland. This was the same percentage that had constituted his own opportunity; obviously, he felt he owed his old friend an equal chance.

Business opportunities continued to be numerous. The Allied Oil Company, founded in 1925 by Messrs. Vandeveer and Newman, who had placed their first order with Blazer, had grown into a formidable competitor by 1937, particularly in fuel oil sales. Early in his career, Blazer had decided that fuel oil was neither a very profitable nor a particularly interesting line; he turned to this product only when all other sales were slack, and considered it at best a seasonal product. Vandeveer and Newman had proven him wrong, in a very large way. Allied Oil was selling immense quantities of fuel oil all the year around; selling, under his very nose, in markets he considered his own: in Pittsburgh, and in southern Pennsylvania generally, to the great steel companies. Blazer watched this traffic constantly.

In addition to this periodic and irritating stream of sales information, he had his nephew, Rex Blazer, to remind him of Allied Oil's growth. Rex, who had been directed to Allied for a job when he applied at Ashland in 1928, had established himself as immensely capable; had zoomed, at Allied, to vice president in charge of sales. From time to time he appeared in Ashland on a visit, happy and prosperous, waxing as a competitor.

Vandeveer and Newman, the founders and owners of Allied Oil, were both extremely individual. Vandeveer was a salesman to his toes: gregarious, charming, interested in misty vistas and large visions, a sportsman and a "man's man," he could make sales by the sheer force of his personality. Newman, on the other hand, was introverted, analytical, concentrated. A man of infinite complexity, he operated like the head of a general staff. Almost everyone who knew them liked them both, and recognized them as opposites. Rumors that they had difficulties with each other were universally credited; the wonder was how they had ever arranged a partnership in the first place. But their talents were so clearly complementary that the secret of their success was equally obvious.

Intrigued by widespread rumors of friction at Allied Oil, Blazer made a trip to Cleveland to see if the partnership would sell out. He tiptoed diplomatically all around the subject in his conversations with the two men, and according to a letter he sent Bill Freeman on the subject, found Vandeveer quivering to sell. But Newman, whom Blazer described as "the principal driving force and a very busy man," was abstracted and plainly not particularly interested. Blazer withdrew to bide his time a while longer; he continued to hear about Allied fuel oil sales in markets he coveted.

That year, 1937, *Gone With the Wind* sold a million copies within six months of its appearance. Intrigued, Blazer picked up a copy. Mrs. Blazer recalls that he was puzzled by the outcry. "How could anyone be fooled by a woman like that?" he asked, mildly indignant. "I don't understand why anyone would bother to write a book about such a person."

It was probably the last novel he bothered to read; the world in which he lived was both too interesting and too important for fiction. For his real information, he depended upon the friends he had made in Washington during his NRA days, his many contacts throughout the industry, his associates. He watched, with a particularly close eye, developments in Kentucky and Ohio politics, and in Congress.

Throughout the United States most people were similarly engrossed in basically domestic concerns: *The Music Goes Round and Round* filled the nation's airwaves; Shirley Temple was seven years old; Mae West was Hollywood's biggest moneymaker; Santayana's *Last Puritan* delighted the longhairs; knock-knock jokes convulsed the young. The resignation of Edward VIII was still being reviewed in the press (it occurred in December, just before the flood); Dale Carnegie produced *How to Win Friends and Influence People*; Benny Goodman and his orchestra astounded the New York Paramount Theater by attracting hordes of adolescents. The era of big bands arrived, when horn and reed sections were synchronized into symphonic precision. Columnists replaced the old fashioned editorial writers; Walter Lippmann, David Lawrence, Dorothy Thompson, Drew Pearson & Robert S. Allen, Westbrook Pegler, Walter Winchell—even Eleanor Roosevelt. *Fortune* magazine made a dent in the thinking of the business community, and older writers wondered whether the vogue of writing magazines within offices might not kill off the independent journalists. The radio enthralled millions and its comedians came into their own: Jack Benny, Fred Allen, Edgar Bergen & Charley McCarthy, Burns & Allen, Fibber McGee & Molly; soap operas enthralled listeners and replaced pulps; movies became sentimental, elaborate, rich and beautiful.

Yet times were still so difficult the nation's marriage and birth rates had fallen seriously; manufacturers of children's clothes saw their volumes declining. The CIO multiplied and so did strikes; violence and animosity poisoned the industrial landscape. *Pins and Needles,* the first frankly propagandistic labor revue, was a great success; Joe Louis knocked out Jim Braddock for the heavyweight championship, a glory less important than in former years, but this time no White Hopes were sought. Maurice Evans portrayed a slender and sophisticated Richard II. A recession began.

The slump started, as usual, with a drop of values in the stock market; prices dropped by two-thirds, to within a third of the real Depression lows. The White House's favorite economists were taken by surprise; much of their prestige dropped with the stocks. An emergent and rambunctious CIO and a whole series of strikes did little to assist the situation, particularly since the government seemed sympathetic to labor in most instances. The business community, extremely bitter, refused to accept Presidential overtures.

At this point, FDR decided the Supreme Court should be changed. The timing was unusually maladroit, especially for a leader of his usual skill; the proposal fell miserably flat and hurt many of his personal relationships—to the detriment of the nation.

At Ashland, Blazer kept mainly to housekeeping. His associates brought him news that a six-story building on Winchester Avenue, the city's main business street, was available; he bought it for $77,500. Minimax, John Dalton's company, that had once almost been in Blazer's grasp a few years before for $100,000, finally sold

out to him for $80,000. Blazer described both purchases to Jim
Martin. He thought the building could harbor tenants in addition
to Ashland Oil & Refining; he had long considered John Dalton
"a good business-getter but an extravagant operator"; and was delighted to obtain the firm. He detested extravagance. One happy
circumstance occurred: oil was found in southern Illinois. That
relieved the crude oil situation for Ashland Oil & Refining; the
timing was just right.

But the end of 1937 found Blazer gloomy about business conditions and prospects, although profits amounted to $694,228 on
sales of $5.5 million. Judging, as he was, by domestic indicators,
he had good reason for being pessimistic, but in common with the
rest of the country, his eyes were fixed too close to home: events
far away were to change all the rules.

LEGISLATORS ON THE MOVE

In early 1938, with values depressed, Blazer made some excellent
acquisitions. He bought a majority interest in the Mt. Pleasant
Aetna Company, a distributor; bought the Burning Fork Oil
Company and the Boston & Southwestern Oil Company, two producing firms with wells in western Kentucky; established a new
river terminal in Covington, Kentucky. He was also elated that
Hugh Jenks and his men had beat out, by a razor-thin lower bid,
a large contract to sell asphalt to the state of West Virginia. They
had outdistanced Standard of N.J., Standard of Indiana, Atlantic
Refining and the Texas Company to get that rabbit.

Then in March, Blazer was horrified to learn the United States
Senate would consider the Petroleum Divorcement Act, aimed at
splitting the oil industry into various sections and breaking up
integrated operations. Sentiment for such a measure had been
widespread since before the days of the Standard Oil ruling in
1911; was responsible for charges that business was becoming too
big; had support not only from the traditional Populist quarters
and parties, but also from the more fervent among the New Deal
economists.

In essence, it was a movement against efficiency, and therefore
anti-progressive, but it was popular: the villains under attack had

long been identified as such in the popular press. Congress, in 1938, was top-heavy with young legislators anxious to prove their vanguard status; in such an assemblage, an upward bidding of reform measures takes place spontaneously.

Not all sections of the oil industry were opposed: the Independent Petroleum Association, consisting of small producers who felt the cards were stacked against them, was heartily in favor of the wonderfully titled Divorcement Bill. The majors, as the parties under attack, were not in the best of positions to have their arguments credited. Blazer, as head of an independent but integrated company that was modest in size, was in an excellent position to expose the inherent fallacies of the measure.

In April, he appeared before a Senate hearing and testified on the subject; his remarks were so clear and so pertinent, that they seem well worth repeating:

"The problems of the other fellow," he said in part, "always appear quite simple; it is easy to tell him what is wrong with his business and how to correct it. That is a common trait of human nature, and especially if some of those urging the change believe they have something to gain, personally, by changing or destroying that which has been built by others . . . (this Bill) would require the transfer of hundreds of millions of dollars worth of property; both large and small companies would have to discharge thousands of employees, upset pensions and stock purchase plans . . ."

"Only a person who has not had the privilege," he continued, "of building a business involving the bringing together of not only properties but of a great many individuals, gradually and painstakingly fitting and molding them into a smooth-running organization, can fully appreciate the tragedy and brutality involved in tearing an organization apart. Even granting that in many instances entire transportation and marketing operations can be transferred, more or less intact, to other owners, thousands of those employees will not be able to adjust themselves to new management and changed conditions. The relationship between management and individual employees is often a personal one, the results of years of association. Who has earned the right, as the result of only superficial thinking, to reshuffle the lives and properties of others in such an off-hand, casual, thoughtless manner? Who has the right to heedlessly and heartlessly destroy overnight that which has resulted from many years of conscientious and successful effort on the part of thousands of others?"

Then, in similarly lucid language and clearly defined terms, Blazer explained that there existed thousands of independent marketing companies in the oil industry whose members were prospering; described how, if Ashland Oil & Refining's operations were divorced from its transporting, distributing and producing properties, it would be "helpless."

Yet in the domestic atmosphere of the times, it is doubtful that Blazer's eloquence would have had much effect. The legislators had their eyes fixed on public sentiment; the man in the White House, generally credited with the same fixity, was instead, far more interested in events abroad. The maestro of the New Deal was among the first to realize its time had passed, though many of his bright young men and supporters in Congress were slow to get the message. FDR was intent upon international developments.

THE WORLD MOVES

In many respects, the 1930s was the decade of the Germans; from 1933 on, the events inside that nation evoked mounting horror and amazement throughout the rest of the world. In the United States, where sentiment against international involvements was strong after World War I, it was never clearly understood that Great Britain had, in that holocaust, largely lost its pre-eminent position in the world.

The Crash and the Depression had ended many social patterns not only in the United States, but in Europe as well; Americans watched the rise of Hitler and then of Franco with a sense of bewilderment. They could not understand why these emerging forces were not repressed; they could not understand that their own inaction had contributed to their rise. This inaction, largely introspective in nature, had so infused the nation with a sense of non-involvement that it had resulted in the Neutrality Act of 1935. By 1936, anti-war sentiment was so strong in the country that college students demonstrated for peace wearing World War I gas masks and Marxist groups called stridently for peace at any price. By 1937, the pendulum swung rapidly in the opposite direction: Italy's invasion of Ethiopia had taken place; in 1936, Hitler occupied the Rhineland without meeting resistance; in 1937 Japan invaded China and Franco launched his rebellion: America turned on the radio.

By 1938, the radio brought the unmistakable sound of marching boots into the homes of America. Hitler's speeches before chanting crowds on Saturday or Sunday afternoons held persons in the United States transfixed before their sets staring at one another in amazement. Suddenly, the world seemed mad.

In the same month that Paul Blazer read his statement in his low, well-modulated tones before the Senate Committee, Neville Chamberlain made his pilgrimage to Berchtesgaden and Hitler moved into Czechoslovakia. By the end of the summer, the world witnessed not only the shame of Munich, but the cheering throngs that greeted Chamberlain on his return, after having achieved "peace in our time."

The whole question of dismembering American industry in the interest of a more equitable economic mix became less interesting to FDR; the President was no longer concerned with subjugating industry: he wanted to spur industry into greater effort. Overnight, Efficiency moved from Pariah to Idol.

By July 1938, the technological race was on: projects that had been confined to blueprints and scientific laboratories in every industry began to take shape and form. Developments that corporations had been reserving until their capital positions improved were being dusted off and measured for size. The rubber industry turned its attention toward synthetic elastomers; the airplane industry was feverishly planning; the automotive industry began to plan vehicles of strange new shape and function; the oil industry began to gear toward high octane gasoline production to fuel military vehicles; all under the urging of a government suddenly aware that greater dangers loomed than partisan defeats.

The reversal did not penetrate all the reaches of government by any means; there are too many persons with one-gear minds for that. The nation, too, was not to be suddenly switched from doctrines with which it had been indoctrinated into attitudes permeated by international considerations. The nation was still extremely parochial in its interests, provincial in its attitudes; many different ethnic and cultural groups continued to reflect, in attenuated form, the prevailing winds in their lands of origin. Isolationism was so strong and well established a tradition that some persons identified it with patriotism, and the weeds of suspicion sown through decades of criticism and finger-pointing were hard to overcome.

Within the ranks of industry, however, where men had long been aching to work all-out, the jobs at hand overcame larger issues. The oil industry, Blazer wrote to Jim Martin, was on the verge of tremendous technological change, especially in refining. This threw him into an agony of indecision. Blazer was too good a manager not to know the stakes: expand or die. He consulted with Fred Irwin and men from the UOP, the Lummus Company; he pored over the trade news; traveled to other refineries; anxiously questioned men at American Petroleum Institute meetings; consulted with Ben Vinson and Art Points and Ed Emrick and Everett Wells, then finally wrote his decision to Jim Martin.

Ashland Oil & Refining would undertake its first real modernization since its birth in 1924 by installing a combination atmospheric and vacuum unit for $222,000, $10,000 more than the refinery itself cost 15 years before. Since the Lummus Company had a slow summer that year (Blazer being ahead of the tide), it was able to spend untold manhours toiling with him, had originally proposed two units costing an aggregate $400,000. Since Lummus was one of the better-known petroleum engineering firms in the world, accustomed to working on major projects for major companies, its engineers must have found Blazer an extraordinarily tough nut in his mountain fastness, but engineers the world over become more enthralled with projects than with their meaning: the outcome was of interest to them all.

After all these years, Blazer decided to abandon his antique shell stills. The Dubbs cracking plant, built in 1926, was better than good; designed to handle 750 barrels a day, it could still handle 2,300 barrels. "We are fortunate," said Blazer, his tone implying that willpower alone could force inanimate objects to function in an extraordinary way.

His other plans for Ashland Oil & Refining were proportionately scaled to the refinery improvement. Discovering that American Barge Lines was going to raise its rates, he cited that as a reason to order two new barges at a cost of $45,000; then declared the *Senator Combs,* at 750 hp, was insufficient and ordered a new, larger boat at 1,000 hp to augment his transportation force. Blazer announced that employees would subscribe to the Ashland O&R preferred stock (having finally persuaded Bob Gordon to allow this extension of capitalism); bought 12 small houses to resell (at no profit) to blue collar employees on long, low payment terms; hired Alex Chamberlain as personnel director away from Emerson Engineers and immediately put him on insurance and a number of other tough jobs as well. Then Blazer plunged into long discussions with Vinson, Points and Emrick, together with Ned Seaton, on new financing problems.

In November, the corporate general counsel Edward L. McDonald informed Ashland that the federal appellate court had sustained the accounting system used by Ashland in its tax case, and sent it back to the board of tax appeals for reevaluation. McDonald told Blazer this meant they could expect substantial recovery of the heavy tax payment the firm had made: it was news that came at a good time.

In addition, to Blazer's considerable relief, the union again signed a contract without a strike. His attitude towards these periodic sessions was always ambivalent; he dreaded them and he loved them; he expected the worst at all times but was usually highly pleased at the outcomes.

Europe bubbled and seethed; Hitler and Mussolini held their shivery conferences in the Alps; the world welcomed the snows of winter because they made military adventures unseasonable.

Ashland Oil & Refining ended the year 1938 with earnings of $566,242 on net sales of $6.6 million. Many changes had taken place within the company: Bill Keffer and Everett Wells had joined the board of directors; the refinery's capacity had been not only modernized but expanded by 80 per cent—almost double;

now it would be necessary to stretch the transportation, crude oil and marketing extensions to match this new, larger refinery body.

THE WINDS OF CHANGE

Blazer turned his attention to crude oil and transportation first, increasing his crude oil inventory, mainly from the southern Illinois oil fields, by some $300,000. He also ordered more barges, and plunged, zestfully, into the fascinating details of a new and larger towboat to supplement the *Senator Combs*. At the same time, he moved into a negotiation already underway between the Illinois Pipeline Company and Standard of Ohio, over the possible purchase of its Owensboro-Ashland system, and provided a good example of how a small company can tip a larger company off-balance simply by moving faster in a fluid market situation.

Briefly, the situation boiled down to the fact that the burgeoning crude oil production in the fields of southern Illinois made it necessary for the Illinois Pipeline Company, subsidiary of the Ohio Oil Company, to build a great many new gathering lines; these cost money. Then, the same increased production caused a competitive price situation to develop between the southern Illinois oil well operators, who began to offer their crude oil at competitively lower prices. This caused the Aetna Oil Company, formerly a heavy purchaser of western Kentucky crude oil, to drop these purchases and begin to buy the bargain crude oil from Illinois. By this switch, the revenues of the Owensboro system, which gathered oil in western Kentucky, began to drop—just when the Illinois Pipeline Company needed money.

The Standard Oil Company of Ohio owned a pipeline system that competed with the Illinois-Owensboro system and began to dicker with the Illinois Pipeline Company to buy the Owensboro line altogether. As it was, Standard of Ohio used about two-thirds of the capacity of the Owensboro system; Ashland Oil & Refining used the remaining one-third. If Standard Oil of Ohio completed the purchase, Ashland would be left in a highly vulnerable position. The sale was almost closed.

Blazer sent Bill Keffer and Everett Wells to the scene, keeping in touch by telephone, as was his custom. While the Standard of Ohio men were waiting for approval from their home office—a routine that had already slowed the pace of the negotiations considerably—the Ashland men, operating in their instantaneous fashion, offered to buy the Owensboro system for $250,000: the deal was closed over the telephone.

When Sidney Swensrud of Standard of Ohio learned of the transaction he was upset; he feared that Mr. Holliday, the president of his company, would be even more upset, with good reason. The crude oil supply leverage which Standard of Ohio formerly held over Ashland was wiped out. Blazer, savoring the switch in the scales, as well he might, suggested that Standard of Ohio become joint owners of the Owensboro system, but also allow Ashland to become joint owners of the Ohio's competing system, as well. Swensrud and Holliday, both sensible men, decided it would be the better part of wisdom to agree to this split rather than to fight. Thus, in one stroke Ashland had moved from a one-third user in the Owensboro system to one-half, had the resources of a second, parallel system available when they needed it and had moved from a minority customer in one line to half-owner in two.

A few months later, the two companies put together the Owensboro-Ashland Pipeline Company; appointed Joseph Pogue, a vice president with the Chase National Bank in New York as mediator.

The maneuver was an almost classic turning of the tables. Fortunately, Blazer was far too sophisticated and innately too courteous to allow himself or his men any visible crowing. He miraculously managed to maintain his cordial personal relationship with both Holliday and Swensrud—under the circumstances, no mean feat.

Clearly, Blazer's management team had, by this time, attained maturity; it could clear the way, soften the atmosphere and reach understandings that required only his assent. In many respects, beyond the achievement itself, the Owensboro pipeline deal was a bench mark of Ashland Oil & Refining's progress and proved that an executive group existed that could carry the firm past the one-man stage.

Meanwhile, Alex Chamberlain,[8] the new personnel manager, visited a "half dozen" colleges that spring to recruit some bright young men for the expanded operations; snared some seventeen (most of whom departed when the war reached the United States). One young man in particular proved an exceptional find: Joe Davis.[9] At Purdue, Chamberlain met Dr. Joseph Tiffin, a psychologist, who had done some work in pre-employment testing, then a new field. Chamberlain, intrigued, returned to Ashland with the Tiffin & Lawshe tests (Dr. Lawshe was Dr. Tiffin's associate), and later worked out, together with the psychologists, some simple variations to select skilled workmen for the refinery. He set up a follow-up and comparison record system; established ground rules for screening employees; created a master file of extra talents that later became helpful in transfers and promotions; in general, Chamberlain established the first scientific rules for employment at Ashland Oil & Refining.

Since most of these accomplishments have since been paralleled by virtually everyone, it is difficult to give them proper credit; in 1939, most men were hired at factory gates; even the government's employment rules until shortly before this period were lax to an extent that would astonish today's young people. The fact is that Chamberlain was far ahead of the average personnel manager in

[8] Alexander Scott Chamberlain, of English descent, was born in Pittsburgh, Pa., in 1900. One of his grandfathers was a famous circuit-riding preacher in the middle of the 19th century. Chamberlain was in the U.S. Navy in World War I; received a B.S. in chemical engineering from Yale in 1922; worked three years for Proctor & Gamble, then became a partner in the engineering and management consultant firm, Emerson Engineers, in New York City. Prior to being employed by AO&R he undertook a long analysis of their operations; impressed Paul Blazer with his abilities; had a variegated experience with the company; was president of Louisville Refining (a subsidiary) at his retirement two years ago, is still a consultant to the firm and will reappear later.

[9] Joseph C. Davis was born in Pittsburgh in 1916. His mother having died when he was young, he was raised by an aunt whose husband was a salesman; Davis' grandfather emigrated from Wales. Young Joe graduated from the Mt. Lebanon High School in Pittsburgh, long rated one of the nation's top schools; was recruited at Carnegie by Chamberlain; started in the accounting department; expressed an interest in sales and was switched in 1940. He is a vice president of Ashland Oil & Refining today and heads Refinery Sales. His progress will reappear later.

1938. Nevertheless, the difference between Chamberlain and Blazer and their approach to both problems and people was in the order of the differences between a political scientist and a working politician. The scientist is baffled by the intuitive approaches that the politician finds successful; the politician is impatient with the cool methods of the scientist. Nevertheless, both have need for one another; so it was with Chamberlain and Blazer. The two men never totally agreed, but they muted their disagreements to work together. Both maintained their reservations about one another's methods; together, they accomplished a great deal.

While Blazer was becoming adjusted to new management men, and his team was developing rapidly, other changes on other levels were taking place. Mr. Lamprecht, the last of J. Fred Miles's old supporters, head of National Refining Company, was leaving the Ashland board of directors. National Refining, furthermore, had been slipping for a number of years: the investment firm of Ford, Bacon & Davis had stepped in and placed one of their men, a Mr. Hill, temporarily in charge. (Lamprecht was chairman of the board.) The wheel took a savagely ironic turn: the financiers offered the post of president of National Refining to Paul Blazer.

Their second choice was Sidney Swensrud, and word came back that Swensrud had said he would be willing to work—not as president—but as assistant to the president, if Blazer accepted the offer: a stupendous compliment.

Blazer, although naturally enough pleased, was not interested in the job. Neither, after considering the matter, was he interested in merging Ashland Oil & Refining with National Refining, although National had many advantages to offer: it had $2.5 million in the bank, a well-known gasoline—White Rose—on the market, a large refinery in Coffeyville, Kansas, and other lures, including capital and surplus of some $16 million. Blazer's major reason for declining the merger, which would obviously have lifted his operations by many times overnight, seemed to consist mainly of the fact that the Lamprecht family still owned 35 per cent of National; he probably assumed this would lead to management difficulties in operating the merged companies. Also, Blazer was notable in his patience: National was receding as a competitive force (although it was still large); perhaps it would, in time, recede further. Whatever his reasons, he remained aloof, and in due course the firm hired Paul Ryan as president. Mr. Ryan received Blazer's congratulations.

Blazer in April began to stir the bankers; he made trips to New York and talked to the Chase National about a million dollar loan, then went to Chicago to relay their terms to the Continental Bank there. He showed both the offers he had received from Walter P. Andrews, the assistant cashier of the Bank of Manhattan, who was soliciting Ashland's business: it had taken him fifteen years to reach this point, and he was shopping assiduously. "I don't know where Paul learned about finance," said Bill Freeman, "but he knew that the time to borrow money is not when you need it, but *when it's available.* When hard times come, it's cash that gets the bargains."

Meanwhile, Washington was still pursuing its schizophrenic course. While the situation in Europe grew more ominous by the hour, Burton K. Wheeler, Senator from Montana, a notable reformer and (at that time) isolationist, introduced a bill to extend the provisions of the ICC to cover oil pipelines, and to divorce the oil industry from their ownership.

To combat this perennial nightmare, the American Petroleum Institute, the National Petroleum Association and even the Independent Petroleum Association (perhaps Blazer's spadework had helped turn their thinking) rose as one man in opposition; Blazer was among those called to testify before the Senate Interstate Commerce Committee. His statement on April 11, 1939, was, as usual, hard-hitting. The same month another branch of the government, the United States Supreme Court, refused the Internal Revenue Service's plea for a review of the decision in Ashland's tax case; there now seemed no further reason for delay in the return of the $500,000 overpayment.

Blazer seemed more interested in the details of the new towboat. This enthusiasm puzzled some of his associates, but he was serious; his letters to Jim Martin are packed with marine details—draft, engines, and future performance. He also, however, proposed that the stock in the Ashland Transportation Company be purchased back by Ashland Oil & Refining: consolidation of resources was still very much in his mind.

In June, he appeared before the sub-Committee of the Committee on the Judiciary as a witness against Bill 2318—called the Harrington Measure—which proposed to divide oil companies from marketing companies. On this occasion, he and Mr. William Farish, then head of Standard Oil of New Jersey, were the only two witnesses called in the morning; Farish was so impressed with Blazer's statement that he had his firm later ask for reprints. Again, the Senators were told about the structure of the industry and the impracticality of amputation as a method of achieving order.

A newcomer who started in modest circumstances that summer was strapping Franklyn (Chub) Moffitt;[10] hired after a long chat with Paul Blazer, who was highly impressed. Moffitt, a dapper but athletic type, was put to work in the refinery blending gasoline, unloading cars, and making himself generally useful. Few college men today would feel this a proper start; Moffitt was to build it impressively.

On July 1, 1939, Ben Vinson, the Ashland auditor, was at the refinery to measure the contents of gasoline tanks, a necessary part of inventory-taking. ". . . he was on top of a 25-ft. tank watching the gauging by the regular refinery gaugers," Paul wrote to Jim Martin later. "Apparently, for the purpose of facilitating his notations, he sat down on the short nipple of pipe extending out from a vent valve, which extends above the top of the tank approximately 2½ feet, and is located near the edge of the tank. It is reported that the pipe broke under his weight and that he fell off the tank backward. His neck was broken and he died immediately. Ben is survived by Mrs. Vinson; there are no children."

[10] Franklyn M. Moffitt, born 1914, in Lynbrook, Long Island, is a descendant of what he calls "original clam diggers," Long Island and Brooklyn settlers from before the Revolution. His father was a dairy farmer in Rockville Center, N.Y. Moffitt attended Oceanside High School, was an all-letter student: basketball, football, golf, polo, baseball. He was sent to prep at Ft. Defiance Military Academy in Virginia; once broke in wild horses for the cavalry; graduated from Duke University with a B.A. in 1938; married Nancy Webb, the daughter of Earle Webb, at one time president of Ethyl Corporation. Moffitt is today a vice president of Ashland Oil & Refining and a senior vice president of Ashland Chemical Company.

Blazer went on to describe Ben Vinson's duties at the company: "He was assistant (corporate) secretary, auditor and chief accounting officer; handled insurance, taxes and miscellaneous government reports . . . His first cousin, Fred M. Vinson, is a Justice of the District of Columbia Federal Court of Appeals; Ben came with us with the Tri-State Refinery purchase at the age of twenty-eight, nine years ago"; Blazer ended, saying, "He was one of the kindest, most likeable and most capable men I have ever known."

Vinson left a tremendous vacuum; many men moved up. Ed Emrick, who became chief accounting officer, assistant secretary and transfer agent was also made office manager and put in charge of government reports as well as deposits, reports and payrolls. Blazer gave him *carte blanche* to sign checks up to $500.

Art Points, who had formerly assisted Ben Vinson in accounting, was given expanded responsibilities, told to work parallel with Emrick and report directly to Blazer; Alex Chamberlain was given responsibility for insurance in addition to his other work; Bill Keffer of pipelines and Mr. Brakefield, the chief clerk of the refinery, had to resume some functions in their areas.

Thus Ben Vinson's death, which saddened the Ashland community,[11] had a direct effect upon the lives and careers of at least four men, and probably affected more men indirectly.[12]

In addition to shifts of personnel, Blazer contemplated even more sweeping changes. He wrote, "At times I can look from my office window and see barges moving down the Ohio River to Cincinnati carrying gasoline which originated at refineries on the Atlantic seaboard, and also see barges moving up the river carrying gasoline from points on the Mississippi River as far south as Baton Rouge. In fact, some gasoline from the Gulf Coast points moves as far north as Pittsburgh." In other words, other companies had discovered the waterways; he was losing his geographical advantage.

Furthermore, industry sources told him that competitors, spotted all around, were making exchanges on an unprecedented volume

[11] The congregation of the First Presbyterian Church in Ashland issued a special statement of grief.

[12] The company had 700 employees in July 1939; Blazer anticipated an increase of another 400 by year's end.

—and there were plenty of competitors. There was Standard of Ohio at Latonia, just across the river from Cincinnati, Gulf in the Cincinnati district, as well as Standard of Kentucky, National Refining, Louisville Refining and Standard of Ohio with whom to contend.

He read, somberly, where the Shell Oil Company expanded its Wood River, Illinois, refinery to the extent of $8 million, more than his own total volume of sales.

Looming even larger was the technological revolution introduced into the industry by Sun Oil Company, employing the Houdry catalytic process.[13] The new process produced gasoline with an octane rating higher than any that could be achieved by thermal cracking. (Since octane is an engineer's term, let it suffice to say that a high octane gasoline makes engines perform better; the higher the octane the better the performance.) Blazer had his men check out the cost of installing a new Houdry process plant; they came back with the answer: $2 million.

TWILIGHT OF AN ERA

In January 1939, Barcelona fell to Franco; the Spanish Civil War ended in a Falange victory. In March, Germany overran Czechoslovakia; in April, Mussolini fell on tiny Albania. On April thirtieth, the New York World's Fair opened; in June, the King and Queen of England made a visit to the United States and the Roosevelts served, at one point, hot dogs; Brenda Frazier was the

[13] Thermal cracking, as its name implies, is a means of refining crude oil by subjecting it to intense heat and obtaining various products (thermal heat and pressure = cracking). Catalytic cracking is based on the introduction of catalysts into the process, using air as well as heat, changing gases into liquids. Sun Oil, Socony-Vacuum and Houdry combined to create this system, which gave rise to the Houdry Process and Chemical Co., named after the French engineer Eugene J. Houdry who was the prime inventor. Many difficulties had to be overcome before the process became commercially practical; listing of the persons, companies and details would be voluminous.

Its introduction began in November 1938, when Ashland's modernization expansion was almost complete, when Arthur Pew, of Sun Oil, told an API meeting his company had three commercial Houdry units in operation. By 1939, the race to convert was in full swing.

debutante of the year; Bette Davis made women weep in *Dark Victory*. Thomas E. Dewey was the hope of the Republican Party, and rumors of a third term for FDR began to agitate Democratic hopefuls. In August, the Soviets and the Nazis signed a non-aggression pact; on September first, Hitler's hordes marched into Poland; on September third, England declared war.

In 1939, however, geographical distance still counted. The world within the United States looked the same on September second as it had the day before; the country was still saddled with an enormous work relief program that was growing more expensively bedraggled monthly, as were the persons whom it supported. Business was still far from healthy; new investments had remained slow despite considerably more money in circulation and in the banks; big companies still seemed big and the small companies were still small; the powers of the government had grown immensely, as had the national debt, but the results seemed mainly that there were more rules; no real path from the morass had been found.

At Ashland, despite Blazer's forebodings about competition and the technological race, the company was still advancing: September earnings were the highest in the company's history—$105,000—almost as much as it made in the entire year of 1931. Ashland Oil & Refining had grown more than tenfold in fifteen years. The new towboat, fascinating details concluded, was ordered for a sum of $175,000; it would have two 600-hp diesel engines. Jim Martin was regaled with further details by Blazer, dictating to Miss Hallnan at top speed; young McBrayer Burnam, a lawyer from Richmond, Kentucky, who had worked for a large firm in New York City and had been in private practice in Kentucky for a year, was hired at a salary of $2,700 a year; he would handle government reports and serve as a liaison with general counsel E. L. McDonald in Lexington. In November, three more barges were ordered; "one half our crude oil now reaches us by river; more than half our gasoline leaves the same way"; the refinery was processing 9,000 barrels a day.

The Kentucky Oil & Gas Association (independent producers) complained that the Ashland Oil & Refining Company, price-poster for their crude oil, was making its profits at their expense:

as proof, they paralleled with their falling prices the rising annual earnings of the company; the Board of Tax Appeals, although directed to recompute the Ashland tax payment of $500,000, was finding new avenues of difference with the company; the company's two largest independent distributors decided to deal with competitors, and despite the fact that the Ashland earnings were high and the volume highest ever, Blazer gloomily contrasted the earnings of competitors: "Sohio (Standard Oil of Ohio) had earnings of $5 million, their highest since 1922," he concluded. He also took care to inform the board that Elk Refining, Louisville Refining and Aetna Oil & Refining, all close, cheek-by-jowl competitors of Ashland, had enjoyed record earnings in 1939.

Ever since the crash of 1929, the chorus that demanded a new world had been swelling; the events in Europe were to usher in changes far beyond the expectations of even the most eager. At no time did these onrushing new tides rise higher or hit harder than in the first six months of 1940. Yet, in the United States, there were many who seemed strangely slow to recognize this; domestic life continued to the accompaniment of the same rhetoric as before, although the shape of the world began to alter. The United States, in September 1939, had 55,000 men in its armed forces, and only 189 airplanes ready for action.

Within the Department of Justice, the beavers working under Thurman Arnold, assistant attorney general, prepared a series of anti-trust suits against the nation's oil industry, intended to completely disintegrate the integrated companies. According to Platt's *Oilgram*, these suits were ready to be filed at any moment; the *Oilgram*, usually reliable, said its sources predicted the filing would take place "any minute."

At about the same time, Hitler threw his armies against Belgium and The Netherlands, outflanked the Maginot Line, and within six weeks reduced and overran both these nations and France itself, as well. The British army barely escaped annihilation at Dunkirk; within less than a year after the war's start the previous September, England, the nation counted the most powerful in the world twenty-five years before, had been reduced to fighting for its survival.

While the attention of the White House and the State Department was riveted upon the events taking place in Europe and Asia, the machinery of domestic change set into motion by the New Deal continued to alter the shape of the American economy. The introduction of the excess profits tax in particular made an enormous impact upon corporations; the explanations for this measure ranged from the philosophic to the empirical.

The administration had discovered that large corporations—the very largest, in fact—had increased their efficiency of operations during the 1920s and the 1930s tremendously.[14] The restrictions on public funding (stocks and bonds) did not affect these giants as much as had been expected, because they were generating huge funds from their earnings. Instead of expanding, however, they were accumulating reserves or issuing heavy dividends to their shareholders. Exactly how these companies could expand in advance of their markets or when they were already under attack for bigness is a contradiction that only politicians could answer; the Administration felt big business was frozen in subtle opposition and refused to do its part toward recovery: a recovery that had thus far escaped all the efforts of the Administration. The excess profits tax was designed to reduce the accumulation of corporate reserve funds by forcing the corporation to pay heavy taxes on such accumulations, taxes heavy enough to keep them from becoming mountains: at the same time it was to reduce the return to shareholders to a "fair" percentage. The corporations were thus placed neatly within an economic trap where they would have to spend instead of save. The fact that this constituted a considerable alteration of some basic ideas in the U.S.A., especially on the unlimited rights of investors to make profits, was beside the point.

Whether the measure would have survived in normal times is a

[14] According to the ratings of industrial efficiency, usually based on productivity per man, the increase from 1920 to 1930 was 21 per cent; from 1930 to 1941, 41 per cent. Ashland Oil & Refining was not the only company where fewer men were working harder than ever, Blazer not the only manager driving for economy and increased production as parallel needs, although the greatest contribution was not by increased effort on the blue collar levels, but due to the innovations of science and engineering; and, in general, increased grasp of scientific principles on managerial levels.

question that would tax the ingenuity of science fiction writers: the fact was that the times had not been normal for a considerable period, and showed no signs of ever becoming "normal,"—if normal is taken to mean pre-1929. Those days, the days of the virtually free and unfettered market, were gone forever; its place was taken by a "mixed economy," part public sector and part private; the intermingling became closer and more complex.

To men like Paul Blazer, Everett Wells, Ed Emrick, Art Points, Ned Seaton and others, these extra-circumstantial considerations were relatively unimportant: they were a young, aggressive management team operating a small company in a very large industry heavily populated by giants. The odds are that the excess profits regulation came close to a pattern they would have followed if left to their own choices entirely; certainly they wanted to invest to expand. The tax enabled them to do that; in fact, it forced such action.

But the impact of the tax was even greater than its planners envisioned, because it was enacted just at the time that the impact of the events in Europe reached this nation. The White House and the State Department had no intention of allowing the Axis Powers to take over the world; vast sums began to pour forth to assist England, and a tremendous portion of these funds were returned to the United States for the industrial sinews, arms and implements of England's defense. The total effect was of a shot in the arm, an incredible stimulant to the nation's industry, and its economy.

In April 1940, after a vacation, Paul Blazer spent almost a week in Washington discovering the pattern of some of these events; when he returned to Ashland he called in his team and they began to examine the situation of the company in the round. The extension of the Ashland transportation network by the purchase of the Owensboro pipeline system enabled the firm to tap the crude oil fields of western Kentucky in addition to its already large share of the eastern Kentucky fields. Although a new, larger towboat, dubbed the *Jim Martin*, in honor of the chairman of the board, had barely settled in the water, it was decided to either build, rent or lease still another large towboat, and add a number of barges to the burgeoning waterways fleet. Then the Lummus engineers were called back to begin a second expansion of the Catlettsburg refinery; initial costs were estimated at $350,000.

Ashland was going to gird itself for the emergency, the length and extent of which no man could foresee.

By mid-summer 1940, Blazer learned that the $500,000 refund the government had returned to the company was, under the rules, taxable as income (under the excess profits tax). He got in touch with Fred M. Vinson, his most influential Washington friend, who arranged for him to have a talk with the Acting Secretary of the Treasury. The Secretary listened sympathetically, sent him on to the Senate Finance Committee, which promptly wrote an amendment to the measure, exempting such refunds from taxation as income. Otherwise, according to the figures Art Points worked up, Ashland would have fought its long, bitter fight for exactly nothing.

That summer, the attention of the nation was fixed on the election campaign. Both parties were internally split between isolationists and interventionists; the Republican Convention was stampeded by spontaneous sentiment that swept Wendell Willkie aloft; war bulletins and newsreels of the Battle of Britain continued to compete in the news with more mundane matters.

In August 1940, Paul Blazer wrote Secretary of the Interior Ickes a letter proposing that a program to salvage oil from stripper wells throughout the nation be mounted by imposition of a minor tax on all wells on a *pro rata* production basis. He had the figures worked out and believed the nation could benefit from this recoverable oil. In response, Secretary Ickes asked him to come to Washington. Hard on the heels of his invitation from Ickes, Blazer received a wire from W. C. Teagle, chairman of the board of Standard Oil of New Jersey, the industry's largest American company, inviting him to a private dinner at the Carleton Hotel, in Washington, D.C., to confer with him and Messrs. Roeser and Mattei before all of them saw Ickes the next day. Large matters were afoot: in September 1940, FDR declared an official state of limited emergency.

At Ashland, the *Independent* carried the story of the Ashland Oil & Refining Company's expansion program: $350,000 for the refinery, $250,000 for a new towboat, $50,000 for two new barges, increase of storage facilities by 25 per cent, and a 25 per cent increase in the amount of crude oil to be handled; all adding up to a $650,000 program.

Blazer also established a terminal in Pittsburgh. He sent bright young Moffitt to be manager, and Joseph C. Davis was later sent to help him. Moffitt said he began to feel like a "messenger" in Pittsburgh: Blazer would call him on the phone and talk for two or three hours at a stretch; in self-defense Moffitt began to keep a book in which he would record everything to keep abreast and answer Blazer's perpetual rain of questions. He was not the first man to adopt this resort, nor would he be the last.

In October 1940, troubled by continuing, although minor, health disabilities, Blazer checked into the University of Chicago clinic at the insistence of Dr. Winans, and had a week's check-up and rest. He reported the doctors considered his health excellent— no organic troubles whatever; he was in the best shape "in years." He was fifty years old, and in good trim at a time when the nation sorely needed industrial managers.

A LOOK BACKWARD

In December 1940 Blazer was invited to give a talk to the Kentucky Chapter of the American Association of University Professors. The talk is interesting because of the glimpse it gives of America that year, a year in which an era ended, as surely as the year 1914 marked the end of an earlier era. It is also interesting for the light it throws upon the needs and attitudes of business, as contrasted with academia:

"It might interest you to know," Blazer said in part, "that of the more than four thousand men who have applied for jobs this year with the company with which I am associated, approximately half, when asked concerning the kind of work for which they were best qualified, replied that they could drive a truck. Probably not one out of fifty of those men was really a trained truck-driver. The other forty-nine merely were telling us that they were not prepared to hold any kind of a job except unskilled labor, for which there is a steadily decreasing demand . . . I presume the same proportion holds true for other companies. That situation presents a real problem. I believe it can be solved only through our public school system. Our schools should prepare young people to fit into our present day economy. The boy who finishes high school and does not go to college should not have to seek a job as an unskilled laborer . . . The need for high school teachers with a better understanding of the economics of the world in which we live is a problem for our institutions of higher education. . . .

"Logically, there is no reason why we should have idle capital and idle men coincident with the unfilled wants of millions of underprivileged people. In my opinion, one of the important causes of the economic dislocations of recent years has been the failure of our educational system to equip young people to do the kind of work that is required by our present industrial civilization. Education has not kept pace with industrial progress. . . .

"I believe that artificial social distinctions between different occupations account for some of the overcrowding of certain professions. I suspect that some of the dissatisfaction with our economic system springs from the fact that many people who would have made good foremen or supervisors in some plant or office are living an unsatisfactory existence as inadequately paid members of one of the learned professions . . .

"That this country still has millions of unemployed while the physical needs of still greater millions are poorly provided for, is often pointed out as an indictment of our system of private enterprise, but in my opinion the responsibility lies fully as much with our educational system and its administration as with industry."

Then, after these blunt words to those inveterate critics of business, the professors, Blazer expressed a viewpoint widely shared among the men of business, even now: ". . . I believe that modern industry is seldom understood by people outside of industry. Industry is constantly changing; it isn't the same as it was twenty or ten or even five years ago. Management looks upon itself . . . as trying to coordinate many different forces and endeavoring to correlate and focus on each day's problems as accumulated from many fields of knowledge. Sometimes men from outside business say to a businessman, 'Why do you work so hard? You have all the money you need.' Perhaps he has more money than he and his family should ever need, and is aware of that fact; probably he has far less personal interest in money than his questioner, who, though he might easily understand why a scientist could work fifteen hours a day without thought of financial reward, cannot visualize a businessman as one whose principal incentive may be a pride in his workmanship, a desire to offer greater security to his employees and their families, and an obligation to give his best to the stockholders who have invested their savings in his enterprise."

They were words he wrote himself; it was the credo by which he lived.

THE END OF THE OLD: 1941

The year 1940 ended with net sales for the company of $8 million, another high, and net profits of $696,938. The board of tax appeals, after all these years, finally handed over the refund check: it amounted to $626,176.89. Blazer commented drily that the first step upon receipt of the check was to return $245,000 of this amount; then he computed aloud, taking in consideration the number of years it would be before the government received the balance back. He felt that the victory had been mainly moral. He also worried over the interest being shown by the government in the Ashland Oil boats: he feared they would be requisitioned.

Perhaps he was feeling more than his usual year-end gloom; his health continued to be mysteriously bad, although the doctors could find nothing specifically wrong. Also, these were the beginnings of long, trying days: shortages of men and materials, unknown before, had begun to appear.

In part the shortages could be traced to the draft, in 1940, of 900,000 men for limited service (prior to this the nation had only 55,000 men in its armed forces), and to the flood of British war orders that exceeded $5 billion; industry confronted an enormous backlog of both men and materials that seemed to appear overnight.

In January 1941, the year opened with FDR's announcement of the Four Freedoms, and with Lend Lease pouring $7 billion more into the economic stream.

At Ashland, the new year started out seeming deceptively much like the old. Once again we find Blazer announcing the delivery of a new towboat; this one is named, simply, *The Ashland*; in almost the same breath he declares his intention to have a fourth boat built. New barges (one almost says, as usual) are ordered. The refinery is being expanded some more; these expansions seem to have become continuous.

The discovery of thefts at the refinery disturbed the management considerably. These are far from unknown at refineries (gasoline being a ubiquitous commodity); they disturbed Blazer most because they revealed that Fred Irwin, the superintendent, did not know everything that took place; Blazer regarded this as a serious management error.

The press of war-laden events was by now full upon the nation; Japan signed a non-aggression pact with the Soviet Union; a great clamor within the United States had resulted in FDR calling for a voluntary embargo against that nation: the embargo left Japan with only 2 years of oil on hand; seven months of aluminum.

In May 1941, Harold Ickes was appointed Petroleum Coordinator, a revival of his NIRA organization, of the oil industry. He summoned Ralph Davies, of Standard of California, to be his deputy again, and in June summoned 1,000 oilmen to Washington, Blazer among them.

"The NIRA had prepared us for war," he said later, "without our realizing it. By the time the war came along, we all knew our way around."

While the oil (and other) industries were being coordinated and prepared for national effort, an Office of Production Management was prepared; priorities were arranged, and planning on a scale hitherto undreamed of began. If President Wilson thought he had turned a corner in World War I, then his ghost would have been awed at the extent of the government's activities in pre-World War II days, to say nothing of what came later.

In June 1941, Hitler created a sensation throughout the world by invading the Soviet Union. Even the most dull could sense the scales of history moving.

In July, the United States landed troops in Iceland, in what was described as part of a hemispheric defense plan. By that time our destroyers were already cruising the Atlantic with the British, in search of German submarines.

That same month, Ralph Davies summoned a blue-ribbon oil group to his offices to discuss a pipeline to be built, and to extend from the Gulf coast to the Eastern seaboard. Ashland Oil & Refining was the only small company present; the rest were giants: Standard Oil of New Jersey, Socony-Vacuum, Texas Oil, Gulf Oil and Shell Oil. The proposition, created to overcome a tanker shortage because of the diversion of tankers to England, was to convey refined products from Gulf coast refineries to a point fifty miles east of St. Louis, straight across southern Illinois, southern Indiana, southern Ohio, northern West Virginia, southern Pennsylvania to Philadelphia and New York. Financing had already been arranged and a great deal of the engineering work done as well. Blazer sat there aghast as the details of this plan were revealed: Ashland Oil & Refining (as well as Standard of Ohio) might as well close its doors when this venture came into being.

Blazer's first reaction was to point out that this proposition would hurt the crude producers of Kentucky, Indiana and Illinois, their pipelines and the refineries that bought their oil. Davies gave him a sympathetic ear, but the men from the major companies, whose plans were obviously far advanced, and who had attended the meeting merely to pick up their "certificates of necessity" which would enable them to receive priority steel and rights-of-way for their pipeline, were taken aback. "Farish (N.J.) and Rodgers (Texas Co.) were scarcely able to be courteous," Blazer said later.

The interjection of crude oil production proved an excellent diversion; Harry Sinclair and Mr. Farish, in fact, fell into a side-dispute on this point, and Blazer, abetted by Sidney Swensrud, who spoke on behalf of Standard Oil of Ohio, created a diversionary group consisting of Sinclair, Tidewater and Atlantic, on the spot.

Finally, Colonel Drake, president of Gulf Oil, suggested that Davies take a poll of the men present to find out who would financially support the pipeline: a move designed to reveal that Blazer and Swensrud were simply spoilers with no financial involvement. Second to be called, Blazer immediately said he would commit his company to between 5,000 and 10,000 barrels a day through a crude oil line; Standard of Ohio made a somewhat larger offer. The poll continued, and the supporters of a crude oil line were revealed, unsurprisingly, to be in a minority.

Then Davies polled the supporters of a product line, and asked them if they would boycott or join in a project to build a crude oil line. Farish of New Jersey said his firm would participate for 40,000 barrels a day, the balance of the major companies said they would participate also; by the end of the second poll, almost everyone would participate in a crude oil line, although admittedly as a second choice for the majority.

The meeting adjourned with the nature of the venture in doubt, although Blazer and Swensrud, still nervous, had reason to be pleased. A few days later, Ralph Davies, after reviewing the matter, called and said he would, himself, recommend that a crude oil line be built. The day was saved.

The debate had been sharp; at one point, one man asked how Ashland could participate in a crude oil line since it had no wells in Texas and no refineries on the East Coast, the terminus of the line. Blazer answered calmly he was sure he could buy what he needed in Texas from producers in the field and could barge his crude from the east back to Ashland; Ashland Oil & Refining already barged both crude oil and refined products on the Ohio to and from Pittsburgh and other points on the river.

Altogether, it was a meeting to test one's mettle.

Later that month, Blazer was appointed Refinery Committee Chairman of District Two of the Petroleum Administration for War. The District consisted of 15 states: Oklahoma, Kansas, Nebraska, North Dakota, South Dakota, Minnesota, Wisconsin, Iowa, Missouri, Illinois, Indiana, Michigan, Ohio, Kentucky and Tennessee. The area was similar, and his functions similar, to the NRA set-up. Blazer was pleased, because at one point it looked very much as though Ickes would draft him as a deputy administrator; Blazer did not want to leave the company. The post he received would, he said candidly, ". . . not require too much time, but will leave access to inner circles." These were important considerations; the company chief executive who could not get a hearing would not contribute much to the war effort.

In August 1941, FDR and Winston Churchill met at sea, and as a result, issued what was termed the Atlantic Charter. This document, which intermingled New Deal concepts with the war effort, was cloudy but irresistible to the press; it had a magnificent ring but was strangely irreducible. The Charter was, in effect, a declaration of a compact. Strangely, the majority of persons in the United States did not seem to so view it, although by then the sentiment of the nation was strongly against the Nazis.

That same month, an office of Supply, Priorities and Allocations was announced, and the Administration made secret plans to raise eight million men under arms.

By October 1941 the Germans were within 100 miles of the gates of Moscow, and United States materiel was flowing to the Russians as well as the British. Late in the month, FDR ascended the podium and addressed the nation: he called for a defense program of Brobdingnagian proportions: 50,000 airplanes, and a quantity of other instruments to create "an arsenal of defense." At almost the same time that he spoke, the American destroyer *Kearny* was torpedoed in the Atlantic; a state of undeclared war was well under way.

At Ashland Oil & Refining, few of the management men had time to discuss politics. They bought crude oil as far afield as Mississippi, where it was shipped by rail to Vicksburg or Memphis and then barged upriver to Ashland. Harry Blackstone, the number two man in the refinery, was seriously hurt in an automobile accident and Fred Irwin, who had lost Mr. Blazer's confidence, was finally let go. A reorganization of the refinery management was launched.

For tax reasons, the fiscal year of the company was changed from January to January, to September to September. As a result, the annual statement for 1941 showed nine months instead of a year's earnings. From the oil industry the news came trickling that the major companies had completely dropped their great pipeline project; they had decided instead to lay a pipeline from Salem to the East Coast bringing oil from Oklahoma, Kansas and

Illinois. The new line would not be a common carrier (which meant it would carry oil that belonged to its owners only).

Late in August 1941, the government needs for 100 octane aviation gasoline became clear; at least double the national output was needed, and refiners were asked to submit plans to participate in such a program. Blazer, delving into the subject, decided that it would cost the company a total of $2 million to construct such a plant itself, but he began to discuss with the engineers ways and means of combining his operation with a government-built aviation gasoline plant. These conferences interested Washington as well; not every refiner was interested in this part of the program, and Ashland Oil & Refining had established an inventive, alert and progressive image.

By the end of 1941 the aviation gasoline project began to appear quite possible; Blazer announced he would include in bonus payments Everett Wells and Bill Keffer, together with himself: clear indication that he considered these two men as important to the company and entitled to an irreplaceable worker's share in the profits. These, at the end of nine months, amounted to $632,779 on net sales of $8.2 million—almost as much as the previous (1940) twelve-month period.

Despite its significance, 1941 is a year whose historian has not yet arrived. Unlike 1929 or 1914, few elegiac accounts exist. On the airwaves, *One Man's Family, The Aldrich Family* and *The Goldbergs*—all nostalgic recreations of a vanished America—were immensely popular; Glenn Miller, Benny Goodman and Artie Shaw competed with Guy Lombardo and Kay Kyser; *Citizen Kane* appeared on the screen with grainy, newsreel-type scenes and a startling resemblance to William Randolph Hearst; Sherwood Anderson, early sensation of the 1920s, and F. Scott Fitzgerald, the epitome of the Jazz Age, both died; *Pal Joey,* the first of many heel-heroes, appeared on Broadway; so did *Arsenic & Old Lace,* so did *My Sister Eileen.*

In Asia, Japan's ruling circles viewed their situation with somber eyes. The invasion of Manchuria in 1931 and north China in 1937 had bogged down; their New Asia program needed alteration. The informal, but highly effective, embargo declared against them by FDR had put their economy in a precarious position: to

their south, the rich colonies of England, France and The Netherlands contained tin, bauxite, oil, rubber—all materials Japan
badly needed—sat, virtually unprotected. France and The Netherlands were both occupied by the Germans, and England had her
back to the wall. Their way seemed clear, and in retrospect, obvious.

The Japanese reasoned that if they struck first and hard, they
could obtain enough *de facto* control of the Pacific to impel the
United States to recognize at least a large portion of their claims;
this was their war aim.

Militarily, their reasoning resembled the Germans': a lightning
series of strokes and a quick war.

They began with Pearl Harbor, on December 7, 1941. Although our Pacific forces were on 24-hour alert and our intelligence had cracked the Japanese codes, their boldness caught
our military by surprise; the immediate result was a United States
disaster. Within hours after the Japanese attack, Hitler and Mus-

Blazer assesses the condition of the Catlettsburg refinery on the eve of
the U. S. entry into World War II.

solini removed what might have been a difficult dilemma for FDR by declaring war on the United States (their reasoning, to this day, remains obscure), and all debate within the nation was ended for the duration.

The situation was dark: Japan was moving in Asia; all Western Europe with the exception of Axis-friendly Spain was in the control of Hitler and Mussolini; German armies were close to Moscow and in the oil-rich Caucasus; Rommel's advance to the Middle East oil fields was being disputed in the bloody sands of North Africa by General Auchinleck; the issue was still undecided. On all sides, the totalitarians seemed supreme.

Section Five—Inside the War

1942–1945

During the 1920s and 1930s, industry not only increased its efficiency, its scientists had worked miracles in the laboratory. Germany, a small country with an awkward shape, squeezed into the map of north central Europe, sought to avoid the shortages of natural rubber and petroleum products that had stalled their military machine in World War I, by developing substitutes. For several years during the 1930s, news that the Germans were making ersatz commodities at first astonished and then impressed the world: synthetic rubber from butadiene and styrene, synthetic gasoline from coal and a variety of other achievements were disclosed.

So successful were the Germans at propagandizing these accomplishments that even the suspicious Russians were lulled. The oil fields of the Caucasus, otherwise an irresistible lure, seemed unnecessary to a nation that had a substitute within its own industrial reaches.

But in actuality, the German synthetic programs were barely equivalent to an American pilot-model. It is difficult for the average American to bear in mind the smallness of Germany, the relatively short distances within its borders, and the smaller quantities of materials it handles. The entire German oil industry, for instance, consumed only 5 per cent of the normal peacetime requirements of the U.S.A.

The innovative achievements of German industry during the

late 1920s and early 1930s[1] attracted intense attention within U.S. and U.K. business and industrial circles. So spurred, they began to launch similar programs of their own. In a very short time, extending roughly from 1934 to 1939, the Germans were outstripped at the game they started; the U.S. and U.K. scientists in industry duplicated and then exceeded many of their advances. Again, it must be borne in mind that the differences in scale were immense, and the U.S. efforts in their aggregate were larger. But these researches were conducted by business at its own expense, in the interest of efficiency, and without the assistance of the government.

Relatively little attention was paid to these efforts by the man in the street, perhaps because the literati of the U.S., unlike their counterparts in Germany and Russia, have never considered our industrial accomplishments a particularly noteworthy topic. Since 1929, in fact, U.S. industry had been mainly a target for criticism, and its advances took second place to the sins of business.

As the crisis in Europe deepened and extended, however, the eyes of the British and American governments began to turn toward the war-essential subject of industrial efficiency. Beginning late in the 1930s, the British began to pour a flood of war orders into the U.S., and industry here began to expand its advances from the laboratory to the plant. In Washington, some of the early New Dealers had revised their opinion of industry as the result of their NIRA observations, and as the tides of war came perceptibly closer to our shores, conferences between governmental officials and industrialists began to change in tone and content; became warmer and more fruitful.

The Petroleum Administration under Harold Ickes was, fortunately, based on the assumption that the men who comprised a particular industry were best equipped to assess its capabilities and most aware of its limitations: boundaries that must be based

[1] Contrary to widespread myth, most of the German accomplishments took place before Hitler. Once the Nazis came to power, their selective terror effectively inhibited experiment, decimated the ranks of the capable and froze advance. The overwhelming majority of the famed marvels that emerged from Germany under Hitler were conceived and developed before he and his fellow tyrants took office; Naziism and intellectual advance were antithetical.

on realities and not wishes, to be effective in planning. Mr. Ickes had selected very capable men from within the oil industry itself to assist him; these men had drawn together a variety of committees staffed by men from the industry itself. As a consequence, the Petroleum Administration was much further ahead than some other sectors whose government administrators had less faith in cooperative methods.

The phenomenon did not pass unnoticed; Congress contained many members who felt that bringing businessmen into these plans in any but an involuntary way was fraught with peril. From virtually the onset of our entry into the war, through its duration and beyond, the oil companies were regarded in some civilian and political quarters with distrust and skepticism.

The military, however, had no time for such considerations. Its needs were so desperate and so many that its attention remained fixed on the need to get the right petroleum product to the right place at the right time.

Unlike many of the Congressmen or the man in the street, for instance, the Air Force knew that the Battle of Britain, which evoked Winston Churchill's famous tribute to the RAF ("Never . . . have so many owed so much to so few") was, like many of the events of history, told to the average man in simplified terms. The essence of the Churchillian rhetoric was true, but some important details had been skipped. The Royal Air Force pilots were able to soar into the skies and defeat the Luftwaffe because they had three vital weapons in addition to their skill and courage: radar, the first successful air-cooled engine, and 100 octane gasoline.

Radar enabled them, literally, to see in the dark, while their opponents were limited to ordinary vision. The air-cooled engine and the 100 octane gasoline, interdependently important, enabled them to soar faster, higher, to stay aloft longer and maneuver more quickly than the Germans. The combination of sight and speed enabled these heroes to avoid the fates of equally courageous fighters in, say, Poland, who were simply shot out of the skies in greater numbers.

It is not surprising, therefore, that when Secretary Ickes called 1,000 oilmen into Washington the summer before Pearl Harbor (when he was still simply Petroleum Coordinator and not yet the chief of the Petroleum Administration for War: PAW), the subjects uppermost in his mind were transportation and 100 octane aviation gasoline.

The creation of a 100 octane facility was not a simple undertaking: the entire question of catalytic cracking introduced enormous problems. A single giant cracker could soar as high as a 20-story building, use 100 miles of pipe, include more steel than a cruiser, take as long to build as an airplane carrier. Furthermore, it used more special equipment, such as pumps, generators, compressors, electrical instruments and the like, than it did the materials of construction. These required time to construct, and had to be coordinated into the whole.

THE OIL OF WAR

The discoveries of the 1930s introduced more than oil into the industry: the bewildering variety of new products came to the attention of mankind, ultimately, under the embracing term petrochemicals. The title gives the story: oil plus chemicals, or chemicals from oil.

In World War I, oil had been a vital ingredient, ranking with rubber and bullets. In World War II, oil was *the* vital ingredient: rubber and carbon black were made from it, and bullets could not be made without it.

Neither the wheels of industry nor the arms of war could move without oil. Civilization itself depended on oil, and the nation without oil was defenseless against its enemies. The ships at sea, the planes in the air, the trucks on the highway, the tanks in the field and the locomotive on the track—all moved on oil.

It brought the ingredients of life as well as of death. Medicines and anesthetics were made from oil. Oil heated the home and the barrack and the tent alike; oil produced the asphalt for highways and landing strips, was the basis for waterproofing uniforms, for rayon parachutes, for lubricating machinery and greasing wounds, and for DDT.

As a weapon, oil was fearsome. Jellied, it went into flame throwers and was dropped to ignite enemy installations. Trinitrotoluene—TNT—was made from oil, and comprised the stuff of bombs. Europe was blasted from the air with TNT.

Perhaps the greatest vulnerability of oil was in the immense quantities needed for all these purposes. One armored unit, in one day's combat, used 60 million gallons of gasoline. Ten thousand gallons a minute were consumed during a bombing raid. One battleship carried enough fuel to heat 500 homes for 100 years. During World War II, the U.S. Air Force *alone* used 14 times as much gasoline as this nation shipped to Europe during all of World War I for all purposes.

The need for oil had grown with the knowledge of its special uses. In 1936, it was estimated the petroleum industry produced 500 different products; by 1942, it was producing over 1,000.

Each of these special products required a special process of manufacture. A bewildering subdivision of special uses required particular blends and combinations. For instance, diesel fuel used in a ship differed from that used in a tank or truck; the diesel fuel used in some of these varied for different terrains or climes. As the use, number and types of vehicles multiplied, so did their special fuels.

Then there remained the agonizing process[2] of arranging to transport all these products: none were of any use unless they were available in quantity, at the right time. This required a continual cycle of taking crude oil out of the earth, sending it to the refineries, manufacturing and transporting it to all the users of all these products. The labyrinth had to be kept open for traffic.

If the U.S. had had one war on its hands, either in the Pacific or in Europe, it could have concentrated in that direction. But it had two wars. In addition, both these wars fragmented into many fronts, and as the war extended, new fronts kept opening. On no front could troops move without oil, in all its protean forms and products, moving with them in a continuous stream.

The Petroleum Administration for War confronted a U.S. industry that consisted, in 1942, of 20 major companies and 520 smaller independents, with 10,000 to 15,000 jobbers and 40,000

[2] There were no computers in 1942.

retailers. As a whole, the industry was rated at $15 billion; it owned 54 per cent of the world's known oil reserves at the time, and 60–65 per cent of its wells were owned by independent producers.

Great confusion reigned in transportation. Blazer was worried that his boats and barges on the Ohio and Mississippi would be commandeered, but he was, clearly, already using them along the lines the government effort needed. Instead of losing his fleet, he was given Certificates of Necessity and allowed to lease several more boats and another string of barges.

The East Coast refineries and markets had been, along the years, served by tankers that brought crude oil from the rich fields of Texas, as well as gasoline, kerosene, fuel oil (for homes) and lubricating oil and fuel oil for industry.

With the declaration of war, the German submarines had moved against these tankers. The result is informally known as the Battle of Florida, but it might as plausibly be called the Battle of the Galveston Bar, or the Battle of Port Arthur. Under whatever name, it was not recorded by the press until after the war, because the military did not want the enemy to know how badly it had been hurt.

A torpedoed tanker is the closest place to a Fundamentalist Hell the earth can provide. A hit is usually followed by the cargo exploding, then fire emerges, and asphyxiating, heavy black blankets of billowing smoke. The steel decks and bulkheads turn white hot from the heat; often the waters around the ship, slimy with escaping crude or gasoline, become lakes of flames. The vessel itself turns into a torch. Watchers along the beaches saw these great flares ascend toward the heavens, and later watched detritus and the bodies of men wash ashore. One out of every six U.S. merchant seamen died at sea in the year 1942.

ASHLAND MOBILIZED

The company Christmas parties in 1941 were held against a backdrop that included the fall of Singapore to the Japanese, and attacks launched against the Philippines and Wake Island.

Bill Keffer became a member of the PAW pipeline committee,

Dupree of the towboat and barge committee. Blazer, already deeply entangled in PAW as head of District Two and its refining committee, was spending long, stretched days at a time in Washington and Chicago.

By telephone, he conferred constantly with Boyd Morgan, the new superintendent of the refinery, Everett Wells, Art Points, Ned Seaton, Ed Emrick, Jim Martin and the other directors, and men throughout the industry. The problem that engrossed their attention was one of alternatives: whether to enter into the manufacture of butadiene, an essential product in the production of synthetic rubber, or 100 octane aviation gasoline. The production of 100 octane required a refinery that was already producing a high quality gasoline, and could, through additional facilities, add blending agents such as iso-octane and tetraethyl lead. The extension would lead Ashland into catalytic cracking, and into the mainstream of technology in refining. Butadiene, on the other hand, was equally complex and essential to synthetic rubber, a product of more than wartime need. Nationally, their importance was chicken-and-egg. Without rubber, the war machine and the nation could not move; neither could they move without oil.

Blazer, finally, inclined toward the 100 octane solution. He examined his men with eagle eyes, trying to discern whether they could cope with the problems entailed. For their part, they were confident they could. Blazer's team by this time was expert enough to allow him to leave them alone for days at a time, though he would not allow himself such a luxury. His telephone calls became more extensive, if this were possible, as the weeks passed. Nevertheless, he was *not* on the spot and his men were; necessarily they made decisions that in the normal course would have been bucked to him. They learned to endure his critiques and comments as part of the normal vicissitudes of life.

In the midst of these pressures, the union dragged its feet on signing a new contract, and meetings were held without results. The men did not particularly want to go out on strike, but were in no hurry to sign a contract. Although only a very few had been involved in the plant thefts that so astonished Blazer, these had poisoned the atmosphere; many felt they were under suspicion; rumors were rife; the departure of Irwin and the entry of a new chief at the refinery carried the usual insecurities of change in its wake.

The company had created a house magazine in early 1941, in order to keep abreast with the trend throughout the nation. Labor experts in Washington were very keen on such academic measures to enhance "communication." But the *Ashland Log* did not really seem to make much impression.

It was obvious that the structuring of relationships between the plant and the management, once an inseparable duo, had not really assisted the situation, however much it had codified and made legal the union representation. In this, Ashland Oil & Refining was undergoing change, in common with—although certainly not to the same degree as—most other companies. U.S. industry was beginning to stratify, but Blazer did not adapt to the new distinctions. He maintained his personal contacts and learned through his old friends at the refinery everything that happened in the union. They were still his men, but new faces were arriving.

Beneath the unanimity of the war effort, there was an unrest in the men in the refinery that had been growing since the middle 1930s; by 1942, it had become endemic. As a result, there was much bickering over relatively minor issues. The disputes, which arose with increasing frequency, seemed more and more often to revolve around the figure of Willy Anderson, a worker at the refinery since 1930.

Willy came from the same home town as Lew Ware: Shelbyville, Kentucky. "When he was a boy," Lew said, "Willy was tragically shy. As youngsters we became accustomed to the fact that Willy would not only remain silent at social gatherings, but would often slip away to walk home alone without even saying good-bye.

"When the union movement came into being in Kentucky under the aegis of the NIRA and then the Wagner Act, Willy seemed to flower. He proved a great arguer, and plunged into union work with zest. He was fast on his feet, quick-witted, and he soon had most of the men behind him. He almost held his own with Paul Blazer, and he could compete with him in intimate knowledge of the refinery's operations."

The contrast between Willy Anderson's concerns and Blazer's at this time was a microcosm of the world. In New England, a fuel oil shortage developed (in part because of the cindering of merchant seamen in tanker sinkings the newspapers could not report), and housewives demonstrated in protest. PAW, juggling problems, asked the industry to create a pool of its transportation facilities. The industry did so; dug deep into the coffers of individual corporations and ran many millions of dollars into the red before the slow disbursement wheels of Washington caught up.

In February 1942, as though to balance the scales even more heavily against us, Singapore fell to the Japanese who continued their drive in the Orient. From their bases in French Indo-China (now Vietnam) they entered the neighboring areas and strutted into Bangkok without encountering resistance.

Meanwhile, in the U.S. the mobilization of industry proceeded; Washington seethed with arguments over priorities. Ed Emrick of Ashland was placed in charge of the heartbreaking and exasperating responsibility for purchasing and priorities.

By this time, Blazer and his men had decided in favor of 100 octane aviation gasoline; he had conferred with experts of all types, and was sure.

Ashland barely qualified in terms of size to be included in such a program: the minimum size refinery eligible was one that processed 15,000 barrels of crude oil per day; Ashland was processing 16,000 barrels.

On April 14, 1942, Blazer wrote Jim Martin one of his voluminous, single-spaced, detailed letters, saying that the refinery profits were running at the rate of $165,000 a month—the excess profits tax would take care of most of it. It was the first day he had been in his office in Ashland, he continued, in two weeks.

He considered his refinery very lucky to be running at all. "Some large refineries are shut down, and others are running at one-half their capacity," he told Martin. The East Coast was severely handicapped by lack of crude oil. Some ports were blockaded by the Germans for days on end, a fact of which many of their occupants were not aware. Such is life without full news coverage.

That same month, the Japanese captured Rangoon, capital of

Burma, and in an air strike at Ceylon, similar to that on Pearl Harbor, sank the British aircraft carrier *Hermes,* two heavy cruisers and many lesser vessels. In Southeast Asia, they had already sunk the British heavy cruiser *Repulse* and the new battleship *Prince of Wales.* In their various attacks the Japanese succeeded in effectively destroying the supremacy of the British Navy in Asian waters for all time.

In the U.S., the Mississippi was crowded with more vessels and cargo than Mark Twain ever knew. Those who thought the glory of the river had ended with the era of the nineteenth century paddlewheels were confounded. Towboats, such as the monsters Ashland Oil was constructing, were actually misnamed, should have been called "pushboats." Constructed for strength and not grace, they squat in the water. In their bows are two "knees"— upright irons positioned against the rear ends of a barge: the boat pushes. The barges are lashed together in pairs, six or eight to a "tow." The boat and barges together make water vehicles larger than most ocean liners. Photographs abound in the Ashland Oil offices of its towboats pushing barges, the whole assemblage larger than the *Queen Mary.*

The river, notoriously meandering, with riptides and cross currents for much of its length, foggy, carried more than 200 million barrels of crude a year and 21 million barrels daily from 1942–1945, when the figures were later totaled and averaged.

Railroads sidetracked crack passenger trains in those days to allow tank cars, loaded with crude oil, to redball through. It was not unusual for motorists to wait, sitting in their gas-rationed cars in which they were forbidden to travel more than 35 miles an hour (to conserve tires), while as many as 70 tank cars in a series trundled past.

Ashland Oil & Refining, located beside the Big Sandy River just below its union with the Ohio, with the C&O tracks running alongside it, was ideally situated to receive and refine crude oil, then push its products toward the eastern industrial belt where fuel and lubricating oil had never been more sorely needed. It could ship gasoline into the numerous towns of southern Ohio, eastern and western Kentucky and southern Pennsylvania.

But the overall size of the Catlettsburg refinery was too small.

Blazer wrote Martin, "We must expand to survive." The major oil companies were pressing Washington daily. The industry—together with everyone else—was feeling the initial impact of the $34 billion the government was shoveling into the economy in 1942 to help the nation step up its pace.

Unemployment, a running sore on the body politic since 1930, was shriveling under the effects of this mighty medicine. The gross national product (a term not then in the ordinary vocabulary) in 1939 was only $91 billion. By 1942, the money of the nation had been increased by more than a third; more funds were to come. One of the most extraordinary industrial flowerings of all time was to result.

In April 1942, the Reconstruction Finance Corporation sent Ashland contracts for the 100 octane aviation gasoline plant. The Lummus Company, already weighted by commitments to build similar plants for Continental Oil, General Petroleum, Globe Oil and Magnolia Oil, was selected by Ashland to be the engineer.

Altogether, Lummus had some $300 million of such contracts on its hands. Its staff and management were severely overworked, as were most mature men with skills during this period. Willy Anderson and his boys had reason to feel aggrieved; they had barely dragged themselves through the nation's longest and most enervating depression, with its stringent economies, corner-cuts and pressures, to find themselves plunged into the long, hard hours and the seven-day week of the war effort.

Labor, however, experienced its own flowering. The wage and price freeze combined with full employment and the creation of new skills and new standards to elevate the living habits and incomes of millions. World War II brought a change of status to millions in the U.S. It was, paradoxically, during this period that the assumptions of a better life became firmly imbedded for most American families. The belief was encouraged by some of the most extraordinary exhortations of which government was capable. FDR had produced, within days of Pearl Harbor and during a conference with his allies in Quebec, the draft of the United Nations, unveiling for the first time his plan to reintroduce international law to the world. Essentially it was a structure to outlaw aggression and aggressors, based on the cooperative leadership of the Big Four: England, Russia, the United States and China. In 1942, the nation found itself grappling with the forces of darkness as a prelude to a rainbow-hued world to come. It was a heady vision.

The nation did not entirely drop its disputatious habits, however. Congress, some of whose members were still mightily suspicious of the ogres of industry, launched a series of hearings into PAW, motivated largely by distrust of committees staffed by men from industry. By war's end, 100 such hearings were held on oil. No large fault was found, but it could not be said that a search was not made.

At Ashland, Blazer was absent more than he was present. He kept in touch by telephone—an instrument that some men thought he wore, personally, as other men wear wristwatches—and a stream of memos. Even *in absentia,* his was a constant, brooding presence. Ed Emrick, in charge of priorities, presumably had a month's time, according to the government, to draw up a list of the materials and supplies needed for the construction of the 100 octane plant. Under his speed and Blazer's goad combined, he and his men produced the lengthy, fearsomely detailed document *in five days.* Blazer personally rushed it by cab to the proper office, arriving ten minutes before Continental Oil. Continental, who had been scheduled first, protested. But the office of materials and supplies pragmatically said, "First come, first served," and Ashland had stolen a large march on time.

At the refinery, capacity was increased another 15–20 per cent; a pipeline to Kenova was built so the new high octane plant would be able to load and unload from river barges. Another new towboat, *The Tri-State,* was received after making the run from Memphis to Ashland in 9 days, half the expected time.

New problems and new orders poured out of Washington in a stream. Ashland was forbidden to continue the production and sale of coal spray oil, a highly profitable product, and was ordered to redirect this production into fuel oil, a badly needed but less profitable item. "Our choice is to do government business or go out of business," Blazer wrote Martin.

In common with other industrial plants, Ashland now had guards at the gates. The entire country experienced, in addition to other advances, strides in authoritarianism. The government establishment, one million strong in 1940, was to expand more than three times during 1942–1945, not counting the armed forces; these reached twelve million. Altogether, the increase in federal authority, size and complexity was awesome.

Early in May 1942, American forces surrendered at Corregidor and the Bataan death march started; Rommel led a force of three German and seven Italian divisions to capture Tobruk; Japan appeared solidly ensconced amid a bead of islands that spread across the southeast Pacific north of Australia: Sumatra, Java, Lumbok, Flores, Timor and New Guinea.

Late in May 1942, the first stemming of the tide appeared. The U.S. Navy won a great engagement over the Japanese in the Battle of the Coral Sea and followed that in early June by another naval victory in the Battle of Midway. Montgomery, heading a revitalized British force, started toward Rommel.

Through June and July 1942, Chamberlain, Ware and Morgan watched, agonized, as the local draft board took, in batches, their most experienced men. "We are a young company," Blazer wrote, "and we have a larger than average number of young men. We are losing more men, therefore, than most other firms." Most of the young engineers whom Chamberlain had recruited had turned out to be reserve officers; they had long ago left for the conflict.

Art Points and his assistants had figured out the effects of the excess profits tax on the Ashland earnings. They concluded that 75 per cent would be subject to a tax of 87½ per cent, leaving 12½ per cent, a figure Blazer grumpily described as "no great incentive."

In July 1942, Rommel was stopped by Montgomery in the Battle of El Alamein, and for the first time, the German armies began to experience shortages of fuel.

Work began on the Big Inch.[3] It required the digging of a ditch 4 feet deep and 3 feet wide to extend from Longview, Texas, to New York City with a branch from Phoenixville, Pennsylvania. Into that ditch was placed a pipeline 2 feet in diameter to run under 30 rivers, 200 creeks, uncounted streets, highways, railroad

[3] A phrase used by pipeline workers—a colorful group—for any pipe larger than a foot in diameter.

tracks and terrain for 1,400 miles. The pipe weighed 100 pounds to the foot; a ton every 20 feet. Then the ditch had to be covered over. The project was to take 2 days and 2 weeks more than a year and would cost $95 million. The Little Inch, begun earlier, consisted of 1,475 miles of a 20-inch pipeline extending from Beaumont, Texas, to Linden, New Jersey, at a cost of $43.5 million. The Little Inch took 225 days. Both carried crude oil to the East.

By July 1942, the Ashland river fleet consisted of 5 towboats and 34 barges. The sales force had dwindled—during a war, salesmen are eminently dispensable. The work force was being increased; the Blazer team was becoming more expert and skilled in special areas.

The company was undergoing a great shift, psychologically: like the rest of the nation, it was fitting into a harness of responsibility within a framework of national necessity. The oil industry, introduced to the idea of legalized pooling, rate fixing and Washington jurisdiction over their internal affairs during the early New Deal days, was finding itself even more regulated and directed during the war. It was becoming daily more accustomed to the idea that its own wishes and directions were secondary to the national interest.

In Washington, within Administration circles particularly, the switch was extreme. There were men who came into government service during the war period whose ideas of control were more sweeping than the nation had ever before seen. J. Howard Marshall, serving again as Ralph Davies' assistant, said later, "Some of those men wanted to regulate the entire oil industry down to the location of the last filling station pump." Marshall had learned better in the years since 1933; his faith in all-embracing planning had diminished considerably. He and Blazer, who had become good friends, used to lunch and sometimes dine together in Washington, and enjoyed swapping tales about the whims of life under directives.

Ashland Oil & Refining Company had made a jump forward the importance of which was, in later years, increasingly more evident. It had moved from a tiny refinery in a nation studded with them, to a refinery capable of competing with some of the best. Certainly, in its regional location, Ashland had lifted itself beyond its competitors. The excess profits tax had the same effect on its management that the planners in Washington had desired. Not all Capitol plans were, by any stretch of thought, either impractical or unsophisticated: the tax sent Blazer's mind into the direction of new ventures, and in particular, of crude oil.

Ashland men, searching for crude oil, had already gone as far afield as Texas and Mississippi, where they were purchasing large amounts for river shipment to Kentucky. Now the question of actually drilling for oil on behalf of the country began to seem more attractive to Blazer: it was better to drill for oil than to simply accumulate earnings that were paid to the government in taxes. Allowances for crude oil search and drill expenditures were generous.

In this observation, Blazer concurred with the industry. Never before had the need for new crude oil been clearer: to simply rely upon existing national reserves at this period would have been tantamount to national suicide. Exploration teams appeared all over the landscape; a record number of new wells were being drilled. In the period between 1941 and 1945, more wells would be drilled than in any other four-year period in the nation's history, a record that included the periods of earlier booms.

In August 1942, the preliminary cost estimates for the 100 octane plant were totaled and approved. The government would put up $6.7 million, and Ashland itself $250,000 toward the installation. Blazer was beginning to think that it was all proceeding too slowly, and he wondered aloud if the man Lummus had put in charge was up to the task.

That month, Stalin charged Churchill with cowardice because a second front had not been opened in Europe. Later in the month, the United States and England together landed three expeditionary forces in North Africa. One, entirely American, landed at Casablanca; two mixed forces landed on two points on the Mediterranean portion of Algeria. Despite the forebodings of the military experts, the raw U.S. troops conducted themselves creditably; fighting ended in three days.

The following month, September, was 1942 fiscal year's end at Ashland. For the first time, the company's net sales had exceeded seven figures. They had, in fact, more than doubled, going from $8.2 million the year before, to $16.7 million. Net profits had not increased proportionately, but were still impressive in terms of ratio and totaled $1.1 million. It was to be several years before they would reach such a total again.

Despite the fact that government business was booming, not all aspects of the market kept pace. Hugh Jenks found his asphalt sales burgeoning, because the military need for asphalt for new landing strips, roads, camps and other uses was enormous. But civilian gasoline purchases had been sharply curtailed by the limitations on individuals and pleasure driving. With no new automobiles being produced by Detroit for the duration of the war, people treated their cars with a loving attention never before accorded.

In order to make improvements in the refinery, Ashland had to describe them in detail and apply for permission from Washington. It is revealing of the period that Blazer was elated enough to report to the directors when this approval was received: at a cost of a price hike of between 1 and 2 per cent, the efficiency of the refinery was raised another 15 per cent.

Blazer's trips to Chicago during this period were motivated by the need to keep in touch with his directors, and also to line up financing. The pressure cooker of war forced expansion, and government contracts did not alone answer the question of capital funds. These had to be raised either from earnings, borrowings or the sale of issues. This took thought, time and effort. As usual, the whole management team was involved. We find a good friend of both Blazer's and Everett Wells's, Ross Shoolroy, receiving a welcoming letter because he bought a large block of Ashland Oil & Refining stock. The purchase was especially gratifying because Shoolroy operated a string of Fair Price gasoline stations selling gasoline in Ohio and was a stout competitor on his home ground.

In the last month of 1942, due, according to a letter to the directors, to "the great number of inexperienced operators with whom we now have to work," a fire broke out in the refinery. Fortunately, there were no casualties, but "flames shot a hundred feet into the air."

By the end of December, the men were struggling against still another Ohio flood. The firm's towboats and barges were fogbound somewhere on the wandering reaches of the Mississippi. At Ashland, the men laboriously packed and piled sandbags, constructed boats with which to travel around when the waters came, built a temporary structure to house perishables, removed gasoline pumps to spare their motors from inundation, drained the underground tanks and refilled them with water. The ordinary vicissitudes of life, vexatious at all times, seemed especially onerous when added to the strains and tensions of a nation at war.

In January 1943, Roosevelt and Churchill met at Casablanca, a location their joint expeditionary forces had liberated in November, and issued a communiqué stating that their war aims included the unconditional surrender of the enemy. Some experts, then and now, took a critical view of this statement and position, claiming that it reinforced the dictators' holds on their people, but it seemed to most persons a proper stand to take. How could anyone treat the Nazis as though they were responsible leaders of a nation?

In far-off Russia in January 1943, the Soviet armies started a drive to recapture Rostov. Under their pounding, the Germans began to retreat through an ever-narrowing corridor to the east. In early February, after getting 34,000 men out by air and losing 100,000 dead, the German General Von Paulus surrendered with 93,000 men. The high tide of German advance in the east began to ebb.

In the United States industry continued to rise. Unemployment disappeared by early 1943. Production of tanks grew beyond 2,000 a month; planes were heading toward 7,500 within 6 months. Hotel rooms and restaurant tables were alike beginning to be hard to get; stores were selling items held in stock for years; wages were on their way up by 86 per cent, while the cost of living, restrained by price controls, went up only 29 per cent. The result was an enormous increase in the purchasing power of millions of wage-earners. Millions were learning new skills, gaining new views.

In the midst of war, a new sort of revolution was taking place. Men in government, in the sciences, in industry, in academe and in business were commingling as partners on an immeasurably expanded scale. This had always been true to some extent, but mainly for the men at the top. Now these contacts extended downward to the middle section of the pyramid, which itself had been expanded. Some observers, dazed by the phenomenon, thought the whole country had turned middle class, but this was an exaggeration based on appearances.

A divide between the sciences and the humanities, centuries long in building, began to close under the pressures of wartime cooperation. In the process of this collaboration on a variety of levels, it was to be learned that the naiveté of science was balanced by incredible advances in physical knowledge; that the social expertise of the humanities was marred by a childishly limited knowledge of the physical facts of the universe. The shock of these disparities and differences was to give rise to considerable difficulties later, but during the war, the combinations were fruitful beyond all previous imaginings.

Into this common effort were swept propagandists, engineers, administrators, technicians of all types, professors, academics, salesmen, businessmen. Practically every profession emerged enhanced. All branches of learning were expanded; medicine took a giant step forward; chemistry came into its own; physics—at the end of the war—would dazzle everyone. Yet it is not understood that the greatest combinations that were created functioned not under military methods but under the businessmen, that the largest contributions were made by the corporation executives who were able to harness these various talents by applying the subtle systems of peace under the urgencies of war. These were the men who took a labor force predominantly untrained and unskilled, and equipped it with the training and the skills to supply a war machine mightier in weapons and logistics than any the world had ever seen.

Perhaps because the miracle was so widespread, it remained largely invisible to many, including the experts. Few top businessmen have been asked to describe their methods or their discoveries during this period.

Nevertheless, the war days exposed many to new patterns of thought and attitude that were invigorating though sometimes shocking. Blazer thought some of the men in Washington leaned toward the view that the oil industry should operate its crude oil properties and transportation facilities in one great, commonly held pool. He was astonished at the concept, because he knew that these combinations would have to be untangled after the war if the competitive enterprise system was to be restored.

The year 1943 started off fairly auspiciously, as far as he was concerned, with the union automatically renewing its contract. War regulations forbade strikes during the emergency, and substituted instead arbitration procedures. But Blazer was disturbed over what seemed to him the slowness of the work on the 100 octane plant.

He was disquieted to discover the costs were 40 per cent higher than Lummus—and hence Ashland—had anticipated. Apparently he had not yet realized that this was to be true generally: estimates were made in one time and clime, and work done in another. Not even the most rigorous price controls could restrain the effects of the vast monies pumped into the economy, or the human effects upon productivity of long hours, tired specialists, and a work force that was using everyone—competents and incompetents alike.

In early March 1943, the firm hired Harrison O'Rear, of Mt. Sterling, Kentucky, an old wildcatter who had enjoyed, at times, considerable success, and had retired to a profitable farm. O'Rear was made head of a newly formed Land Department, and was already making plans to drill two wells. By this time, even Ned Seaton, ex-banker and treasurer of the company, was deeply involved in details of crude oil negotiations and searches; so were Art Points and, of course, Bill Keffer.

But progress in the 100 octane plant was rapid compared to that in other locations. The firm benefited from being in virtuous Ashland, where the usual attractions of sin were notably absent. A letter to the directors describes how the original simple plant had now come to handle atmospheric crude oil distillation, vacuum distillation, cracking, vacuum distillation of cracked residue, and manufacture of cumene and codimer from cracking plant gases. Products included gasoline, naphtha, furnace distillates, feed stock for the new 100 octane aviation gasoline plant, cylinder stock, lubricating oil, straight reduced asphalt, cracked gasoline, cracked furnace distillate, industrial fuel oil, reduced cracked asphalt, cumene, codimer and 3 million cubic feet of gas per day. The Dubbs unit, designed in 1926 to crack 750 barrels of reduced crude and to produce 350 barrels of gasoline a day had become, 17 years later, with additions, improvements and ingenuity, one of the most sophisticated crude oil and cracking units to be found, operated with only 5 men to a shift. Other new installations at the plant included a 130-foot tower upon which auxiliaries were hung. When the new 100 octane plant was complete, the entire installation would begin to resemble some great, sprawled destroyer at night, with lights and flames flickering, and the smell of oil hanging heavy in the air.

Then, on June 15, 1943, Boyd Morgan, the general superintendent, became impatient with what appeared to be some delay and, pushing aside a workman, started to remove a manhole cover to help cool a flash chamber. Blazer happened along, in company with two men from Louisville, and saw a knot of workmen standing around watching their energetic superintendent. He noted a man was standing by with a steam hose in the chamber. A careful man, Blazer ordered everyone to get back, then turned with his companions and walked away himself.

"I was about thirty feet away," he wrote, "when there was a flash; I turned to see Tom Brown running toward me with his clothes afire. I rolled him on the ground and extinguished the flames, then noticed Crosby Rogers lying on the pavement with his clothes burning, not ten feet from me. I helped several other men beat these flames out. His clothing was almost completely burned away. A few minutes later, Mr. Morgan, who had run in the opposite direction, came walking from the other side of the cracking unit. He was almost completely naked and his skin and hair showed evidence of severe burns . . . None of the three lived through the night."

It was the worst catastrophe the refinery had experienced.

Fortunately, Blazer had met and talked with E. A. Brown, an experienced superintendent at Sohio, some time previously, and Brown chose the next day to call up and say he was available. A combination of union trouble and the shutdown of three Sohio refineries had combined to squeeze him out. Blazer hired him immediately.

In July and August 1943, Montgomery and Patton, each with a flotilla of ships and a quarter of a million troops, landed in two places on the island of Sicily. But the German and Italian troops, some 100,000 strong, evaded battle, escaped to the mainland, and lived to slow the occupation of Italy later.

The German lines were stabilized, at this point, but Hitler had lost thirty-eight divisions and thirty-eight satellite divisions, and had been driven away from the invaluable—to him—oil fields of the Caucasus. The military men of Germany, with North Africa lost and the drive into Russia at a stalemate, recognized that their cause was lost. Their hands were not strong enough politically, however, to overthrow Hitler. The Allies had already declared total surrender to be their objective, and Hitler's internal terror machine was operating at top efficiency. It was at this point that the Nazis, insane and determined to carry their suicidal doctrines to their logical end, launched a campaign of extermination within their sinister empire. They began the slaughter of Jews, Poles, Russians, Slavs, political "unreliables" and dissidents within their ranks. The horror was to begin methodically and become intense.

Mussolini fell in late July 1943; the council in Rome, composed of men who had followed him faithfully for twenty years, stripped him of his power and had him arrested after he left its presence. His jail was a comfortable hotel suite.

FDR and his intimate advisors, at the same time, produced two further fill-ins on their UN plan: one was a UN Food and Agricultural organization, called FAO, and the other was a UN Relief and Rehabilitation agency—UNRRA. Their minds were occupied with the shape of the postwar world, but, along the lines of President Wilson in a bygone era, with singular altruism. The role of the United States, in their view, would be mainly eleemosynary.

At Ashland, contemporary events shadowed Blazer's activities. He wrote Jim Martin at one point that "management seems to have become mainly a defensive operation." The phrase was well put. He had the union arising with a petty grievance on every occasion on one side, and Washington seeking renegotiations almost in advance of orders on the other. Between the two, management found itself answering a variety of questions regarding its operations, systems, plans and directions a good deal of the time.

It is no wonder that Blazer wrote back warmly when he received a pleasant and unexpected note from Joe Levin of A. G. Becker & Company in Chicago expressing admiration for Ashland's 1942 annual report, and discreetly mentioning, in passing, that he was connected with a potentially useful financial firm. Blazer had worked closely with Levin years ago at the *Cap and Gown* yearbook when they were fellow students at the University of Chicago in 1916; Levin's note seemed like a reminder of simpler and more friendly days.

The differences between those days and the autumn of 1943 were almost as great as those between civilizations. At this point in time during World War II, the country was spending money at five times the peak rate during the first war. Unlike World War I, however, stockholders were not benefiting from the greatly increased activities of corporations: the stock market was extremely listless. Some small manufacturers were benefiting, but other small businesses were languishing. Tourist camps, for instance, were mainly vacant; firms that could not shift into war work were hard hit. But farmers prospered, also engineering firms of every type.

In September 1943, reflecting this situation, Ashland net profits amounted to $733,865 on net sales of $17 million. The Company had spent, since the previous September, almost $2 million in improvements and additions to the Catlettsburg refinery—more than at any previous similar period—and the 100 octane plant was on the verge, counting two months as a verge, of going onstream.

The new Land Department had increased the crude oil reserves of the firm by 50 per cent; the number of towboats the company was operating had increased to seven. The cost of the 100 octane plant, in dollar terms, had almost doubled from original estimates. To Blazer, this was a source of mortification, but Ashland was far from being at the head of the list in this respect in the industry. The Company debts, mainly to the Equitable Life Assurance Company, had grown to $4 million.

The management group at Ashland regarded its labor relations with pride in its 1943 annual report. One suspects that the twenty-year record of continuous work at the refinery without a stoppage or a strike, unique during the turbulent thirties, was inserted in presentiment of imminent labor trouble: it was Blazer's way of reminding the directors that management had done well in this respect. Behind the scenes, the argumentative Willy Anderson had checked out the strict new general superintendent, Mr. Brown, and, through channels equally informal, had asked for his head. It had been refused.

In October 1943, FDR, Churchill and Stalin met at Teheran and issued various communiqués dealing with the United Nations, and agreed that Iran would remain independent. This was virtually the only nation bordering Russia to be so spared. It was a victory for the West that shone more brightly against the dark fates of its neighbors.

In the Pacific, the U.S. and Australian forces had thrust northward in two great forks from Australia east and west of Truk. They had recaptured New Guinea after frightful struggles against the enemy and disease, then worked through the Solomon Islands and the Marshalls to attack the Marianas.

Stilwell and Mountbatten had penetrated Burma from India, were attempting to cut their own avenue through to China: the Burma Road. In 1943, they were far from their goal.

The year 1944 saw the mounting of the real Allied offensives; the 100 octane plant at Catlettsburg came onstream at exactly the moment when its production would be most helpful for the effort.

Nevertheless, in January 1944, the union refused to renegotiate a new contract, and by the nineteenth of January voted to give Willy Anderson and his aides the right to strike. Blazer called upon the international officers, some of whom came in to see him from Oklahoma, and found, to his pleasure, that they shared his views: the war effort could not afford such luxuries. Meantime, new employees were added for the 100 octane unit; Ned Seaton was joined on the board of the Second National Bank by Everett Wells; Bill Keffer's son-in-law was president of the Third National Bank in Ashland, and he was on that board: the management of the company was completely integrated in the city.

And by this time, the question of Blazer's health had recurred often enough to give the directors food for thought. Informally, they suggested that it might be a good idea to search for a possible successor. All men are mortal, and Blazer was showing signs of strain. He was fifty-four in 1944, and retirement age no longer seemed so far away that it could be ignored. He himself voiced no great objections to these speculations. He mentioned that he lacked an engineering and a legal background. It seemed to him that in the years to come, the new head of the company would need one or the other. In this he was, as usual, ahead of the men of his time, who bitterly resented the appearances of suddenly paramount specialists.

Nevertheless, signs of cresting success were abundant for Ashland. In May 1944, Blazer was a naval guest aboard a flattop in the Atlantic, together with the head of Standard of New Jersey; he received a letter from the New York Curb informing him that out of their 676 common stocks issued, only 194 had paid dividends every year for the previous ten years, and that Ashland was among them. That same month, Blazer wrote Jim Martin that he was now on a fruit juice, buttermilk and black coffee diet, and felt better than ever.

A sad letter reached him a few weeks later, from Joseph Halle Schaffner, nephew and executor of his uncle's estate. Mr. Halle, whose opinions had always meant much to Blazer, and who had been a most valuable and important man in his life, had died.

Life, however, provides replacements for us all. The previous summer, Mr. and Mrs. Levin took a trip to Colorado on the Rock Island railroad. Trains then were crowded with servicemen and women; civilians had low priority and were in the minority. The Levins were sitting in the observation car, and Joe's attention was drawn to "a very attractive woman traveling with a very tall young boy, whose legs extended well into the corridor. From their resemblance and her fond looks at him, it was obvious they were mother and son."

A Wave asked this attractive passenger if the train stopped at Aledo, Illinois. A bell rang in Joe's mind, and he asked the woman with the boy if she came from Aledo; he had gone to school with a man who had. The passenger said it was her husband's hometown.

She was, of course, Mrs. Paul Blazer, traveling with their

youngest son, Stuart.[4] Levin, delighted at the coincidence, enjoyed the conversation.

"It also," he said later, "reawakened my interest in the Ashland Oil & Refining Company."

When the Ashland annual report reached Levin's desk at A. G. Becker & Co. in early 1944, Levin did not content himself with simply writing a note, but impulsively picked up the phone and called Blazer. The conversation led to an invitation to come to Kentucky, and their business relationship began.

That summer in 1944, the wars on both the Atlantic and the Pacific fronts became arenas of Allied initiative. Normandy was invaded by forces directed by Eisenhower on June sixth. Nine days later, the U.S. Pacific forces mounted an attack on the strongly held island of Saipan, and at almost the same time launched drives against Tinian and Guam. In the east, the Russians began a drive on all fronts. In Italy, mixed U.S.-British forces had drawn a line north of Rome and were battling stubborn German forces in the center of the boot. In the welter of wartime dispatches, it was hard for the average person to understand the grand design in progress. To this day it is not widely realized that Hitler threw his strongest forces against the west, rather than against the east.

At Ashland, the refinery was running all out; the new 100 octane plant was designed to process 3,080 barrels of crude a day and, in a manner to which the firm had become accustomed, had already exceeded its designed capacity. It was producing an average 3,800 barrels a day. In one 24-hour period, it had processed between 4,000 and 5,000 barrels but Blazer admitted this was extraordinary, and not to be normally expected. The plant was inherently dangerous, he said. "Hardly a day passes without a fatal accident in one or another of its counterparts in the rest of the industry." It handled hydrofluoric acid, which produced one of the most dangerous of all gases. Contact was fatal.

[4] Young Stuart had a chronically dislocated shoulder, and Mrs. Blazer was taking him to the Medical Center at Davenport. When the train stopped at Rock Island, they were leaving for Aledo to see the Blazer family.

Nevertheless, the war was going to end in the foreseeable future. Jesse Jones, Secretary of Commerce and of almost every other aspect of the business side of the FDR Administration, sent Ashland a letter questioning their intentions for the plant after the war—did they plan to buy or lease it? The old world was drawing to a convulsive end; nobody knew the form of the new.

Blazer assured the government the company would want to continue operating the 100 octane plant after the war. In the meantime he sent letters to the directors discussing the problem of postwar financing. As time passed, he looked at Joe Levin with an increasingly speculative eye: A. G. Becker & Co. was one of the largest handlers of commercial paper (short-term business loans) in the nation, and was known to be an excellent brokerage firm and a strong underwriter of new issues. Blazer began a cautious game of "let's bid" between Jim Martin, who was anxious that his associates handle whatever new issues the company introduced, and Joe Levin, of Becker.

By September 1944, some other conversations held during the summer bore fruit: J. Howard Marshall, who had been an assistant to Ralph Davies and Harold Ickes during the petroleum administrations of the NIRA days as well as PAW, was out of government and back at the practice of law in San Francisco.[5] Marshall, who by this time considered himself in the oil industry, had probably the broadest personal acquaintance with the men and conditions of the industry of anyone, and it was natural that Blazer would turn to him for help in finding a successor. The more often the two men discussed the problem, however, the more obvious it appeared that Marshall himself was most eminently qualified. Blazer talked to the directors, who were delighted, and Marshall came to the Ashland Oil & Refining Company September 1, 1944, as president.

Some rearranging was necessary, of course. The wage stabilization board was still in existence, and Blazer had to have their approval of salary. The board refused to allow the company to go beyond $25,000 a year. Blazer, who by then was making $75,000, asked if he could reduce his own salary $25,000 so the new presi-

5 As a partner in the firm of Pillsbury, Madison & Sutro.

dent could come in at $50,000 a year. That, it seemed, was all right.

That left only the question of rearranging the titles. Jim Martin agreed to relinquish the post of chairman of the board, and became vice-chairman and Paul Blazer was made chairman.

This was a considerable step. In its entire existence, the company built around the refining and marketing operations at Ashland had never known another chief: there had been a difference in age and experience between him and his closest assistants. It was not that Blazer himself created the distance: in terms of compensation—and that is one measurement—the second highest salary in the company until September 1, 1944, was paid to Everett Wells, who held the title of vice-president and received $20,000 a year. Then came Bill Keffer, with $17,000. Then there was a sharp drop to the next level, in the $10,000 to $12,000 range, occupied by Alex Chamberlain, Art Points, Ned Seaton, Ed Emrick, Palmer Talbutt, Hugh Jenks and M. C. Dupree. It was not that Blazer was parsimonious. This was the salary scale under which he had, himself, developed. Until World War II, the top man received a top wage, but there was a great divide between his wage and that received by the number two, three and the rest. The war was to change this considerably: middle salaries were to expand as the middle group itself expanded; the top did not go higher, but the middle moved nearer the top.

Howard Marshall came to Ashland Oil & Refining in September 1944, at the close of its fiscal year. Net sales were $18.7 million, and the net profits $771,939—little more than the year before. It was a wartime year; there was another wartime year yet to come. Great shifts and changes were taking place, but the majority of these were the results of wartime violence; their significance would not be apparent for a time. Internally, as far as Ashland Oil was concerned, Marshall's arrival closed the pages in a long and interesting, but extremely difficult chapter.

Reading that chapter, with its beginnings rooted in the careless 1920s and post-World War I America, and carrying it through the terrible thirties with their sour taste and drab problems, was like reading of another world and another time. The young man

Blazer, with his snapping eyes and collar-ad appearance, all brisk and go-gettum, the protégé of Senator Combs; the diligent young refiner, who hardly counted as a factor in the expansive J. Fred Miles's activities, changed during this period into the solid citizen of Ashland, the executive who haunted the refinery day and night, slowly maturing into a seasoned veteran with graying hair and a smiling reserve even financiers found formidable. The tiny refinery on the banks of the Big Sandy, once described by Palmer Talbutt as "little better than a skimming plant," had become a great complex: a scientist's wonderland of pipes, towers, separators and chambers, at which passing motorists in the evening would stare as at some monster bubbling mysteriously away in a continuous process, altering the hydrocarbons of oil into a continuous stream of petrochemical products.

By following his own star instead of one selected by another, Blazer had turned away from the pursuit of wealth and become a professional manager. But until the war, his management method was essentially a one-man show; his top team consisted of assistants. During the war, they became managers and specialists in their own rights; both because the company became too large for Blazer to personally operate, and because his own long absences left them on their own.

But the hiring of J. Howard Marshall was recognition that even in theory Blazer alone was no longer sufficient. Marshall was thirty-nine to Blazer's fifty-four; he knew even more people in government and business; he was well-known and liked in Washington and academia alike; he was a lawyer with a lawyer's keen eye for the significance of a detail and the meaning of relationships; he was experienced with the oil industry and with other managements, other firms.

It started out as a great combination.

END OF THE OLD ORDER

In October 1944, when Howard Marshall was still getting settled, the refinery at Catlettsburg consisted of the enlarged original plant No. 1, and the new 100 octane plant. To the naked eye, and especially to an engineer's eye, they looked like one continuous plant. But Blazer and his men had made a distinction. Such a distinction existed legally, of course, and the men of the union under Willy Anderson were outraged to discover that this distinction would be used to separate the workers in that plant from theirs.

Willy's response was to pump more air into the minor grievances that arose, and in the course of his enthusiastic, minor warfare, made the error of encouraging some men to refuse to obey orders he considered beyond their sphere of specific duties. For this encouragement, he and his handful of followers were dismissed, in the middle of October.

Immediately, all the men walked out. The International officers, alerted by both sides, informed Willy the work stoppage was illegal, that he had recourse to the federally established mediation proceedings, but not to a strike. Willy, however, was too angry to arbitrate, and seventy-two hours after they had walked out, the men walked back. The major part of the union trouble was eliminated, a victory that greatly relieved the harassed management. No trouble of this sort was to arise again. In comparison to the vast upheavals that took place elsewhere, it hardly merits comment, but in the close-knit relationships of the tiny valley, it is still a subject of conversation when unionism arises. Willy Anderson today, living in another city, is in the insurance business, and from all reports is a solid citizen; one speculates he may even be a conservative citizen. Such are the lessons of life.

The pace of the refinery operations continued to quicken. Increases in this center of the company operations were equaled by corollary increases in transport efforts, sales, and the volume of crude oil. Throughput picked up to 22,000 barrels of crude a day. In one 72-hour period at this time, the firm processed 66,000 barrels, almost twice as much as the operations throughput the first month the firm was in business.

This expanded volume was fed, not only from Ashland, but from virtually every other functioning refinery, into the military machine put together by the Allies. The machine had grown to monstrous proportions, and the time of its strongest application against the enemy in both the Pacific and the European theaters had arrived.

In the autumn of 1944, when the demand for oil was not only

at its peak but headed for a long period of continuous production, the Rumanian, Bulgarian and Finnish governments attempted to extricate themselves from the Nazis and sued for peace. The effort did not deflect the Soviet juggernaut, which moved into Sofia, crossed Bulgaria, entered Yugoslavia, and occupied Belgrade by the middle of October. That meant that Hitler lost the oil fields of Rumania: a mighty blow against his military position. At the same time, the remnants of Poland's last army were extinguished between the Russians and the Germans.

At the time that the Ashland refinery experienced its tiny strike, the U.S. forces in the Pacific invaded Leyte in the Philippines, and for the first time Japan astonished the world with its kamikazes.

Late in the fall of 1944, the Allied armies in the west of Europe began to penetrate the body of Germany itself. Hitler was still holding the survivors of 8 million civilian slaves of various nationalities: 10 million Jews, 5.7 million Russian prisoners, and millions of prisoners from other armies. Extermination of these peoples was accelerated.

By this time, the U.S. was producing 75 per cent of all the petroleum products employed by the vast armies and farflung operations of the Allies, a production three times the combined production of all its allies together.

Despite the fierce struggles that were to continue on both sides of the world, parallel plans for the postwar world were underway on almost every planning level. In Kentucky, Paul Blazer was appointed a member of the Kentucky Postwar Advisory Planning Commission, and made chairman of its transportation committee, as well as vice-chairman of the commission itself. Howard Marshall was spending a good part of his time in Washington, attempting both to unsnarl the inevitable tangles regarding materials, men and supplies, and trying to anticipate postwar developments.

The business brains of the company toiled with a suggestion relayed from Mr. Holliday of Sohio, who thought drilling costs should be capitalized instead of expensed, an accounting approach that took cognizance of the government tax experts—those busy beavers.

In Europe, although reeling in the east from the hammer blows of the Russians across a broad front, Hitler, reflecting his deeper hatred of Western civilization, mobilized his forces for a counter-attack on the west. The Battle of the Bulge, an alarmingly power-ful try, began in December 1944, and Christmas for countless families in the U.S. was darkened by telegrams of death.

The year 1945 entered the world to find the men of Ashland engrossed. Eighteen thousand barrels of crude a day were pouring into Catlettsburg by barge alone but they were not enough. Marshall had been plunged into the crude oil situation, and Blazer wrote to Jim Martin that "Marshall has proven to be a tireless worker."

So tireless was he, in fact, that gossips in the oil industry whispered that Ashland Oil & Refining had actually been sold to one of the major companies. Marshall, they said, was a big com-pany man, placed with Ashland by the mysterious new owners.

In February 1945, Marshall, Everett Wells and Blazer, after some secret conversations, concluded a deal with the Texas Company that provided more crude oil. For a price of $700,000, Texas sold Ashland 300 to 400 stripper wells in eastern Kentucky, a pipeline system and a small refinery at Pryse. The pipeline ran from the oil fields to Beattyville, Kentucky, and the refinery had a small 1,600-barrel-a-day capacity. The properties had belonged to the long-defunct Great Southern Oil & Refining Company, founded by a group of Kentucky businessmen and Paul Blazer and Eric Shatford. He remembered the construction of that line vividly; recalled selling the output of that refinery through Kentucky, southern Pennsylvania and Ohio as a beginner in the industry. Palmer Talbutt had learned his refinery knowledge at the Pryse refinery; he grinned when he heard about the purchase.

In Europe, the Battle of the Bulge came to an end the same month; the struggle had lasted for weeks. February 1945 departed and March arrived, bringing another flood in Ashland, but a relatively minor one. In Washington the Circuit Court ruled that oil companies could not write off the expenses of oil well drilling. "Some companies will be caught," Blazer predicted. The decision was so broad—no exception being granted for dry holes—that Blazer made a special trip to Washington to discuss the matter with his friend Fred Vinson, now Secretary of the Treasury, and returned to tell everyone that Vinson said a new law should be drawn. On March 6, barely a month after the Texas purchase, the company bought the F.H.E. Oil Company for $500,000.

In April 1945, Marshall expanded the crude oil department by the addition of a Mr. Arnold, from British American Oil Producing Company who came in as a vice president at a salary of $22,500. Arnold was dispatched to set up an office and work from Tulsa, Oklahoma; Sam Wells was to do the same in Evansville, Indiana.

An equally large step was taken in a business sense: the bidding between Martin and Levin had ended, with A. G. Becker handling a new issue. The ending had come about when Levin suggested that Ashland replace its $1 million shares of preferred stock outstanding with an issue of $4,060,000 in convertible preferred stock. Jim Martin wanted to handle the new issue, but moved too slowly. Blazer, after creating the competition, decided in favor of Joe Levin and A. G. Becker. Once the decision was made, Levin recalls, Martin and his associates became very eager, and protested, but Blazer held firm. He had made his commitment, and he would not swerve after that. "That was characteristic of Paul," Levin said. "But the terms were good, too."

Levin recalls that the sales were slow. He thought afterward the price had been set too high (at $101.50 a share), but despite the effort it required, the issue was finally sold.

One result was that Levin was invited to sit in on the Ashland Oil & Refining board of director meetings. Blazer told Joe that it was against his policies to have a financial man sitting on his board. "I prefer to have complete freedom to shop around for the best available groups with which to arrange financing; I do not believe in being tied down." He also warned Levin personally: "Don't believe you have any prior claims on this company."

Levin thought this was logical; he was not dissatisfied with the arrangement.

While these efforts were underway, a series of events took place that fell upon the tired attention of the world like so many hammer blows. On April 13, 1945, President Roosevelt was suddenly felled by a cerebral hemorrhage that struck him without warning, so suddenly he could not even be transferred to a bed. Many voters could not recall when he had not been President; to them it was strange that Harry Truman ascended to the Presidency.

On April 25, the Russians surrounded Berlin; three days later Mussolini was shot by partisans in northern Italy, and his body hung in the marketplace. On April 30, 1945, Hitler took poison.

In the Pacific, the Philippines had been liberated from the Japanese and MacArthur returned in March; Tokyo had been firebombed, and on April 1, the battle of Okinawa—longest and bloodiest of the Pacific Island efforts—began. It was to last three months, lead to the deaths of 77,000 Japanese, and 40,000 U.S. casualties. The supply oil tankers brought in 8.75 million gallons of fuel oil, and 21.5 million gallons of high octane aviation gasoline to this engagement alone; the men of Ashland had produced both products to the best of their abilities.

Early in May 1945, Howard Marshall told Blazer that Ed Pauley, a well-known oil man and once one of Marshall's law clients, had been after him from Washington to work on the reparations situation. Marshall was tired of Washington, and wanted no part of it.

"If he calls you, tell him no," Marshall urged Blazer. "I've done enough for the government. I've just started here; I like it, and I want to continue."

Blazer agreed. "Most ridiculous thing I ever heard of," he said. "Of course they can do without you. Be sure I'll turn them down."

Then one afternoon, the telephone operator at the Ashland Oil & Refining Company was told the White House wanted to talk to Mr. Blazer; she made the connection. Blazer could not, of course, refuse a direct request from the President, and Howard Marshall left, in the spring of 1945, on a secret mission that was to culminate at the Potsdam Conference.

In early May, just ten days after Hitler had committed suicide in his underground bunker in Berlin, Marshall and several others in the group visited this site. Walking through Hitler's apartment in the bunker, Marshall sighted a strange-looking telephone: it was Der Führer's private phone; his only link with the outside world during his hysterical last days. Marshall picked it up, together with one of Eva Braun's bed lamps "and some odds and ends," gave the Russian guard a couple of packs of cigarettes, and carried the things off.

By this time in 1945, the great movement of oil products had been reversed within the United States. During the period leading up to the Nazi and Fascist defeats, the greatest part of the flood had been directed to the East Coast and from there to Europe. Now it was flowing toward the west, and the war in the Pacific.

Discussions in the industry, as well as in Washington, centered around the nature of the postwar industry, the use—or non-use —of the Big Inch, the size of the postwar market, and other matters of pressing and immediate practicality. Blazer told Jim Martin the postwar market would be "three or four times the 1940 size."

In the meantime, despite the desperate nature of the fighting in the Pacific and the decidedly murky eastern European situation, labor in the U.S. was breaking its wartime bonds. There were strikes, disputes and threats of strikes in all directions; Blazer was alarmed to see that his large neighbor in Ashland, American Rolling Mill Company (Armco), was shut down by a strike. John L. Lewis' famous District 50—the beetle-browed labor leader's answer to the CIO—was not only active, but popular in the region.

In late June 1945, the United Nations Charter was adopted at San Francisco with reams of newsprint serving as confetti. Then, in the middle of July, a series of events took place that changed the course of the human race. Rarely has such a change occurred so abruptly.

On July 5, the English held a general election for the first time in ten years. Because the overseas troops voted, as well as the people at home, it took several weeks for the returns to be recorded and the outcome to be made known. Thus, the conferees at Potsdam included Churchill, whose party was up for reelection, as well as Stalin and Truman, and their entourages.

The Potsdam Conference started on July 17, and lasted until August 2, 1945. Howard Marshall was there, and sent a telegram to Paul Blazer, saying that he hoped to be home soon. He strongly implied that the war couldn't be over soon enough, as far as he was concerned. This was a hope shared by millions; they had no means of knowing that some scientists, gathered some distance away from a steel tower one hundred feet high in Alamogordo, New Mexico, had unwittingly and innocently destroyed mankind's ability to enjoy its dream of peace, the day before.

There, on July 16, the scientists had put together and detonated an implosion type, 12 lb. plutonium bomb at 5:30 in the morning. The result has been described often since. At the time, it amazed its makers. A fireball 2 miles high arose within milliseconds; the light was so blinding it was seen 180 miles away; the sound was the greatest made by man in the history of the world; windows were split at a distance of almost 200 miles; a great cloud of radioactive smoke ascended more than 7 miles into the heavens.

The theory behind the manufacture of the bomb had been well known to the scientists of the world since 1939, but few persons in military or political circles knew this, or were ever to credit it. The project to manufacture the bomb in the United States cost its government $2 billion and considerable effort in terms of people, materials and the creation of new systems of secrecy.

At Potsdam, the information of the success of the program had most effect upon Harry Truman, who quickly issued approval of plans to bomb Japan. His reasoning: the Japanese invasion was expected to cost a minimum half-million American lives.

Before the Potsdam Conference ended, Mr. Churchill was informed the electorate had defeated the Tory Party that had selected him for Prime Minister, and he and Anthony Eden withdrew. Their places were taken by Clement Attlee and Ernest Bevin.

On July 29, 1945, the heavy cruiser *Indianapolis* delivered all except the uranium of another bomb to the U.S. forces at Tinian, in the Mariana Islands in the Pacific. Japan had rejected an ultimatum. The cruiser departed and was torpedoed by a Japanese submarine three days afterward, losing all but 316 men out of 1,200.

On August 6, four days after the Potsdam Conference ended, the B-29 *Enola Gay,* under the command of Lt. Col. Paul W.

Tibbets Jr., who had been told he had a new bomb aboard and little more, roared down the runway at Tinian and took off for Hiroshima at 2:45 A.M.

At 9:15 A.M., precisely on schedule, the *Enola Gay* was over Hiroshima. Following his instructions, Tibbets brought the plane into a bombing run at 31,600 ft., going 238 m.p.h.; banked right 150° and departed from the scene after the bomb was away. The bomb, shaped like an egg, 5 ft. wide and 9 ft. long, weighing 9,000 lbs., fell 5 miles to 2,000 ft. altitude. The two masses of uranium came together to become instant energy; the fireball appeared, as did the sound and the radioactive pillar. Half the city was destroyed; 40,000 were killed at once and 60,175 at length; the center of the city vanished.

Three days later, on August 9, 1945, the third bomb was released over Nagasaki; 30,000 were instantly killed and 60,000 injured.

On August 16, 1945, on the battleship *Missouri,* under the 31-star flag that Commodore Perry had flown 92 years before, the Japanese formally signed the papers of surrender. The greatest war of them all was over.

At almost the same moment, as though to illustrate the vagaries of fate and the closeness of mankind, J. Howard Marshall, back in Kentucky, gave Paul Blazer the telephone that Adolf Hitler had employed to scream his farewells to the world.

Section Six—The New World

1945–1950

World War II changed more than the map of the world: it altered the internal structure of world society. What this change meant to U.S. industry can be illustrated by the circumstances of the Ashland Oil & Refining Company in the last year of the war, 1945. Net sales at the firm had soared to $34.8 million from $18.7 million the year before. Yet the net profits of the company were lower than in 1942 because of the heavy wartime taxes laid upon industry and the people alike. In 1942, net profits had been $1.1 million: in 1945 they came to $980,000.

J. Howard Marshall and Paul Blazer, sitting together chatting until the small hours of the morning, speculated on ways and means to help the company grow; they hoped they could bring profits to a million dollars in peacetime.

Even under ideal circumstances this did not appear an easy task. For one thing the firm had been pushing its equipment as well as its men since 1941. Replacements and repairs had been obtained for years from secondhand parts scrounged everywhere. Even the high octane plant had been erected for one purpose only: to produce 100 octane aviation gasoline—and it belonged to the government. It was operated by the company on the basis of a thirty-day lease. Now these orders, like the emergency itself, were part of the past. It was true that millions of men and women were being demobilized from the armed services, and that the nation was anxious to resume peacetime life, with all its amenities.

A great industrial complex glowed and bubbled beside the Big Sandy
River. (After the war)

But Detroit had to retool and regroup to make new cars. Business
cannot function in advance of orders; normal resumption of
markets appeared at least a year away. Manufacturers of every
description were searching for capital with which to reform their
operations; money was not searching for companies.

Fortunately, through the good offices of Joe Levin[1] of A. G.
Becker & Company, Ashland had been both astute and fortunate

[1] Joseph J. Levin, born 1897, in Chicago, Ill., graduated from the
University of Chicago in 1917; went to work for the firm of A. G.
Becker & Co. in 1922; is still active with the firm; is listed in *Who's
Who* as an investment banker; has many interests.
A. G. Becker & Co. itself was founded in 1893, and was therefore only
four years older than Mr. Levin when he was accepted. The firm has had
considerable dealings with Ashland over the years.

enough to cap its April preferred stock issue with a $5 million debenture at 3½ per cent to an insurance company in August. The two issues refunded and recapitalized its position, and in that respect, at least, the company was well situated.

For the immediate future, it looked very much as if the 100 octane plant might have to be cut back; it was already heading toward an operating loss. That would mean letting a number of men go, and Blazer, aware of the repercussions in such a small and relatively isolated community, was reluctant to do this.

On the plus side, Ashland enjoyed high-octane production facilities superior to those of its neighbors: National Refining, Louisville Refining, Aetna, Allied, Frontier and other small independents. The full engagement of these facilities meant, however, that it would have to come to royalty agreements with Houdry and Sun Oil.

The Catlettsburg plant—now referred to as plant No. 1—was running 25,000 barrels of crude a day. It seemed likely this amount might have to be reduced; certainly a sales staff would have to be reestablished. That was a problem Everett Wells was able to solve.

Unlike many companies during the war, Ashland had enjoyed the intangible but nonetheless real advantage of having a strong executive group whose ranks had not been decimated. Wells, Points, Emrick, Seaton, Keffer, Chamberlain, Dupree, et al., were used to working with one another and the chairman; they were all equally seasoned, but also young, energetic and alert.

J. Howard Marshall, the new president, brought more with him than Washington expertise and knowledge of the industry: his was a new, fresh presence. For many years, Blazer had played the role of teacher, goad, coach and father to his men; he dealt constantly in specifics, toiled unceasingly with problems. Marshall, however, was an ambassador from a larger, more interesting world. His anecdotes, insights and cheerful presence did much to lift Blazer's spirits and expand his horizons. In addition, his interest fell into an area that Blazer had personally neglected: production.

Joe Levin had discovered, and reported, that the investing public—a group whose central ideas are directed, to a large extent, by brokers, bankers and customer's men—had a fixed idea that an oil company is, simply, a company that drills and finds oil.

The far-flung networks of gasoline stations and the flood of petrochemical products notwithstanding, this fixation upon crude oil was deeply rooted. Generations of stories about gushers, great discoveries, boom towns and fast money had left imprints. In vain, Levin described the Ashland earnings over the years and its profit ratios and equity return; discussed marketing, transportation and refining—the points he had absorbed in long discourses with Blazer. The hard-headed men of business, caught in the aura of legend like so many boys, wanted to know where Ashland's oil fields were located, and turned away, uninterested, at the description of hundreds of small stripper wells and long lines of barges moving unromantically into the refinery at tiny Catlettsburg on Big Sandy, in obscure eastern Kentucky.

Blazer listened, smiled and nodded. Mr. Marshall would help to solve that problem.

In the interim the company lost the powerful 2,000 hp towboats temporarily leased to it by the government. As the autumn lengthened into winter, the refinery showed its first operating loss in many years, although—thanks to the mysteries of tax payments—the final figures exhibited a profit.

It was decided to cut the labor force by 25 per cent—and for the first time in the history of the company, to reduce refinery output.

The end of the year found Marshall accompanying Bill Keffer and Alex Chamberlain in a round of out-of-town company Christmas parties; he was fast becoming a member of the Ashland family.

A new union contract had been signed with the refinery workers. They had received an across the board 17 per cent increase, and it speaks volumes for the relationships that season between management and labor that Blazer considered this a triumph. Labor, it seems, was of the opinion that the scales of equity would have to be greatly changed. Millions of persons emerged from the war with a sour conviction that the world was unfairly organized, and would have to be put into a new condition altogether.

In the ordinary course of events, with war orders stopped, a flood of demobilized persons entering the labor market all at once, with industry forced to readjust, regroup and reform peacetime ventures, there seems little doubt that there would have been a hair-raising depression.

But events were not ordinary. Domestically, government had drawn so close to business that even experts could no longer discern clear boundaries. The nation had witnessed the introduction of a mixed state and private enterprise economy in the early New Deal days that had become symbiotic by war's end. A similar amalgam had been created with the universities and the government; vast research funds and the expansion of governmentally sponsored programs had altered the ivory tower into a virtual extraterritorial area of government.

In terms of the individual citizen, the government had moved far. The income tax base had been extended downward during the war: most persons became intimately acquainted with this institution during those years for the first time. The phenomenon of a stated salary in excess of the sum received each payday struck most people as odd indeed.

The government also assumed responsibilities for returning servicemen and women that exceeded, both in purpose and scope, the rewards previously granted those who had served the nation in war. The G.I. bill assured health benefits, assistance in buying homes, attending school, unemployment compensation, going into business or entering the civil service.

In order to keep the economy from toppling, the Administration retained many wartime features into the peace, including the Office of Price Administration. The retention of this and other administrative features introduced during the war produced some muted outcries from some businessmen, but in the main the majority of these measures were heartily approved.

The most important developments during the fall of 1945 and the spring of 1946 took place internationally. In Europe, the war-toughened armies of the Soviet Union were located in Poland, Czechoslovakia, Bulgaria, Hungary, Yugoslavia, Austria and eastern Germany. Far from being sated with wartime advances, the

Soviets put strong pressures against Iran and Turkey. From bases in Albania and Yugoslavia, the USSR fed material and propaganda, and more direct assistance, to an insurrectionary movement in Greece. In Italy, France and Belgium, Communist members of coalition governments began agitating to achieve complete control.

Domestically, discussion of these developments was obscured by a strong national reaction and concern over the atomic bomb. A nation that had been neither bombed nor invaded during the holocaust was greatly shocked at the use of this weapon, although it had been developed for use against the Germans and was used against the Japanese to spare American lives. A noisy debate between the antis and the pros regarding the atomic bomb, couched in apocalyptic terms, succeeded in diverting public attention from the realization that only America's possession of this ultimate weapon prevented the Russians from achieving Hitler's goal in Europe.

In Asia, where the United States returned millions of Japanese soldiers to their homeland and occupied Japan itself, other immense problems arose. The Nationalist and Communist Chinese forces engaged in civil war: rising nationalist groups in the Dutch and French and British possessions emerged to prevent their former colonial masters from returning.

In the Middle East, the Zionists stepped up their campaign against the British in Palestine, and the Arab independence movement grew mightily. Central Africa began to stir and seethe.

The United States poured money into UNRA: it went primarily to Poland, the Ukraine, China and Italy. Enormous credits were opened to Britain. Men from the largest United States corporations traveled throughout Europe, assisting that continent to rebuild its shattered and semi-obsolete industries.

Since the United States still constituted the world's major resource for food, finished goods, and the hardware of life as well as war, a great deal of the funds disbursed found their way back through the channels of American industry. The effect of these orders and this activity cushioned the shock of peace for the American nation and recreated, in effect, the fuel upon which the war itself had been fought. There were some who thought a new form of economics had been created, but in essence it was simply a continuation of the war. There was no peace. By the time the realization of this began to dawn, the nation was well launched in a new style of life, to which we have all become accustomed.

POSTWAR PAUSE

In late March 1946, Ashland completely shut down the high octane plant—now called plant No. 2—and reduced the throughput at plant No. 1 from 25,000 barrels to 13,000 barrels. Crude oil drilling and exploration efforts, greatly expanded in the fall with the opening of offices in Tulsa, Oklahoma, southern Illinois, Texas and western Kentucky, were already being "streamlined" by Howard Marshall.

The men at Allied Oil were irate over the fact that Ashland salesmen had followed the trucks from their terminals, tracked down some of their unbranded gasoline customers, and persuaded them to switch by offering a lower price.

For its part, Allied Oil was causing grief in the sales offices of Ashland. Rex Blazer and his men, during the shortage days of fuel oil, had signed their large customers to a long-range, five-year contract, in which they protected the purchasing agent by agreeing to meet any lower price offered by a competitor. Thus, they cut the ground out from under Ashland when it became anxious over the fuel oil market and sought large-scale reentry. Wells and Blazer fumed, but they had been outmaneuvered.

Blazer began to have, and to express, doubts about the wisdom of buying the high octane plant. Both he and Howard Marshall beat their way to Washington almost as often as before to take part in meetings over OPA ceilings. The government was, in effect, ratifying labor contracts that included whopping wage increases, while seeking to hold the line on the prices of goods. The Reconstruction Finance Corporation reduced the rent on the high octane plant, but that did not seem to assist much. Specialty products were in demand: asphalt, kerosene, fuel oil. But fuel oil was a sore subject.

Then in May 1946, markets and activities began to quicken.

Production profits began to go up: the refinery runs were increased. Howard Marshall, at the suggestion of Blazer, joined the Ohio Valley Improvement Association, a nonprofit organization that attempted to persuade various agencies and communities to improve the condition of the waterways. Ever since the terrible floods of the 1930's and their smaller but similar recurrences during the early 1940s, Blazer had been quietly working to improve the condition of the canals and locks on the river: Howard could do some good in this effort.

In the meantime, the company poured money into an effort to find oil. Despite the fact that it went into partnership with all sorts of drillers and drilling companies, wildcatters and corporations, the number of dry holes seemed to exceed good wells, and the good wells seldom seemed large. By June 1946, out of a total fiscal investment of $8 million, more than half was tied up in production. Blazer intended that the company would find and use its own oil. He confidently predicted to the directors that crude oil production would be the future area of highest profits for the firm. He had, however, little real patience or liking for the crude oil search: he deplored the wheeling and dealing that prevailed in this sector of the industry, and was particularly uncomfortable with the uncertainties. Blazer preferred to work with facts and factors that were either known or could be learned: he chafed at the guesses and errors of geology, which smacked to him more of art and intuition than of science.

Once, when a well that everyone had seemed unanimously to consider an almost sure shot came in dry, he turned to Marshall with annoyance and said, "Whose fault is it?"

"Fault?" Marshall echoed, with ready wit. "The fault was made, oh, probably, about 80 million years ago, Paul, in the Cenozoic Era."

Blazer didn't smile. For distraction, he turned his attention toward the refinery. There, in the precisions of processing, he could always find comfort. As usual, he had some young men in particular over whom he was brooding. One of these was Bob Yancey. Yancey had joined the refinery in 1943. His was the voice on the other end of the phone, night after night. (Blazer would call from wherever he was, asking how the refinery was functioning.) According to company legend, Yancey[2] acquired a memorandum book in which he jotted down the state of the refinery when he reported to work and thus impressed Blazer with his prodigious memory. He denies this, and fact seems to bear him out: he *has* a prodigious memory.

"If anything is important enough to recall, a notebook shouldn't be necessary," Yancey remarked, when told about the fable. Then, with an engineer's typically detailed conception, he added, "Suppose the phone is in a dark corner or the light goes out? What good would a notebook be then?"

Another was Chub Moffitt, who had returned from the Navy and the war, and was back in Ashland. The more Paul talked with young Moffitt, the more impressed he became with his general abilities. He involved Moffitt in a light octanes program being developed by some of the company process engineers, including Arnold Leas[3]—one of his particular favorites. Moffitt found him-

[2] Robert E. Yancey, born 1921, at Cleves, Ohio, cannot recall when he did not live in Ashland, Ky. His father came to the area in 1916, set up the first laboratory the American Rolling Mill (now Armco Steel) installed in their local complex. Yancey Sr. was a chemist. Despite the fact that he worked at Armco during the summer while attending Marshall University in nearby Huntington, W. Va., he preferred to apply for work at Ashland Oil when he received his B.S. in chemical engineering in 1943: more independence. While in college, he graded physics papers and played professional football, a combination that epitomizes his brains and brawn. He is not tall but extremely sturdy; moved upward rapidly at Ashland: became a vice-president in thirteen years. Today one of the top four men in the company, he is a senior vice president and president of the Ashland Chemical Company as well.

[3] Arnold Leas, born 1915, in Fort Wayne, Ind., was one of 11 children raised on a farm, and worked his way through the Tri-State College of Engineering. The Leas family emigrated to the U.S. from Germany before the Civil War. He worked at a family-owned Shell station during adolescence; attended an API meet in Chicago in 1937, where he approached Paul Blazer who hired him. He spent his first five years in the laboratory; worked in the refinery during the war as a shift foreman; had at least one long conversation a week with Blazer during this entire period; in the postwar period became operating head of Technical Service. In the refinery, he served as part of Blazer's team of observers and commentators; was Yancey's boss in 1946; early felt Yancey capable of any job in the company. Leas felt his association with

self working temporarily with Willis Munro, the company advertising manager, and the marketing division headed by Earl Weaver, in the reintroduction of branded gasoline. Together they launched some radio advertising and devised new print campaigns —but this was frothing.

Their real project was to create new fuels the aviation industry and the railroads needed. This was to engross them, and delight Blazer for some time to come.

Oliver Zandona, another young process engineer who had joined the refinery brain trust in 1944, was delighted to be part of these backstage efforts.

Roland Whealy,[4] by now operating superintendent of the refinery, kept a keen eye on all of them.

While Blazer was prodding his young men into new directions, he was also pleased that director Gordon, in Chicago, sent his son, Robert D. Gordon Jr.,[5] to apply for a job. Young Gordon had become a geologist, and the moment could not have been more propitious. He was sent to Oklahoma to become part of Howard Marshall's crude oil domain.

Blazer was a better education than continuing in school; says Blazer provided him with more than a Ph.D.; later he became head of Research & Development of Ashland Oil & Refining.

[4] Having survived the rigors of the laboratory, Roland Whealy had been made road oil foreman until fall 1939, and then was titled assistant process superintendent—a post in which he was assigned to anything that looked promising, and that he could be held at least partly responsible for the outcome. Then he actually managed to get out of the refinery and into sales for a year, but the war eliminated the need for salesmen, and he worked through the war as a senior engineer. From July 1944 until May 1945 he was a process supervisor, then was made responsible for refinery operations.

[5] Robert D. Gordon Jr. was born 1920 at LaCrosse, Wis. Early in childhood, young Gordon was afflicted with progressive myopia, and therefore had to select subjects that did not entail too much reading or close eye work. Outdoor interests led to geology. During World War II he served in a limited service capacity: was an instructor at Ft. Sheridan, Ill. and in Puerto Rico. He received his degree in geology at Cornell University. He worked in the exploration division of Ashland for various heads over the years; was in charge of the Tulsa office from 1947; was made a vice president in early 1967; is a director.

The atmosphere at Ashland Oil, in fact, seemed to suit a young man's fancy. Blazer's letters to the directors were brimming with new plans, new directions and a new spirit.

In June 1946, while Winston Churchill was acquainting the American public with the new and terrible facts of international life in his Iron Curtain speech, Blazer was writing Jim Martin that OPA might soon be ended; that gasoline demand had gone up and prices, not illogically, had gone down; that the proposed $80 million canalization program of the Big Sandy had been voted through the House but seemed doubtful of passage through the shoals of the Senate; that it had been decided to create the Ashland Drilling Company and a rotary rig had been purchased for $70,000; that adding propellers to the towboats could improve their performance by at least 50 per cent; that refinery margins were thinner than before the war but that this might be balanced by larger margins of profit on the waterways.

In the background of all this, secret talks were being held with Flood Newman and W. W. Vandeveer, the principal owners of Allied Oil. Allied was doing well, but it had problems. Its refinery at Canton, Ohio, was becoming obsolete and would require large sums to modernize—but Allied was not primarily a refiner, anyway: it was a reseller of fuel oil. That business was excellent. The two owners had their entire personal assets tied up in the company; they were moving well into middle age and estate problems had become foreseeable. Neither could afford to buy the other out. Problems of how to realize their earnings without losing them again in taxes were beginning to constitute a dilemma, and they had personal difficulties with one another. Blazer, who had known them both since the early 1920s, played his cards very coolly, but he was not able to conclude the negotiation.

At the last minute it fell through. The difference between prices quoted and rejected came to $500,000: all three were men of extraordinary stubbornness.

By September 1946, though, the curve of business was visibly rising. An expanded exploration and production department was turning up oil. Not in spectacular amounts, but in promising quantities. The overall value of the Marshall efforts were gratifying. Blazer felt strong enough, in fact, to resist the powerful Superior Oil Company when that firm wanted to increase the price of Illinois Basin crude oil, and was rueful when Superior, angry, cut off their crude oil sales to Ashland altogether. These amounted to 3,000 barrels a day, a considerable part of its daily requirements, and Ashland had to scramble for a different supplier.

Nevertheless, matters were going well. "Roland Whealy is doing an excellent job at the refinery"—words as rare as diamonds from the unblinking watcher of that end of the operations. As a consequence, Whealy was made General Refinery Superintendent, a post somewhat fraught with peril.

Turning to the annual statement of 1946, we see the reason for the cheerful tone of Blazer's commentary: despite a drop of almost $15 million in net sales, from the 1945 high of $34.8 million down to $20.4 million, profits were up to $1.3 million, $345,000 more than in 1945. Companies, like individuals, can exist only on what is left over.

In the remaining fall of 1946 and early winter of 1947, the signs of a quickened tempo throughout the land continued to be reflected in the circumstances at Ashland. After much wrangling, counter-suggesting and soul-searching between the oil industry and the government, a decision was made to convert the Big Inch and Little Inch pipelines into gas carriers: a decision which did not displease Blazer and Marshall. The company exploration and drilling efforts continued to be strenuous, both because the tax laws encouraged such activities and because the firm wanted to balance its integration.

The company Christmas parties, the gayest in a number of years, were held at Grayville, Illinois, as well as Owensboro, Beattyville and Ashland.

The year 1946 ended with the announcement in the Kentucky press that Paul Blazer had been appointed chairman of a committee for a state Constitutional Convention to be voted upon the following November. In his office, Blazer toiled over campaign literature and sent out letters at a pace he had not pursued since his days with Curtis before World War I. The state had not changed its ground rules since the 1890s; he was eager to help it catch up with the twentieth century. Mrs. Blazer,[6] the same year, was reappointed a trustee of the University of Kentucky in Lexington; the family was numbered among the important and more public-spirited in the region.

Signs of the effects of the international situation came with the information that Ashland Oil in February 1947, was shipping steam-refined cylinder stock to the railways of France and Czechoslovakia. Shortly afterward Ashland sent an additional 500,000 gallons by barge down the Mississippi River to New Orleans, and from there by tanker to Italy.

Arrangements were made to obtain crude oil in St. Paul: the crude would be shipped through St. Louis. This replaced the quantities formerly supplied by Superior. And toward the end of the month, the high octane plant was reactivated.

At this point, all the visions about the high octane plant came surging back. Discussions about improvements and the variety of products that could be thus produced returned. And for the first time, elements of nervousness began to appear.

"There is a rumor," Blazer wrote darkly to the directors, "that Standard of Ohio has expressed an interest in our high octane plant." *Our* plant?

By March 1947, news arrived that an especially good well had been brought in in Baylor County, Texas, and that the Dubbs unit had operated for a straight four months without having to be shut down for a cleanout: a record. Under Roland Whealy, the first general superintendent to mature under Blazer, the refinery was operating exceptionally well. Nevertheless, these items of good news did not calm Blazer's nerves.

He busied himself with the Constitutional Convention issue, made speeches, wrote broadsides, dictated letters. The previous Conventions had been held in 1792, 1799, 1849 and 1891, but the modern Kentuckian seemed less inclined to experiment than his forebears. "The corporation laws of this state are particularly onerous," Blazer explained later. "They were passed when anti-railroad

[6] Mrs. Blazer was first appointed a trustee of the University of Kentucky in January 1939—the first woman to receive this honor. She was reappointed several times, and served until January 1960.

agitation was at its height: we pay a premium for having our headquarters in this state as a result."

His views, like his person, had become well known: he had established strong political friendships, although he was careful to remain bipartisan in internal political issues. One man he found particularly helpful—and with whom he shared many views— was John Diederich, another Ashland resident. Mr. Diederich, his contemporary, was a potent political force. Like Blazer, his methods were often oblique, but never his objectives.

Then in June 1947, unable to bear the suspense any longer, Blazer traveled to Washington to discuss the high octane plant with the War Assets Administration, and took Roland Whealy, by now one of his favorite men, along for aid and comfort. This is the first time we notice this, but it will not be the last. From this point forward, Blazer will travel with the men he raised, so to speak, to business maturity: he will seldom make a trip alone.

By this time, his telephoning—an ingrained habit for many years—became truly phenomenal. His calls were not only frequent and widespread, but longer. Joe Levin of A. G. Becker would find himself listening to Blazer on the telephone for as long as two or three hours at a stretch. "My ears got tired," he said. "I would squirm around, trying to get comfortable. But those calls kept coming."

Once in Washington with Messrs. Hobday and Rossinger, the War Assets Administration experts, Blazer employed every ruse to discern their thoughts regarding a fair price, but they played excellent poker, maintaining impassive and impenetrable expressions. "They use a theoretical figure of $3 million in explaining the computations," he fretted. "I guess they expect something between $1 and $2 million. We have about $4 million in hand, but of course we will have to make additions and improvements in both plants."

The longer he contemplated the situation, the more it vexed him. With horrid clarity, he could visualize a competitor buying the high octane plant from under the very nose of Ashland: shipping, from this jugular point, higher octane gasoline than plant No. 1 could produce, to the Ashland territorial customers. The vision curdled his nerves; he communicated it to his men, who

sat up till unreasonable hours night after night, calculating feverishly against the menace.

The governmental gavotte had its own curious steps and
rhythm. An informal offer was expected first. Then, if the figure
was considered generally reasonable, the government would
publicly announce that a sale would be made, and ask for bids.
The highest bidder would receive the plant, provided the Department of Justice approved. It was generally believed that Justice
would not look with favor upon a very large company acquiring
the plant, but Blazer, determinedly gloomy, didn't believe this.
"I wouldn't be surprised," he wrote the directors, "if some large
company might bid on our plant."

The alternative was a long-term lease, whose terms would constitute, in effect, a down payment on a purchase price. However,
this left many matters still open for governmental objection, at
least in theory. Then, if the plant was not obtained, the men
figured out the costs of creating a comparable installation, at
1946 prices. Much higher; much, much higher.

ADVENTURE OVERSEAS

Kuwait had been under British domination since the late nineteenth century. It supported a little over 320,000 citizens, consisted of 5,800 square miles, extended along the northern end of
the Persian Gulf, was bordered by Iraq, Saudi Arabia and a
Kuwait-Saudi Neutral Zone. Its ruling family, the Al-Sabahs, had
enjoyed the palace since 1756. It was a land inhabited, as far as
the world was concerned, by djinns and genies, sandstorms, veiled
women and men in burnooses: obscure, unimportant and remote.

By 1947, against all the usual probabilities, it had become an
object of envy and desire. Blazer said that the Gulf Oil Company
was rumored to be "taking 100,000 barrels of crude a day out of 6
wells" in Kuwait.

It had been learned, through a grapevine of contact and comment too elaborate to deserve retelling, that the Sheik might grant
another concession in the Neutral Zone. The situation of the
major oil companies regarding another concession was complex:

although each of the majors could be interested, each would rather see an independent obtain it, or a group of independents, rather than one of their own ranks. Blazer explained this to the directors of Ashland. "At this time," he said, "only major oil companies have foreign reserves, and, thus, ordinarily are the only importers. They would be subject to less criticism and their political position would be much improved if a number of independent oil companies operated in foreign fields."

Blazer was putting the situation in extremely simple, but essentially factual terms. Ralph Davies, the former deputy administrator of PAW and once a top executive with Standard of California, was the guiding spirit in the formation of a group of independents. He had discussed and invited into the consortium Phillips Petroleum, Signal Oil & Gas, Allied Oil, Ashland—through J. Howard Marshall—and others. Marshall had been told—and relayed to Blazer—that Ashland's participation would be limited to 5 per cent, amounting to $500,000, in a corporation to be formed with a capitalization of $10 million. Initially, only $50,000 would be expected; the balance could wait until the project showed indications of success.

Continuing to pour cooling waters over the heated reaction of the directors of Ashland, Blazer went on to say, "from the standpoint of money involved, it is not outstanding in a company that is doing a business of more than $2 million a month. The transaction is much like a $25,000 investment in a wildcat well, which, if it should happen to open up an oil field, would commit us, with pleasure, to a half million dollars for development. Our participation in the 'American Independent Oil Company' sounds big and glamorous, but, as a practical matter, unless we get a concession, it is probably of less importance than many transactions in which our directors show little more than a casual interest. If we get a concession, it will be worth much more than we have invested."

Almost immediately after Marshall had received authorization to proceed, the members of the consortium met at Bartlesville and decided to subscribe the entire amount for the new company. A committee of three men were named as trustees, pending the organization of the company. The three were J. Howard Marshall,

Paul G. Blazer (early 1950s)

Bernard Majewski and K. S. (Boots) Adams. The trustees were empowered to spend up to half the capitalization of the new company, without any further formalities, if this appeared necessary.

Blazer pointed out that this sweeping authority, in advance of the selection of the officers and directors of the new company, was typical of the manner in which the men of the oil industry operated. "The explanation," he said, "is that the oil industry gives the right to speak only to those who have earned it by past performance, and those people make important decisions with a minimum of red tape." This rather broad hint was received by the directors with silence; Ashland had moved far.

The American Independent Oil Company, shortly afterward, selected its directors, who included J. Howard Marshall from Ashland, and Ralph Davies as president.

Meanwhile, Blazer sketched out a plan to extend the Ashland regional properties by a series of new terminals. One, he explained, was to be in Paducah, Kentucky, others in Evansville, Indiana, Louisville, Covington, and Maysville, Kentucky, Marietta, Ohio, and Pittsburgh, Pennsylvania. The company already had small terminals in Pittsburgh and Cincinnati; these would be enlarged.

He also said it had been decided to bid $1,642,271.13 for the high octane plant, adding, gloomily, "It is quite possible we will be outbid."

Messrs. Whealy, Leas and Bill Humphreys,[7] he explained, had worked out the final figures for the bid.

When the news of the formation of the American Independent Oil Company was announced, it seemed to surprise a goodly number—among them, the *National Petroleum News*. That publication, widely respected and a considerable authority in the industry, exhumed the experience of the major oil companies overseas.

"Aramco," it said in part, "arrived on the Arabian scene in 1933, yet a round decade had elapsed, and nearly $100 million was expended, before the first barrel of marketable oil was laid down at seaboard."

Then, after making this point—which seemed to bear out the

[7] William Howard Humphreys was born in 1908 at Columbus Grove, Ohio, where his grandfather and grandmother, both from Wales, England, had met and married. Bill graduated from the Case Institute at Cleveland, Ohio, receiving a B.S. in mechanical engineering in 1930. He worked two years for Babcock & Wilcox in Barberton, Ohio; went to MIT and received an M.S. in 1933. Back in Ohio, he received a job at the Findlay Refinery owned by National Refining Company; was put on the Dubbs unit. During World War II, when National built a 100 octane unit at Coffeyville, Humphreys worked on this with the UOP men; went with the plant when it was sold to the Consumer's Cooperative; came to Ashland in November 1946, when a friend in the Defense Supplies Corp. brought him to the attention of Paul Blazer; Humphreys was hired to be chief Catlettsburg engineer under Roland Whealy.

most gloomy predictions—it listed the officers and the directors of
the new company. These consisted of Frank Phillips, the board
chairman, K. S. Adams, the president, Don Emery, the vice president and general counsel and Paul Endacott, a vice president and
assistant to the president of the Phillips Petroleum Company;
A. C. Mattei, the president, and L. A. Cranson, the vice president
of Honolulu Oil; the president, Will J. Reid and vice president
John W. Hancock of Hancock Oil; I. A. O'Shaughnessy, the president, of Globe Oil & Refining; Ralph K. Davies; C. H. Wright,
the president of Sunray Oil Company; J. Howard Marshall, president of Ashland Oil & Refining; Sam B. Mosher, president and
Russell H. Green, vice president of Signal Oil & Gas; W. W. Vandeveer, president of Allied Oil Company; Jack Blalock, director
of Premium Oil Refining Company; Vernon Barrett, of Los
Nietos Producing & Refining Company; J. S. Abercrombie, of
Abercrombie & Harrison Oil Company.

While the *National Petroleum News* was thus reporting and
shaking its head over the Neutral Zone venture, Blazer and his refinery men were going through the last stages of their chase after
the 100 octane plant. The government had announced the sale
and asked for bids; the team worked until late at night preparing
their bid and sealing the envelope, then piled into two cars and
headed for the denouement.

The first car contained one man with the bid and one man
driving; the second car contained several more men and another
copy of the bid—in case the first car and its passengers had some
unbelievable accident. Both cars arrived safely, and the men entered the final room in a high state of excitement; Blazer was

The fleet. (late 1940s)

waiting in his office, and instructions were to call him immediately, no matter what.

The men of Ashland hardly knew whether to cheer or cry when theirs turned out to be the only bid. With typical mystification, it was for a figure different than Blazer had confidentially imparted to the directors: the final bid was $2,153,125.00. The plant was theirs.

THE NEW WORLD

By the autumn of 1947, the postwar world was in full swing. The long literary tradition of cynicism toward persons and matters American had returned, sweeping away the temporary truces of the war as though they had never existed. *The Hucksters* hit the best-seller lists; *Gentleman's Agreement* discussed anti-Semitism; mass magazines zoomed into greater prominence than ever. That year, thirty-eight magazines each had a circulation of more than a million. A college education, until now relatively rare as far as the great majority was concerned, suddenly seemed to become almost universal; the first GI graduates were beginning to leave school. The big homes on Fifth Avenue in New York were deserted, or rapidly becoming so; housing developments began to blossom; book clubs proliferated as though reading was fashionable; stock exchanges were more active than ever before; although the continuance of economic controls distorted the realities of business, business had not been so good since the forgotten 1920s. Management schools began to bloom; the Depression and the war had interrupted the continuity of experience taught by one generation to another (when jobs had been scarce, many young men missed the normal mentors of men in business); instruction resumed under a new type of business academician whose lessons were based on such sources as *The Theory of Games and Economic Behavior,* by John von Neumann and Oskar Morganstern, and Norbert Weiner's works on cybernetics (computers).

The government apparatus not only continued; it expanded. Further, the exigencies of the cold war introduced into American relationships between citizen and government a new element: secrecy. New categories of citizens came into being: the cleared and the uncleared; the knowing and the unknowing; the expert and the mass.

Yet in everyday life there seemed fewer distinctions than before. Clothing and manners alike became more casual; class symbols and differences became more subtle.

MERGER TALKS

The high octane plant—plant No. 2—was obtained in September, the month that Ashland's fiscal year ended. Net sales for 1947 had gone up to more than $29 million; net profits had more than doubled, to reach $2,898 million. Furthermore, the eager brains at the refinery were enthusiastic over the modernization program being encouraged; the refinery itself was operating with a capacity of 24,000 to 25,000 barrels a day.

Despite the intense efforts being made in the drilling and land departments, the corporate crude supply could not keep pace with the continual refinery expansions. A large percentage of wildcatting was undertaken—140 wells were drilled—55 per cent were productive. Wells in which the company had an interest were producing 7,773 barrels a day—less than a third of the refinery throughput. But Howard Marshall and his men were not having any trouble in buying oil; they would never encounter too much difficulty in this respect. It was ironic that the Ashland drilling in Oklahoma and Texas, both famed oil areas, was disappointing, while the drilling in Kentucky, Illinois and Indiana—where laymen seldom think great oil fields exist—was much better.

Blazer, Marshall, Levin, Points, Seaton, Emrick, however, were more engrossed in fascinating discussions about financing: the Allied Oil merger was getting hot again.

In November 1947, the firm suffered a loss when Bill Keffer died. Older than the majority of the Ashland executives then, Keffer had been one of those rare men who had no enemies; Blazer was particularly affected.

Fortunately, he had Marshall to sustain him. J. Howard Marshall by this time had established himself as a creative and energetic man. His phone was apt to ring at any time; his wires went far and deep throughout the industry. In this, he differed from the rest of the team, whose contacts were mainly obtained from their experience at Ashland itself.

One proposition that Marshall brought to Blazer's attention was the tanker situation. The government had created hundreds of tankers during World War II; now they were being offered to the industry on relatively attractive terms. The companies most in need of these vessels were the large majors. But again we find the War Assets people were encouraging smaller groups to make these purchases. The American Independent Oil Company under Ralph Davies had, in fact, taken advantage of the situation to create a subsidiary and obtain nine tankers, which it then put out at charter. Thus, Aminol found a means of sustaining itself while the tortuous course of obtaining a concession in the Neutral Zone wound its complex path.

Marshall told Blazer that in order to obtain two tankers, it would be necessary to apply for eight. And it speaks volumes for the conditioning a businessman receives in the course of dealing with Washington, that Blazer received this information calmly. But when the application was accepted, and the company was informed it could purchase all eight tankers, Blazer was aghast.

Marshall got busy while Blazer fumed. Fortunately, Allied Oil and its owners, Vandeveer and Newman, were also interested in the tanker situation. Working together, the men formed the Independent Tank Ships Company, and succeeded in getting all the tankers accepted by the Standard Oil of N.J., at rates that would pay them off and assure a profit.

Nevertheless, the situation troubled Blazer. Years later, he would harken back to this incident as a turning point in his relationship with J. Howard Marshall. Had the situation not been satisfactorily resolved, it would have been difficult for Blazer to explain to his board or, for that matter, to himself. The fact was that he had relied upon Marshall and his advice, and had nearly been landed in the soup. The net effect was what the psychologists call a traumatic experience; it left its scar.

There was, however, an unexpected side result which was to divert attention away from the subject of the T-2 tankers, now happily out of sight. And that was the Allied Oil–Ashland merger conversations, which began in earnest.

On the Ashland side, there were experts. First of these was Paul Blazer himself, who in hundreds of negotiations had developed the arts of examination, bargaining and closing. At his elbow were men who had worked and studied under him for years, and knew all the steps in a merger minuet. Everett Wells knew virtually every marketing group in the Middle West, including their sales manager's preference in neckties; Art Points could read balance sheets with eyes that x-rayed assets; Ned Seaton was a treasurer who always knew Ashland's position and resources; Joe Levin, of A. G. Becker & Co. constituted a shrewd ex-officio member of the team. J. Howard Marshall and Joe Levin had taken to each other from the first. Marshall himself was valuable in negotiations because he was a legal eagle as well as an oil executive. Behind these members of the top team were other men whose names are omitted for reasons of space: individual specialists who had developed, under Blazer's tutelage, into men who could analyze and interpret a situation quickly.

Allied Oil had, however, very strong men of its own; men who were highly gifted and individualistic. The combination of Vandeveer and Newman was one of those rare complementary associations few teams could excel.

Newman was analytical. A Cornell graduate, he started his career with the Standard Oil Company of N.Y. in 1912—the year after the Supreme Court issued its famous decree of dissolution. Standard of N.Y. was left with the overseas properties of the old Trust, particularly with its Far Eastern arms. Newman, who had been sent to Shanghai in 1912, became one of the old China hands. He knew and worked with the husband of Alice Tisdale Hobard, who drew upon her observations of her husband's duties to write *Oil for the Lamps of China*.

When he returned to the United States and looked for newer fields, Newman found himself invested with the aura of "a Standard Oil man."

After World War I and service in the Army, Newman went to work in Cleveland for the American Petroleum Products Company—oil resellers. There, equipped mainly with a desk and a telephone, he learned the sources of supply, the freight rates and a great deal not written in any book.

"The region from Chicago to Buffalo," he said later, "and then south to Pittsburgh, across the Big Sandy and the Ohio, then up the Mississippi to Chicago again, encompasses the industrial heartland of America. Within the region is the great steel industry; the mines and mills and smelters; the machinery manufacturers and the heavy equipment and fine tool makers; the automobile industry and many of its suppliers. All of these use fuel oil, and fuel oil was then considered almost a waste product. It was the residue from refining; the bottom of the barrel; the lowest price item in the line."

Newman reasoned that if he could assure these users a steady supply of fuel oil, he would become a success at American Petroleum Products. He became acquainted with all the various refineries —and fifty years ago, there were almost a hundred small refineries dotted along the periphery of this region—and with freight rates. He discovered that river terminals and transport by boat could reduce transportation charges and enable him to sell fuel oil below prevailing rates and with enough margin of profit to lift it from a negligible market item to an excellent one.

Despite the fact that he developed a brisk business in fuel oil, however, he could not interest his employers in his larger observations. Eventually he decided to go into business for himself. But he was not the world's greatest salesman, and he knew it. He looked about for a salesman, and found an ideal man in a neighbor named W. W. Vandeveer.[8]

[8] Welzie Wellington Vandeveer, born 1887 on a farm near Haubstadt, Gibson County, Ind., descended from a family whose history constitutes a microcosm of the United States. The Vandeveers were established here by Cornelius Janz van der Veer in New Netherlands in 1659. Descendants settled in North Carolina, Kentucky and Indiana; are mentioned as having engaged in the Revolutionary War and all those since.

W. W. Vandeveer, co-founder of Allied Oil Co., graduated from Haubstadt schools with honors, received a teaching certificate from Southern Illinois Normal in 1910; spent three years as an instructor in County schools in Illinois. In 1913 he was a telephone linesman, where he received an injury that kept him out of World War I. He worked for the B. F. Goodrich Co. from 1916–1921, and for Republic Rubber from 1921–1923, then for American Petroleum Products from 1923–1925. After the Allied Oil merger with Ashland, Vandeveer established the Vanson

Vandeveer, when Newman first met him, was working as a salesman for the Republic Rubber Company. Before Newman could convince his employers of the value of fuel oil, Vandeveer moved away, to Chicago. But some measure of how much he impressed Newman can be obtained from the fact that when Newman received permission to hire an assistant, he traveled to Chicago to look up Vandeveer. He found that Republic Rubber had folded up, and Vandeveer was selling insurance. It did not take too much effort to persuade him to come back to Cleveland, and go to work for the American Petroleum Products Company in concert with Newman. Their business career together began; Vandeveer learned about fuel oil.

By the time they went into business together in 1925, Newman had scouted the barge situation in New York; had located a representative there; had estimated the length and the conditions of traffic through the St. Lawrence and the Erie Canal; knew where terminals could be located and refineries reached; had toiled and moiled over the specifics of the heartland, its refineries, the nature of the fuel oil employed with different equipment by different industries; was in general a walking compendium of information in a subject that no other man in the world really wanted to know —except W. W. Vandeveer.

Vandeveer was able, armed with this formidable rear-echelon, human computer behind him, to enter into any situation where fuel oil was used and promise the customer that his needs would

---

Production Corp., which consisted of some oil and gas properties and drilling equipment in the southwest; placed Jim Weeks in operating charge for several years. Weeks was replaced in this role by Jim Vandeveer, W. W. Vandeveer's son. Jim Vandeveer has made a notable success of Vanson; is today a director of Ashland, and will enter this chronicle in a later section.

In addition to establishing Vanson, W. W. Vandeveer wrote a booklet called *Mergeritis,* in which he discussed the tax laws that forced entrepreneurs such as him and Newman to either sell or merge their properties. The booklet created considerable flurry, was reported in *Time, Newsweek, Fortune* and other sources, brought him a flood of business fan mail, resulting in his being called to testify before both Senate and House groups—but did not particularly change the tax laws. After the merger, "Van" also functioned as a director of the Ashland Oil & Refining Company.

be met. As a combination, they were miraculous. Vandeveer was all man; though interested in dogs, horses, hunting, golf, sports, he was probably most interested in divining other men. This intuitive insight into others was Vandeveer's native gift.

Once he had to see a tax man, who was scowlingly positive that the high Allied Oil salaries were disguised dividends. Vandeveer listened while the tax man presented his case, and then asked him what part of Indiana he came from. The tax man, surprised, told him. Then Vandeveer quoted a Whittier poem—just a snatch—so wonderfully evocative, the atmosphere in the office suddenly lightened. The tax man began to discuss the situation in an entirely softened, civilized way. Jim Weeks, the Allied Oil attorney, who had accompanied Vandeveer on this occasion, was never to forget this illustration of Vandeveer's lightning ability to unlock men.

Weeks himself is one of a kind. Born and raised in Akron, he knew Vandeveer from childhood. The two men met on Euclid Avenue in Cleveland after Weeks had graduated from law school and gone to work for Thompson, Hine & Flory, one of Cleveland's largest law firms. Shortly thereafter, Vandeveer called young Weeks in to do some legal work. In time, Allied Oil became Weeks' largest client; he actually moved into the corporate offices in the Standard building, and became a resident idea man and sounding board for the partners. In time, he became more: he served as their liaison, their interpreter, their negotiator. He never became an official member of the firm; he charged legal rates for his time and fees for his special efforts. Weeks is eloquent to a stupendous degree; one of the rare men capable of expressing the subtleties of thought aloud. He became a member of Allied's top team, especially helpful in matters of financing, but he never left his law firm.

The fourth man in this curious arrangement was Rex Blazer. As tall as his uncle, with whom he shared some family resemblance and characteristics, Rex had a highly developed ability to see the relevant detail in other men, as well as considerable persuasiveness. Unlike his uncle, Rex was shy and had developed a habit of open self-deprecation that was extremely disarming. It helped him to be a wonderfully effective salesman, especially because it covered a tremendous amount of drive and ambition, coupled with great energy.

Weeks's peculiar ability to get along on equally warm terms with men as disparate as Newman and Vandeveer—especially when they grew apart—made him a mysterious figure to the rest of the Allied Oil men; such skill in personal relationships is often distrusted. But Rex also got along extremely well with both Vandeveer and Newman. He started out as a salesman under Vandeveer, but within no more than four or five years, was actually doing much of Vandeveer's work. He became widely known throughout the region and in the oil industry; and was enormously successful. His income leaped upward, year after year, during the bitter brew years of the Depression, when most men could hardly earn a decent living.

But his activities were in marketing; in customer contact; in hiring, training and running the sales of Allied Oil—a company that existed almost entirely on such efforts. The maneuvers that accompany financing: the long secret sessions and the mysterious calculations: the trips to banks and investment houses, involved Weeks and Newman. There was a conspiratorial air about these backstage rustlings that became noticeable from time to time.

Over the years, Allied became eminently successful, but its company form became a financial corset. With sales for 1947 amounting to $40 million, as compared to Ashland's $29 million, its net profit was $1.8 million compared to Ashland's $2.9 million. In real profit terms, therefore, Allied was half Ashland's size. In large measure this was due to the difference between the small-margin product upon which Allied mainly depended (fuel oil) as compared to the large profit items that Ashland marketed (gasoline, special aviation fuels, etc.). But a deeper reading of the books and a review of the assets of the two companies showed a considerable difference between their complexities. Ashland was a public corporation, with stock traded, with connections and a reputation with brokers, with a number of astute financial advisors on its board and near its management. Its avenues for expansion and capitalization were extensive; its structure complex. Allied Oil, on the other hand, operated along the lines of a simple partnership, although technically it was a corporation. The stock was largely owned by Newman and Vandeveer, and neither wanted to enter the complicated world of shareholders, directors, public reports and exposure involved in a publicly held corporation.

Allied Oil was primarily a salesman's company. The terminals, ships, pipelines, oil wells, and refinery it obtained were mainly purchased to enhance its sales position. Its owners worked backward from sales. About "half a dozen" prima donnas made these sales—with Rex Blazer as their star performer and leader under Vandeveer. These men could travel as and where they pleased; could entertain widely; could strike bargains and close deals they reported to the owners after the event. Both Vandeveer and Newman had started out themselves as salesmen; they never forgot it. The firm was highly informal, although from time to time a salesman's ideas of formality would emerge.

Whether a simpler form of enterprise is better or worse than a more complex is a matter for business moralists to decide. Neither Ashland Oil & Refining nor Allied Oil could be said to be better or worse. A salesman would certainly find Allied more congenial, but an engineer would feel in the shadows there; Ashland's internal climate was more rigorous, but contained a wider diversity of ability.

By 1947, Allied's two owners were in a corner. They had plowed back most of their profits into extensions of the company and its assets; it was the repository of their earnings and their savings alike. Although they gave themselves fairly large salaries (they paid their men well, too), the government's experts viewed extra large salaries as concealed dividends, and made minatory noises. Refinery modernization was overdue at Canton, Allied's refinery— and would entail large sums. Both Newman and Vandeveer could see the time ahead when they would have to organize their estates, but their assets were intermingled into the company. Neither could afford to buy out the other, because the man who sold out would have to pay enormous taxes; the other would be saddled with enormous debt. Neither wanted to go public, although Jim Weeks rationalized the reasons and the methods aloud for each man, many times.

A merger, preferably with a firm not too much larger, that was already public, would solve all problems—because in such a move, the partners could obtain both cash and stock. The stock would be an equity for the future: the cash would solve immediate problems. It was a way to eat and keep their cake.

Some time before 1947, Newman and Vandeveer had given Jim Weeks a small percentage of stock. This percentage actually gave Weeks the balance of power in the corporation, for the owners' shares were exactly equal. Weeks, siding with one or the other, could (if he wanted) determine the course of any decision. Remarkably, he avoided this temptation, and although a liaison between the two, managed to retain the respect of both.

The merger talks slowed, however. Paul Blazer, who preferred, naturally enough, to deal with principals, finally made a trip to Cleveland and talked with Newman. The subject was the future of the men within Allied, should the merger be consummated. Blazer assured Newman that he had observed the Allied men in action over the years and had the greatest respect for their abilities, and that they would have excellent futures within the combined companies. This conversation warmed Newman[9] considerably, and helped the situation to move forward.

[9] Floyd "Flood" R. Newman, born 1890 in Casnovia, Mich., raised in Churchville, N.Y., where he graduated from high school, entered Cornell in 1907. Learning Standard of N.Y. was recruiting a special group in his senior year, he took his first sleeper train to New York City, was tested at 26 Broadway, headquarters of Standard Oil of N.J.; eventually landed in Shanghai.

In 1916, Newman relocated in Cleveland, worked for the American Petroleum Products Co., a stint interrupted by service overseas in France and Germany for the Quartermaster Corps; was part of a special Gas & Oil branch that extended and deepened his oil industry contacts and knowledge.

Returning to American Petroleum Products, where he had almost been forgotten, he rediscovered the fuel oil situation; hired Vandeveer in 1923 as his assistant. By 1924, both Newman and Vandeveer were ready to go into business, took the final step in June 1925.

By 1948, when the company merged with Ashland Oil & Refining, Newman was 58, received (as did Vandeveer) $5,750,000 in Ashland Oil & Refining securities consisting of preferred and common stock. Newman attended only two directors meetings of the merged company; early decided Blazer neither wanted nor would heed his comments.

Having, some years earlier, purchased a small estate in Medina, Ohio, he busied himself with this; planted flowers and trees, changed the

A little while later, Blazer spotted Vandeveer at an API meeting, drew him aside, and told him, in effect, that a merger as potentially useful as the one under discussion should not be allowed to fail because of minor differences. Vandeveer, never a man to allow details to impede progress, was in hearty agreement. Thus Blazer managed, in effect, to reach his principals.

By this time, the conversations between the two companies had ranged over many different possibilities and prospects. At one point, it seemed likely that Jim Weeks would go along, as executive vice president of the merged company.

During this period, Weeks visited Ashland. While dining at the Bellefonte Country Club with Paul and Georgia Blazer, the subject of vacations arose, and Weeks waxed enthusiastic. He dwelled—perhaps a little too long—on how much he enjoyed vacations. Mr. Blazer, whose enthusiasm for Mr. Weeks was wearing thin, frowned.

"At Ashland Oil, Jim," he said, "our work is our vocation, our avocation, *and our vacation.*"

MERGERS

Ashland purchased three LSM boats from the government, replaced the engines in the *Ashland,* installed Kort nozzles and redesigned 30 feet of the stern, at a cost of $325,000. The improvements made the *Ashland* "as powerful as any boat on the river,"

---

course of a small river that flowed through it, hired a staff to conduct his horticultural experiments. A year after the sale of Allied, he agreed to donate $1 million to Cornell to assist the creation of a nuclear research laboratory now known as the Newman Laboratory of Nuclear Studies; later gave the school another $1.75 million to create the Helen Newman Hall; has assisted the Cornell Plantations. His holdings have grown immensely in value over the years as Ashland Oil & Refining has grown; one consequence being he is one of the handful of men in the U.S. who, by giving away 90 per cent of their income to charity, pay no income tax on the residue. He is today a happy millionaire nearing eighty—much to the surprise of those who knew him as an around-the-clock toiler.

Newman describes himself and Vandeveer as "a couple of lucky salesmen. If this can happen to us, perhaps it will give others some hope to learn about it."

said Bob Gray, marine engineer with the company. The *Tri-State* and the *Paul Blazer* would be remodeled next, at a cost of $125,000 each. In addition, fifteen new barges had been ordered, each one 585 feet long; the *Ashland* alone and the new barges would be able to push 140,000 barrels of crude oil to the refineries in one trip. Altogether, the barges would cost $800,000: total river expenditures in new equipment and upgrading another $1 million. In the meantime, the Cumberland terminal was expanded; a new terminal was purchased at Evansville, Indiana; contracts had been signed with the Catalytic Construction Company to repair and remodel one of the kilns on the TCC unit; costs originally estimated to run $500,000 had been whittled, via a saving here, a saving there, to $370,000 by the Ashland refinery men.

Talks with Allied, Blazer reported, were proceeding so well that they had reached the stage where the Allied Oil debts were being discussed with its creditors by Ashland Oil.

Blazer and Mrs. Blazer, after having seen these projects almost to their conclusion, decided to take a combined business and pleasure trip to the Southwest. For the first time, the chairman would visit the company exploration and development divisions; see for himself the offices at Henderson, Kentucky, Jackson, Mississippi, Baton Rouge and Crowley, Louisiana, where his youngest son, Stuart, was working for an Amerada seismograph crew. (Stuart, who had attained the height of six feet six, was especially valuable on the crew because he could carry instruments through swamp waters where other men could barely hold their heads above the surface.) The Blazers would then proceed to Galveston, Texas where the Western Petroleum Refiners Association was meeting, go on to Shreveport and to Tulsa . . .

J. Howard Marshall was spending most of his time in western Kentucky, "making a number of crude oil deals."

Paul Blazer Jr.[10] was being married that spring at Georgetown,

---

[10] Paul Blazer Jr. was born in Chicago in 1919, raised in Ashland, Ky., attended Western Reserve Academy at Hudson, Ohio and graduated from Hatch Preparatory School at Dexter, Maine, then entered the Virginia Polytechnic Institute at Blacksburg, Virginia; from there entered the Army during World War II, was sent to the Philippines six months before the war ended, returned and decided to finish his schooling at

Kentucky, a town located near Lexington. Vandeveer was an invited and special guest; Paul Jr. met his prospective bride through the Vandeveers. She was, in fact, the sister of Vandeveer's son-in-law. This did not hurt the conversations being held between the two companies.

The advantages of acquiring Allied Oil Company were considerably more attractive to Ashland than to any other company. "Their Canton refinery location is more favorable than ours," Blazer wrote. "Their geographical locations are likely to continue. They are located on trunk pipelines extending to the Gulf of Mexico and the Atlantic seaboard . . . Howard and I may well recommend this acquisition; we are negotiating with Jim Weeks who represents Allied, and is in a similar position regarding his principals—that is, holds their voting trust rights, as does Howard Marshall regarding mine, in case of my disability . . ." That is a curious piece of side information; later its meaning will become clearer.

Then, toward the end of March, we find Blazer writing more about the Allied situation. "One of the problems involved," he said, "is the fact that my nephew, Rex Blazer, exercises a high degree of control of their fuel oil brokerage business, which, ordinarily, accounts for approximately half their total earnings. That character of business is more closely associated with individuals than, for example, a manufacturing business. Recognizing the possibility that Rex and his salesmen might decide to go into business for themselves and doubtless would be able to carry a substantial part of the business with them, I have asked for a five-year employment contract with Rex. He has been making between $30,000 and $35,000 per year, a part of his compensation being in the form of a bonus. We have agreed that his salary is to be $30,000 per year for five years, plus such bonuses as are customary . . . on the basis of current payments, his salary will be increased eight or nine per cent . . . Allied's salaries are considerably higher than ours . . ."

---

the University of Kentucky in Lexington. He received his B.A. in 1946. In September 1947, he joined the Ashland Oil & Refining Co. and received no favors from management; is today Manager of the New Products Development department; was elected a director in early 1967.

Then he continued. "It is not proposed that Mr. Vandeveer or Mr. Newman become members of our board, although they own more than 90% of Allied's stock. Probably Mr. Vandeveer would like to be a member, but that would mean that Newman also would be a member. They do not get along well. I have let Van know that I do not favor their being on the board. They have agreed to that. I have advised that I will recommend increasing our board to 15 members, permitting four Allied department heads to be directors in the parent company. There would be Cobb Marshall who heads the Central Pipelines operations: Jonassen who is head of Cleveland Tankers; Rex who is operating head of Allied Oil Company, which is principally the purchase, transportation and sale of petroleum products. Those three operations could be continued through the present subsidiaries which would continue as separate companies. The Canton Refining Co. would probably be merged into the Allied Oil Company, or directly with Ashland Oil & Refining. Mr. Vandeveer, who appears to be partial to Rex, would prefer that their refining operations would be under Rex . . .

"I agreed with Vandeveer and Weeks that because so much of the business of Allied pertains to purchase and sales agreements with other oil companies, many of which are closer and more friendly to them than to us, it is highly desirable to keep certain of their operations. There is little resemblance, I believe, between the character and psychology of their operations and ours. One of the assets we will acquire will be a framed copy of Allied Oil Company's Purchase Order No. 1, pertaining to the first business transaction of their company, which was the purchase of ten cars of fuel oil from the Ashland Refining Company. That was in 1925. They built their business solely from their original investment, which was modest. Jim Weeks and Rex are the only stockholders other than Van and Newman, who own equal shares."

Meanwhile, the internal operations at Ashland seemed to have reached new heights of efficiency. Art Points had discovered a legal provision in the tax laws—resisted by the Treasury, but admitted by that department when it was insistently pointed out—that led to the recovery of $177,000 in tax relief to the firm: a coup by any standard. Howard Marshall was lending money to crude oil producers at the rate of $750,000 for the next six months: $1 million was being spent at the refinery.

Measures against the floods on the river had become, over the years, more and more elaborate. In late April, another flood had arrived, but although the waters rose higher than in 1943, when the refinery was shut down, and quite a bit higher than in 1945, when it was partly shut down, operations on this occasion continued without interruption. But Roland Whealy and his men had set pumps at the sewer catch basins and pumped water back into the river fast enough to keep the levels at normal depth, below the refinery yard. "They saved us many thousands of dollars," Blazer wrote exultantly. "It was their decision to keep operating; Howard and I were away. I am very proud of our refinery organization."

Furthermore, Points and Mac Burnam, the company counsel, spent weeks in Washington pushing the acquisition papers for the high octane plant from desk to desk and bureau to bureau, and avoided the freeze on government plants that went into effect, by fewer than ten days. The Wilshire octane aviation gasoline plant in California, whose purchasers were less eager—or less prescient —were not so lucky: that sale was stopped at the last minute. The atmosphere in Washington was changing: it was now obvious that prewar days would never return, and the government was not anxious to get out of industry anymore.

Nineteen forty-eight was a Presidential election year. The Republicans were confident, but the Democrats moved disconsolately toward their convention in Philadelphia, unhappy that Harry Truman was to be their standard-bearer. Yet, looking back, it is hard to recall the platform differences—other than their personalities—between the candidates.

Great advances were being made industrially throughout the country. Myriad labor-saving devices introduced by the logistics of the great war were beginning to emerge in industry: gravity rollers, conveyor belts, power-driven hand tools, forklifts; training films for factory workers and photographic charts from which to assemble components. Automatic milking machines appeared on small farms, as did new tractors, disk harrows, hay driers. Electrification proceeded incredibly rapidly; so did the installation of indoor toilets and regular bathrooms in homes in rural communities. In a few short seasons the entire nation would forget that the outhouse had been a fixed feature of the U.S. landscape since colonial days. Consumer goods spread throughout the land; automobile dealers began to smile at customers as their waiting lists disappeared. The birth rate did a complete reversal and so did the population experts: births per thousand rose from 17 or 18 in 1939 to 23.3 in 1946; 25.8 in 1947; 24.2 in 1948. The long-delayed marriages of the depression and the postwar boom combined to make the large family popular again; the experts would soon keen on the other side of the wall. The long westward drift of the population continued; in the postwar years, more young people went to the West Coast than to the East; California began to overtake New York as the Union's most popular state. The introduction of science into business and of government into both, extended rationalism both as a method and a form: logical sequences and mathematical forms continued to grow rapidly. An alarming increase in specialists' jargon began to appear. Unscientific in nature but sounding fearsomely scientific, charts, graphs, and equations began to appear in what purported to be descriptions of human behavior and attitudes: the social sciences vied with schools of engineering for young students. In April 1948, the Communists in Italy suffered a resounding defeat at the hands of the electorate; the Nationalist Chinese were rapidly losing their last footholds on the mainland of their nation; Russia undermined the free government of Czechoslovakia and Jan Masaryk, son of the founder of that nation, suffered a mysterious and fatal fall from a window; the Soviets instituted great pressures in Berlin and the Air Corridor began; the United States' defense establishment underwent the pangs of reorganization. Most persons worked hard, kept their heads down, and hoped for the best.

By summer 1948, Ashland Refining negotiations with Southern Pipeline Company began to bear fruit. Southern Pipelines actually consisted of three companies managing separate lines. The companies, Eureka, Southwest Penn and Southern, were all managed by Theodore Towl, son of Forrest Towl, the elderly Standard Oil executive from whom Blazer had purchased the Cumberland Pipeline many years before. Control of the Eureka Pipeline had been obtained by Quaker State, Pennzoil and Elk Refining; another group had obtained Southwest Penn.

Ashland managed to become a one-third owner of Southern by buying shares from the Rockefeller Foundation. The pipeline carried oil from western fields to Philadelphia and to Marcus Hook from Toledo, Ohio, during the war. Now, oil in the lines was flowing west, from Marcus Hook through Philadelphia westward, at the rate of 12,000 barrels of crude oil daily. Marshall and Blazer hoped to increase this traffic to 19,000 barrels a day: both men became directors of the Southern Pipeline Company. The extension of the Ashland interests carried the company much farther east than ever before, bringing it in touch with the Atlantic.

Union negotiations continued as smoothly, conducted by a group consisting of J. Howard Marshall, Alex Chamberlain, Lew Ware and others, with Blazer advising in the background. Marshall, who by this time had become well known within the company, proved to have a deft touch in bargaining; some men enjoyed working with him—others did not.

Chamberlain liked him. "He would pound the desk," he said of Marshall, "but then you could present your side."

Meanwhile the refinery men investigated the Allied Oil refinery in Canton, Ohio, and determined to their own satisfaction that by adding some heat exchangers they could both reduce the costs of its operation and double its capacity.

Meanwhile, Paul Blazer, studying the proposed agreement with Allied Oil, suddenly noticed a new clause. He read it with mounting anger, and then reached for the phone. Weeks was in Connecticut, attending an important meeting on behalf of some other clients. He was annoyed at being called to the phone; the protracted merger negotiations and the strain of matching wits with Blazer were beginning to wear on him. On this occasion, he answered the call to find an irate Blazer on the other end. "You and Marshall," Blazer started, "have conspired—" and Weeks, aware even in his anger that he was probably ending a relationship, hung up.

In his office, Blazer scowled at the agreement. The section that had aroused his anger and suspicion centered around the voting rights of the Vandeveer and Newman stock; stock they would receive for the Allied Oil Co. and its subsidiaries. Weeks had drawn up the agreement together with Marshall, and in it he had retained his privilege of voting on behalf of Vandeveer and Newman. Combining their votes of a large bloc of Ashland Oil stock (in exchange for Allied), together with his perception of the fact that Marshall and Weeks seemed congenial, Paul Blazer mentally put all these men together in some future period in his mind, and foresaw a struggle for control. There had, after all, been conversations with Mr. Weeks[11] regarding the possibility of his becoming an executive vice president of Ashland Oil; Marshall was already president of Ashland. With a large amount of stock behind them —perhaps the largest single bloc in the company—it was possible these men could unseat Blazer completely, and change the direction of the company.

Himself a man who seldom took a single step without having a journey in mind, Blazer could not believe the clause was innocently inserted.

Shortly after this exchange, on August 3, 1948, the principals met in the Chicago offices of the A. G. Becker & Co. to conclude the merger. Blazer was extremely cool and self-possessed.

After other details were concluded, he produced a paper, read its contents aloud and handed a copy to Vandeveer and Newman. "This," he said in effect, "is a voting trust. It is to endure ten

[11] James A. Weeks, born 1901 in Akron, Ohio, where he graduated from high school and where Vandeveer lived for a period. Mr. & Mrs. Vandeveer, in fact, rented an apartment from Weeks' mother, a widow. Weeks attended the University of Akron, received a B.S. in chemistry; was a member of Goodyear's Flying Squad; studied law at Western Reserve University, received his LL.B. in 1923, went to work for Thompson, Hine & Flory, a Cleveland law firm that represented the minority stockholders in a tangled dispute involving Dillon, Read & Co. in the aftermath of events that unseated Goodyear founder F. A. Seiberling.
In 1926, young Weeks met Vandeveer in Cleveland, did some legal work for Allied Oil and eventually became its legal counsel; maintained an office with the firm for years, became friendly with Newman as well as Vandeveer; is today executor of Vandeveer's estate.
Although his own participation in the merged company ended, Weeks remained the Allied Oil counsel in the merger. Today, Mr. Weeks is a senior partner in Thompson, Hine & Flory—a firm that employs approximately 65 lawyers; is still a close friend of Mr. Newman's.

years, and transfers the voting rights of your stock to me. Unless
you sign this, *right now,* the deal is off."

A blind man could have seen he was in earnest; both Newman
and Vandeveer were surprised. They left the table and huddled
together. Neither had ever heard of such an instrument before;
both were extremely anxious to conclude the sale. Vandeveer
said, "Let's get the money and get out." Newman, to whom the
business had stopped being fun, agreed.

They returned to the table and signed the agreement. It made
them both multi-millionaires. Yet both were to later regret having
signed the voting trust, for it effectively ended their influence over
the enterprise they had built, and limited their influence in the
merged company.

The following morning, John G. Clymer of Allied Oil was in
the dining room of the Mayo Hotel in Tulsa, Oklahoma, having
breakfast, when a friend stopped at his table. "I see your company has been sold to Ashland Oil," his friend said casually, and
Clymer almost choked on his Cream of Wheat. Years later, he
could still recall his dismay with retrospective amusement.

The merger changed a great many lives, and among them that
of Rex Blazer, who became president of the Allied Oil division of
Ashland. A week later, Rex was in the lobby of the Bethlehem
Steel Company, waiting to see the purchasing agent. He was called
to the phone. It was his uncle, and by the time Rex replaced the
receiver, he knew that Mr. Blazer would, henceforth, call a lot
of the shots Rex had previously fired.

But the world changed for the men of Ashland Oil also. The
combined companies represented more than $100 million worth
of business. It extended Ashland Oil from a one-refinery company
to a company with almost double its former resources. Lake
tankers, pipelines, barges, tank cars, salesmen, new customers, new
banking connections, more oil and gas leases and partners, and
more crude oil and wells entered the firm. The psychological problems of the acquisition were considerable; Blazer wanted to establish, as deeply and as soon as possible, the concept of the merged
company as Ashland Oil & Refining Company.

A relatively minor problem of nomenclature—because there
were to be two men in the firm named Blazer—seemed to resolve

Wedding photograph of the marriage between Ashland and Allied Oil.
(1948)

itself. By common consent, Paul remained Mr. Blazer; in later years this was often (out of earshot) softened to Uncle Paul.

Feverish coordinating activities took place. Art Points, who had the task of combining the accounting systems of the two firms, discovered in his Allied counterpart Sumner Hippensteele, a top man. The sales departments began to sift one another's ranks; the refinery at Catlettsburg began to schedule the production of more heavy fuel oil for Allied.

Shortly after the official signing of the merger, Mr. Blazer, J. Howard Marshall and Everett Wells attended a farewell dinner in Cleveland, given in honor of Vandeveer and Newman, by the Allied supervisory employees. At this dinner, Mr. Blazer invited both men to become directors of the Ashland Oil & Refining Company, and both accepted.

A photograph was taken of the group standing at the head table. It shows a younger Rex Blazer smiling hopefully, J. Howard Marshall looking, as ever, alert, Everett Wells, lean and dapper. Mr. Blazer, however, looks surprisingly pale and thin.[12]

A month later, the combined companies earned $1 million— the sum that Blazer and Marshall had hoped, only four years before, they might someday realize for Ashland Oil in a year.

Year-end statements, in September 1948, showed net sales of

[12] Soon after, the doctors discovered Mr. Blazer had diabetes.

$63 million, net profits of $7.8 million. Blazer could not resist calculating the combined earnings and profits of the two companies based on a year-old combination; he could hardly wait for the time to pass and these figures to be realized.

His letters to the directors spell out the details of the expanded enterprise jubilantly: the Catlettsburg refinery throughput was increased to 39,000 barrels of crude a day—almost double its previous ability. "Unusual credit is due to Roland Whealy and his assistants," Mr. Blazer wrote. "Before January first," he added, "we will have functioning facilities for fractionating a complete line of naphthas—taking advantage of our proximity to Akron and other large naphtha consuming areas—catalytic desulphurization of naphtha and gasoline, restoration of cracking plant, thus increasing the yield of diesel fuel for the Pennsylvania railroad (Moffitt and *his* men were selling greater amounts all the time) . . . all of which will add to our flexibility."

The sales department had done especially well; Allied was selling 75 per cent of Ashland's heavy fuel production . . .

In addition, the Ohio Oil Company decided to sell their distribution properties in a dozen or more Kentucky counties; from Covington through Lexington and the Blue Grass country, southwest to the Bowling Green region. To reproduce these networks, Blazer added, would cost at least double the asking price of $375,000 (plus inventories). These properties represented sales between 600,000 and 700,000 gallons of petroleum products a month: Ashland did not hesitate to make the purchase.

The Lake tankers intrigued Blazer tremendously: he had many sessions with the bluff and blunt Captain Jonassen—some of them argumentative—and he told the directors about the purchase of a converted LST for the Lakes; Allied had an excellent crude oil man named Colbert H. (Cobb) Marshall who was placed in charge of exploration and production for Ashland under Howard Marshall. "For all practical purposes," Blazer said, "Rex Blazer and Captain Jonassen can handle their own operations (Allied Oil and Cleveland Tankers)."

The Allied merger overshadowed other events during the year. One of these had been the acquisition of a small refinery from Western Reserve Refining, in Niles, Ohio, with a capacity of 2,000

barrels a day. It was small but profitable, Ashland discovered—
and operated with only twenty men. Another unremarked event
was the meeting between Edgar Kennedy, of Lehman Brothers,
and Messrs. Blazer and Marshall.

Mr. Kennedy, an oil buff, knew Bill Bennett, a partner in Frontier Oil, of Buffalo, New York. Frontier, a competitor of Allied
Oil—although Allied had originally helped it get started—operated a refinery in Buffalo, and sold fairly large quantities of fuel
oil and gasoline in northern New York, Pennsylvania and Ohio.
The minority partner, Bennett, was in poor health and anxious to
sell; the majority partner, Jim Breuil, had lost some money in
some other ventures—notably the Buffalo Bills, a professional football team—and might be willing to listen. Kennedy called Mr.
Blazer from New York during the summer, and was invited to
Ashland for a discussion. When he arrived, he was taken to one
of the towboats, where he, Mr. Blazer and Howard Marshall had
lunch.

Mr. Kennedy described Frontier Oil—a company that regularly
made money, but not in tremendous quantities. Mr. Blazer, who
seemed interested, said, "Well, let them come to us. We'll be happy
to talk to them."

But, Kennedy[13] said, he only knew one of the partners. He

---

[13] E. L. Kennedy, a partner in Lehman Brothers in charge of their
Oil Department. Mr. Kennedy was raised in Ohio, and came to New
York City in 1929, where he went to work for a financial publishing
house. His first boss had once been a drilling contractor, and his tales
aroused an interest in Kennedy "in the glamor and hidden mysteries
below the surface of the earth." Later, as a bank officer in Scranton, Pa.,
Kennedy became involved in the liquidation proceedings of 8 banks
that failed as an aftermath of the 1929 debacle. The largest single
asset of these banks, he discovered, was oil stocks. Confronted with
the necessity to learn about oil companies, he began reading everything
on the subject available; succeeded in retaining, for the banks, those
stocks that could (and did) recover. Joining Lehman in 1941, he at
first handled part of their investment portfolio; gradually became their
leading expert in oil. By 1948, he had been watching Ashland quite
some time. "Ashland had a *compelling record,*" he says, "it gave high
returns, equity profit, even through the Depression. Very few oil companies could make the same boast." His trip to Ashland included considerable curiosity about Mr. Blazer; he was not disappointed. The Frontier

didn't know whether the other partner was aware what Mr. Bennett was seeking; he thought—hesitantly—that the tactics of the situation would encourage Ashland to make overtures. To his great relief, Mr. Blazer nodded calmly and said, "In that case, we'll go to them."

By December, the company had more interests than ever before; 1948 had been a tremendous year. Ashland had almost doubled its size; grown beyond the $100 million volume figure. Its market area had been extended from the Ohio River valley north to Chicago, Cleveland, and the Great Lakes; its pipelines had been stretched east of Pittsburgh to the Atlantic seaboard, south to Louisiana, Texas, the Gulf, west to Kansas and Oklahoma. It had added two more refineries and more specialists to its group, extended its products, increased its capacities, added more executives and more young and ambitious men; its employees grew to 2,000; its stockholders to 9,600. Mr. Blazer and his associates had accomplished this, moreover, without losing control; without even sharing control.

MORE MERGERS

Early in 1949, Mr. Blazer, Art Points, Ed Emrick and others visited Frontier Oil, and talked to Jim Breuil and Bill Bennett. As Kennedy had predicted, both men seemed receptive; the industry climate was turning cold for small companies. The great consumer demand that arose after the luxury famine of World War II had peaked and was declining; business was becoming more competitive and the prices for oil products were beginning to crack in all areas. With the passing of the boom, those firms that could not afford large capital sums for modernizations and improvements thereby found themselves unable to meet lower prices and make a profit. It was becoming more evident with every passing quarter during the postwar period that simpler

---

deal was noteworthy for him, because it was the first deal in the oil business he helped to put together; a landmark in his career.

Lehman's present Oil Department is Mr. Kennedy's handiwork. Of Lehman's philosophy, he says, "We bet on men: try to find out where they want to go, and how they want to get there. Then we help."

forms of competitive enterprises—such as closed corporations, partnerships and one-man ownerships, were losing the capital race to larger public corporations. This had been true of Allied Oil; it was to be true of Frontier Oil, of Freedom-Valvoline and Aetna Oil as well.

An additional circumstance mitigating against the individual entrepreneur was the cobweb of estate (death) taxes and inheritance taxes. In their zeal both to collect taxes and prevent the growth of individual oligarchies, the planners succeeded in creating a situation where the individual enterprise would be destroyed by the death of its owners. This ensured the eternal enterprise—the corporation—which could outlast its founders. Nowhere was this clearer than in the instances of Allied Oil, Frontier Oil, Freedom-Valvoline, Aetna and other small independents—all individually owned, or owned by a few persons—competing against a publicly owned company such as Ashland Oil & Refining. The owners of these firms had reinvested the earnings of these enterprises into continuing operations and expansions. The assets of the companies were their personal assets. In order to realize these assets, however, they would have to dissipate their companies, a course that would have dissipated the assets. If they simply worked until they died, their heirs would have to dissipate the assets to pay the estate taxes; accomplishing the same short-sighted economic end. If the owner-operators sold outright while they still lived, the taxes would be severe. The only remaining resource was to sell to a publicly owned company, receiving payment in the form of stock, whose dividends would provide an income. This would, in effect, allow them to retire and retain an equity in the property they had built. Of course, if the enterprise to which they sold lost, they would in the end lose also. The problem was complicated by the fact that a major oil company seeking to buy these small independents might be refused permission, on the grounds that it was lessening competition in the industry.

Most of the owners of these small independents knew Paul Blazer, Everett Wells and the other men at Ashland personally; they did not view them in the same light as they did the managers of the majors. There was the fact that, if Ashland did not purchase them, they might well go out of business altogether; a cir-

cumstance that would lessen competition (and eliminate jobs)
more clearly than any other.

All told, it was a situation in which Ashland Oil & Refining
had a better position than appeared even on the surface; a position that Mr. Blazer appreciated. It is to the credit of the company
that it did not seek hard bargains, although its offers were highly
realistic.

Frontier Oil had developed an excellent domestic fuel market
in western New York state; operated a refinery with a capacity
of some 8,000 barrels a day that had been uplifted with a vapor
phase cracking unit in 1940; obtained crude from Illinois and
Michigan and Breuil's own producing company, operated inde-
pendently; owned a subsidiary called Frontier Transportation
Company that conveyed crude oil to Buffalo through the Erie
Canal; once operated terminal facilities in New Jersey with Leon
Hess; competed with Allied Oil, but not directly with Ashland.

After the Allied Oil merger, the acquisition of Frontier Oil
seemed eminently logical. Mr. Breuil,[14] the creative mind and
majority owner of the enterprise, had more than enough extra
interests to keep himself occupied, but because he had lost a large
sum of money—almost $1 million—backing the Buffalo Bills, a
pro-football team in Buffalo, he was in temporary difficulty. The
conversations soon resolved into a question of specific price. Mr.
Blazer, no man to push a negotiation if he thought a little more
time might worsen his opposing bargainer's position, established
contact and then withdrew to let nature take its course.

The year had begun with more crude oil available than for
many years; "Howard made a great trade with Phillips Petroleum,"

[14] James F. Breuil, born 1901 in Philadelphia, Pa., is a direct descendant
of the Marquis de Breuil, who fled the Terror in France in 1789. He
attended Staunton Military Academy, left without leave to join the
Army in World War I. His father was a mining engineer who, says
Mr. Breuil, "chased dreams around the world," found an Aztec gold mine
in Mexico and blew it in to keep it out of the hands of Pancho Villa.
Mr. Breuil founded his company with the help of Vandeveer and
Newman, sold out to Texas Co. in 1930; started up again in 1931. He
has long been a director of Ashland Oil & Refining; is still active in
oil production.

Mr. Blazer reported, "and we can now curtail drilling operations." The great point of contact, apparently, had been through the Neutral Zone venture, Aminol. That enterprise had yet to drill a well, though a concession had been obtained. Mr. J. Paul Getty had a concession also in the Neutral Zone. He proved a gentleman of strong opinions. Mr. Getty insisted that his opinions be consulted. Neutral Zone concessions represented an undivided half interest from King Ibn Saud of Saudi Arabia and the Sheik of Kuwait. Neither half could be separated from the sovereigns; the concessionaires had to cooperate to operate.

Mr. Blazer and Howard Marshall, when they entered the consortium, had made an agreement to stick with Signal Oil & Gas— and Ralph Davies—on all issues that came to a vote before the directors. The general purpose of this understanding was to prevent Phillips from dominating the company and its strategy. By 1949, Mr. Blazer was showing some signs of being dissatisfied with Mr. Davies, who had also become president of the American President Lines, and who had other business interests. Mr. Blazer was consistent in his opinion that men who operate corporations should have no other interest; but because Mr. Marshall and Mr. Davies were very good friends, and Howard Marshall was certainly working hard and well for Ashland Oil, he held his peace.

Meanwhile, taking advantage of a temporary market lull, the refinery was being modernized and upgraded again; new river equipment was ordered, and capital expenditures at the rate of $1 million a month were being poured into the company.

In early January, Mr. Blazer accepted the post of chairman of the Cincinnati branch of the Federal Reserve System. At this point memories were sharpened when the towboat *Senator Combs,* was sold. Mr. Blazer wrote, "It is with considerable regret, that I report the sale . . ." It was too small for the company requirements; it was losing money because the crew was as large as those of the larger boats.

Steadily through the winter, Allied Oil was marking down the values of its inventories; Howard Marshall was busy in Texas; the manufacture of jet fuel began to quicken at Catlettsburg; $200,000 was being spent to enlarge the terminal at Nashville; land for a new terminal at Paducah, Kentucky, was acquired; Shell Oil sold some of their distribution in western Kentucky. One suspects one of the reasons that Shell and Ohio were selling these distributorships was because they were tired of meeting Ashland's competition in this, its home territory. The Louisville and Evansville terminals were coming to a completion. The Ashland Drilling Company, with its rotary rig for which so much had been hoped, had proven unsuccessful: Howard Marshall recommended its sale. The American Independent Oil Company had decided to drill in Mexico, and Mr. Blazer wrote the directors: "I read about this in the newspapers," and followed up this frowning comment with the statement that "The mideast situation looks less promising because of the world-wide oversupply of crude oil." His irritation was growing.

By June 1949, operations were down; the company was refining only 36,500 barrels a day, but the new terminals had expanded gasoline sales. Overall, the company was refining six times its crude oil production, and Mr. Blazer complained that crude oil prices were being maintained by proration, which he said, "puts the burden of price breaks on refiners." This was an old observation of his; he preferred the old days of the open market, although he seldom stated it openly.

His practical interest in politics remained keen. He both enjoyed and benefited intellectually from his conversations with Chief Justice Fred M. Vinson, who provided him with an overall understanding of the drift of events. But at home, his younger son Stuart was proving a product of the times; Mr. Blazer, telling his wife he himself had been "radical" when he was young, did not mind from an intellectual standpoint. But the discussions sometimes grew heated, and he found these tiring.

In terms of Kentucky politics, he had found a gold mine in John Fred Williams, who joined the company in 1948.[15] Mr.

[15] John Fred Williams was born 1904 in Volga, Ky. Originally from Wales, the family arrived in the U.S. sometime before the Revolutionary War; his great-grandfather was born in Virginia in 1793; his grandfather came to eastern Kentucky in 1864 to join and fight with the Union Army during the Civil War, bringing his son born in 1859 with him. Thus, only three generations separate John Fred Williams from the founding of the country. John Fred Williams taught in a one-room

Williams' background as an educator struck a sympathetic chord with Mr. Blazer, whose own family had been deeply involved in this profession and its results; the two spent hours together, with John Fred talking and Mr. Blazer asking questions, about the people, feuds, marriages and mores of Kentucky.

Mr. Blazer felt this was all essential information toward getting a new Kentucky Constitution. It was not an easy task; the voters had most recently rejected this proposition in 1947. Then a Review Commission was established, upon which Mr. Blazer was active, and an attempt was being mounted to ease the process of amendments to the Constitution. If this effort was successful, change could be introduced piecemeal. John Fred Williams' store of knowledge about the state and its people could lead Mr. Blazer to many avenues. But the conversations were interesting in themselves; the two men enjoyed them hugely.

Mr. Blazer had, though, a private worry. In the course of a visit with Dr. Leslie Winans to get a routine checkup, he had received a rather clear warning. Dr. Winans, who said that Mr. Blazer seldom stopped talking, had difficulty in concentrating during these visits. On this particular occasion, the two men left the examination room and walked together down the hall. Mr. Blazer was, as usual, speaking; Dr. Winans' attention was obviously elsewhere. Finally, Mr. Blazer and Dr. Winans entered the doctor's office, and Mr. Blazer said, "Leslie, you seem to be deep in thought. What are you thinking about?"

Winans, who like many physicians is apt to be more busy than diplomatic, said bluntly, "Your heart attack."

"Am I going to have a heart attack?" Mr. Blazer asked. "When?"

"In about a year," Winans said. He then proceeded to give instructions on what to do—including a suggestion to line up

---

rural school in the hills of eastern Kentucky from 1924–1930; earned a B.A. from the University of Kentucky in 1931; taught high school in Johnson City, Ky.; was principal at Paintsville, Ky. from 1932–1933; then superintendent of schools in Johnson City for 10 years (1933–1943); was elected Superintendent of Public Instruction of Kentucky from 1944–1948; narrowly missed obtaining the Republican nomination for governor. He is fascinated with the history of Kentucky, knows the state and its people in encyclopedic fashion; is today a vice president of Ashland Oil & Refining.

"some good heart men" out of town. In the event the attack occurred when he was away, he gave him an injection kit and some morphine.

Mr. Blazer was not a good bet to survive a heart attack. A year before, it had been learned he had developed diabetes; his hours remained as idiosyncratic as ever; his diet had to endure many adjustments. But Dr. Winans' information was unsettling; he kept it to himself, for the most part, excepting for a very few men to whom he felt particularly close.

But now the question of a successor was upon him, and Mr. Blazer was reluctant to see J. Howard Marshall chief executive at Ashland Oil & Refining. This presented some difficulty, because Mr. Marshall had been engaged precisely for this succession. Not only that, his abilities had attracted considerable and favorable attention. Some of the directors seemed convinced he was the right man; Art Points and Ed Emrick played golf with Marshall and enjoyed his company; Roland Whealy got along well with him; so did Alex Chamberlain; so did Joe Levin of A. G. Becker; so did W. W. Vandeveer and other men. There were, of course, men who had different opinions, but Mr. Marshall was president of the company, and these opinions were muted. Mr. Blazer's dilemma was more personal: he did not want to step aside—for Mr. Marshall. As the time to do so came closer, the thought became increasingly less appealing. A heart attack would bring the move terribly close, but Mr. Blazer did not fear a heart attack.

On the surface, other matters dominated the stage. "Many independent refiners appear willing to merge or to sell," he wrote the directors. One such lead came to him from Joe Levin. An A. G. Becker man, working in Indiana, had to make frequent trips to Louisville, Kentucky. There, the Becker man, Charley Ritter, discovered that Henry Offutt, president of the Kentucky Trust Company, was holding a half-interest in the Aetna Oil Company because one of the firm's principals had died. Levin discussed this with Blazer, who suggested he go to Louisville and talk to Hoffutt about a merger between Aetna and Ashland. Levin met Hoffutt at the Columbia Club in Indianapolis, and the merger was discussed. This discussion in turn led to other conversations with Walton Davis, the other major stockholder. Mr. Davis, who managed the company, was experienced and skillful, and had done a good job. But in 1948, Aetna had experienced a damaging fire, and one of the principals died. This left the future management and the ownership of the company in some question; when Ashland acquired 46 per cent of the stock for $1.8 million, Mr. Davis was in an obvious position to sell. The firm had a refinery at Louisville, but was more attractive to Ashland because it had 220 owned or leased service stations, located in central and western Kentucky and southern Indiana, as well as a barge fleet, bulk stations and other properties.

Freedom-Valvoline, another independent, was in a position similar to Allied Oil. The owners were Earle Craig and William Bechman. Mr. Bechman, older by about a decade than Mr. Craig, was in bad health, and the question of his estate and the subsequent taxes loomed large. Freedom-Valvoline was a larger property than Aetna; like Allied Oil, it served a special market. In this instance, it was important in the manufacture and marketing of motor lubricating oils. Both names were, in addition to being company names, brand names as well; both brands were very well known.

Mr. Blazer had known Earle Craig,[16] the majority owner, for

[16] Earle Craig, born 1894 in Newcastle, Pa., is a descendant of a family originally from Chester, England, that emigrated to the U.S. from northern Ireland in 1822, settled in Allegheny County, Pa., in 1829–1830. Craig attended prep school at Lawrenceville and went to Yale, where he was a classmate of Ned Seaton's. Neither man saw the other again until after the merger between Freedom–Valvoline and Ashland Oil became effective. Craig received a Bachelor of Philosophy degree (that is no longer issued) in 1916, was accepted for training by the Field Artillery Officers in 1918, graduated after the war was over.

After Freedom Oil Works was established by Earle's great-uncle Joseph W. Craig, the family obtained the Newcastle Gas Company and the Fort Pitt Gas Company (now part of the Columbia Gas System); Fort Pitt Gas had Andrew Mellon as a vice-president. Joseph W. Craig died in 1912, his brother Percy (Earle's father) became president of Freedom Oil Works, and the balance of the properties were sold.

Earle Craig himself began his working life with Freedom, starting in the summer of 1914 as a bookkeeper for $50 a month ("overpaid," he says many years. Conversations with Freedom-Valvoline were begun at the Duquesne Club in Pittsburgh, and included sessions in Freedom, Pennsylvania. Final Freedom-Valvoline merger talks began on a Friday. On Sunday, Mr. Bechman called Ben Heath, who was by then a vice president of Freedom-Valvoline, and told him Paul Blazer wanted to see him the following day. Heath went to the hotel the next day, and found Mr. Blazer, Arthur Points and Joe Levin. The three men quizzed Heath about Freedom-Valvoline until five in the afternoon. Finally, Mr. Blazer turned to Heath, and said "I'll pay so much," naming a figure.

"I'm not the owner," Heath said.

"Do you think they'll accept that figure?" Blazer asked him, and Heath, feeling harried and still a loyal member of the Freedom-Valvoline team, said, "No, I don't think they will. It's not enough."

Mr. Blazer turned to Points and said, "Art, get the plane. We're going home."

Heath, shaken by all these maneuvers, left. As soon as he reached home, he found the president of Freedom-Valvoline on the line, wanting to know what was said and by whom, and he gave his report. From then on a curtain dropped between him and the negotiators, and he remained in the dark until the board of directors of Freedom-Valvoline met, were informed of the offer, and voted to accept. Heath was, by that action, working for Paul Garrett Blazer again.

Although agreement to merge was reached between the companies, it had to await a tax ruling from Washington. This did not arrive until after the Ashland fiscal year ended. The annual report, therefore, discussed the acquisition of Freedom-Valvoline as a strong probability, and not a fact. Otherwise, the results at the end of September 1949 were as glowing as Mr. Blazer had, a year before, exultantly predicted in the wake of the acquisition of Allied Oil. Net sales were $102.3 million; net profits $9.3 million.

---

today). After the acquisition, Mr. Craig remained as president of Freedom, but considered his methods too different from Paul Blazer's for true harmony; he believes progress for Freedom began later, under Rex Blazer. Mr. Craig is a director of Ashland Oil & Refining today.

While these advances were being made, the world as a whole was making others whose import and direction were by no means as clear-cut. On September 23, 1949, President Truman revealed to the general public that the Soviet Union had detonated its own atomic bomb. The news sent a chill around the world, since the implacability of the Soviet state had long ago established itself in the minds of observers.

Within the United States this circumstance coincided with a rash of revelations; for the first time in its national history, the country was confronted with the spectacle of spies and traitors. Voices of alarm and indignation began to be raised. The closing days of the Chiang Kai Shek regime in China—the greatest single change in Asia and the world situation—also helped usher into being a new and even more dangerous era than that which had gone before.

The spirit of the nation in the face of these circumstances was not assisted by the fact that the press, in a variety of oblique but obvious ways, began to attack the White House itself more bitterly than at any time since the early 1930s, when Mr. Hoover was its unhappy occupant. The circumstances of the nation were not otherwise analogous, but the citizenry was made psychologically unhappy by the agitation.

One result, predictably, of the advances by the Soviets and the international Communist ideology, was a marked increase in United States defense appropriations and spending. The Air Force was to be greatly increased; so were the number of nuclear reactors and explorations into nuclear fission. The one development affected the aeronautic, fuel, fine tool and allied industries; the other was to have a tremendous effect on hydroelectric projects; together, they sent large amounts of money coursing through the nation that quickened industry, increased inflationary forces and in turn led to more agitation in the ranks of labor as the ordinary circumstances of life became more difficult.

In financial terms, the nation had received another booster shot, especially since these efforts were accompanied by rising welfare and eleemosynary programs. The stock exchange began to move upward and increase its trading; the nation was moving at a rate that caused many economists to glow, although others, over-aware of automation and the emergence of computers, began to keen about the rapidity of obsolescence in industry.

Internationally, 1949 ended to the echoing collapse of Nationalist China, eight years to the day after Pearl Harbor, less than that since FDR confidently included that country in the Big Four, and America began its great effort of money, arms, men, and support to free that country from invasion and tyranny.

At Ashland Oil & Refining, the men of the company began to plan their usual round of year-end Christmas parties.

In January 1950, the imminent purchases of Aetna and Freedom-Valvoline made new financing necessary; for the first time, Mr. Blazer began making appearances before underwriters. In Chicago, he addressed a group of analysts, accompanied by Howard Marshall, Rex Blazer, and Walton Davis (of Aetna), and another group in New York, this time with Ben Heath along. While going from one point to another, he also found time to have another conference in Buffalo with Messrs. Breuil and Bennett; on this occasion, Mr. Blazer was accompanied by Art Points and Walton Davis. The flavor of a large enterprise was becoming more evident with every passing season.

In January, also, both the Aetna and the Freedom-Valvoline mergers were officially cleared, signed, and sealed, and Mr. Blazer felt it was the "greatest growth in our history," a statement we have heard before, and will hear again. Aetna's Louisville refinery added eight thousand more barrels a day of refining capacity to the company—and we know by now that Mr. Blazer operated from refining as a base—some crude oil wells in the Illinois Basin, a small fleet of river barges, and distributing properties in southern Indiana as well as western Kentucky and central Kentucky.

Freedom-Valvoline was a larger acquisition and involved a step in new market directions for Ashland. Essentially, the company manufactured lubricating oils from Pennsylvania crude oil obtained in the western fields, conveyed to its refinery through a 1,400 mile pipeline through western Pennsylvania, West Virginia and southern Ohio, that culminated in Freedom, Pennsylvania. The refinery had a capacity of 4,000 barrels of crude a day. Ethyl Corporation made a study of its best-known brand, Valvoline motor oil, and discovered that it could be traced back, in a direct line of descent, to Continuous Oil Refining Company organized in 1866. The company's oil, developed by Dr. John Ellis, was named Valvoline by George Corliss, the inventor of the Corliss steam engine, in 1868. A trademark was obtained in 1873; and in 1903, the company itself adopted the name. Dr. Ellis' son was still active in the company when control was acquired by E. S. Edwards (a steel executive).

Thus, Ashland Oil had become owner of one of the oldest and best-known motor lubricating oils in the country; in years to come it was to push this brand to the national forefront again.

Then in April 1950, as though to cap progress, the Frontier Oil Company in Buffalo, resistance satisfactorily over, sold to Ashland. Against the backdrop of these relatively large negotiations, the purchase of the Findlay, Ohio, refinery from National Refining—the Lamprecht family's company—seems almost anticlimactic.

Nevertheless, Findlay was a significant purchase. It included a refinery with a crude oil capacity of 10,000 barrels a day, and the brands White Rose gasoline and Enarco motor oils and lubricants. These had been big names when Mr. Blazer entered the industry: trees were falling before the traveler in all directions.

The refinery at Catlettsburg was producing one million gallons of gasoline a day; all the refineries together were processing in the neighborhood of 75,000 barrels of crude oil daily.

The company had grown large, and it was time to move up: Ed Emrick and Mr. Blazer spent some time with Mr. John West, the Director of Listing at the New York Stock Exchange—the Big Board itself—and a formal application was filed March 28, 1950. Approval from the Board of Governors for an issue of common stock and $1.20 preferred, was received on April 6. The N.Y. Curb required thirty days for formal delisting; the transfer went through smoothly and without incident. The transfer agents were the Second National Bank of Ashland, the Chase National Bank and the Morgan Bank were co-transfer agents and co-registrars. Steps were also taken, at the same time, to be listed on the Midwest Stock Exchange.

Against all this, the news that the first well drilled by the

American Independent Oil Company in the Neutral Zone was a dry hole hardly seemed to ruffle the waters.

In discussions with the Department of Justice over the purchase of Frontier Oil, it informed Mr. Blazer that Ashland Oil & Refining now ranked nineteenth in the nation's oil industry. He was surprised.

"There is no virtue in acquisitions," he wrote, "as such. I believe these have strengthened our company."

Then, in the next paragraph, he takes pride in having acquired, for $65,000, "44 miles of pipeline connecting the eastern terminus of the pipeline to a point near the Delaware River at Marcus Hook. An important acquisition, since I anticipate that eventually this line will be handling foreign crude. Heretofore, we have depended on connecting carriers for the approximately 50-mile gap between our lines and deepwater navigation."

The ink had hardly dried on the sale to Ashland when Mr. Bennett, who had been serving as president of the Frontier Oil Company, asked to be relieved, and asked that Rex Blazer be his successor. Since Frontier's operations were very similar to Allied's, Mr. Blazer approved of this—so did the Ashland board.

By July 1950, Rex Blazer was spending several days a week in Buffalo looking after the affairs of Frontier Oil, as well as several days in Cleveland watching Allied Oil, when he had information that his life would be further changed.

It came on July 19. Mr. Blazer had, by this time, discussed his heart condition with a number of persons, and Vandeveer, a man whose instincts were always kindly, suggested he see Dr. Roy Scott, a leading heart specialist in Cleveland, later President of the American Heart Association. Mr. Blazer was accompanied by Rex, who stayed until the examination was over. Then the two men left together: Mr. Blazer was slightly pale, and somewhat shaken.

"I wasn't prepared for what Dr. Scott told me. I knew I had a serious heart problem, but Dr. Scott thinks a coronary accident is imminent." He paused, and then continued slowly, "I'm not afraid to die, but the company is in the hands of Howard Marshall."

There was another long silence, and he continued. "I'm not

concerned about my family. They're well provided for. Georgia is strong and intelligent. But the company concerns me. Rex, you will have to come to Ashland later in the year. Is that agreeable to you?"

Although content in Cleveland, Rex, faced with this unexpected turn of the wheel said, "Yes, of course I'll come."

The conversation between the two men came a little over three weeks after the North Koreans invaded South Korea with sixty thousand troops, spearheaded by one hundred Russian-built tanks. On June 27, 1950, the UN Security Council, boycotted by Russia because Red China had not been admitted to membership and Nationalist China booted out, voted to assist South Korea by all necessary means. The same day, President Truman ordered General MacArthur to Korea as Commander.

Internally, the Ashland organization made a number of shifts; Alex Chamberlain was made an executive assistant to relieve both Marshall and Mr. Blazer; John Fred Williams was made Personnel Manager. Mr. Blazer, in describing Chamberlain's duties in a letter to the board, declared him responsible for insurance, pensions, safety, industrial engineering, efficiency studies and also the operations of the pipelines—but he hoped to relieve him of that.

By August, sales were moving at the rate of $175 million annually, a pace that would have seemed incredible only a couple of years before; a new fluid cracking unit and accessories had been ordered at a cost of $2.5 million; the refinery at Findlay was being started up; "Whealy, Cecil West and I have looked it over and spotted fifty improvements that will enable it to pay out." Heart trouble or no, attack coming or not, Mr. Blazer was still working around the clock. He continued on the Findlay refinery: "It is now capable of processing some 8,000 to 10,000 barrels of crude; we will lift it (via the improvements spotted) to 20,000 barrels."

Sohio decided to participate in the Mid-Valley Pipeline, to carry its crude oil to their refineries all the way from Louisiana. As a consequence, Mr. Blazer wondered whether they would still need the new towboat and barges they had constructed, and just received. He caught the scent of a bargain for Ashland Oil . . .

At the 1950 fiscal year's end, annual net sales soared to $145 million; net profits were over $10 million: a new high.

In September 1950, Rex reported Allied Oil had its biggest month in history; the directors were told "we are now visualizing our ultimate marketing territory as extending from the Mississippi River eastward to the Appalachian mountains, including Buffalo." The visualization was a reality.

In fact, the company was viewing new business in Southern Illinois. There was a small refinery at St. Elmo, located on a trunk line of the Ohio Oil Company, ninety miles east of St. Louis, that looked interesting: it could process 4,000 barrels of crude oil a day, but was poorly designed. It was owned by the Northwest Refining Company, and included a river terminal in East St. Louis. Mr. Blazer stated, "We should have a terminal in East St. Louis. Ten per cent of all the crude oil in the United States crosses the river at this point . . ."

In late October 1950, more internal changes were revealed. Mr. Blazer recommended to the board that Everett Wells, until then a vice president, be made executive vice president. "He will," Mr. Blazer explained, ". . . take over most of my work in operations." The balance of the operating group: Whealy in charge of refining, Dupree in charge of all transportation except pipelines, Bolton head of marketing, Luthy in charge of all crude oil procurement except pipeline transportation, to continue as before; Rex to coordinate sales and operations for Freedom-Valvoline, Allied and Aetna as well as Frontier; ". . . this is not to affect J. Howard Marshall, Ned Seaton, Art Points, Ed Emrick or Rex . . ." But one has a feeling it was designed to affect Mr. Marshall.

In December 1950, Mr. and Mrs. Blazer were in their beach apartment house in La Jolla, California. As usual, Mr. Blazer was working; he and Mrs. Blazer were composing an Employee-Dividend letter, which would accompany a year-end bonus to all employees. The routine was familiar to them both; he would dictate and Mrs. Blazer would transcribe it directly on the typewriter. Then he would amend and she would retype. He was meticulous and exacting, but she did not mind; she knew he tried to do his best. This time both the letter and the typing went well, and they completed their master copy.

They mailed the letter as they drove to a cocktail party at the home of some friends. Uncharacteristically, Mr. Blazer was feeling depressed, and his wife tried to cheer him up as they drove. But at the party, shortly after laughing uproariously at some chance remark, Mr. Blazer suddenly turned very pale, and said, "I feel very queer."

They drove back to their apartment almost immediately, in order to reach the oxygen tank (they had not yet formed the habit of carrying it almost everywhere), and the short distance—three blocks—seemed many miles to Mrs. Blazer. Back in the apartment, Mr. Blazer rested against some cushions and inhaled oxygen, while Mrs. Blazer called Dr. Herbert McCoy, a young heart specialist they had located only three days before. The call reached Dr. McCoy just as he himself was leaving on a dinner date, and he came over immediately. He was a very young man—not yet thirty —and very calm. By the time he arrived, Mr. Blazer was obviously seriously stricken. "He was," Mrs. Blazer said later, "in heart failure."

Dr. McCoy made his examination, and then said to Mrs. Blazer, "I'd like to see the rest of this apartment."

In the next room, after Mrs. Blazer had pulled the door shut, he told Mrs. Blazer he didn't expect her husband to live through the attack, but warned her not to tell him.

Mr. Blazer was taken to the hospital in an oxygen-equipped ambulance that traveled very fast. By the time Mrs. Blazer arrived, driving after the ambulance, he was already in a room and under an oxygen tent.

Section Seven—Corporate Life

1951–1955

Physicians know the will to live has a large bearing upon the outcome of a critical illness. Mr. Blazer's will was highly developed. When death, the greatest of man's adversaries, moved to take him from under his oxygen tent, he assessed his own position coolly.

"Would you consider this a serious heart attack?" he asked young Dr. McCoy.

"Oh, yes."

"What are my chances?"

"Getting better every hour. You can live another five to eight years."

It was a reply that might have daunted another man, but Mr. Blazer's struggle was not diluted by fear. It might well have been, though, for the struggle back from the brink was a long one that extended for weeks. Mrs. Blazer rented a small apartment on the ocean front, just below the hospital; she could see the lights of his room from there. She spent her days with him, and relayed messages. One—an early one—was to Palmer Talbutt, instructing him—to that gentleman's amazement—to get an immediate physical check-up.

After a few weeks, Mr. Blazer was improved enough to feel restless. Young Dr. McCoy forbade any real work to his patient, but when queried, could see no real harm in at least some business fun. Accordingly, a bright young broker was summoned, and Mr. Blazer amused himself by playing the market for small sums.

Back in Ashland, the letter to the directors appeared in January over the signature of Everett Wells. The story it had to tell reminds that new faces and new negotiations had obscured the overall story of the firm's progress, and the day-to-day work that was continued.

The company that emerged from the pressures of World War II to earn net sales of $20 million in 1946, increased by almost a fifth in 1947 to reach $29 million, more than doubled to reach $63 million in 1948, more than doubled again to clear $145 million in 1950. From a company operating one refinery, it operated seven.

A domain once comprehensible enough to be managed by one man and his associates had extended far beyond that stage by January 1951; entire reaches were being managed by men unknown to Ashland Oil a few years before. The reports to the directors had grown from a few pages to great stacks of dense statistics.

Years later, when asked his thoughts beneath the oxygen tent, Mr. Blazer said simply, "I thought about the company."

Because he had set in motion some developments that did not emerge until January 1951, Mr. Blazer had plenty of material upon which to speculate in his oxygen tent. Back in Ashland, at the annual meeting, Rexford S. Blazer, forty-three years old, had been elected president of the Ashland Oil & Refining Company. In the same meeting and at the same time, J. Howard Marshall was made vice-chairman of the board.

For Mr. Marshall, it was difficult to precisely define this shift in status: titles alone are seldom the keys by which the mysteries of corporate influence can be deciphered. He had worked well for Ashland Oil, and in the process, Mr. Marshall had changed his own fortunes as well. He started out in 1933 as a professor on leave in Washington, had become an oil company house counsel, then a partner in a law firm with oil industry clients, had served the nation as a Petroleum Administration for War official. Then he became, at Ashland Oil & Refining and with Paul Blazer, a full-fledged oil industry executive; president of a firm that seemed to soar after he joined it.

For a long time, Marshall and Paul Blazer worked together very closely; they found one another mentally stimulating and congenial. The consensus of most opinions was that Marshall had helped the firm through his contacts and activities; had bargained hard and often on its behalf, and had established himself as a hard-driving, astute executive.

Now the situation at Ashland had subtly altered. The chairman was no longer either vocal or laudatory about Mr. Marshall's accomplishments; praised other men instead.

Since Mr. Blazer had never really established clear-cut channels of delegated authority, the change did not entail a great shift in day-to-day duties. It was assumed that Mr. Blazer would cross lines, change assignments, quiz assistants, launch new projects and redirect older ones, as before.

The vice-chairmanship was, therefore, an ambiguous honor: one that could be construed by its recipient as either a designation of official heir apparent, or as a loss of the presidency. Mr. Marshall, an intelligent man, had his own thoughts. But he had been maneuvered into a position he could only smilingly accept.

Rex Blazer, on the other hand, was in no such quandary. He had received a signal honor, a little over two years after Allied Oil was acquired by Ashland. In addition to becoming president of Ashland, he remained president of Allied Oil and Frontier Oil; had behind him the support of men at Allied with whom he had worked for years—many of whom would join him at Ashland—and was fresh to the situation. His sponsors Vandeveer and Newman were delighted.

Newman, in fact, visited La Jolla not long afterward, and dropped by to pay a call upon Mr. Blazer, who was by now out of the hospital and back in his apartment.

"He said he was going to take things easier," Newman reported.

Mr. Blazer, who was somewhat out of the mainstream in La Jolla, was loath to allow Newman to depart; he delighted in conversations about the oil industry. At thirty-minute intervals he would excuse himself and go into the next room to take oxygen, then would return.

Back in Ashland, men remained busy. But in the background, a new sort of war was being conducted by the United States. Allied Oil and the other subsidiaries, and even the refineries, were losing young men to the armed services. These young men were being sent to fight in Korea, to take part in the United Nations resistance to North Korean aggression. Officially, the United States was at peace.

The United Nations authorized military action to protect South Korea, but not to overcome the aggressor beyond South Korea's borders. In other words, the military action was approved only to restore peace, and not to win a war.

Our young men were fighting, but the nation was not officially at war. Therefore there was no wartime censorship, nor did the government issue rallying statements calling for the defeat of the enemy. The general public, unused to such distinctions, fell into confused, highly charged and partisan debate, exacerbated, as usual, by the press.

Since the economics of the situation had the same effect as a war, the government established price controls over a number of essential commodities, established priorities and Certificates of Necessity, and restored the excess profits tax. The whole circumstance was termed an emergency.

At Ashland, Art Points and Ned Seaton, toiling over the complexities of the tax regulations, forecast enormous taxes that would substantially reduce the earnings of the company. Then a boom started in the Spraberry fields in West Texas. J. Howard Marshall flew down at once, and began negotiations with Tex Harvey, who had a field fifteen miles from Midland, Texas, in the Spraberry sands area. Some sixty oil rigs were working in the area; Ashland soon had gathering lines from which it was collecting some 8,000 barrels of crude a day; plans were made to drill a number of wells.

Mr. Blazer was most excited at the possibilities, and they looked highly attractive. It was his dream, by this time, to realize some substantial discoveries; the company had spent millions in crude oil searches. Furthermore, the excess profits tax would allow part (but not all) of the cost of these efforts to be, in effect, expensed from revenues that would otherwise go to the tax collectors.

To take charge of this campaign, Mr. Blazer recommended Colbert H. (Cobb) Marshall, formerly of Allied Oil. In fact, so enthusiastic did he become that he thought Cobb Marshall should be made a vice president. He sent Roy Ralston, another produc-

tion man, from Henderson, Kentucky, to the southwest to work
with both Cobb and J. Howard Marshall.

In order to balance these activities with the overall direction of
the company, Mr. Blazer—for the first time—found it necessary
to call for capital budgets from his department heads. Ed Emrick,
his head of purchasing, and one of the top team in the company
during this period, was one of the few who noticed that this was
not the only change.

In 1951, Emrick, probably as a hangover from his wartime stint
in charge of priorities, was in charge of getting pipe for the company; pipe (for pipelines) was in short supply, and the Ashland
need was growing by the hour. In addition, Emrick was a special
assistant to Paul Blazer; he had been relieved of his duties as
assistant treasurer in "1948 or 1949."

"I liked Howard Marshall," Emrick said, "but the fact that we
worked together so well began to irritate Mr. Blazer. He resented
the time I spent with Howard, and even the fact that we played
golf together. But Howard was, after all, my boss . . ."

Years before, Emrick had been given the responsibility of signing the company checks; in the earlier days in amount up to $500.
In 1943, Mr. Blazer—who until then had insisted on discussing
amounts beyond that sum—gave Emrick permission to sign checks
up to $1,000. In 1944, he lifted the ceiling to $5,000. But after he
came back from La Jolla and his heart attack, he said, in effect,
sign them all.

"Mr. Blazer was for years the most cautious man I ever knew,"
said Emrick. "When I first started working for Ashland, Mr. Blazer
examined everything; took no chances; moved very carefully. He
remained that way until he had his heart attack. And after that
attack, he began to do things in a different way. He became
more—" Emrick stopped, unwilling to go too far, and finally said,
"—expansive." He dropped his voice and said, "almost reckless."

After several more moments of reflection, Emrick added, "Paul
changed. I have never known a man to change as much as he did
after his heart attack."

"We will drill," said the new Mr. Blazer in a letter to the directors, "twenty-five wells in the Spraberry area between April and
September." He also outlined plans to build a pipeline between

Toledo and Detroit, and another between Louisville and Lexington. He discussed the fact that a new cracking unit was needed at Buffalo, and that the refineries at Findlay and Louisville should be modernized. He also stated that he was actively seeking small companies whose owners had estate or tax problems and that he had decided the company should advertise more extensively and should issue credit cards. He informed the board that for these and other purposes, Art Points had asked the government for $21.5 million worth of Certificates of Necessity.

Mr. Blazer's letters read as though he were charging across the landscape on a white steed; it is hard to realize that he was virtually bedridden; he did not go to the office at all during this period; he lived mainly with the telephone with papers spread before him.

Rex Blazer was staying at the Blazer home until he could find a suitable house of his own, and at dinner in the evening he would often find that Mr. Blazer would lead the conversation into avenues of oblique inquiry regarding the course of actions taken in the office. One evening Mr. Blazer asked Rex if anything had happened during the day that was of interest, and Rex replied that he had held a conversation with Ed Emrick who had expressed grave reservations about the Spraberry field. Mr. Blazer was astonished, and Rex, unaware that he was conveying new information, went on to say that the elevation of Cobb Marshall, who had been placed in charge of the company's crude oil efforts, and in particular the Spraberry project, had also been questioned. Mr. Blazer was thunderstruck. The fact that such conversations were being held without his knowledge was wounding enough; the knowledge that their gist was being conveyed almost by accident was even more so. He had always expected his associates to voice their opinions openly; Rex's information underscored his isolation. Unaware of this reaction, Rex continued with the conversation. It was only later when he saw Emrick's responsibilities drastically narrowed that he realized he had unwittingly contributed to this development.

In April 1951, the month that Mr. Blazer unfurled his plans and projects for the perusal of the board of directors, a young lawyer particularly knowledgeable in price regulations, and who had worked briefly for Allied Oil, joined the firm. William J. (Bill) Hull impressed Mr. Blazer, and he decided to use him as a special assistant.

A year previously, under no such towering auspices, another young attorney named Orin E. Atkins[1] joined the firm. Young Atkins, barely out of the University of Virginia Law School, had heard from his grandmother's nurse that Ashland Oil was looking for a young lawyer. He applied immediately, to the astonishment of the Legal Department, since they had not yet announced their need. Alex Chamberlain interviewed him as did Mac Burnam, and because he showed obvious signs of intelligence he was hired almost on the spot. He was twenty-six.

By July 1951, Cobb Marshall's reports on the company's crude oil efforts were enthusiastic and optimistic. In the west Texas Spraberry region, arrangements were well along to drill seventy-five wells; drilling was underway—with an assortment of partners —in various parts of the country.

Shifts in the corporate line-up continued. Mr. Davis, of Aetna, wanted help, and Dr. Clive Alexander, until then a vice president of that company, was elevated to executive vice president. "A good man," Mr. Blazer wrote, ". . . with better than average executive ability. His training has been principally as an engineer and technologist; so far as I know, he had no sales experience (a handicap, in Mr. Blazer's view) . . . Like most well-trained engineers, he is a logical thinker and has an excellent sense of orderliness and system . . ."

This was a new tone; from this point on Mr. Blazer's evaluations would go beyond the immediate, and into larger principles of

[1] Orin E. Atkins, born in 1924 in Pittsburgh, Pa., grew up in Huntington, W. Va., a city located only a few miles from Ashland, Ky. He graduated from high school in Huntington, where one of his teachers, Mrs. Henryetta Hager, described him as quiet, a bookworm: "highly honorable." He entered Marshall University but his education was interrupted in 1943 by service in the U.S. Army, where he was wounded in action in the European Theater. In 1946 he reenrolled at Marshall and majored in political science and economics. In the fall of 1947 he transferred to the University of Virginia and received an LL.B. in 1950. Atkins is tall, quick-moving and fast thinking: his rise in the company will be described.

management assessment. Perhaps the oxygen tent reflections were responsible for this, or perhaps the development would have been reached in any event. For whatever reason, his thoughts began to revolve, more and more openly, toward the matter of a succession in management. And in looking around, he made the same observation that struck most others in the 1950s: the nation seemed woefully short of well-rounded men. The results of specialization, started in the early 1940s under the pressures of war and continued by the educators as an excellent means of both staffing and operating intellectual factories, were beginning to appear.

Mr. Blazer began to search for younger men, men still plastic enough to learn more than suffer from new experiences. Until the early 1950s, his closest associates had been men of experience like Ed Emrick, Ned Seaton, Everett Wells and others; now he began to tutor younger men. His methods were unique.

They began, usually, with having the young man read his mail. Then Mr. Blazer would discuss possible responses to these letters. The conversation might then range into the activities of the company—and often the men—then the possibilities of the market and political situation; the general trend of events; possible new directions. Mr. Blazer treated an assistant as a personal collaborator; it became a custom for him to look around a roomful of men and say, "You gentlemen might be interested in knowing the next president of the company is probably sitting right in this room," or to put his arm around a young man and say, "I wouldn't be surprised if this young man doesn't become the next president of the company."

These were flourishes, of course, intended mainly to encourage. Nevertheless, they evoked tremendous dreams and efforts to match while the senior executives, already installed, left no effort untried in order to prevent the future from overtaking the present.

And since business, like time itself, equals motion, changes continued.

Earle Craig of Freedom-Valvoline was not anxious to continue as operating head of that company; Everett Wells became president in his stead, and operations were entrusted to executive vice president Harry Johnston.

At Allied Oil, Frank Colegrove[2] became executive vice president and operating head, while Rex Blazer moved into the president's chair at Ashland Oil, and into a Georgian colonial home he bought in the town.

At Frontier Oil, all was running well; at Ashland, backstage conversations were being held with companies that seemed likely prospects for acquisition.

And despite the slightly feverish activities in the Spraberry region down in Texas, where drilling crews were at work, and the landscape was littered with oil pumps rocking away, Mr. Blazer wrote the directors that, ". . . barring unforeseen developments, crude oil is not a problem now, nor does it appear likely to become one . . ."

Aware, as ever, of the refinery men, Mr. Blazer invited the union bargaining committee members to his home for a steak dinner; the occasion was as social as could be, while John Fred Williams did the actual negotiating.

In many ways the summer of 1951 was excellent. Mr. Blazer, whose life had dangled by the thinnest of threads the previous winter, was more frail but in good spirits. The house on Bath Avenue in Ashland, with its fairly spacious grounds, was the scene of a number of good-natured gatherings.

At one of these, young Bob McCowan was present with some other men, when young Stuart Blazer[3] emerged. His father was

[2] Frank Colegrove was born 1910 in Portsmouth, Ohio, was raised in Pittsburgh, graduated from Westminster College in 1931 and went to work as a high-school mathematics teacher. A gifted amateur musician, he played cello in the Methodist choir; worked up a musical program with his sister; was invited to Texas City by Mr. Robinson to put on a program and wound up with a temporary job surveying and obtaining orders for barge delivered refinery products from Texas City along the Mississippi. He became permanently employed by Republic Oil; wound up as assistant to vice president Henry Baskerville for five years; came to work for Allied Oil in 1944 under Rex Blazer. He was manager of supply until July 1948. After the merger, he was assistant to the president 1948–1950; made vice president in 1950; executive vice president in 1952; president in 1959—a post he still holds.

[3] Stuart Blazer, born 1927 in Ashland, Ky., attended Exeter and St. George (in Newport), and Princeton, where he majored in political science. At Princeton, he was a leader in a student-liberal onslaught against the restrictions then prevalent in fraternities, a movement

leaning on his arm; young Blazer was in his second lieutenant's uniform. While the men sat around, enjoying their drinks, Stuart, who had graduated from Princeton that year, surveyed them and listened for a time, then walked over to his father's chair, and putting his hand on Mr. Blazer's shoulder, said, "I can't tell you how happy this makes me. To see my Dad here, back with all of you, and to realize that we are all involved in this great enterprise. We have a lot to be thankful for in this country and I am very thankful to be a part of it; I thank all of you for being a part of it, too . . ."

"It was," said McCowan, "the sort of impromptu speech that is not usually made, but that one might think to himself. I actually got a lump in my throat, and I remember thinking that he was a hell of a guy. His father just beamed."

In July, the ever-active J. Howard Marshall appeared before a Senate Finance Committee to add his voice against a proposed tax on the water transportation of petroleum. He appeared also before a House Committee on the Merchant Marine and Fisheries against a similar measure, created in the larger chamber.

The first Spraberry wells were beginning to come in, and their yields were disappointingly sparse: the geologists were beginning to frown. Joe Levin and Mr. Blazer, Bill Freeman, Jim Martin and others were beginning to discuss the possibilities of a new stock issue, and Mr. Blazer took notice of comments about his health.

"During the past few weeks," he wrote, "I have made trips to Cleveland, Evansville, Houston, El Dorado (Ark.), New York and Washington . . . At El Dorado I saw Charles Murphy, Senior and Junior (of the Murphy Oil Company) . . . in Washington I visited with some of the Kentucky Congressmen and our Kentucky Senators Clements and Underwood, friends of mine for some time. Through Messrs. Clements and Underwood, I met a number of other Senators, including Senator Kerr of Oklahoma and Senator Lyndon Johnson of Texas . . ."

---

that succeeded in establishing the campus rule that all students should receive at least one bid. He was attracted to journalism and to politics; was highly aware of having been fortunately born, and anxious to be a creative force in society.

By September 1951, the fiscal year's end, net profits were running at the rate of $1 million a month; net sales had soared to $205.9 million, net profits reached $12 million. Sales, still mainly under Everett Wells, with the exception of Allied Oil and Frontier, were up 41 per cent over the previous year.

Expansion movements were well along regarding the Buffalo (Frontier) refinery; the engineers agreed that a new catalytic cracking unit was needed to improve the gasoline yield and quality, but the sales organization at Frontier was displeased because they weren't being consulted in their share in these plans. In the western and upper part of New York State, they reported, the automobile driver seemed almost entirely a puppet of massive advertising. As a result, the brand stations of the major companies seemed to do better than independents. Their fears were reported and ignored.

The Spraberry area continued active; the company had combined with Tex Harvey to obtain some gathering lines in the district; a new towboat, the *Aetna-Louisville*, was in service; the christening was attended by hundreds, and caused a great stir in the Ohio valley; Joe Levin was busy among underwriters in preparation for a new stock issue; Everett Wells's department was a full year ahead on orders for the product output of the Catlettsburg and Louisville refineries, and J. Howard Marshall was in Texas again. The Spraberry sands were producing disappointing yields.

Once in Texas, Marshall was appointed chairman of a producers' subcommittee to make recommendations to the state regarding the spacing of wells. Mr. Blazer explained his appointment by saying that Ashland Oil was, in size and in the nature of its activities and interests, somewhere between a major oil company and a host of independents; but personality, reputation and drive undoubtedly counted also. The basic purpose of the subcommittee was to keep the spacing of one oil well to 40 acres; this restriction (one well) was in danger of being reduced. Efforts were underway to allow one well to every 160 acres; a move that would have cost Ashland a considerable amount of money. Marshall worked hard to prevent this from happening; the subcommittee was really his creation; he and men he persuaded made a number of appearances and representations before groups and officials. After several weeks, the effort was successful, and Marshall returned to his home in Ashland.

He was having dinner at home when Mr. Blazer called and asked for a detailed, step-by-step description of how the matter had been handled. Marshall gave a description, and Mr. Blazer thought the methods employed could have been different, better, smoother. "I would have done it another way," he said. Marshall, his patience and his nerves already strained, cracked. Caustic words were exchanged; suddenly the men were openly at odds.

The break had been a long time coming, and had many roots. Later, Mr. Marshall thought that perhaps Mr. Blazer's heart attack had caused his viewpoint to change, but then he recalled that, even earlier, Mr. Blazer had erupted over other matters.

At one point, J. Howard Marshall, W. W. Vandeveer and some other men had discussed a business plan to establish a gas pipeline running from the southwest to Cleveland, Pittsburgh and several other eastern and midwest points already served by Ashland. The general line of reasoning behind the project was to switch the large steel firms—already fuel oil customers—to gas for the balance of their operations. As a business proposition, both Marshall and Vandeveer thought it excellent; their error was in discussing the proposition before telling Mr. Blazer. He was taken aback, and was both surprised and angered. He felt it would disrupt fuel oil sales efforts, but Marshall believed he was more annoyed that business plans were being projected and explored without his participation. Mr. Blazer ordered Marshall to drop his efforts immediately, and Marshall had said, half facetiously, "Is that an order?"

And Mr. Blazer, his expression leaving no doubt of his sentiment, replied, "Yes, that's an order."

"I think," Marshall said later, "that was the first direct order I had ever received. I told Vandeveer and the other men I had been ordered to drop the matter. But, looking back at it, I can see where it made Paul wonder what other propositions were being entertained of which he was unaware . . . I think our break, therefore, started at lower and more internal levels than the Spraberry matter, which actually came out the way we wanted."

Yet, Marshall did not regret the experience. On the contrary, he said, "Blazer was the best man with whom I was ever associated. He had no formal training or background in oil, but he made himself into the most knowledgeable man I was ever to know. He knew every piece of equipment in the refinery, and what it could do, to an extent I have never seen since. I don't suppose I have ever learned more, from any person I ever knew, than from Paul Blazer . . ."

They were together seven years. "We spent twelve hours, sixteen hours a day together, seven days a week, for years. I spent more time in the office than I did at home; my wife told me about that . . ."

Each morning, Marshall's first task had been to check on the crude oil situation. When he joined the company, it was operating one refinery running about 18,000 barrels of crude oil a day; when he left, the company had six refineries running 150,000 barrels a day. "I had to get that crude oil," he said, "to fit what I used to call his accordion-pleated refineries."

"We worked together without a cross word for years," Marshall said, "in close harmony. But in the last year, we could hardly talk without an argument. *I was ready to leave, and Paul was ready for me to leave.*"

The parting between the two men came in December 1951. They discussed the manner in which Marshall would leave, and it was agreed that he had matters to clear first.

By the time the annual meeting was held in January 1952, the directors were able to read J. Howard Marshall's resignation. Mr. Blazer, aware that there were shoals in the water, discussed the general management state of the company cautiously. "We are," he admitted, "a little thin at the top, but we have many good younger men."

Marshall, too, found time for reflection, and in later years, was to prove that he had put it to good advantage. The postwar period had done much to convince the former professor, dean of law and government official of the fallacies inherent in detailed plans for the future; of the swiftness with which the unobserved reality could wreck blueprints.

"All of us," he said later, "relied on the economists, who themselves relied on the patterns of previous postwar periods. We assumed, as did they, that when the war ended the bottom would drop out. What we forgot was that gasoline restrictions during the war had artificially retarded its consumer use. As soon as gasoline rationing ended the curve went straight up—and there wasn't enough available gasoline to fill the demand. In other words, the public resumed the use of gasoline, at the point it would have reached had there been no war at all. This was the exact reverse of what the best economists in the country had predicted.

"Paul and I," he continued, "were knee-deep in deals; we financed deals all over the place. We lent men money to lay pipelines, extend their services, expand in all directions. At one time we had $8 million in receivables out—a tremendous sum for a small company—for crude oil drilling alone. When the dust settled, we found we had lost about $200,000 from these investments—but we made millions for the company.

"I would say that men like Paul Blazer and Charley Jones of Richfield (another empire builder) knew practically everything there was to know about the oil business. They had done everything at one time or another; they were broad scale men with great experience. Today, we have the narrow scale men, who know only one sector of an industry. Good God," he ended, with a typically persuasive burst, "I saw the Russians with their 5-year plans that never worked! In industry today we have men who think they can, actually, project what is going to happen in a market for years in advance. What a waste of time; what a waste of money and men . . ."

Mr. Marshall, in other words, lost his vestiges of academia at Ashland Oil; he left the company a seasoned, rounded businessman versed in the realities of the oil industry. He was to put his knowledge to excellent use; Ashland Oil and its men were to meet him often in the future.

Meanwhile 1952 sales continued to mount; Allied was up 22 per cent over the previous year; most areas of operations seemed good—too good to last.

Crude oil was plentiful with the result that prices were weakening all the way down the line; product prices began to crack. Mr. Blazer wondered aloud if, with crude so abundant, it was necessary to continue with the American Independent Oil Company and its long, expensive search for oil in the Neutral Zone. He grumped about the Middle East and its "perpetual territorial claims and rivalries." One wonders if he was not reluctant to continue a venture in which Howard Marshall had played so prominent a part.

Then, just when one least expects it, the curtain parts to reveal the circumstances in which he had been working. "I am feeling *exceptionally* well," he wrote. ". . . but do not plan to engage in any activities that will tire me. I enjoyed being in the office Saturday, which is the most I have been there in eighteen months . . ."

The war in Korea was beginning to affect the industrial landscape seriously; Everett Wells, in a notably concise, clear and descriptive letter, reported that it was becoming very difficult to obtain young men to work in service stations, and in his regular letters to the directors, Rex Blazer took the unusual step of naming the men who helped prepare the reports on Allied and Frontier, and to give them due credit.

Early in May 1952, their plans completed, Messrs. Levin and Paul Blazer unleashed their new preferred convertible issue, priced at $30. In New York or other large cities, the details would have been handled differently, one suspects, but an idea of the basketball team methods still employed at Ashland Oil in 1952 is given by the record: "Mr. Trout and his assistants did a wonderful job of getting the rights written, completing the work after midnight Tuesday, May sixth. He flew them to Chicago early Wednesday morning, and at approximately 8:30 he was in the office of the American Bank Note Company where the warrants were overprinted. Before the day was over they were in the mails, together with an accompanying letter and prospectus, thereby enabling us to comply with the requirements of the New York Stock Exchange that notice be given them prior to 10 o'clock Thursday morning that the mailing had been completed."

Orin Atkins was discovering, at the same time, that Ashland Oil's creative system extended to the Legal Department.

"Mac Burnam," Atkins recalls, "was a complete nonconformist. The legal staff wasn't even supplied with forms (those frames without which no lawyer can easily function). Without standard forms, it was necessary to be creative on almost every occasion."

This had its benefits. It meant the young lawyer who worked for Ashland Oil had to rediscover the principles underlying each circumstance, and had no stereotypes upon which to rely. The situations that arose ran the gamut from the personal—involving employees—to the highly impersonal. The fact that there were no ready-at-hand tools helped Atkins and his colleagues to develop their own methods of quick search; sharpened their ability to move and think on their own feet, instead of on the shoulders of precedence.

News appeared in the trade press that J. Howard Marshall had become a director of the Signal Oil Company, had been placed in charge of mid-continent exploration efforts for that firm, and was working out of Houston, Texas. Mr. Blazer mailed the press clipping to the Ashland board.

Meanwhile, the military demand for jet fuel had sharply increased; the United States Air Force had been expanded from 48 wings in June 1950, to what would become 110 wings by the end of 1953; the military pace, due to Korea, was quickening.

Roland Whealy, Bill Humphreys, Bob Yancey and the other engineers were knee-deep in plans to expand and improve the refineries; Buffalo in particular came in for special attention. In the meantime, a combination of circumstances—some obvious and some unknown even at Ashland—combined to bring the drive to improve the canalization of the Ohio River to the forefront of attention.

One of J. Howard Marshall's duties had been to maintain a close working relationship with the Ohio Valley Improvement Association, a group formed to push for river improvements. Because of the weight of his other duties and the time they entailed, however, Marshall had not really done too much in this area, and Mr. Blazer was aware that more hands were needed. After Marshall departed, Mr. Blazer called Alex Chamberlain and suggested that he look into the OVIA.

During the latter part of World War II, Chamberlain had, in the course of his activities, undertaken a cost analysis of the Ashland Oil Marine Department. In the study, he worked out a system that enabled the company to keep track of individual boat costs and their performances; this established him, somewhere in the intricate Paul Blazer mental file, as a man with a knowledge of the river.

Chamberlain, delighted, as usual, with a new job, looked up the Association's offices, and attended a meeting. Only seven or eight other men appeared, and they were mainly connected, either directly or indirectly, Chamberlain said later, with the Youngstown Sheet & Tube Company. This firm was especially interested in seeing a canal between Lake Erie and the Ohio River improved for reasons that were fairly immediate; such a canal would help their operation. However, the Association had only $13,000 in its treasury, and the canal project about which Youngstown Sheet & Tube was concerned had just been rejected in Congress. The OVIA, founded in 1895, had once been able to attract widespread support, but its influence faded when the canalization of the river seemed complete in 1929. For years the Association had been drifting slowly downstream, like a log on one of the rivers to which it was presumably devoted. Chamberlain began what he calls a "study"—an undertaking considerably more energetic than the term usually implies.

In this context, it meant that Chamberlain made trips to Pittsburgh, Wheeling, Louisville and other cities along the Ohio, to begin proselytizing, with Mr. Blazer active in the background, directing. He devoted, he said, about 25 per cent of his time to these efforts. Fairly shortly he succeeded—together with others, of course—in enlisting Wheeling Steel and the largest of all steel companies: United States Steel. Both were potent additions.

While Chamberlain was busying himself in this direction, Bill Hull, the attorney whom Mr. Blazer had appointed as his executive assistant, was feeling the chill winds of disapproval. "I knew that I wasn't working out," Hull said, "but I couldn't seem to improve. Mr. Blazer wanted me to become a businessman, and to think like one—but I persisted in thinking like a lawyer. He would ask my opinion, and I would discuss *both* sides. That was not what he wanted." He paused, and said, "I began to think that he didn't like *me,* and of course I was unhappy. But then Mr. Marshall left, and that left a great many details open for handling in Washington. Mr. Blazer began to suggest that I go to Washington to discover what Committee or group was handling a particular piece of legislation that might affect the company. In time these trips became frequent, and I found myself spending a lot of time in such efforts. I also discovered that when I began to discuss the pros and cons of *these* situations, Mr. Blazer was an excellent listener, and a highly intelligent and tactful commentator. I began to enjoy myself again, and Mr. Blazer's attitude toward me became quite warm."

"It's curious," Hull concluded, "that this should have happened. I finally realized that Mr. Blazer's regard was based on one's usefulness. He did not like waste effort, nor men in the wrong place; he had strong opinions that everyone was useful, and that all men were talented. The challenge was to combine the circumstance, the talent, and the man. He had never disliked *me;* he had been annoyed that we were wasting our time together on the wrong matters."

Some idea of how closely Mr. Blazer followed the men can be gathered from a letter of his to the directors. "We are setting up a management group which will be over all our refineries," the letter reads. "Roland Whealy . . . will be responsible . . . Bill Humphreys will be chief engineer for all our plants . . . Arnold Leas will head our technical service . . . Whealy will report to Everett (Wells)."

Then, going down the line, the letter details how Walker Marx would become superintendent at Catlettsburg; John Rosson would be assistant superintendent; Bob Yancey (now coordinating new construction at Buffalo) would be operating superintendent of both Buffalo and Catlettsburg reporting to Marx; Herb Czeskleba would become assistant operating superintendent of both plants; Stewart McHie would become maintenance superintendent reporting to Marx; Gus Litton would become chief engineer of both plants; Milton Bradley would become assistant superintendent at the Findlay refinery; Eldon Sloan would be made a shift foreman, Pete Sutton would be transferred from Findlay to assist Brooks, and Henry Hays, a machinist, would be made foreman of that department to report to McHie.

These men were watched with unblinking attention. The detail

and variety of the names listed for the board of directors, aston-
ishes. It is obvious that shifts of responsibility are only surface
indicators. Practically all of the men listed were originally hired
by the company as youngsters fresh from school (Humphreys being
one of the few to come from the outside with an extensive background of his own); they were products of the company and the
highly individual, personalized training that had come to mean,
and many were being groomed for larger responsibilities in the
future. They were being shifted and sifted, tested and tried, as
well as being placed in operational positions.

Behind each of the transfers were hours of conversation with
and about the men; Everett Wells, John Fred Williams, Palmer
Talbutt and others had been consulted; the men were consulted
about one another and themselves. Managerial development that
other firms expected colleges, psychologists, special courses and
formalized indoctrinations to achieve was accomplished at Ashland
Oil more personally, more subtly, and perhaps, more surely.

In the meantime, a peculiar geologic condition prevailing in
the Spraberry oil fields was becoming more evident. "The greatest
non-commercial oil field ever discovered," said Rex Blazer, sum-
marizing. Oil was there, under the surface. On that point the
geologists were agreed. But for reasons known only to Nature,
it was trapped, never fully to be released. The result was many
rocking oil pumps producing small trickles.

To further complicate matters in 1952, the steel industry labor
union, deciding it had a war of its own to win, embarked on what
was to be one of the longest and most bitter strikes in the history of that turbulent sector. That immediately affected Ashland
Oil fuel sales; a considerable portion of the company's earnings
dropped.

Mr. Blazer, whose personality seemed to contain a subordinate
labeled Owner, began writing lengthy descriptions to the directors
about his efforts to economize. This was an old custom of his
whenever business conditions appeared to tighten; he drenched
his observers with detail, and detailed corner-cuts that were both
imaginative and impressive. At the same time, aware of the difficult labor climate, the company granted its unions wage increases;
offered the Lodestar for sale at $100,000, and spent an equal

amount for a new De Havilland Dove. The passenger capacity of both planes was the same, Blazer explained, but he cited the lower fuel requirements of the new plane over the old as an additional economy, and since Roy Ralston had clearly become his latest in a long string of men who would completely resolve all crude oil exploration problems, Mr. Blazer was filled with praise for Mr. Ralston's abilities.

Meanwhile, events on a level far beyond the mundane were having a silent effect upon the efforts of Alex Chamberlain and Mr. Blazer on the Ohio Valley Improvement Association—although this does not imply that their efforts were not successful. By persuasion and diligence, they had managed to increase the budget of that organization to $55,000, and had become acquainted with a number of the industrial groups whose activities could be quickened and improved by a new river canalization program.

But the government had other and very serious problems of a technological nature to face that revolved around the spinning web of the cold war. The news from Russia was dark and menacing; the Red Chinese had thrown their military might behind the North Koreans. The United States public, aroused and alarmed by the outcries of Senator Joe McCarthy—an advocate whose methods obscured some stark realities of the time—became increasingly confused.

Early in 1951, the United States had attempted to fuse tritium and deuterium into helium to create a larger nuclear bomb; had succeeded, at Eniwetok, an atoll in the Pacific, in creating fission but not in reducing the physical dimensions of the pile employed. At the same time that these efforts were underway, however, the United States Atomic Energy Commission had obtained $2 billion to erect and install reactors at Portsmouth, Ohio, and Paducah, Kentucky, as well as on the Savannah River. These projects required hydroelectric power; in turn, the stations would operate from coal. Coal was brought in by water. Thus, the condition of the rivers became of paramount national importance, for reasons that few of the persons located along the valley knew.

And in midsummer 1952, with Mr. Blazer directing Chamberlain and Hull in their efforts for the OVIA, the refinery men, all newly appointed new brooms, were sweeping busily. They recom-

mended the installation of an alkylate plant (used in the manufacture of aviation gasoline) at a cost of some $2 million. The effects
of the steel strike were hurting industry badly, and Ashland in
particular. Mr. Blazer wrote: "Although our cash balance of $34
million is impressive, we continue to keep in mind the desirability
of conserving our cash and making only such capital expenditures
as are dictated by circumstances . . . Competition is never static;
in transportation and refining we have some increasingly exposed
flanks which will require protection." Past experience indicates
these words meant Mr. Blazer would move to protect these flanks.

In July, a month of respites, Rex Blazer traveled to Cornell,
where Mr. Newman had given the school, his alma mater, $1.5
million for the Helen Newman Hall, in honor of his wife.
(Mr. Newman had previously given Cornell $1.75 million for a
nuclear research center.) Both he and Mr. Vandeveer had sold a
block of their Ashland shares. Mr. Paul Blazer was impressed with
these proceedings, but more pleased to swap two shareholders for
the thousand by whom their stock was purchased.

The following September, 1952, a graduate student at the University of Chicago named Joseph L. Massie wrote a letter to Ashland;
he wanted to write his doctoral dissertation on the management
methods employed by a small oil company. In response, he received
a lengthy letter from Mr. Blazer, in which he was not only invited
to Ashland, but told what trains ran through the town and which
one to take. He arrived dutifully a few days later, met Art Points,
and was ushered into Mr. Blazer's office for what he expected to be
a fifteen minute interview. The resulting conversation lasted three
hours; Massie left with a mass of notes, a sense of amazement, and
a determination to return.

Fiscal 1952 came to a close with results that reflected the problems that existed: net sales were up slightly to $229 million, but
net profits were down to $5.7 million, the lowest in five years, less
than half the amount retained after taxes the preceding year.

In the nation, the clock moved toward national elections.
Dwight Eisenhower, a bipartisan hero, was elected in a tidal-wave
of national hope; the nation, almost to a man, was tired of partisan bickerings and anxious for a period of calm.

But the extent to which the national condition had changed

since Mr. Truman had entered the White House on the death of President Roosevelt in early April 1945, was only beginning to dawn on the general public.

In that fall one event occurred, however, that was not included in the letters to the directors, but which affected Mr. and Mrs. Blazer profoundly. Their youngest son, Stuart, anxious to do his part in Korea, had been sent to that remote Asian country. In his first engagement with the enemy on October 14, 1952, he was shot in the forehead and dropped, killed instantly.

The news reached Ashland, Kentucky, in a telegram from Washington addressed to Mr. Blazer. But, such are the intimacies and the humanity of small towns, the local Western Union operator knew Mr. Blazer, knew of his heart condition, and did not feel he should receive such news in so blunt a manner. She called his secretary and family friend, Mrs. Phyllis Geyer. In turn, Mrs. Geyer called Rex Blazer, who started out in his car to find Mr. Blazer, after first alerting Dr. Leslie Winans. Rex arranged to have the doctor go to Mr. Blazer's home. Then, driving, Rex overtook Mr. Blazer, who had just left the barbershop, and was walking toward his residence. When they arrived there, Dr. Winans went inside with Rex, and the men broke the news.

The house was festive, in preparation for a party to be held that night in honor of Earle Webb, head of the Ethyl Corporation. Mr. and Mrs. Webb, unaware, were preparing for the party.

When Dr. Winans came downstairs, he told Mrs. Blazer, who had just entered the house from some errand or another, about Stuart. He said Mr. Blazer had taken the news very well; very calmly. But he had murmured, as though to himself, *"I was counting on him."*

When Stuart's will was read, it was found to contain legacies to Exeter and Princeton, and even to St. George's at Newport and a summer camp he had attended as a youngster. He had devised it when he was twenty-one. Interested in education, he was himself an excellent example of the fact that a good education includes a sense of responsibility.

His parents bore their loss proudly; established the Stuart Blazer Foundation to continue his interests. But they were hard hit.

After this event, Mr. Blazer's concentration on the company became even more intense. Another, and equally natural result, was that he began to take an even deeper interest in younger men. He began to seek them out; to watch them closely for signs of talent and ability.

These conversations disclosed that many had keen interests in petrochemicals, an area that Mr. Blazer, previously interested only in oil and oil products, had neglected. He set about to repair this omission, and invited Herman Nieuwenhuis, an expert then with the Walter J. Levy Associates, noted in the oil industry, to study and recommend his services to Ashland in this respect. But Nieuwenhuis' terms were, Mr. Blazer thought, too high.

Mr. Blazer, speaking that fall before the Kentucky Broadcasters' Association, voiced aloud some thoughts that many other top management men held silently.

"Who knows," he asked the broadcasters, "what kind of social order the young people will be living under twenty years from now? . . . Will personal and corporate taxes be supporting agencies of education, public information and spiritual need, which we as a free people have nurtured through so many generations?"

And after these somewhat surprising questions—provoked, perhaps, by the impact of Stuart's death in Korea—Mr. Blazer (who either wrote his own speeches, or spoke extemporaneously from his own notes), said:

"I speak as one manager of a business, recently small enough to permit typical and somewhat skeptical appraisal of the great corporations, and now large enough to appreciate and be sympathetic with the problems of these managers . . .

"The development of mechanical power is the basis for our progress; the change from simple tools into vast machines doing the work of hundreds. . . . Not only does the manager today not know his employees, *but the worker does not know management* . . . is no longer aware of its problems. The growth of labor unions competes with machinery as an amazing development of this century . . . and has helped to create powerful entrenched interests that thrive on industrial dissension.

"Management today," he added, and it is evident he was describing himself, "is now an umpire between labor and the shareholders. Ordinarily, stockholders are inarticulate. But if they don't like the way things are run, they switch their investments. The real

problem, therefore, is to satisfy employees and customers . . .
Salesmanship and skill today is most important with employees.
You can get another customer easier than another employee."

Then, still thinking aloud about the complex and increasingly
dissatisfying area of employee relations, he said, "The loss of (employee) confidence and friendship results in their selection of
unreasonable leaders, who by fostering suspicion and hatred, per-
petuate themselves." He looked at his audience gravely, and said,
"It is easier to build another plant elsewhere."

"Seniority," he said, and suddenly one wonders what would have
happened to Palmer Talbutt[4] under modern rules, "advances the
incompetent. Many productive talents lie unused. Many business
men feel caught between labor and government, sabotaged by men
with little understanding of a system predicated on personal initiative, with rewards for success and penalties for failure."

Inexorably, his words led him toward an attempt at instructing
the audience in the essence of the system to which he had dedicated
all his efforts. "Frequently," he concluded, "the most brilliant are
not successful. It has been my privilege to know a number of the
most important leaders in American industry. I have been interested in studying them. Their most prominent characteristic is
their ability to inspire confidence.

"Yet, there's a shortage at the top. Perhaps too much emphasis
on technical training and not enough in those qualities which
make for leadership. We live in a world of people," he concluded,
"not things. Others can do more for us than we can do for ourselves."

He sat down. The audience had heard a man who was raised
during a more democratic period, and who was finding the stratifi-
cation of labor stifling to his instincts as a leader. He simply could
not accustom himself to the theory that his interests, and the
interests of the enterprise he had grown to love, could be considered inimical to labor.

By this time, it was becoming obvious that the extensive Ashland
operations in the Spraberry region were going to cost the com-

---

[4] Mr. Talbutt, a senior executive, was once an operator in plant No.
1; under today's system, his counterpart will remain there, unless he
goes to college.

The board of directors of the Ashland Oil & Refining Company in Chicago, Illinois. (November 13, 1952)

pany substantially. After lengthy huddles with Art Points and Ned Seaton, Mr. Blazer wrote gloomily to the board: "The excess profits tax accelerated our drilling program, but when this program is reduced, tax liabilities occur. Our drilling program over the last eight years is not, in my opinion, anything of which we can be proud." This was crow indeed.

By early 1953, the peculiarity of the Spraberry region had become evident, and the geologic explanations appeared in the trade press. At hearings held before the Texas Railroad Commission, the engineers stated that each well drilled in the Spraberry region could be expected to quit producing oil shortly after the pressure around the well reached a bottom hole pressure of approximately 1,000 pounds per square inch. The whole problem, the press went on to explain, was similar to an automobile vapor lock. In the Spraberry sand, when the pressure reached a critical point, the gas could move out of the sand, but the oil was locked in. None of the production methods known to the industry circa 1952–1953 could extract an estimated $2.5 billion worth of oil.

Estimating how that oil could be unlocked and recovered provided a fascinating parlor game for a number of geologists, but their employers—like Ashland Oil—had to toil with the problem of explaining the state of affairs to their stockholders. Mr. Blazer and his associates composed a special letter explaining the sequence of events. In September, the company's Spraberry wells yielded 109,000 barrels. In October, the yield was 108,000 barrels.

But in November, there was a drop to 96,000 barrels, and in December, 80,000 barrels. For the last quarter of the company's fiscal year, the Spraberry loss amounted to $810,000. Reluctantly but inescapably, in view of sharp drops in production to be expected, the great Spraberry effort had to be written off.

By this time, Mr. Blazer's experience seemed fairly clear: he had consistently taken losses in crude oil exploration and development efforts, and just as consistently made profits in refining, transportation and marketing. In this respect, his conclusions came out very close to those of John D. Rockefeller, who decades before had employed refining and transportation as the two levers by which profits could best be obtained in the oil industry. Both men considered the theory of industry analysts, who believe all but completely integrated firms to be in a precarious position, to be a cliché. Integration was fine—if you had it—but it was not a *sine qua non* of success: the record proved that.

With so much emphasis on refining and marketing, however, there remained the pressures of the technological race to consider. "The TCC unit at Catlettsburg needs replacing," the engineers told Mr. Blazer. This could cost anywhere between $2 million and $5 million. At the same time, agitation arose regarding pollution of the Ohio river; oil that enters water is alarmingly visible. Several accidents revived that eternal problem.

The two T-2 tankers—a problem once solved by charter to Esso —returned to haunt the profit pages. "An idle T-2 tanker," Blazer told Jim Martin, "is almost as bad as a shutdown refinery." Then, adding to a host of vexations, the American Independent Oil Company directors decided the firm needed another advance from its backers; Ashland's share of an extra $1.3 million would only come to $169,000, but the view was frankly expressed, in the company's seventh floor executive offices, that it was throwing good money after bad. "What I fear," Blazer said, "is that if these two additional wells are unsuccessful, we must drill two more . . ." All in all, he found drilling for oil an exasperating business. The whole subject of Aminol (the name finally agreed upon) was one that did not sit well, in fact. J. Howard Marshall was back on its board of directors representing Signal, and had recently endorsed an employee incentive plan. This incensed Mr. Blazer, who argued that these rewards were in advance of accomplishment; furthermore, he, Ashland and J. Howard Marshall were embroiled in a dispute regarding whether the Bank of Commerce, in Houston, and the Banker's Trust, in New York, had or had not been guaranteed by Ashland Oil against loss on a loan. Mr. Marshall and Mr. Blazer were at opposite poles on that situation, and it did not help the Aminol climate.

Then as so often happens in life, the situation suddenly changed. A telegram arrived from San Francisco, from Ralph Davies, regarding Aminol. It read:

WAFRA FOUR FLOWING APPROXIMATELY TWO THOUSAND FIVE HUNDRED BARRELS PER DAY THROUGH QUARTER INCH TUBING CHOKE STOP PRESSURE FOUR ZERO TUBING FOUR ZERO ZERO CASING STOP GAS OIL RATIO PROBABLY LESS THAN FIVE HUNDRED STOP NOW RUNNING PRODUCTION TEST.

The Wall Street Journal, already far along its postwar path of lively journalism, reported in sprightly fashion on Monday, August 20, 1953:

AMINOL DISCOVERY
WILL IT BE COLOSSAL
OR MERELY TERRIFIC?
Success of Kuwait Independent Zone Field
To Determine Independent's Role With Giants

Kuwait (AP)—The latest oil discovery at the head of the Persian Gulf may put some of the little fellows in the industry right up front with the giants, oil men say.

"Terrific" is the way some engineers describe it. Others say further tests will prove that the new discovery in the neutral zone is not terrific, but "colossal."

What they're talking about is Wafra No. 4, the new well recently brought in by a combination of independent U.S. oil companies in the neutral land between the rival nations of Saudi Arabia and Kuwait.

If it turns out to be just "terrific," the American independents will regard themselves as real competition for the world's largest crude oil producers. If it turns out to be "colossal," and some experts think it will, the independent combine figures to rank with the industry's leaders.

Signs point toward it being colossal. It has all the characteristics of the famed Burgan field in Kuwait, the largest known single oil reserve in the world. It's only 20 miles south of the 15-billion-barrel Burgan reserve. It came in from the same prehistoric formation as that of the Burgan—the Cretaceous. The oil is the same. The oil column is more than 250 feet.

Over 5,000 Barrels Seen

The Burgan field is producing virtually the same amount of petroleum as Arabian-American Oil Co. wells in Saudi Arabia—800,000 barrels a day. Kuwait Oil Co., jointly owned by Gulf Oil Corp. and Anglo-Iranian Oil Co., is pulling oil out of Burgan with more than 135 wells, each producing slightly more than 5,000 barrels a day in a series of test flows.

The independents are planning to drill the next well two miles away from Wafra No. 4 on what they describe as the top of the dome. After pacing a half dozen wells at strategic spots on the Wafra structure, the independents figure they will know for certain whether the Wafra field is simply terrific or colossal. It will be months before this is finally determined.

The neutral zone oil concessions are held by nine American independents under the name American Independent Oil Co. (Aminol) and by Pacific Western Oil Corp.

Yacht Thrown In

The neutral zone is a sandy waste of 2,200 square miles lying south of Kuwait with one side on the Persian Gulf. It was created by British mediation following a dispute between King Ibn Saud of Saudi Arabia and the Sheik of Kuwait. Both rulers retained an "undivided half-share" in the neutral zone.

Aminol terminated the first concession with the Sheik of Kuwait for his share five years ago. The terms of the concession included a $7.5 million cash payment, $625,-000 annually, minimum royalty whether oil was found or not, 34 cents a barrel on all oil found, plus a 15% interest in the company. All of this, plus a million-dollar yacht thrown in for good measure, went to the Sheik.

American Independent Oil Co. is owned by seven companies and two individuals, Ralph K. Davies of San Francisco, president of Aminol who owns 8.25% of the stock, and J. S. Abercrombie of Houston, and Signal Oil & Gas Co., and Hancock Oil Co. with 14.65% each. Other owners are Ashland Oil Co., Globe-Lario Oil Co., Deep Rock Oil Corp. and Sunray Oil Co.

On the world scene, the largest news in the spring of 1953 was entirely different in nature; beside it, business was the most innocent of activities. The news was of the death of Stalin, ogre of the Soviet Union, and a large part of the rest of the world besides. The internecine struggle that this event released behind the walls of the Kremlin, and the purges it sent coursing through the subterranean reaches of the international Communist movement, did much to relieve the pressures on the West—temporarily. This relaxation assisted President Eisenhower to make good on his campaign promise to reach a peaceful settlement in Korea, and made the world an easier place in which to stay alive, the spring of 1953.

At Ashland, the news about the oil strike in the Neutral Zone was received with more reservations than in the press; the company was too well aware that much remained to be done before any advantage could be realized from the discovery. In general, the major attention of the management centered around the details and progress of the great modernization programs underway at Catlettsburg, and the improvements and additions in the Buffalo refinery.

Union negotiations—another area that J. Howard Marshall had occupied—reengaged the personal attention of Mr. Blazer, together with John Fred Williams, John Rosson (in charge of labor relations) and Walker Marx, the superintendent of both the

Buffalo and Catlettsburg works. They lasted over one hundred hours; an exhausting and nerve-wracking ordeal, whose outcome was largely affected by the increase won by labor in the recently settled steel strike.

Then, in a letter to the board, appear some details of an incident that was to send shock waves through the refinery staff and the engineers for some time to come. "I have been surprised to learn," Mr. Blazer wrote, "of a very substantial overrun in the cost of the Frontier plant. I can assure you that I am terribly embarrassed to have to report that the cost of the Buffalo improvements will exceed $10 million . . . It will be recalled that we discovered a year ago that the original estimates were two or three million dollars too low and now we find they have been raised another two million dollars. Apparently those of our organization directly in charge of the construction have known of this situation for some months, but only within the last ten days has that information been given to Rex, Everett and myself. I understand that a very small part of this last increase can be accounted for by additions and changes in design . . . The work of the Catalytic Construction Corp. in some instances, has cost two or three times as much as anticipated. I consider the situation very serious . . . Some months ago . . . I had Whealy remove Catalytic from the job and turn it over to an Ashland contractor . . . I am told Whealy was displeased with my action and felt my criticism of Catalytic was not justified . . ."

The balance of the letter discusses a seamen's strike that immobilized the Cleveland Tankers, and details of the construction of a new Universal Oil Products fluid unit at Catlettsburg. But one's attention returns to the description of the Buffalo expansion, and the explanation of why the costs had risen so far beyond the original estimates. This was unprecedented; in the past, almost all the work done in the refineries had cost less than expected, and not more. It is even more surprising to learn, later, that these costs ran closer to $12 million than $10 million, and astonishing that Mr. Blazer, Everett Wells and Rex Blazer were not informed. Explanations of this unprecedented situation would undoubtedly be demanded by the board.

The men at the upper levels of the refinery operations were

surprised; they had carried each plan in to Mr. Blazer, and spent hours poring over the details with him. As was his custom, Mr. Blazer continually suggested additions and improvements; the "Blazer factor" was notorious throughout the industry: every item of equipment was expected to perform at least 25 per cent better than rated capacity. Even the manufacturers, contractors and suppliers knew this. At the same time the mounting costs, clearly escalating beyond the original framework and estimates, worried almost everyone involved. Ed Emrick, a man who kept an extremely close eye on such matters, had, in fact, discussed the situation with Rex Blazer and Everett Wells. Both men thought Mr. Blazer was cognizant of the situation, but neither man had discussed it with him. This oversight was later a matter of regret.

Several other factors contributed to the situation. One—and one that Mr. Blazer, of all men, could not for a moment forget—was his health. To say that it was precarious is an understatement. Death literally walked beside him; he could not for a moment ignore its presence.

Another factor was the change in the board of directors. When Senator Combs died, years before, and Mr. Blazer had succeeded him, there were men on the board who would have preferred another, but they had neither a candidate nor expertise in oil. Now, in mid-1953, Ashland Oil & Refining had become a composite of several companies. These companies were brought in by their creators, and these creators now sat on the board. They were shrewd, capable and experienced; they were knowledgeable in oil and its various facets; they knew Mr. Blazer's health was bad. There was a definite and growing undercurrent of opinion among them that he should retire.

Mr. Vandeveer and Mr. Newman, both directors, were openly of this opinion. Furthermore, although they had lost their voting privileges through the agreement Mr. Blazer had devised, they were by no means without influence.

But Mr. Blazer's energies had become centered around the company; its problems and situation had become the instruments by which he kept himself from succumbing to his physical disabilities. Although many of the men in top management were the results of his training, there were others who had been trained elsewhere. He foresaw, if he stepped aside prematurely, struggles for control. He considered his own abilities to be sufficient for the challenges ahead; he did not believe his physical condition was dire. While he was of this opinion, he would neither recognize nor make accommodations for death.

The occasion for management to admit a multi-million dollar error at Buffalo could not have been worse timed, as far as Mr. Blazer was concerned. Yet he did not hesitate to call the matter to the attention of the board; he did not hesitate to place the responsibility upon the refinery management. Later, no man could say with absolute certainty that Mr. Blazer had been informed of the totals of the mounting costs; each thought someone else had called it to his attention. Intent upon other weighty matters, Mr. Blazer did not focus on the overall costs of the Buffalo expansion. Later, when caught by surprise by the total, he decided he had not been told. At this point, shock waves reverberated throughout the organization.

Virtually the whole Ashland team during a combined inspection trip and a board meeting at the Canton refinery. (1952)

After launching his attack, Mr. Blazer departed on a trip to Texas and California. It is hard not to suspect that his trip was taken as a silent demonstration of his physical ability to keep on top of all situations. If so, it was an impressive one.

Taking along Mrs. Blazer and Mr. and Mrs. Mac Burnam, Mr. Blazer passed through Texas and reached a compromise while there with the Houston Bank of Commerce regarding their loan dispute. Then he attended an Aminol board of directors meeting, and listened in disapproval to that management's request for more money for Neutral Zone exploration efforts. "Extravagant and impractical," he said in an aside to the Ashland directors.

At the same time, modernization efforts at Catlettsburg proceeded: a new catalytic cracking unit was being installed at a cost of $3 million. The union local there, warned in advance by Mr. Blazer that no such improvements would be made as long as they followed disputatious leaders, had elected a new slate of more conservative officers; Mr. Blazer was pleased.

Only a few days after his return from the West Coast, Mr. Blazer went to Washington, D. C., where he testified eloquently before the Senate Interstate & Foreign Commerce committees against new proposals to divide the industry into competitive segments. First giving an outline of the company, ". . . We operate two refineries in Kentucky, three in Ohio, one near Pittsburgh, Pa., one near Buffalo, N. Y.; refine over 100,000 barrels a day; own less than 10 per cent of our own crude oil; have extensive transportation and refinery facilities, and . . . must sell through independents," he proceeded to give the lawmakers still another of his descriptions of the intricacies of the industry. "Oil is a highly complex industry," he said. "There is little similarity between exploration efforts to find new fields, and the operation of pipelines, boats and barges; the manufacture of petroleum products; marketing of gasoline, tires and accessories through service stations.

"Thousands of persons are engaged in each branch of the industry, and there are many divergent opinions and views. There are important differences between independent companies and the majors, and between the majors themselves. The oil industry is not homogeneous. Branded gasoline prices are fairly close," he admitted—this being a point the solons were particularly suspicious about—"but this is a result of competition, not cooperation."

He gave a practical man's tip on how the situation might well have been different had not the men in the industry obeyed the law. "Leaders, otherwise," he said, "could easily stagger their prices to foil suspicion . . ." This caused a great flurry of comment in the trade press covering the hearings.

Less attention was paid to his description of the economics. "Recent advances in crude oil prices have cost Ashland about $25,000 a day," he said. "Although crude oil prices and gas prices were almost stationary for the last 5½ years, wages, employee benefits and the cost of materials has consistently risen. In 1948, the refineries received 12.3 cents a gallon; in May 1953, refineries received 12.2 cents a gallon for their products. After deducting the cost of tetraethyl lead, added at the refinery, we receive a net realization one-third of a cent less than in 1948. During this period, crude prices remained constant, but the selling price per barrel of products declined 57 cents: from $4.79 a barrel to $4.22 a barrel. The shrinkage was 55 cents. By spending millions for equipment, we managed to reduce costs a few cents, but wages were increased by 56 cents an hour. If we had the vanished profit, our earnings before taxes would be up $60,000 a day. The public benefited."

Then he gave overall figures. "In the last 5½ years, Ashland earned $52.2 million, and disbursed $23.7 million in dividends, which left $28.5 million. We invested $31.8 million; then $28.9 million—a total of $89.3 million. Counting all our investments and reinvestments during this period, we put $138 million into our operation—and we are less than 1 per cent of the oil industry.

"We have never had a shortage of petroleum products in the U.S.A.," he concluded drily. "Had one developed, *prices would have gone up*."

As though to illustrate the difference between myth and reality, late that summer in 1953, Walter Winchell, in his Sunday night broadcast, excitedly declared that Amurex—a Canadian exploration venture in which Ashland had a minority interest—had properties near a newly-found oil strike in Canada. The stock of Amurex shot up enormously; Mr. Blazer issued a statement pointing out that Amurex was not close enough to where the oil strike had been made to be significantly affected. In the interim, reports coming in from the Neutral Zone had some deflating effect upon that exciting news: the oil being produced was discovered to have a high sulphur content. This made it less desirable to the world oil market. Nevertheless, the Neutral Zone continued to look promising.

Mr. Blazer continued to spend much of his time thinking about the management. To take up the slack in his own increasingly rare public appearances, he was pushing Rex Blazer into the limelight; he wrote Jim Martin this would help Rex to know and be known throughout the industry, and would, in the long run, be of great benefit to the company. "Everett Wells," he remarked, "is overworked." It was an observation that could have been made at any time in the past twenty-seven years; it made no perceptible difference to Wells's work load.

In 1953 the Korean conflict came to a halt; an armistice was signed and peace talks were begun. The fighting had lasted three years and a month, cost the United States 25,000 dead, 115,000 casualties and $22 billion. No peace treaty has ever been signed.

In Ashland, Jimmy Blubaum, a refinery worker with fifteen years' service, came to Mr. Blazer's home to discuss whether or not to accept a job offer he had received from the Goodyear Atomic Corporation. Mr. Blazer assured him he would always have a job at Ashland Oil. After thinking the matter over, Jimmy decided to leave. The old order was passing.

In August 1953, because a hydrogen bomb was carried aloft, loosed and detonated from an airplane in a military test in Siberia, shock waves went coursing throughout the United States defense establishment. This nation did not have the ability to create a hydrogen bomb either that light or that compact; the test was chilling evidence that the Soviet Union had outstripped the United States in nuclear weaponry. The general public in the United States, however, largely unaware of the implications of the Soviet achievement, was beginning to grow bored both with the cold war and the Red Menace and turned its attention elsewhere.

By September 1953, when the company's fiscal year ended, net sales were $238 million and earnings after taxes were $8.4 million.

These figures, which on their face represented an advance over the previous year, were actually reached after agonies that only professional accountants and corporation managers can appreciate, for in 1953, the acceptance of the Spraberry loss had to be faced by the management.

The problem that faced the management was how to itemize that loss. If it was all charged against 1952, the shareholders would, in effect, be told the company hadn't made any money at all—and that would have been misleading. The loss had been over a period of time.

But in the meantime, sales had been good and other parts of the operations had been successful. Arthur Points and his contacts at Ernst & Ernst, the firm's outside accountants, decided to switch some $8.5 million in assets to the loss side of the ledger. But because the loss had occurred before 1953, they decided to apply it retroactively against the previous year. This called for a restatement of the previous year, a practice now common, but then quite rare. The result was both more realistic and more candid; the annual 1953 report showed a healthy company continuing to expand. But a loss is a loss, and Spraberry was to remain, like a dark, undissipated cloud, on the horizon for a long time to come.

In addition to Spraberry leases and equipment the company was still active in Canada with the Murphy Oil Company in Amurex: was waterflooding its Kentucky wells to squeeze more oil from them. But despite these efforts, crude production remained approximately the same as for many years: 10 per cent of its refinery needs. On the waterways Ashland continued to operate a large fleet, and this traffic amounted to $2 million in leased equipment alone during the year 1953. Obviously, leased equipment of such magnitude meant it would be practical to build more barges and tows.

But other problems retarded this solution and the largest of these was the insatiable needs of the refineries.

In October 1953, Walker Marx disciplined a persistently unsatisfactory worker for an unauthorized absence from the job; as a result, one hundred men walked out of the Catlettsburg refinery, and the company had a wildcat strike on its hands. Orin Atkins, working with the legal firm of Gray & Woods, went to court and obtained a temporary injunction against a picket line the union threw up. Young Atkins, by this time, was attracting attention within the company.

The strike proved to be merely a spark and not a fire; the men came back to work. But the company realized that union relations at Catlettsburg were delicate; the days when difficulties could be talked out informally were over.

By December 1953, Mr. Blazer was still answering the rumors about his general state of health obliquely: "My health has been exceptionally good lately," he wrote, "as attested by the fact I attended Christmas parties last week in six different cities, including afternoon and evening parties at Ashland on Saturday."

He spent the latter part of the holiday season, moreover, composing a twelve page reply to NLRB charges, the gist of which had amounted to a complaint that the management persistently attempted to contact the workers in its refineries on labor issues, without going through the elected union officials.

THE RIVERS

The awful floods of the 1930s had faded from the memory of the country by the early 1950s, but every winter they threatened to return. Alex Chamberlain and Bill Hull, both directed closely by Mr. Blazer, worked to create sentiment in Congress for flood protection, but the men did not find their path easy. Such appropriations are traditionally called "porkbarrels" by the press; a term that withers the projects it describes.

Yet, year by year the river traffic was increasing; it was greater than during the emergency days of World War II; greater than ever in the history of the country.

Occasionally, a letter would reach the offices of Ashland Oil, asking if a writer or a photographer could take a trip on one of the Ashland tows—each of which is equipped to carry a few passengers. One such passenger amused himself while sitting in the wheelhouse watching Captain Eddie Shupert of the *Valvoline* steer his way expertly downstream, by leafing through the chart books. The names alone evoke the history of the region, and recall the

incredible mixture of people, events and cultures that went into
the taming and settlement of this region.

Along the upper Ohio, they include Opossum Hole, Little Step-
son, Rag's Run, Little Indian Creek, Kinney's Run, Painter's Run,
Ball's Run, Herringer's Run, Graveyard Run, the Little Miami
River, Licking River, Scott's Landing, Hogan's Creek, Kirby's
Rocks, Shannon's Landing . . . ; towns with names like Rabbit
Hash and Gunpowder Creek, the Patriot Bend Light, Sugar Creek
Light, Wiley's Hollow, Big Bone Lake (a famous resort in the early
1800s; then past the confluence with the Mississippi and down the
reaches of that Father of Waters, past Cairo, Illinois (pronounced,
in the region, Kay-Row), the ships slide past Reelfoot, Tennessee,
and Heloise Bar Light, past the mouth of the Obion River and the
River Styx and the Shoo Fly Bar.

In some of these stretches, whole herds of deer and wild turkey
can still be seen along the banks; the deer come down to the river's
edge to escape swamp flies. From a towboat, a searchlight trained
in their direction at night will reveal their eyes, shining flatly back
like so many reflectors . . .

Bends in the river have, through the generations, been eliminated by the engineers by what are known as "cutoffs." Some of
these have shortened or eliminated loops in the river by as much
as 150 miles. This work has proceeded, piecemeal, for decades.

Then, as the tow proceeds downriver, it passes the Choctaw Bar,
Spanish Moss, past Ark, Mississippi, the Skipworth Crevasse and
Bunche's Cutoff, Acadia Point, the Indian Mounds, Omega Land-
ing, Terrapin Light, the Yazoo Cutoff, past Togo, or Big Black,
Hardscrabble, Cerro Gordo Landing, Pandella Landing, Black
Hawk Point, past Tunica Bend down to Alligator Bayou, Point
Menoir, Devil's Swamp, Point à la Hache and Bayou La Loutre and
Lagier Light through New Orleans and on down toward the
sea . . .

These are more than names from the past—they are names of the
present, just as solid as Louisville and Pittsburgh and Ashland and
New Orleans itself. At Vicksburg, Mississippi, the Army Engineers
built models of proposed dams and used soap chips and bleaches in
an attempt to duplicate the flow of waters and currents: no two
dams occupy exactly the same sort of location. When the waters

begin to rise, the freshets, rivers and streams come sweeping into the Ohio and the Mississippi carrying debris of all sort: branches, old boxes, drifts of every sort. One recalls the millions of dollars worth of damage these waters have carried to the valley. Yet the proposition that the canals should be modernized to handle the industrial needs of an exploding population and a gross national product expanded beyond even the levels of World War II met considerable opposition. Congressmen were afraid such measures would be scorned by the muckrakers as porkbarrel; the electric utilities management men, sensitized by the TVA and similar projects, were wary that the government would use the improvements as a means of moving farther into the electric power business; there were many others who felt that tolls should be applied. This latter argument had particular appeal to the railroads, themselves saddled with every conceivable regulation. The truckers, who might in principle have been expected to agree (since toll highways were rapidly coming into existence throughout the nation) were, on the other hand, indifferent—probably because the sulphur and molasses and petroleum products, and the coal, that moved up and down the waterways was not cargo they were equipped to handle.

To the electric power plants, and to such operations as Ashland, the issue was crucial. With profit margins in refining being shaved with every passing quarter, the transportation margin enabled the company to keep its operations profitable; add a tax to this, and the company might well begin to choke.

Mr. Blazer, Bill Hull and Alex Chamberlain spent countless hours in discussions; they telephoned and exhorted. One particularly important individual who became convinced by their argument was Mr. Philip Sporn, president of the American Electric Power Company, one of the great engineers and businessmen of the United States, and a man of towering prestige in the utilities industry. Mr. Blazer and Mr. Sporn both spoke and corresponded on the subject; once convinced, Mr. Sporn swung many men and interests in his industry.

But in the foreground, other matters competed for attention. The program regarding the waterways was a background one.

One of the situations that confronted Mr. Blazer at this period concerned Aminol. When J. Howard Marshall was the Ashland representative on Aminol's board of directors, the company was a participant in a voting trust with Signal and some others—including Ralph Davies—and excluding Phillips and Abercrombie. But Mr. Marshall had been a close friend of Mr. Davies; Mr. Blazer did not occupy this position. Accordingly, Mr. Blazer began to search for ways to alter Ashland's position on the board. As usual, the arguments he mustered contained considerable force. Boiled down, they amounted to the thesis that a director's duty was to approve worthy projects and disapprove unworthy projects —not to blindly support a particular management. The management was not well served, he added, by having a claque on the board, the stockholders were not well represented by such an arrangement.

To assist this campaign Mac Burnam, Bill Hull and Mr. Blazer,

Rex Blazer alighting in Owensboro, Kentucky. (August 24, 1953)

joined from time to time by Rex Blazer, began to meet with Phillips and Abercrombie on Aminol matters. Signal, Davies, Marshall (now representing Signal) et al., soon heard of these meetings. Perhaps by coincidence, Bernard Majewsky, one of the founding fathers of Aminol, approached Ashland Oil at about this time, and wondered if they might not like to sell their interest in Aminol—perhaps to Sohio. The offer came at a time when four wells had come in at the Neutral Zone, and when Aminol's prospects looked better than ever before. The suggestion had the effect of increasing Mr. Blazer's resolution. He and Rex Blazer traveled to an Aminol board meeting in San Francisco, where J. Howard Marshall was also present on behalf of Signal Oil; the business at hand was discussed courteously by all concerned, but undercurrents were unmistakable.

These were not the only undercurrents. Within Ashland itself, the disappointment over the Spraberry field remained keen; to Mr. Blazer the experience was traumatic. Roy Ralston, a strong advocate of the Spraberry development, had also obtained other sites for exploration and development but now Mr. Blazer's enthusiasm had cooled, and he wanted to retrench. Ralston departed, and Ed Emrick, whose original skepticism over Spraberry had been ignored, was appointed to supervise the cutback in exploration and production efforts. The choice was tacit acknowledgment that he had been correct, and Emrick plunged into his new tasks with determination.

Then, proving anew that difficulties have a tendency to group before attacking, discussion again arose in the oil industry regarding the Big and Little Inch pipelines. These lines had been switched from crude oil to natural gas after World War II; the lines were now the objects of a plan, by a group of pipeline operators, to switch the line to petroleum products. This revived an old bugaboo, beside which agitation regarding new taxes and accusations of river pollution seemed almost domesticated nightmares.

During the spring of 1954, Mr. Blazer sought more inviting avenues of interest in discussions with Chub Moffitt, Bob Yancey, Tom Paulsen, Arnold Leas and other members of the younger generation in the management of possible petrochemical ventures.

He had Everett Wells busy; Rex Blazer was watching the sales of Allied and Frontier, and had become active with the Kentucky State Chamber of Commerce, which consumed at least a quarter of his time: the senior men were all neck-deep in work.

Throughout May and June 1954, the rumbling in the background regarding Aminol continued; so did the repercussions of the expanded cost of the Buffalo expansions. Mr. Blazer, in an attempt to throw some quenching water on this latter point, discussed the shortcomings of some Universal Oil Products equipment installed there. He assured the directors he was diligently searching the bushes for new acquisitions, and discussed, at some length, the fact that the tankers were still idle. By July 1954, gasoline price wars and a general industrial decline combined to make cutbacks and layoffs necessary for the first time in several years. Conditions, said Everett Wells, were so bad they reminded him of old times. "We haven't seen anything like this in twenty years," he told Mr. Blazer, who passed this along to the board. Wells was not a man for careless comment; one such quote from him was worth its weight in platinum.

Nevertheless, the pace of technology continued to be fast throughout the industry; the inexorable rule of grow or perish persisted. At the No. 2 refinery, $1.3 million was being spent in modernizations that included a cooling tower and a new catalytic reforming unit; it was reported that the company now had too much crude on hand (for a falling market it might mean writedowns would be necessary); and the company moved on into summer.

The brouhaha over the Buffalo expansion had, undoubtedly, affected the atmosphere. Mr. Blazer's explanations had met with some skepticism at the board meeting.

In July, new events began to turn the edge of attention. Jim Martin, a man who had saved the company during its most critical period, and who had been a tremendous friend to Mr. Blazer for many years, died at the age of seventy-six. Mr. Martin was born in Boston in 1878; had been a partner of Pynchon & Co. when that firm capsized in the great Depression (Bill Freeman refers to it as "The Fire"); he had then entered the insurance business; was for years a member of the board of the Birtman Electric Company of Chicago and the North Shore Gas Company; was first chairman of the board of Ashland Oil & Refining, then vice chairman. His death thinned the ranks of older men to whom Mr. Blazer could turn.

But good news arrived as well. The powers had decided to erect a new dam at Greenup, Kentucky, a few miles down the river from Ashland. If that project was completed, it would be possible to load and unload at the refinery at Catlettsburg itself. The appropriation had been approved by President Eisenhower (a reversal of his position; for some time the General had been singularly unimpressed with the needs of the waterways); it would still have to pass a subcommittee and a major committee, get through the Senate and then go back to the House and be finally approved by House and Senate before it would be a reality. Nevertheless, Messrs. Blazer, Chamberlain, Hull and their friends were jubilant: after years of denial, their efforts were beginning to bear fruit.

The Greenup Dam, in fact, was only one item in a great series of improvements projected for the rivers. Plans were made to build a new Cumberland Dam near Pittsburgh; this would mean better protection and an assist to industry in the whole region. The numbers of men who worked to achieve this breakthrough cannot all be listed here; they included John Diederich, the Republican National Committee Chairman for Kentucky, a potent Boyd County political leader and a good friend of Mr. Blazer's; Senator John Sherman Cooper of Kentucky lent his assistance, as did Senator John Bricker of Ohio, and the project was favored by Senator Knowland of California. California is a state that knows both the value and the dangers of waterways. Representative Jenkins of Ironton, Ohio, just across the river from Ashland, was active in the campaign, and did yeoman's work.

In retrospect, one wonders why the improvements were so long delayed and so difficult to obtain. In many locations the river locks were fifty years old. Every day saw long lines of barges lined up waiting their turns to traverse these locks; sometimes the wait literally extended to more than a day. The river itself was rife with snags; the dangers of flood had been dramatically proven, tragically exhibited, time after time.

Late in the month, the chief of the Ohio Division of Army En-

gineers, General Paschal N. Strong, wrote Mr. Blazer asking for a
boat trip for a Mr. & Mrs. Crump; Mr. Crump was described as
a writer. In due course, he proved he earned that description by
producing the history of the Army Engineers, and dedicated it to
Mr. Blazer for his efforts regarding the waterways.

Another writer who brought cheer and comfort to Mr. Blazer
at this period was Dr. Joseph Massie. His dissertation on the
Ashland management methods—methods he regarded as entirely
too individualistic to succeed in a large company—earned Massie
not only his doctorate at the University of Chicago, but more
than usual attention for a dissertation. He visited Mr. Blazer
in his new home in Florida, in the course of his project, and
recorded the interview on tape.

Mr. Blazer encouraged Dr. Massie toward more general publication, and in 1954 the two men began to update the dissertation.

By August 1954, Mr. Blazer was again warning the board that
"competition is larger, stronger and sharper," than ever before. His
vocabulary was, by subtle shadings, becoming more military as
the years passed. He continued to find ways to improve—lessen,
in other words—transportation costs. A new products line was installed between Canton and Findlay, Ohio; the reduction in truck
costs thus achieved did something to balance the fact that crude
oil prices had to be cut in the Kentucky fields for the second time
in six months—a sign of slack business.

In September 1954, Mr. Blazer spoke again at the University of
Kentucky. A look behind the scenes reveals he had sponsored a
lecture series known, eventually, as the Blazer Lectures. But his
gifts to the largest school in the state did not equal his gifts to
smaller schools, and to churches. These latter gifts were personal;
they were unpublicized. He himself attended church in Ashland,
but not every Sunday; he did not discuss religion nor his beliefs.
He seems, in fact, to have been unusually fortunate, in that his
faith was real to him; he did not waver in it, nor did he question
its validity. It bore him along, and he trusted in it.

By this time, Mr. Blazer had Palmer Talbutt watching for
young men; Talbutt told him that Orin Atkins, in the legal
department, was excellent timber. One day late in the fall,
Atkins was surprised to find Mr. Blazer, tall and frail, picking his

way into Atkins' office and carefully seating himself. "I have decided you shall work with me for a while," he told Atkins, who had no clear idea of what this meant, and the two men chatted briefly before the older man departed.

In September 1954, we find net sales of $227 million, and net profits of $6.6 million. Both figures were below the year before; the earnings would have been a matter of pride for many managements. But for the first time they give rise to a question: has the wizard lost the secret of his incantations? Miracles no longer appear.

The absence of miracles also occurred to the board. Orin Atkins, attending his first board meeting in 1954, was astounded when Walton Davis arose and read aloud a lengthy statement whose import was that, for the sake of his health and continued life, Paul G. Blazer should accept the thanks of his associates and retire from the company. He was speaking for several of the directors.

Atkins looked down the long polished table toward Mr. Blazer, whose face showed little more than polite attention. When Mr. Davis was finished and sat down to muted murmurs, Mr. Blazer thanked him for the friendliness of his sentiments, and his concern. "But I believe," he said, looking around the table at the eyes upon him, "that you have exaggerated my condition. My doctors assure me there is no danger whatever; none at all." By his tone, he managed to relegate the suggestion to the status of something sentimental and slightly ridiculous—like a Valentine Day's card unaccountably handed to an adult, or birthday wishes that are too fulsome. Atkins relaxed, sensing that nothing in particular was going to happen, but he had been keenly aroused, where he had expected to be bored. He decided board meetings were more rousing than he had expected—if this was a sample.

After the meeting, however, during an automobile ride, the tenor of remarks by Mr. Blazer and Palmer Talbutt left no doubt *they* considered the situation serious; even critical.

While normal and continuing situations evolved during the autumn and into the winter, quiet conversations were held between Mr. Blazer's emissaries and members of the board of directors. Mr. Blazer did not believe in letting situations get out of hand.

He selected as his agents for some of these talks Palmer Talbutt and Rex Blazer. Sending Rex was an extremely astute move; no other man could reassure Mr. Vandeveer and Mr. Newman more than their candidate himself. For Rex Blazer, who had neither created nor fostered the situation, it was all embarrassing. But the outcome was all that Mr. Blazer could have hoped. He earned more time; the directors decided to drop the subject of his retirement, temporarily. Although the board as a whole relaxed into its customary posture of approval, it remained vigilant and there were scars.

Mr. Blazer moved, as usual, on several fronts at once. Announcing the Ashland organization had grown too "static," he shifted Roland Whealy from general superintendent of the refineries to the post of special assistant to Everett Wells, executive vice president. Bill Humphreys, who had been chief engineer of the refineries, became an assistant to Chub Moffitt, head of National Accounts. Gus Litton, formerly an assistant to Humphreys, was made chief engineer; Bob Yancey became coordinator for the refineries—Whealy's old post—with a subtle difference.

That November, Mr. Blazer spent almost an entire day talking about petrochemicals with candidate Tom Paulsen,[5] pressured him

---

[5] Thorwell H. Paulsen was born 1922, in Detroit, Mich.; attended Michigan State University from 1940–1943; was in the army as a 2nd Lieutenant in World War II; returned to school and graduated in 1947 with a B.S. in chemical engineering; studied at the Illinois Institute of Technology later. Paulsen went to work at the Sinclair Research Laboratories in Harvey, Illinois, and revealed talent; was transferred to the New York branch of the organization and became assistant to executive vice president W. M. Flowers (now president); worked closely with E. W. Ison, then chairman of the board, now deceased. When Sinclair Chemicals was formed, Paulsen became its chief process engineer, was in charge of technical and economic evaluations, also served as a liaison between the organization and ongoing research projects at the Laboratories. Dissatisfied with the tempo of the progress with Sinclair, Paulsen applied to Ashland after reading that it was interested in venturing into petrochemicals in the trade press; wrote a letter and was interviewed by Everett Wells who was favorably impressed and directed him to Mr. Blazer. Paulsen and Mr. Blazer liked each other, but it was a meeting of two worlds: Paulsen later declared Mr. Blazer "used to translate everything into barrels."

into saying he would work for the company before deciding what the salary would be: Mr. Blazer had his eye on petrochemicals.

The year 1954 drew to a close against the backdrop of an industry in the midst of great technological changes and an increasingly sharp market. A 4½ per cent decline in sales during the year had made it necessary to lay off one hundred employees at the Canton refinery, and this led to a worsening of labor relations—already sensitive—in that area. The No. 1 plant at Catlettsburg was shut down for the first time ever; a decline in crude oil prices was beginning to give rise to great discontent, especially among independent producers, and outcries against the unregulated importation of foreign crude oil began to be directed toward Washington.

Recapitulating the situation in the 1954 annual report, a document over which he toiled even more than usual (and Mr. Blazer usually paid very close attention indeed to this yearly project), the management said, in effect, that when it acquired seven small refineries between 1948 and 1950, it knew these would have to be modernized or closed. For several years, the Report said, circumstances so favored refining that the company made unusually high profits; this led to unrealistic projections and hopes for the future. Now, a modernization program was underway, but to modernize several small refineries was to move in a different direction than the industry—which was moving toward larger, more economical refineries.

Ashland Oil could continue to operate smaller refineries profitably, however—though they had to be modern—by linking them to its water transportation system. The modernization program would cost around $20 million at Buffalo and Canton alone; more money would be needed to upgrade Catlettsburg, but money was not one of the company's problems at the moment: it had some $45 million on hand.

Meanwhile, the refinery workers in Canton decided to go out on strike, creating doubt as to whether its leadership was as well informed on the general state of the industry as it should have been. The National Maritime Union was organizing among the workers on the Ashland towboats and meeting, initially, with considerable success; Aminol had found another well in the Neutral Zone; sales declined even farther hitting an 8 per cent drop by December 1954; Rex Blazer and Lucile Thornton Blazer returned from their honeymoon to reside in Ashland.

In retrospect, it seems clear that a number of misunderstandings had developed between Mr. Blazer and some of the members of his board, and between Mr. Blazer and some of the men in management. The breakdown in communications seems, at least in part, attributable to Mr. Blazer's differences with J. Howard Marshall. Once he developed dissatisfactions regarding Mr. Marshall, Mr. Blazer seems to have transferred some of his dissatisfaction to the men who appeared to work best with Marshall or who saw him most often, or both.

After Mr. Marshall departed, moreover, there were a number of informational channels developed while he was president that were suddenly left either broken or dangling. Rex Blazer, the new president, had to develop his own channels.

Bill Hull, whom Mr. Blazer had hoped to develop as a sort of extra assistant, had proven to be a brilliant lawyer and an effective Washington contact man, but not particularly interested in the sort of business problems that engrossed Mr. Blazer.

It was different with Orin Atkins. He had been added to Mr. Blazer's staff with few instructions at a time when Mr. Blazer seldom left his home. It is not surprising, therefore, that in a few weeks Rex Blazer called Atkins in, and told him that Mr. Blazer was not especially happy with his performance.

Atkins, alerted, seized a notebook, and started to go through the firm. He discovered, to the best of his ability, what the various departments were doing, and when Mr. Blazer called the next morning, Atkins gave him an eagle's eye description. Mr. Blazer was delighted. It took Atkins a little while to discover that some of the information had repercussions. On one occasion, for instance, he learned that asphalt sales were dropping. He told Mr. Blazer. A short time later, he was confronted by a disgruntled Everett Wells, who wanted to know why he had shifted the refineries around. Atkins, amazed, denied responsibility. "I suppose Mr. Blazer ordered some changes," he said.

"On the basis of information you supplied," Wells answered tersely. Atkins realized then that information relayed in fragments was subject to diverse interpretations. He began a more serious and deeper study of how the company worked, and the interrelationships of the technology; became more chary of voicing his observations until he could discern these patterns. His days as an executive were launched.

Meanwhile, evidence within the company pointed inescapably toward the conclusion that Mr. Blazer, far from being faced with incipient rebellion, was regarded by the men throughout the management with a respect that bordered on awe. Far from causing a wholesale departure, his shifts of assignments and duties were accepted without question; men seemed to work harder than ever.

Mr. Blazer was selected by the Kentucky Press Association as Kentuckian of the Year in 1955—an honor bestowed by working newspapermen that is respected because the choices cannot be directed by influence; the recognition delighted the company.

In February, rumors that the White House and the administration generally favored river tolls for bulk transporters of petroleum products cast shadows over the transportation and refining departments of the firm. The Aminol voting agreement dispute boiled over into the courts: Ralph Davies and his colleagues obtained an injunction in a San Francisco court against directors' activities that violated the private agreement. The injunction was, clearly, obtained against Ashland; Mr. Blazer and Rex Blazer had been slated to attend a meeting at which the attorneys believed the papers would be served; Mr. Davies later denied this intention.

The Aminol situation was annoying, but the possibility of tolls on the river was a more serious threat that could affect the economic picture of the entire Ashland Oil & Refining corporate structure. Modernization of the Catlettsburg works, Mr. Blazer wrote, "would be folly" under such conditions. The transportation of large amounts of asphalt and heavy fuel oil was only economical, he declared, as long as the riverways remained open.

But now, larger regional economic reasons were involved. By

the spring of 1955, the Ohio River valley was producing three times the coal and steel of the German Ruhr. Since the end of World War II, in 1945, $10 billion worth of new industries had located or arisen in the Ohio valley: all of these would be affected. The proponents of the riverways tolls, ostensibly anxious to protect the taxpayers, nevertheless carefully exempted from their propositions the Great Lakes and ports handling foreign trade. Thus, their definition of inland waterways was highly discriminatory.

Meanwhile, court charges between the divided groups of Aminol directors (pro- and anti-Phillips) were filed in Wilmington, Delaware as well as in San Francisco. The snarl was a lawyers' delight and had deteriorated into emotional declarations from the participants; Mr. Blazer declared he was not against Mr. Davies—he simply refused to be bound to him—a fine distinction.

These legal arguments consumed time; but at least refinery operations moved more briskly. The Buffalo plant was still undergoing some improvements; Mr. Whealy later was to take stoical satisfaction in the fact that the installations he had supervised were to make that complex one of the most efficient in the area for many years; Tom Paulsen and Bob Yancey had decided that a Udex unit would further improve the installation and were toiling over its justification.

The year 1955 moved into spring. Mr. Blazer arranged that Mr. and Mrs. John Fred Williams, as well as other families in the company, could fly down to Florida with him; he believed the company plane could well be used, when otherwise not filled, to help general morale. Rex Blazer was made president of the Kentucky Chamber of Commerce, a distinction won after he was in Kentucky only five years. A new pipeline was laid between Canton and Findlay, connecting the two refineries at a cost of between $1 million and $1.25 million; the total refining capacity of the company was up to 100,000 barrels a day.

Mr. Blazer, noticing increasing newspaper clippings mentioning himself, Rex Blazer and various other persons both in his family and the company, made explanations to the board. "Many members of our organization engage," he wrote, "in activities of a public or civic nature. I believe this is justified. For many years, large corporations in this section of the country were weak and short-sighted in their public relations. Rex's activities make him known throughout the State; he will develop friendships with leaders for many years to come; John Fred Williams is well known; it would help if we were busy in other areas . . ." One recalls the long conversations with the Vinsons, and the New Deal charges that corporations were devoted only to their own selfish interests: these charges had sunk deep.

Meanwhile, exploration and production efforts were being cut back; crude oil was plentiful and its price was dropping. On the other hand, despite the continuing rumors about river tolls, $1.5 million was being spent on a new tow and barges to fit; the company was actually beginning to tow for other firms. But the marketing department was receiving the pressure: a natural result of having increased the refinery capacity. Everett Wells, Charley Bolton of Ashland, Aetna's Donley, Valvoline's Mohr, Frontier's C. G. Maxwell and others labored hard to extend their territories. In the background, Mr. Blazer fulminated eloquently about the "wasteful and extravagant" practice of the majors, who steadily extended expensive service stations across the land from which they sold their gasoline; every new station nibbled away at Ashland's cherished independent outlets. This was an old theme of Mr. Blazer's.

Then, on July 7, 1955, *The Wall Street Journal* ran the following article:

RIVER RUCKUS

New Battle Brews Over Barges' Free Use of Waterways

By Louis M. Kohlmeier, Jr.

ST. LOUIS—One day this spring the diesel towboat *Aetna-Louisville* cast off from the dock at Memphis bound up the Mississippi for Cairo, Illinois. Her square, ungraceful bow was hard against a "tow" of 13 barges loaded with over eight million gallons—some 30 thousand tons— of petroleum products.

It was a journey of interest to rivermen, railroaders and

truckers. And it was a journey important to shippers, politicians and taxpayers, though they might be remote from life on the Mississippi.

For one thing, this towboat and tow set a record. From barge's bow to boat's stern the tow measured 1,605 feet, one and one-half times the largest ocean-going liner, the *Queen Elizabeth*. For another, she was moving over a "roadbed" dredged and maintained by the Federal Government and the use of which was free.

And thereby hangs a controversy. Last week's Hoover Commission report on water resources and power proposes to change the nation's river traffic habits; it wants Congress to authorize the Interstate Commerce Commission to start imposing tolls, or "user charges," on the barge lines that ply the 28,400 miles of inland waterways kept up by the Government. It's a large question, of course, whether the Administration or Congress will agree; the recent report of the President's Cabinet committee on transportation policy failed to make such a recommendation.

All the same, the Hoover proposal pleases truckers and railroad men who feel this river competition has been subsidized. Shippers are divided, depending on where and what they ship. The romanticists are tangled up with emotions. But rivermen are up in arms; they fear they may be put out of business. Certainly the proposal would change a policy as old as the winning of the West.

* * * * *

The Federal Government has indeed spent a lot of money over the years fixing up the waterways. Exact figures are hard to come by, but an official estimate is that since 1824 appropriations to dig channels, build dikes, dams and locks have added up to $4 billion. In addition, more than $3.5 billion has been spent since 1936 on flood control projects from which navigation also benefits.

* * * * *

Nor is the Government building finished. There are plans, for instance, for four new dams and locks on the

Snake River, a tributary of the Columbia, at a cost of
$400 million. This would make the Snake navigable up to
Lewiston, Idaho. Altogether, Army engineers estimate they
have a backlog of unfinished work on improvements that
totals $8.8 billion. This, of course, is in addition to main-
tenance costs which run about $33 million a year.

*   *   *   *   *

The writer of the article had introduced a semantic switch; he
called the rivers "roadbeds." From this amazing leap into fantasia,
the balance of the article was unrealistically based, but in true
science-fiction fashion, given verisimilitude. The detail was, in fact,
so dense that once the reader accepted the concept of a waterless
river, he was intellectually caught.

Having thus reduced the Father of Waters to the status of a
dry track, Mr. Kohlmeier recapitulated all the money spent by the
government to improve the "roadbed"—from 1787 onward.

This recapitulation carried the reader all the way through the
days of the Erie Canal and the *Robert E. Lee,* the rise of the railroads and shifts in the movements of industrial materials.

But he was heavily impressed by the taxes loaded upon the
truckers using the highways, and the railroads whose tracks
parallel the rivers.

Against these taxes and tolls Kohlmeier contrasted the steadily
lengthening ribbons of heavily-loaded barges that streamed up the
Mississippi and Ohio—ribbons that included many bearing the
emblem of Ashland Oil.

By tolling off these sums spent through the centuries without
mentioning floods, their effects on the ecology, the economy or
the human life of the region; without mentioning the purposes of
dams, docks, dredges or levees beyond improving the "roadbed",
Mr. Kohlmeier managed to relegate these sums expended by the
nation through the centuries from 1787 onward to the status of
a gigantic handout to barge-line operators.

To direct attention away from this reductio ad absurdum, the journalist dwelled, at length, on the colorful aspects of the decades he was describing.

But for a final and convincing gun, he wheeled in a reference to a recommendation by the Hoover Commission—a body whose studies and recommendations through the years have been almost as widely admired and ignored as Sunday exhortations against golfing during church hours.

Mr. Kohlmeier ended his article by saying:

*   *   *   *   *

The resurgence has also been due to several factors: The changing economy, improved waterways transportation, rising rail freight rates and, of course, the improvement in the waterways themselves by the investment of Government money. Today there are some 4,000 towboats and tugs plying the waterways, most with modern efficient diesel engines. They handle a fleet of some 14,000 barges and floats with capacities averaging 1,000 to 3,000 tons each; and one boat can handle up to a dozen of them.

It's this new competition typified by the Memphis-to-Cairo record-breaking tow that has raised the political issue. The Hoover Commission thinks the time has come for the river barges to pay at least a part of their own way. So too, naturally, do the truckers and railroad men who say the barge rates would not be so low if rivermen had to pay for their own roadbed.

"Impractical and Discriminatory"

The barge lines retort that full user charges would be impractical because of the complex, multi-purpose nature of waterways improvements and that to attempt it would be nothing more than a "discriminatory tax." If high enough, a user charge could put them out of business and thus destroy the Government's investment. Finally, they claim it would be an abandonment of a basic national policy that not only is as old as the nation itself but also has helped to build the nation.

In 1953 the Federal Government sold its Inland Waterways Corp., an operating barge line, in an effort to get the Government out of business and the waterways out of politics. River boating is now plainly a booming private business. But equally plainly the barges are as deep in politics as ever.

And as the Administration considers whether to send the Hoover proposal to Congress, rivermen are finding politics as full of shoals and sandbars as the Savannah and the Tombigbee, as tortuous as the Snake.

Mr. Blazer, who read the article closely, had copies distributed to the directors, saying in part, "Cleverly written. But it is mainly propaganda for the railroads."

He had always admired the railroads for the masterly way they could present their causes, and would often darkly observe, when some otherwise inexplicable occurrence would take place, that "the railroads were probably at the bottom of it."

In expressing this opinion, Mr. Blazer was probably reflecting his background; when he was a lad, the railroads had been potent movers and shakers; national symbols of Machiavellian maneuvers.

The article constituted the first shot in what was to become a fusillade in favor of tolls on the waterways. The issue had been a hot political chestnut over a century before; the arguments thoroughly thrashed and, apparently, permanently resolved. But like many other historic matters, the issue seemed novel to the men of mid-century America, and debate arose as though it were all new. The men of Ashland gathered their forces to meet the charge.

By this time, some of the internal management changes had lost their initial shock; new results were emerging. Director Bill Bechman wrote Mr. Blazer and praised the efforts of Ed Emrick in the exploration and production department, saying, ". . . it proves that a man with ability and experience can step into almost any field," added that he thought Bob Gordon Jr. was one of the best men in the company, and then, returning to the subject of Emrick, called him a "deep thinker and a careful operator."

On the other hand, director Earle Craig wrote Mr. Blazer in favor of more gasoline stations, instead of dividends . . . a position he knew Mr. Blazer did not share, but one he felt should be maintained as a goal. The board contained independent thinkers.

But the company was changing. Mr. Blazer described the workings of the new: ". . . the coordination of demand for our refined products, our available refining capacity, transportation of crude oil and refined products, the matching up of yields of the various products with sales and storage facilities, and the procurement of the proper quantities of crude oil, present a complex problem. In my experience, we are making marked progress in the development of experienced personnel in the handling of these related activities. *Not many years have passed since I was handling practically all of this coordinating personally, carrying the figures and problems in my head, but as our operations have become more complex it has become necessary to prepare literally reams of figures involving forecasts a year in advance.*"

He then discussed, in some detail, the complexities involved in catalytic reforming, the variety of possible units, the fact that such a unit, installed at Catlettsburg, encountered difficulties with a "poisoned" platinum catalyst, and the inherent difficulties in trying to mesh an organization that consists of so many acquired divisions, with their separate managements, men and systems. Mr. Blazer was beginning to relax both with the board and his various associates; reading between the lines, one is relieved to see the discursive, almost chatty way in which he thought aloud in these great, lengthy messages, which seem to have become almost a form of thinking aloud for him. The years had brought him increasing fluency; he now dictated these missives.

Although not many persons outside of business seem to have heard of it, the Newcomen Society in North America is extremely well known in business circles. Mr. Blazer said its purpose is "difficult to describe." To a neutral observer, it would seem to fill a human need of businessmen and the enterprises they form and direct, to be given some sort of credit for hard work and accomplishment. Since the late 1920s this credit has been largely withheld by the great communicators of our time; business reaches the front pages usually when a scandal erupts. Otherwise, the charge that business is for the dull or the greedy, or both, is generally so widespread in the art of our times that arguments against it seem almost quixotic.

This harsh circumstance, however, has been a blessing for the organizers of the Newcomen Society, who, to simplify their function, arrange for banquets, speeches, and booklets describing business or industrial achievement. The subjects wind up paying some rather heavy charges for this pleasure, but their friends enjoy it, and the Society, knowledgeable in its sector, performs its functions with dignity and tact.

Ed Dabney suggested to the Society that it approach Mr. Blazer and create a celebration to be built around the Ashland Oil & Refining Company. Mr. Blazer was pleased and interested. By the time he realized the booklets would run into some fairly large figures (although of course, the figures are not too onerous to prevent the Society from arranging similar gatherings practically every day in the year, and to be booked years in advance), it was too late for him to tactfully withdraw, had he been so inclined. The odds are that he was not. The dimensions of business are more extensive than chess; they include the most changeable and fluid of all living organisms: humanity itself; the oil industry is one of the most intricate and challenging, and almost every successful industrialist and businessman in it has—like a chess master—developed some fascinating methods of play that can only properly be appreciated by his peers. Thus, the Newcomen Dinners are probably one of the most instructive series of gatherings possible to find: those interested in the Harvard School of Business and similar management-oriented factories might be well advised to follow the activities of the Newcomen Society instead, for a more interesting and less didactic course. Blazer signed Ashland up for a Dinner in 1956. Dr. Charles Penrose, head of the Society in the United States, would be back from a trip abroad then; both men looked forward to meeting one another.

Thus the year 1955 passed; the ever-shifting tides of business kept the men busy; new shoals to avoid and rapids to shoot seemed to appear at every bend. Rumors swept through Wall Street that the company was on the verge of merging into the wake of a larger corporation; speculators began to buy Ashland stock, and the price moved up sharply. When the management denied the rumors the stock fell several points, abruptly, giving short sellers a profit and catching, as usual, those who trust in gossip.

At the end of August 1955, the company bought the River Company, Incorporated, a subsidiary of the Jordan River Lines. It consisted of two towboats and eight integrated barges; a new company was set up to operate this property. Everett Wells was made its president, and M. C. Dupree, long the transportation chief of the company, vice president of the new company.

The end of the fiscal year in September 1955 found net sales of $245.9 million, net profits of $10 million—the second highest figure for profits in the history of the company, and a new high for net sales. The wizard's incantations were working again, excepting for a decision during the year to reduce the dividends on common stock from 25 cents a share to 15 cents. Understandably, this produced sharp cries of pain from the shareholders, and led to a coolness on Mr. Blazer's part toward his old friend Joe Levin, who endorsed the step. The reduction lasted only nine months.

The coolness was not improved by some points of difference regarding the best course of action to take in the Amurex venture which was not proving particularly productive as far as Ashland Oil was concerned. Despite Mr. Murphy's considerable success in discovering crude oil, he had not been successful, or at least not notably so, in combination with Ashland Oil. At the Amurex board meetings, Joe Levin somewhat rashly found himself taking opposing positions to Mr. Blazer in a number of instances; along with the contretemps of the untimely dividend reduction, the combination created a visible rift.

Meanwhile the forward momentum of the company continued. A trunk pipeline running 48 miles into Kentucky was purchased for $600,000; a catalytic reformer was selected for the Buffalo plant at a cost of $2 million; the second step of this would run another $1.5 million. Some cutbacks in labor accompanied these advances; the Aetna refinery in Louisville was closed down, and the men were offered jobs in other refineries. Only six elected to move, although thirty openings existed at Catlettsburg, eighteen at Buffalo, six at Canton and six at Findlay.

In October 1956, *Fortune* magazine carried its first Directory of the 500 Largest Industrial Corporations in the U.S., listed in order of sales (with the exception of those that do not publish these figures).[6] Ashland Oil & Refining was listed as Number 134, based on a sales volume of $227.9 million (the figures of 1955), 146th in terms of assets; 211th in terms of profit before taxes and 210th after taxes; 65th in number of shareholders (30,800); 381st in number of employees (4,200). Not bad for a firm that started as "little better than a skimming plant."

"I am taking steps," Mr. Blazer wrote at the same time, "to obtain more administration assistance. Orin Atkins, who is one of the most capable, aggressive young lawyers, will become my personal assistant . . ." Mr. Atkins had met the challenge.

The room at the top is a small area, but Atkins had assumed a position in this magic circle that was unique; Mr. Blazer had employed assistants before, but none had earned the title "personal."

The fact was the two men complemented one another. Atkins' legal training equipped him to concentrate upon the issues that arose: to examine them for avenues and means of resolution and this was valuable. But even more important was the fact that his was a fertile and creative mind in finance; Atkins brought insights to Mr. Blazer that had not been taught him, but that he discovered for himself. In addition, his manners were good and his instincts gentlemanly; the combination to Mr. Blazer was most attractive. His eyes, experienced in reading men, saw the outlines of a possible corporate heir, and all his faculties began to assess, to weigh and to consider this possibility.

It was, after all, more than time. That September in 1955 Mr. Blazer had reached another great meridian of time. The traveler was now 65 and across the river. Middle age was over, and old age had begun.

[6] The figures and relative positions were obtained from 1955 activities, and therefore are included in that year instead of in the 1956 section.

Section Eight—How to Win Friends & Influence a Region

1956–1960

By the middle 1950s, the world had so altered that a man reincarnated from 1939 would have had difficulty locating, let alone recognizing, many old landmarks. The western colonial system was in disarray. The people of the western world, far from mourning its condition, seemed anxious for its demise.

The Eisenhower administration had devised a foreign policy based on "massive retaliation," at a place and time of its own choosing, against either Soviet adventures or Soviet-inspired adventures. This policy was coordinated into an interlocking series of alliances, plus missile bases, with non-Soviet nations around the world, backed by a great variety of nuclear weapons. The policy, the pacts, the arms, and the bases combined to create a feeling of security within the government. Unfortunately, the security system prevented an open discussion of these matters, and the public, lacking knowledge of its protection, did not share the government's confidence. For the first time in the history of the United States, an informational gap of considerable size had opened between the government of the United States and the people; it rendered many official statements cryptic and oblique, and made many public attitudes difficult for the government to accept sympathetically. This unfortunate by-product of the cold war is still with us.

Confident of the efficacy of his defense posture, President Eisenhower moved to cut the conventional military establishment. He reduced the Truman defense budget from an average of $43 billion to an average of $37.5 billion a year. He cut the armed forces by more than a million persons, leaving 2.5 million persons in uniform.

Because the Administration had entered office after publicly promising to reduce the sprawling governmental apparatus erected during the New and Fair Deal tenures that stretched from 1933 to 1952, the President also introduced similar economies in this area.

Here, the anomalies of the Administration's position resembled those of the public, who wanted bureaucrats to disappear but the services they administered to remain. The White House found it could not dismantle the interlocking network of agencies, bureaus, commissions, and directorates without crippling the government. Neither could it separate cold war issues from their domestic effects. But it made a valiant effort.

With the reduction in the defense budget and the cutback of the armed forces, the nation felt twin impacts from a lower supply of money and more persons dumped into the labor market. For the first time the momentum of the boom began to diminish, and the economy began to miss some beats.

The oil industry, however, was already in a difficult position, and was hurting in several sections along its incredibly extended length. The majors were finding floods of crude oil in the Middle East, but these imports were hurting the market for the U.S. independents. Thus, the price of crude oil was sinking.

At the same time, the industry was in the painful throes of another technological change in refinery processing. This called for capital expenditures, new equipment, new training of workmen and new products. Pressure from Detroit, which was bringing out new engines that required higher octane gasoline, contributed to this development.

While these efforts were underway, the gasoline market peaked, and customers began to shop for lower prices without regard to brand. This set off price wars.

All this added up to circumstances no industry enjoys: competitive pressures and a falling market. But they usually go together.

The market squeeze was especially hard on Ashland because it had ventured overseas in only relatively small ways; the bulk of its operating capital and business effort was in the industrial heartland of the United States.

Ashland operated, furthermore, small refineries that were technologically uneconomical in comparison to the giant installations being created by the majors. The main reason Ashland could compete was that it could supply its refineries with crude oil over inland waterways economically and could ship its refined products out the same waterways.

It would not be true to say that Mr. Blazer was the only man to perceive the opportunities presented by these rivers; both Messrs. Vandeveer and Newman saw and exploited the same opportunity on the Great Lakes. The steel companies made use of the rivers. The coal companies sent their long strings of barges, through commercial shippers and barge lines, to the power stations and companies by water. But Ashland was probably the only large oil company in 1956 to whom the waterways were literally a lifeline; without them it could not compete.

One can imagine the consternation in the seventh floor executive offices on Winchester Avenue in Ashland, therefore, when on January 30, 1956, President Eisenhower, in his message to Congress, called for a "user-tax" on the rivers, and a study to determine general tolls. The Eisenhower economy wave had reached Ashland.

Within two weeks, Mr. Blazer was in Washington, testifying before a Congressional committee. "Refineries are supplied with crude oil either through pipelines or by water," Mr. Blazer told the committee. "I selected Catlettsburg as a refinery site because it is located on the water. Over the years, it has grown, until it is now 50 times its size then."

He then described the large amounts that moved in and out of the refinery, and said this traffic could not be handled by the railroads. "The real competitor to the waterways is the pipeline," he said. "If you tax the waterways, you will succeed only in putting the small refiner out of business. That will leave only the majors." Then, in extremity, he revealed an industrial circumstance he had never before openly discussed. "Ashland cannot join the pipeline people," he said, "they keep to themselves."

"I thought," he remarked at one point, "that a policy that was in effect almost 170 years—free waterways—was reasonably stable."

One of the Congressional inquisitors took exception, and wanted to know if Ashland was not, in effect, seeking a federal subsidy.

"The railroads receive assistance from the government," Blazer pointed out, and the Congressman said sharply, "That's not a proper answer. I want to know if you are not asking for a subsidy."

Blazer said he was merely asking not to have his profits cut to the point where his company would have to relocate.

Under more sympathetic questioning by another Congressman, he went into greater detail. "The Greenup Dam," he explained, "will raise the water level 25 feet at that area, and directly help our refinery. That will also help the small oil and gas producers in the hinterlands of Kentucky who depend on our refinery to buy their production."

Then the friendly Congressman put a final question, and it was obvious that he knew the answer: he wanted the rest of the Committee to hear it. "Mr. Blazer," he asked, "does your firm pay the 52 per cent tax on its earning, or does it enjoy the famous depletion allowance?"

"We pay the 52 per cent," Blazer said, "we do not enjoy the depletion allowance."

These were, of course, forays into the outer world to protect the company. Business in the firm proceeded as usual. Bob Yancey bargained—he turned out to be a shrewd bargainer and to have a liking and a feel for business unusual in an engineer—and arranged to have the catalytic reforming unit installed in Buffalo; in the Illinois Basin Ashland Oil was becoming stronger; the waterflooding program for the Ashland wells in eastern Kentucky appeared promising; the management decided to restrict its exploration and development efforts east of the Mississippi for the foreseeable future.

A general stock option plan for key personnel was approved by the board; the list of names extended to seventy-four; this time the board approved without argument: men who could share in the fruits of their efforts worked with a better will.

Then Ashland received an invitation to participate in the creation of a Tecumseh pipeline that would originate in Chicago and terminate near its Findlay, Ohio, refinery. Mr. Blazer was jubilant. "This gives us a chance to break into the exclusive pipeline fraternity," he wrote to the directors. All the partners in the venture except Ashland were major oil companies. As though to deliberately darken the glow that this venture evoked, it was announced in the trade press that the Texas Eastern Transmission Company would convert the Little Inch pipeline to a product line.

The Little Inch, a proposition that had originally attracted Mr. Blazer tremendously when it was first conceived during World War II, was familiar territory to Mr. Blazer. He had intended to be one of the original participants, and actually joined the venture on behalf of Ashland Oil. But the government men informed him he could not retain this participation and obtain the aviation gasoline plant as well. Accordingly, Ashland Oil had dropped out of the Little Inch. But Harley Pope, one of the participants in the line, who decided to buy Ashland's share in the Little Inch, later sold half his stock back to Ashland Oil.

When the majority owners of the Little Inch decided to switch the Little Inch to petroleum products, therefore, they not only posed a threat to Ashland Oil's markets, but voted over the objections of a minority stockholder. No man to abandon even a minority position, Mr. Blazer was pleased when a proceeding before the Federal Power Commission against the line's operators succeeded in moving the plan from the edge of execution into the endless labyrinth of the law.

This maneuver filled Orin Atkins, in particular, with pleasure, for Bill Hull was an active and creative partner in the step. Atkins and Mr. Blazer then turned their attentions toward other problems. Essentially, they were fighting for time to work the company out of its watery trap.

The Chancery Court in Delaware ruled on the voting agreement within Aminol: the agreement that Mr. Blazer found so personally vexatious, was, in effect, dead. Mr. Blazer had won his fight to sever

Ashland from Ralph Davies, J. Howard Marshall, Sam Mosher and company; he switched openly to Phillips and Abercrombie.

By the end of February 1956, the Tecumseh pipeline deal, with partners Pure Oil and Sinclair, was closed. Ashland found itself with 20 per cent of a 20-inch line that would extend from near Chicago to the town of Cygnet, Ohio, near Findlay. The company could count on receiving 8,000 barrels of crude oil a day through this line which would cost, when completed, $15.2 million. The company's dependence on the rivers was that much lightened.

In April 1956, Ashland's long anticipated Newcomen Dinner was held in Lexington; long-time director and friend Ed Dabney, president of the Security Trust Company of Lexington, introduced Mr. Blazer; the dinner was presided over by John E. Tilford, president of the Louisville and Nashville Railroad. Dr. Charles Penrose, the senior vice president for North America of the Newcomen Society of England, was present, and so were six hundred other guests—many of whom had traveled a long distance to attend.

Mr. Blazer had entitled his address "E Pluribus Unum—One Out of Many: An Oil Company Grows Through Acquisitions." The Society had printed booklets that ran, including the cover, to thirty pages. These were decorated with woodcuts; paragraphs were separated for easy reading. Mr. Blazer's description of the growth of the company was lucid, clear and factual. Toward the close he quoted Dr. Joseph Massie, whose dissertation had been entitled "Management of a Growing Company: Ashland Oil & Refining Company." Dr. Massie and he were together upgrading the dissertation with a view toward general publication. ("They seemed to enjoy themselves," Mrs. Blazer said, "Dr. Massie was a charming young man.")

The Newcomen Dinner was a huge success, but afterward Mr. Blazer was prostrated. He had to cancel all his engagements, but he reported stoutly to the board that Dr. Winans had discovered a new medicine that greatly reduced his angina pains.

Meanwhile, Mr. Blazer and a new technical brain trust were deep in plans for the future. These were pointed in the direction of petrochemicals.

Shortly after Tom Paulsen joined the company, Bill Gammon,[1] a young colleague of Paulsen's at Sinclair Research, applied for a job.

Gammon and Paulsen found themselves working closely with Ollie Zandona, Bob Yancey's right arm. Zandona was a product of the Ashland method; he had been one of the men in the car that followed the leader to the bidding on the high octane unit. In fact, Zandona,[2] together with Bob Yancey, had been deeply involved in the installation of the wartime high octane gasoline plant.

Zandona, with Yancey and others, had investigated and evalu-

[1] William H. Gammon was born 1926 in St. Louis, Mo., where his father worked for the Missouri-Pacific Railroad. Gammon, who has always looked older than his years, graduated from high school at 16, attended college for a year then joined the Marine Corps in 1943; saw action at Okinawa and Pelelieu, where he was a reservist; was wounded 31 days after landing in Okinawa by a machine gun spray that left one of his hands injured for a year. Discharged from the service in May 1946, he got a job as an engineer's aid in the St. Louis Water Department, then returned to the University of Missouri's School of Mines & Metallurgy. He was an athletic bug, and wanted to become a professional ballplayer or a coach. At school he was selected by the Steelers, a professional team; began to officiate at high school and college football games, a sideline he maintained for years. After receiving his B.S. he went to work for Sinclair Research, where he met Paulsen; became a protégé of E. C. Herthel, Sinclair Research chief. Herthel retired; changed loomed, and Gammon followed Paulsen to Ashland, where he was interviewed by Houlton, tested by Jim Hiatt of Personnel; had lunch at the Henry Clay Hotel in Ashland where he met Mr. Blazer, Everett Wells, Bob Yancey, Tom Paulsen. At the end of the lunch, Mr. Blazer welcomed him to the organization; his rise has been rapid, and more shall be said about him.

[2] Oliver Zandona, born in Freeport, Pa., in 1922, graduated from Carnegie Tech in December 1943, with a Bachelor's Degree as a chemical engineer. He selected Ashland Oil from what was an almost infinite number of vacancies that then existed, because he wanted a small company with large opportunities. He was plunged immediately into the morass of detail that surrounded the high octane plant project, and has been a happy swimmer in the Ashland technical groups ever since. In 1955 he was assistant to the Refinery General Superintendent; and in 1956 made assistant to the Vice President of Manufacturing. Today he is one of the firm's top trouble-shooters and has responsibility for the anti-pollution program and many other sectors.

ated scores of refineries, technical programs and properties; had been part of the team that had lifted the Canton refinery from 6,000 barrels a day to 15,000 barrels a day within two months. The skill of these men can be guessed from the fact that they considered their improvements at the Freedom refinery a relative failure: they had only succeeded in lifting the throughput from 4,000 to 6,000 barrels a day—a mere contemptible increase of 50 per cent. Zandona, Yancey, Houlton, Humphreys, Leas and the others operated out of their own engineers' unwritten handbook of technical perception and were ahead of the times. "Most of the small refineries that Ashland obtained," Zandona said, "had few or no technical men of their own. The management used outside consultants from Universal Oil Products and other firms, who would be called in to resolve a particular problem. They would improve a section of a refinery, and then, their task completed, leave. We would enter and examine the overall picture; discover the potential, and work toward it. We had learned that you cannot make an entity out of a given unit; you must establish combination units that use energy from one unit to support another. Then you gain maximum efficiency."

Zandona considered Mr. Blazer an engineer. "He learned his engineering by living, studying and working during the period when the industry developed from an art into a science," Zandona observed. "Even his efforts to stimulate people were based on using principles he had observed; he didn't have a cookbook full of recipes. He used his tested and proven principles on everyone—and they worked."

But Mr. Blazer ran a hard school. In evaluating the aviation gasoline plant, Yancey, Zandona, Humphreys and the rest of the team made ninety-two case studies covering that many possibilities, including different types of product distribution, placing various values on each . . . "during a holiday."

This was the team and tempo that Paulsen, Gammon and others found at Ashland. It was, essentially, a young man's pace; especially invigorating because they could go to the top to discuss their methods, discoveries, ideas, and possibilities with men who could say yes or no. Everett Wells's grasp of refinery changes in relation to the market was as sound as Mr. Blazer's. Rex Blazer had grown up in the petroleum business; Mr. Blazer himself would become totally absorbed and as enthusiastic as a boy. But he was apt to switch his position; he always kept his options open.

Mr. Blazer probed for flaws in their presentations, and would then exaggerate them. Essentially, he viewed technological developments as being cyclical in nature. These cycles would last as long as three to five years. "We had to sell him again and again," Zandona said, "but he could move like lightning when he was convinced. That was the big thing we had going for us: we could always talk to the man who made the final decision." As all engineers know, this was a big plus.

Detroit supplied the pressure. The automobile manufacturers had, for decades, been producing new engines that required new and improved gasoline. This kept pressure steadily on gasoline manufacturers—and gasoline was Ashland's bread and butter.

But the young engineers, who inspired each other as well as the company, wanted to do more than simply make refineries more efficient, to produce better gasoline to meet market and sales needs. They wanted to extend Ashland Oil & Refining forward into petrochemicals, and they pushed Mr. Blazer in this direction. He was intrigued; he wanted to go, but he wanted to be sure.

They were delighted, therefore, when their arguments, presentations and persuasions succeeded during the first half of 1956, and Mr. Blazer gave them a green light to go ahead with a $4.5 million Udex installation at Catlettsburg, to convert reformed material into benzene, toluene and xylene, as well as other heavy aromatics. Furthermore, the technical brain trust had an additional pet project, whose possibilities excited them greatly, that was being kept highly secret even within the company. They had wheedled $20,000 from Everett Wells and Mr. Blazer for this baby.

The Udex (a Universal Oil Products unit) would take about fifteen months to install and become operational. In the same period and parallel with these plans and projections, the Ashland company purchased Lynch Oil, a producer with properties in the Mink Island area of White County, Illinois, and Posey County, Indiana; in the Rochester Pool in Wabash County and adjoining Gibson County, Indiana; and with reserves in southern Illinois and southern Indiana, for almost $2 million.

By projecting forward toward petrochemicals, the acquisition teams were pointed in the direction of new markets. Therefore, they began to survey the existing marketing organizations; looking in particular for companies owned by individuals confronted with succession or tax problems. The Ashland reasoning had become highly refined: figure out how to produce, then find those companies with customers willing to sell, and then build.

The organization was moving well. All refineries except the Aetna installation in Louisville were working at capacity; the company throughput amounted to 125,000 barrels a day.

Toward the end of April 1956, to Mr. Blazer's relief, Captain Jonassen of Cleveland Tankers managed to sell the last of the Ashland T-2's, for a price of $805,000. This time, Mr. Blazer did not discuss other sales and better prices made elsewhere; the T-2 had been virtually written off; Captain Jonassen had outdone himself. It was a pity the doctors had forbidden Mr. Blazer to engage in his old double-edged pleasure of arguing with the doughty Captain, but on this occasion his comments were most agreeable.

Nevertheless, a company whose major properties consisted of refining and marketing did not attract great attention from the financial community. Mr. Blazer was keenly aware of this; when Mr. E. L. Kennedy of Lehman Brothers, who remained a good friend, gave a talk before the Dallas Section of the American Institute of Mining, Metallurgical & Petroleum Engineers, Mr. Blazer was so pleased he sent copies to the directors. Mr. Kennedy, who had by this time become a recognized expert on the industry, said in part, ". . . in view of the rising costs of finding crude oil, prejudice against refining and marketing may lessen in financial circles . . ." It was a hopeful prediction. Financial circles do not change their opinions easily.

Meanwhile, ground was broken along the Ohio River for the Markland Dam—a $73 million project that would displace five old locks and dams, that brought the entire Cincinnati area, including the Ashland-Covington terminal, into a single large pool 87 miles long. Other dam projections in 1956 included a new one at Louisville at a cost of $54 million; more millions for a New Richmond Dam that would complete the canalization of the Ohio from Louisville to approximately 97 miles above Ashland—a distance of 366 miles.

Between 1954 and mid-1956, the government had spent more than $200 million for these projects. Ashland Oil was a prime mover, an unobtrusive one, in these developments: they were the first significant waterways improvements since 1929.

The business of the company became sufficiently widespread to make still another airplane necessary; the management selected a second Lockheed Lodestar for $102,500; and—one almost says as usual—the union at Canton was showing renewed signs of restlessness.

In general, the unique position the company had created for itself was still difficult for many to grasp. A shareholder, A. Fletcher Marsh, wrote Mr. Blazer a letter in which he wondered why Ashland Oil was not, in effect, more like other oil companies. Mr. Blazer patiently dictated a lengthy reply, interesting because it describes the complexity of evaluating a large company, which said in part, ". . . our profit in relation to sales is less than for many oil companies. The reason for that is easily understandable. We are less integrated than most oil companies. Our net crude oil production is less than 10 per cent of the oil we refine and our sales of refined products are substantially in excess of our refinery throughput. For example, we have a division (Allied Oil) which is one of the principal suppliers of industrial fuel oil to the steel industry. Its sales are greatly in excess of our production. Much of the oil sold to the steel companies is purchased from other refineries and transported by common carrier and contract carriers to the plants of the steel companies. We never see the oil. The gross profit on the operation may be only 6 per cent of sales and the net profit less than 3 per cent, yet the earnings of that division, amounting to almost $1 million a year after taxes, represents a good profit on our investment in that portion of the business.

"On the other hand, we may have a profit before taxes of as much as 50 per cent on that part of our sales volume represented by the crude oil we produce from our own wells and transport in our own pipelines to river terminals, haul in our own barges to our refineries, and manufacture into finished products which often are transported in our own boats or trucks to industrial customers or delivered to consumers served through our own service stations. Even with such a large percentage of profits against sales, that particular part of our business does not always yield as good a return on our large investment in equipment involved as do some of our other sales.

"It is my observation that there is no single yardstick to use in determining whether a business is healthy. The most important criteria, of course, are whether the business can show earnings consistently over a long period, maintain a sound financial condition, and yield to its stockholders a reasonable return."

Mr. Blazer was arguing, of course, against over-simplification of a complex company. In Washington, the search for a single yardstick of profits had engaged the attention of many; efforts had been underway for a considerable period to establish some mandatory accounting practices by which profits could be measured. Thus far, this magic formula has not been found; Mr. Blazer's description of a part of the Ashland operation gives some indication of why such a formula may never be found.

By May 1956, the petrochemicals program culminated temporarily in the purchase of the R. J. Brown Company of St. Louis, Mo., for more than $2 million. R. J. Brown, whose sales grossed some $15 million a year, had plants and offices in Chicago, Detroit, Lansing, Louisville, Memphis, Cleveland, St. Louis and Decatur, Illinois, as well as a Canadian affiliate. It sold naphthas, solvents and specialty petroleum products in the eastern part of the United States and Canada. It could have been created to fit Ashland's plans. All told, negotiations had lasted between two to three years. Representing the Legal Department, Atkins, who had been in on the proposition from the first, was immersed in this project, learned much and found it whetted his appetite for more. He found the complicated interplay of men, property, bargaining, legality and reshaping fascinating.[3]

Rex Blazer, talking at the dedication ceremonies of the Gateway Terminal at Wellsville, Ohio, a new installation Ashland had

[3] At approximately the same time, Ashland bought the Industrial Solvents plants and distribution of Anderson-Pritchard Oil Co. of Oklahoma City.

recently established, gave some picture of the oil industry context at the time.

"Oil in 1956," the younger Blazer said, "provides 40 per cent of the total energy requirements of the nation; gas 25 per cent and coal a little over 30 per cent. Oil and gas together, therefore, account for two-thirds. Eight million barrels of oil a day are being produced, and the nation is expected to consume 40 billion barrels during the next 10 years; an amount equal to all the oil produced since Colonel Drake drilled his well.

"To meet this need, the industry will invest, in the period between 1950 and 1965, capital to the extent of $100 billion. Compare this with the steel industry, which is expected to invest, during the same period, $35 billion."

Then the president of the company mentioned the growing concentration of refineries: "In 1935," he said, "two and a half million barrels of oil were refined daily with 435 refineries; by 1954, 308 refineries were processing 7 million barrels a day."

He concluded his talk with a mention of the Eisenhower road building program, the most ambitious in the history of the world, due to start. "The government will spend $27 billion in the next 10 years to create 40,000 miles of new highways."

Ashland was deeply interested, of course, in the highway program, because D. Hugh Jenks and his men had succeeded in making asphalt sales by Ashland a highly important factor.

Even the labor front appeared serene; contracts were signed with the unions at Freedom, Canton and Findlay, for a three-year period. "I cannot recall," Mr. Blazer wrote the directors happily, "when we could see labor peace for so far ahead . . ." A comment that would convince a stranger Ashland had experienced great labor troubles when it had, in fact, enjoyed relations more equable than most firms; had never had even a major strike. But it had worried.

Orin Atkins arranged another peace—this time with the City of Catlettsburg, whose fathers had been grousing for some time about water pollution for which they held the company largely to blame. The problem was resolved when it was realized that the city's water treatment system was antiquated, and the little town lacked the money to update; Ashland contributed $40,000 toward a new plant and the dispute dissipated.

Grover (Deacon) Shropshire, of refinery sales, was selected to go to the R. J. Brown Company as Ashland's liaison with that new group; Deacon had joined Ashland in 1949; was an Annapolis graduate and an ex-naval officer; had worked with Ernst & Ernst and with Sumner Hippensteele in the company; had worked well also with Chub Moffitt on problems relating to R. J. Brown Company, its markets and products.

Retracing the growth of the new installations, Mr. Blazer explained to the directors that catalytic reforming units were the first stage for the manufacturer of benzene, toluene and xylene (BTX), and that soon the subject of either borrowing money or obtaining new financing would arise.

While these conversations and problems were underway, crude oil inventories began to mount. Mr. Blazer wrote the directors he thought they would be plagued by excess amounts for crude oil for some time to come, and he discussed this problem with Everett Wells. The result of their conversation was that Ashland reduced the price of crude oil for their Kentucky suppliers. This in turn led to an exchange of letters between Mr. Blazer and O. H. Horne, president of the Kentucky Oil & Gas Association, the producers. Mr. Horne, as president of the Association, was duty-bound to register a protest (his was neither the first, nor would it be the last) when lower crude oil prices were posted. But he pointed up an immediate paradox: the cut came at a time when the price of refined products was being increased.

Horne's statement began by saying that "The recent reduction in the price of crude oil in the Kentucky-Indiana-Illinois area, has caused widespread discussion and dissatisfaction among the members . . . reaches through all segments, including producers, former royalty owners, and many others. The reduction in the price of crude (was) arrived at almost simultaneously with a major oil company's increase in the price of gasoline . . . it is our understanding this gasoline price increase was followed by most other marketers.

"This rise in refined products is only an indication of . . . the upward trend. With reference to the cost of crude, there is . . . a tremendous increase in wildcatting . . . records show that only one well out of nine is productive; many times this proves to be small. A comprehensive, nation-wide study shows the expenditures for exploration, development and production increased by 95 cents a barrel, from 1948 to 1953 . . . in Kentucky there have been additional heavy cost increases . . . a shallow well that could have been completed in 1948 for $9,100 and in 1953 for $13,000 now costs $14,300 . . . an increase in eight and one half years of 57 per cent. At the same time, the increase in the price of crude has been *less than 5 per cent*." (His emphasis.)

Then Mr. Horne discussed the heavy increase in the amount of foreign crude oil entering the country; he said the importers had ignored the President's Cabinet Committee recommendations to keep imports down to the 1954 average of 1.052 million barrels a day, and instead had increased their imports to 1.651 barrels a day; mentions that Canadian crude was pouring into the Kentucky-Indiana-Illinois area through the Great Lakes, and foresaw its increase when the St. Lawrence Seaway was completed.

He ended with a plea to Ashland to remove the basic cause of the Association's distress, the reduction in price, and asked instead for an increase of 75 cents a barrel. The statement was sent, as well as to Ashland, to several pipeline companies and the Representatives of the state of Kentucky in Congress.

Mr. Blazer, for perhaps the fiftieth time, undertook to reply. First he said that the reason crude oil was entering the Kentucky market was that Kentucky crude was overpriced in relation to some of its competitors. He discussed the heavy inventory of crude oil that Ashland obtained from the Illinois pools. He then said that with the price of Kentucky crude reduced, it was placed in a better competitive position, and its sales should improve. He discussed the difference in crude oil quality, and the fact that certain crudes were better for some products than for others. Therefore, the ups and downs of some crude oil production could be traced to the product vicissitudes. He agreed that foreign crude affected the situation, and reminded Mr. Horne that Ashland refineries were the farthest east of any using domestic crude oil; he left the strong implication that the company might be forced, for competitive reasons, to buy the foreign crude oil if its price gave

Ashland competitors an advantage, and ended by saying that only the company's loyalty to the Kentucky crude oil producers kept it from acting more quickly.

All in all, a standoff: a situation in which both parties had plausible positions and neither would move back.

At Ashland, Mr. Blazer obliquely admitted he had recovered from another siege; another struggle with his nemesis. "My health has been slowly improving during the past few weeks, during which I have had no social engagements. I have not been out of the house any evening since the Newcomen Dinner at Lexington. I have conducted most of my business by telephone and memorandum, making only an occasional visit to the office for a half day . . ."

That was the atmosphere by early summer 1956. Then three men, as different from one another as could be, in every respect except determination, sparked a great world crisis.

The first was Nikita Khrushchev, who admitted before a large gathering of Soviet officials what he, they and the world had long unofficially known: that Russia had been ruled for decades by a bloodthirsty paranoid—Stalin—responsible for the murders of countless innocent persons. Khrushchev's reasons were rooted in the politics of the Soviet Empire: Stalin's sins could no longer be supported or hidden—either his fiction or the government would have to change. The net result of Khrushchev's admissions was to sacrifice countless lower-echelon figures who had carried out the orders of the regime, and to maintain at least Stalin's associates in power.

In the United States, the second man, John Foster Dulles, Secretary of State, announced the cancellation of an agreement to help finance the Aswan Dam in Egypt. Dulles was taking this action because Egypt, refused great quantities of arms from the U.S., obtained them instead by barter from the Soviet Union in exchange for Egypt's cotton—its only important crop.

The first repercussions were among the Soviet colonies in Eastern Europe. There, the pot began to bubble and seethe; the sounds it emitted were matched by those emerging from the Middle East.

The news about the Khrushchev admissions reached the U.S.

press in early June 1956, shortly after this country announced it
had dropped a hydrogen bomb from an airplane. The public did
not know how great a relief this accomplishment brought the
White House; it meant that the U.S. had matched the nuclear
super-weapons scale with the Soviets.

The third man, Gamal Abdel Nasser, seized the Suez Canal toward the end of July, and the pot in the Middle East boiled over.
England and France, co-owners of the Canal, made strong representations; India and the nations of Asia, their trade route threatened, were equally alarmed; the United States began a feverish
round of diplomatic talks, and Europe's oil supply—and to a
lesser extent that of the United States—was in jeopardy.

Obviously, all other matters did not cease; the question of tolls
on the rivers continued to gain momentum and support in Congress and elsewhere: Mr. Blazer wrote the directors he considered
the toll situation the most serious threat to the company's existence
it had yet confronted.

For a long time the power industry, still smarting both from
the TVA and the Dixon-Yates controversy, seemed of the opinion
that perhaps waterways users should pay charges; that would at least
maintain the responsibility of private enterprise. But a deeper
examination of the issues persuaded some of their more prominent
men to switch their position, and by late summer of 1956, the
power industry had changed its collective mind, and was in favor
of continued free waterways.

The debate churned through Congress and the press again;
Chambers of Commerce and other groups endured speeches on the
topic. Bill Hull spoke before the Ashland Rotary Club, among
other places. The local newspaper listed Orin Atkins among those
in attendance, but it misspelled his name.

That busy young man was engaged in assisting the reorganization of the R. J. Brown Company. Shortly we read that he drew
up its new papers and table of organization; that Chub Moffitt
became a vice president of the enterprise, Deacon Shropshire
treasurer, Ned Seaton an assistant treasurer. Orin's legal duties
intertwined with his executive functions. He was all over the lot.

Finally the trade press received a release on the new acquisition;

R. J. Brown Company was described as the proprietor, itself, of
Petroleum Solvents, Bronoco Solvents & Chemicals, Michigan
State Solvents, Burke Solvents, Bauer-Brown Solvents. One of the
persons who read the release with particular attention was a tall
young man named Ed Von Doersten, employed by Signal Oil &
Gas Company. Von Doersten had resigned from R. J. Brown because he didn't think they were moving fast enough; soon he
would enter the Ashland orbit.

In 1956, the company planned to spend $10 million for new
service stations within the next two years; $20 million in refinery
improvements; "perhaps" $4 million in petrochemicals; $2.6 million in new pipeline terminals; $8 million in exploration and pro-
duction . . . this last item disturbed Mr. Blazer.

On the vexing question of crude oil, Mr. Blazer expressed his
thoughts to the directors: "It is quite possible," he wrote, "that by
paying a salary of as much as $50,000 a year, or more, we might
find the right man, but I think the chances are at least two-to-one
against our making the right selection." This was a rare mood of
depression. Mr. Blazer never came so close to admitting either
failure or uncertainty as he did in this letter. He continued, "We
have never discovered a major field. Some of the smaller oil operators seem to be excellent oil 'finders' but operating as individuals
they make so much money we couldn't attract them, and even if
they came into our organization they would probably want to
change their method of operation, being influenced by the fact we
are a $100 million company, and presumably have almost un-
limited funds at our disposal . . . it is difficult to get across to our
organization that even though we are a comparatively large company in refining and transportation, we are just a little company
in production, and we must engage in 'poor boy' operations."

August appeared on the horizon to find the No. 1 refinery shut
down for repairs and cleanout; Findlay due to undergo the same
treatment in a month; Valvoline profits off and some of the best
minds in the company toiling with the problem this presented. Its
former chief, Earle Craig, wrote Mr. Blazer that the time might be
ripe for a new debenture issue. Mr. Blazer, for his part, was pleased

to be able to write back telling Mr. Craig that Ashland would open 120 new gasoline stations during the year; gasoline stations was a subject close to Mr. Craig's heart.

To the naked eye, the company appeared to be proceeding along a course it had followed ever since 1924; everyone was busy and absorbed and all was as usual.

But the fact was that serious discussions were underway between the seventh floor offices and the house on Bath Avenue, and Mr. Blazer could be observed entering first Everett Wells's office and then Rex Blazer's, and then the offices of other men. He would draw his chair close, and talk rapidly in his light voice, interspersing his more serious comments with a vein of wit as was his habit, laughing often.

His spirit seemed even more youthful than ever, and the play of his mind was lightning fast. But Time respects neither intelligence or grace of spirit; the calendar is inexorable and the sands were running lower. Mr. Blazer had passed 65—a modern meridian —and change was in the air.

To the average corporate analyst, the management of the company appeared well organized; the senior executives had worked with Mr. Blazer for a number of years and areas of responsibility were sufficiently defined to be well covered. There is little question that Mr. Blazer regarded his team with satisfaction. But his eyes, as usual, were fixed on more distant horizons.

In common with many other top executives of his generation, Mr. Blazer considered many young executives less adventurous and less knowledgeable than men of former generations. But unlike most men of his generation, Mr. Blazer did not blame the young men; he blamed the growth of an organized mass society that did not provide the entrepreneurial atmosphere he had himself enjoyed.

"By the time a man becomes head of a department in a large modern corporation," Mr. Blazer observed, "he is usually in his early fifties, and has expertise—in his department. To take him away from that department would hurt the department. At the same time, to bring him into general management would be unwise, because he would have no background in looking at all the aspects of a problem. I know many companies draw their senior management from the ranks of department heads, but I do not agree with the practice."

At the same time, he did not believe that special courses in schools of business could make up for either the experience of a free marketplace, or the keen tests of competitive enterprise.

He decided, therefore, that special avenues of experience should be opened within Ashland itself, where a bright young man could gain real experience. He would create assistants not just for the men in senior management, but for the senior management level. Instead of an assistant to the president and an assistant to the chairman, for instance, he would create assistants to the *management*. And these assistants would work first for the president and then for the chairman or vice versa; they would become involved and engaged in the problems that engrossed top management.

At the same time, Mr. Blazer had the question of his own future to resolve, and he surveyed his own prospects as coolly as he estimated the abilities of others. Acquisitions, he decided, was an area in which he would like to be allowed to continue. At the same time, confronted with his own restless intelligence and insatiable attraction for more knowledge and new experiences, he found he preferred the companionship of younger men. Privately, he decided to concentrate upon developing reservoirs of future talent upon which his older associates could rely as time passed.

He discussed this with the board members, and found them in agreement; they felt he should retire from the firing line, but none wanted to lose his vital presence for the company.

Then, with all arrangements made, he and Mrs. Blazer decided to take a cruise through the Mediterranean. So many half-planned trips had never materialized because some new and fascinating problem had arisen that their actual departure was a surprise, even to themselves.

The timing could have been more propitious. The consequences of Nasser's seizure of the Suez Canal had begun to affect important parts of the world. With no tankers able to travel through the Suez Canal, a shortage appeared. For the first time in a number of years U.S. crude oil producers were being asked by Washington to increase their production; emergency committees from the petroleum industry were being called to Washington; the atmosphere regarding the Middle East was thick with conjecture, suspicion and apprehension.

At the end of October 1956, Israel attacked Egypt, penetrating the country with terrifying rapidity; England and France joined in by attacking Egypt from the air and landed joint invasion forces on November 5 and 6.

The United States rallied UN support against Israel, France and England, and a cease-fire was effected on November 7, 1956.

This outbreak coincided with a revolt in Hungary against the Soviet occupation; the revolt began October 23, and the Soviets, pouring in additional tanks and troops, crushed it by November 4. Thousands of Hungarians found refuge in Austria, and eventually in the United States, where Congress and the White House joined in special efforts to allow them entry.

The paradox of a situation in which the Soviets could successfully apply force to achieve their objectives, while the leader of the West abjured force although threatening to use force against its own allies, struck some observers as a blurring of the once-clear Dulles policy. From this time onward, situations were to be handled along lines of immediacy; the West lost its clarity; its people became increasingly confused.

For the United States oil industry, it meant that with the Suez closed U.S. capacities would once again be called upon to aid Europe. Economists estimated that the oil shortage on that continent would, or at least could, set back its previously expanding level of industrial activity to that of mid-1954, pushing output down and wiping out millions of jobs. Rationing of oil and cutbacks of oil for heating supplies went into effect almost immediately; cutbacks in refineries were as high as 50 per cent; only the major oil companies with their great tanker fleets could maintain normal or extra operations. As a result, the structure of the industry in Europe was chaotic. For the average person in the United States these conditions were not close; he could not feel their reality, nor sense the extent of the confusion sown by the policy of the United States. Europe was astonished the United States would so strangely exert its influence: force the participants to stop in their tracks in the Middle East; order Israel to return to its exposed and highly vulnerable position; cause England's government to fall, its army, air force and navy to retreat; France to withdraw, embittered anew at another setback—and simultaneously render its own decade-long rhetoric about liberation and freedom in Eastern Europe into vapor. It was a cold, hard winter in Europe in 1956.

When Mr. and Mrs. Blazer returned from the Mediterranean in November—their itinerary having been only slightly disrupted by the Middle East eruption—the Ashland figures for the 1956 fiscal year were totaled and discovered to be $279.9 million in net sales, and $13.5 million in net profits: a record high.

The annual report for the company is usually prepared during the fall and released in late December; on this occasion extraordinary care was used in its preparation. In fact, after a trip to New York together, Orin Atkins and Mr. Blazer joined Art Points in Chicago to see the final printed proofs: they expected the contents to receive unusual attention.

Very late in the year, Senator Thruston Morton paid a visit to Ashland; the company Republicans were guests at Mr. Blazer's home in honor of the Senator. These included Bill Seaton, Orin Atkins, John Fred Williams and others; it was the first time ever that Kentucky had two Republican senators.

1957

Usually Ashland holds its annual meeting in early January, but the annual report appears a few weeks earlier. On this occasion, we read with mixed emotion a special enclosure the Report contained, entitled *A Letter from the Chairman.* "*Having served almost thirty-three years as Chief Executive of Ashland Oil & Refining Company and one of its predecessors, Ashland Refining Company, I desire to turn over to others the responsibilities usually associated with that position,*" said the first sentence. Mr. Blazer believed in getting to the subject.

"*I expect to remain active with the Company as Chairman of the Executive and Finance Committees or in such capacity as the*

Directors may desire. Doubtless I shall continue to devote a considerable part of my time to the strengthening of our Company by the acquisition of properties and other companies principally through an exchange of stock. As will be reported more fully to our stockholders, I entered into an employment contract with the Company earlier this year, whereby my services will be available to the Company over a period of years.

"Many of our shareholders have owned stock in Ashland Oil for a great many years and from time to time have sought my personal assurance that we have officers competent to assume my responsibilities at the appropriate time. I take this occasion to advise all our stockholders of my proposed relinquishment of my most arduous duties, and of my recommendation for the advancement of two of my most experienced and capable associates who are fully competent to manage this Company.

"I shall recommend to our Board of Directors that Rexford S. Blazer, now President of the Company, be elected Chairman of the Board, and that Everett F. Wells be advanced from Executive Vice President to President of the Company."

Then after a description of Everett Wells's and Rex Blazer's backgrounds, the message ends: *"I should mention, also, that our Company is fortunate in having developed capable junior officers and other executives who now head our most important divisions and departments, giving our organization an unusual depth of talent."* It is signed, of course, Paul G. Blazer, the signature heavy, clean, and bold as ever.

The annual report carried the photographs of Rex Blazer and Wells, and was barely in circulation when the annual meeting was upon them.

Over the years this event has become the hub of a series of activities that include not only the board members and officers, but divisional and subsidiary heads, out of town guests and most of the employees located in Ashland. Around the hub spins a wheel of events that includes both official and private parties, and that usually culminates in an affair at the Bellefonte Country Club to which a great many persons are invited and introduced to the directors; day-long presentations are produced by the various divisional and subsidiary managements; the progress of problems of the year are described, and new directions charted.

In early January 1957, the big news was, of course, the shifts in the top positions of the firm. In addition to the new chairman and president, the balance of the executive line-up consisted of five vice presidents: Alex Chamberlain, Palmer Talbutt, Bob Yancey, John Fred Williams and Chub Moffitt; Angus McDonald remained as secretary, Ned Seaton as treasurer, Art Points as controller, Mac Burnam as assistant secretary and chief legal counsel, Bill Hull as assistant secretary, J. P. Trout as assistant treasurer-transfer agent, Charley Bolton as manager of the marketing division, Ed Emrick in charge of production, exploration and purchases, Harold Houlton as R&D director, Hugh Jenks, asphalt, Arnold Leas as technical service director, Roland Whealy as coordinator of refining and sales, Earl Weaver[4] as executive assistant, George Derby as executive assistant, and Orin Atkins as executive assistant.

News that Mr. Blazer had surrendered the top post in the company came as a considerable surprise to many; the press blossomed with articles of his career; his name thereafter virtually dropped from company releases. But it was a most unusual sort of retirement; in effect, it took him off the firing line, but kept him on the team. Over the years, the relationships between Mr. Blazer and the senior men in the company had become very close indeed. Palmer Talbutt, who had the experience of working for years under Mr. Blazer directly, and then under Everett Wells, was struck by their similarity of thought and outlook. One day, he recalls, a man stopped Wells in the lobby of the Blackstone Hotel in Chicago,

---

[4] Earl W. Weaver, born 1908 in Catlettsburg, Ky., valedictorian of his high school class of 1925, went to work at a filling station a block away from Ashland Oil headquarters; climbed the ladder from his first job (with Standard Oil of Ky.) to the post of Terminal Superintendent; switched to Ashland Oil in 1943 after interviews with Alex Chamberlain; was made an administrative assistant; became Operations Manager in the Marketing Division in 1946; after the arrival of Rex Blazer, was moved to the post of special assistant; was made executive assistant in 1955. Earl Weaver was, he says, "still in a departmental trap" at the age of 44, but although a late bloomer, moved fast once started; he is today a vice president; has charge of branded sales and Valvoline; retail propane; industrial and home heating sales.

and asked his opinion about a situation newly arisen in the oil industry. Wells gave him a complicated reply. Then the man went upstairs and called Paul Blazer in Ashland and asked him the same question over the phone. Mr. Blazer unhesitatingly took him through the same course, and came out at the same conclusion as had Wells. Since the situation had just arisen, and the man knew that Wells and Mr. Blazer had not had time to confer, he was thunderstruck. "I have never heard such similarity in approach between two men before," he said to Talbutt.

Great affinities existed between Rex Blazer and his uncle as well, but with a competitive tinge. Both men shared an unusual sensitivity to criticism; both employed oblique methods to achieve their goals, and both were close observers of men. Rex was apt to point out to Mr. Blazer the negatives of a plan under discussion; his independence came through clearly. He also had opinions regarding potential talent among younger individuals. One result was that Rex introduced a number of protégés into the corporate management. His protégés, and those selected by his uncle, comprised part of the next generation of top executives within the company. But group relations can never be simply described; many men and their opinions went into making the progress of Ashland; Palmer Talbutt, over the years, was an astute talent scout; John Fred Williams was a shrewd analyst; Art Points evaluated financial and accounting acumen; Bob Yancey disclosed a large and generous spirit, and uncovered talent in the technical men; Arnold Leas, who sprays ideas all the time, sparked creativity; Chub Moffitt proved a keen evaluator of salesmen.

By early 1957, therefore, the company had not only progressed beyond the one-man, one-leader concept, but it had conceived a method of retiring the man who was virtually the founder without losing his astounding skill and acumen. Mr. Blazer, still operating mainly from his residence and over the telephone, as well as through letters and memoranda, began to create a new role unique in the annals of business: he became the articulator, the rationalizer and the communicator between the officers and the board, without responsibility for the decisions that emerged.

But he had retained control, in an intellectual sense, of one highly significant area; acquisitions. Through the years he had evolved bargaining and evaluative techniques that seemed almost wizardry in this highly involved art; his mysterious position with the firm assisted his bargaining position.

And in evaluating the men, properties, potentials and pitfalls of a possible acquisition, he had at his side young Orin Atkins who was not only armed with a legal background, but who was gradually steeping himself in a sea of esoteric corporate knowledge.

The company was actually, therefore, divided into two main areas of activity. The first was operational, and the executives in charge devoted—as they do in most companies—the majority of their time to supervision, market planning, personnel control and various duties of keeping a large enterprise afloat and prosperous.

The other side of the business was what might be called "new business" in a corporate sense. And in direct command of this activity was the formidable Mr. Blazer with Orin Atkins at his side. At almost any time these two might commandeer the services of a host of specialists: engineers, accountants, merchandizing men and others, who could help them evaluate the properties they examined. Together, this constituted a deceptive total: the company was able to move faster and more directly than most others, while presenting a picture of modest stability to the world.

During the spring of 1957, the price of domestic crude oil soared because of the Middle East situation. But—such are the realities of business under quasi-control of the government—refiners found that although they had to pay higher prices for crude oil, they could not easily pass along higher prices in refined products to customers. The price-watchers of Washington were not swayed, as was the State Department, by the vicissitudes of international developments. Ashland was fortunate enough to have at hand such a large inventory of crude oil that it could actually relieve the situation somewhat by selling some crude oil to companies with whom its relations had been cooperative through the years. But the management knew the squeeze on profits would have an effect.

At Catlettsburg, the refinery was processing crude oil at the rate of 80,000 barrels a day. But it was only natural the company should look around for its own sources of crude, and through an old and good friend, Earl Wallace of Eastman Dillon, it acquired exploration rights in Guatemala. Venezuela, long a private preserve of the Royal Dutch Shell and Standard Oil of N.J., chose this moment to break the spell of these giants, and its government announced it would distribute additional concessions to other oil firms.

Orin Atkins, who found himself sitting at dinner one night next to some men from Phillips, had shortly before the Venezuelan announcement mentioned that Ashland Oil might welcome some joint exploration efforts overseas. As a consequence of this remark, when the Venezuelans issued their invitation and Phillips' interest was aroused, the firm called Orin. As usual, the Ashland management, apprised, went into a huddle, and after some discussion, decided to pursue the matter.

Negotiations between the two companies moved rapidly: Ashland decided to join Phillips and others in Venezuela.

Meantime, the river tolls continued to threaten. Mr. Blazer, with more time on his hands than before his retirement, made a trip to the Capitol and talked to both Dr. Arthur Flemming, director of the office of defense mobilization and to Dr. Milton Eisenhower, the President's brother, who was also an important figure in the defense establishment.

By coincidence, that summer of 1957, Sherman Adams, then at the height of his influence as assistant to the President, came to Centre College to receive an honorary degree, accompanied by Arthur Krock, senior columnist on *The New York Times,* who also received a degree. Mr. Blazer, for years a trustee of this college, was very interested in its progress. Adams and Krock visited with the Blazers; we feel safe in assuming that riverway tolls somehow arose in the conversation.

Within the company, the new regime functioned smoothly. Bob Gordon Sr., in Chicago, was delighted, and wrote Mr. Blazer a letter of congratulations; told him he thought Rex and Everett were a remarkably effective top team. This was high praise indeed, from an unbiased observer.

Mr. Blazer went into specifics in his reply. "Crude oil production, crude oil supply, pipelines, river transportation, refining, wholesale marketing, accounting and part of the activities of the Personnel Department are under Everett," he wrote. "Allied Oil, Cleveland and Lakeland Tankers, our bulk plants and service stations, sales of Valvoline and our other branded products, advertising, most of our public relations and much of our personnel relations . . . come under Rex."

"We have an excellent management team with many years ahead of them . . . Everett is 52 and Rex will soon be 50; Palmer is 58 and his very capable assistant Joe Davis is 41; John Fred Williams is 52, Chub Moffitt is 42, and Bob Yancey is 36; Erskine Owens is 46, Orin Atkins, who is capable of being part of top management, is 33; Ned Seaton is within three years of retirement and thought is being given to his successor. On the death of Mike Dupree (transportation) his responsibilities were split up between John Fox, Bob Gray and Dave Beldon, all of whom are 39, and Bill Meacham who is 40; Ward Disbrow who heads supply and distribution is 40, and his assistant Paul Kinnaird is only 34 . . . I doubt if there are many companies of our size in which the chief responsibilities rest on men of so young an age . . ." In that one must agree.

In the Middle East, the United States picked up some of the responsibilities formerly handled by the British; assumed the subsidy to Jordan that helped the pro-Western ruler to remain in power; and sent a fleet to regularly patrol the Mediterranean. Temporarily, the Arab states seemed to view Americans amiably; U.S. oil companies, formerly trailing the English and French firms, began to find their negotiations easier. Nevertheless, the long, slow disintegration of the Islamic civilization, begun many years before with the collapse of the Ottoman Empire, continued, and the oil men agreed the long-range outlook was not good.

Aminol, still selling mainly to Japan, announced its geologists estimated its crude reserves at one billion barrels and indicated that its future prospects were excellent. Ashland, as a partner in this venture, could look forward to an excellent return on its investment.

Beneath the surface, the area seethed. The Soviet Union, now under Nikita Khrushchev, who had elevated himself into control by instituting his peculiar purge, took advantage of the Middle Eastern crises to make contact with Syria. Thus, Russia had, moving carefully, crossed its bridge with Egypt to reach a second Arab state.

In larger terms, with both super-powers possessing an air-borne H-bomb and thus a balance in terror, the overall situation appeared to be relatively calm. Europe and Egypt proceeded to dig their way out of the debacle of Suez; Egyptian canal pilots began their training; the normal troubles of peace resumed their usual prominence.

In Washington, another series of discussions engaged the attention of the oil industry. This time, the subject was oil quotas. Described by government spokesmen as a "voluntary" program, it was suggested that the industry limit its crude oil imports to a percentage of domestic production. Initially, quotas were granted to sixty-four companies, and "historic" importers were expected to limit themselves to their usual amounts, less 10 per cent. Newcomers to the import situation and hardship cases were to receive exceptions, and the West Coast was to be exempted. The source of the foreign crude oil was not to be a consideration, the government men said blandly, and then proceeded to contradict themselves by saying that Canada and Venezuela would receive special consideration. The program had the sponsorship of the White House, was to last one year, and was to start in the last quarter of 1957. Ashland was, of course, keenly interested.

In the U.S. Senate, Thruston Morton arose and gave a full-dress speech on the growth of the Ohio River Valley, and declared the Ohio now surpassed the Rhine, Europe's "chemical river."

"This rebirth," Senator Morton said, "is directly traceable to the waterways, and the unlimited supplies of coal that it makes available. The vast and growing concentration of electrical energy is dependent upon an adequate supply of process and condenser water, chemical brines, efficient rail service and a labor supply—much of which it obtains from rural communities—and the central market location of the region."

The entire region had finally grasped the vision that caught Paul G. Blazer many years before: that the riverways were the key to industrial expansion in the Ohio Valley. The results were probably

the greatest regional expansion program the world has ever seen
—spurred, conceived and coordinated by private industry. It would
have delighted Lincoln and Twain: they had both considered their
contemporaries benighted for not having seen and appreciated
these mighty waterways.

By this time, the support for waterways improvement was no
longer a subject of whispers. Mr. Blazer told the directors that Bill
Hull had registered in Washington as a lobbyist, and was working
to help obtain appropriations for a New Richmond Dam above
Cincinnati; others were working on this project also. The river
programs no longer suffered for lack of supporters.

The fiscal year 1957 ended in September with Ashland scoring
a record $320 million in net sales, and earning $16.2 million; an
enormous increase over the year before. The refineries processed
50 million barrels of oil, an average of 137,000 a day; catalytic
reforming units came onstream in Buffalo and Canton; the Udex
unit at Catlettsburg was still under construction; gasoline and
heating oils were being sold through 1,100 independent distributors; Ashland branded stations were accounting for 22 per cent
of the company's gasoline sales; Valvoline sales—formerly a matter of concern to the management—had been completely turned
around and were at a new high, selling through 14,000 distributors
and dealers in 43 countries; asphalt sales had shot up 24 per cent;
the advertising of the company spread through 95 radio stations
in the Kentucky, West Virginia and Ohio areas (they broadcast
football and basketball games for 9 state colleges and universities,
as well as telecasts of professional football games); the terminals
had spread to 24 locations, the company was operating 3,491 miles
of crude oil lines and 235 miles of product lines—together they accounted for 30 million barrels; the fleet had grown to 9 towboats
and 101 barges, 8 American flag tankers on the Great Lakes and 2
under Canadian registry . . . altogether, a concentrated and powerful empire.

The American Petroleum Institute, largest and most prestigious
of the oil industry organizations, contains many levels and responsible posts. Mr. Blazer, a member of the organization since 1918,
had been on the organization's board of directors since 1935.

Within the board, membership on special committees constitutes the ultimate honor: Mr. Blazer had been a member of the executive committee for many years. He relinquished this post in favor of Rex Blazer; the API responded by making Mr. Blazer an honorary member of the board.

The Secretary of the Interior, Fred Seaton, appointed Everett Wells to the National Petroleum Council for 1958; Palmer Talbutt was named to succeed Wells on the API general marketing committee. Bob Yancey had succeeded Mr. Blazer the year before on the refining committee of the API. All of these honors, which entailed considerable responsibility as well as honor, reflected the game of musical chairs within the company.

Barely a week after the company fiscal year ended in 1957, the Soviet Union amazed the world by putting Sputnik into orbit. This object, packed with observational instruments, weighed 184 pounds. News that Russia had outstripped the United States in the space race sent a thrill of horror throughout the world. The enormous prestige of U.S. science suffered; public confidence in U.S. superiority in the world was rudely shaken.

A month later in November 1957, the Soviets sent Sputnik II, weighing 1,120 pounds, aloft. It bore a live dog; the dog died in the vehicle.

Within the United States, the achievement was generously praised, but it caused grave doubts about the state of our science and education; efforts in specialization were spurred to greater extremes by this event, which cast a psychological shadow over the country.

Within Ashland, interest focused, naturally enough, on immediate matters. Willis Munro, the popular advertising manager, died unexpectedly; Rex Blazer discreetly began to explore the talent pool on New York's Madison Avenue for a successor.

1958

At the end of January 1958, the U.S. Army launched the nation's first satellite—Explorer I—into space. It weighed $36\frac{1}{2}$ pounds, but was dense with instruments. The Suez Canal resumed operations, this time under the control of Egypt. The crude oil situation in the United States once more assumed secondary importance, as foreign crude began to enter the country again. Ashland, together with some other firms, began to reduce its crude oil prices; as a consequence they received bitter letters from producers. One even arrived from J. C. Miller, a partner of Ashland's in some Kentucky drillings, and Mr. Blazer was surprised. "After all," he wrote back, his astonishment evident, "one shouldn't be too antagonistic toward one's customers . . ."

By February, Rex Blazer had found his new advertising man in the person of George W. Sisler,[5] who moved to Ashland and was studying the situation.

In the background, the long backstage struggle among the directors of Aminol came to a close: Mr. Blazer wrote a conciliatory letter to Sam Mosher, founder and head of the Signal Oil Company. J. Howard Marshall, whom time had also softened, assisted in the reconciliation. It was agreed a search for a new head of Aminol would be undertaken. Mr. Davies, who had actually done quite well with and for the consortium, was also the president of American President Lines, and had widespread interests in other areas. Thus, no great harm would be done, and a new man seemed a good way to resolve the long impasse.

Having discovered the humid Florida air to be unsuitable, Mr. and Mrs. Blazer were having a new home constructed in Scottsdale, near Phoenix, Arizona; Mr. Blazer traveled with his oxygen tank and amazingly managed to make numerous appearances at various spots on the landscape despite his myriad disabilities. In March 1958, he traveled to Washington, D.C., to discuss tolls with the

[5] George W. Sisler, born 1919 at Eccles, W. Va., was raised in Tulsa and Bristow, Okla.; graduated from the University of Missouri School of Journalism, 1941, where he was the first student to major in advertising and business administration. He always wanted to be in advertising. He worked for Continental Oil for $12\frac{1}{2}$ years, and was assistant advertising manager of the company when he decided big-city, big-agency experience was essential to his career; wound up at McCann Erickson; was there 5 years as an account man for McCann client Standard Oil of N.J. when Rex Blazer appeared with blandishments. Sisler is now Director of Advertising.

Undersecretary of Commerce after receiving an honorary degree—
an LL.B.—from Marshall University in Huntington.

Throughout the nation, the cold winds of a recession blew,
particularly in the oil industry. On March 9 and again on March
16, 1958, *The New York Times* carried long articles on the situation. The articles pointed out that crude oil prices appeared to be
firm, but product prices were dropping—a situation that put a
profit squeeze on refineries.

By April, the full force of the chill hit the company earnings:
March earnings after taxes were $564,000, compared to $1.58
million during the same month the year before; profits slipped
11 cents a barrel, according to Art Points' regular report to the
directors.

Internationally, the situation remained dark and murky. In the
Middle East, silent struggles over sands suspected of concealing
vast petroleum wealth continued; the USSR, feeling itself ahead
in the technological race, gestured menacingly on the world stage.

By April 1958, news came that Ashland had lost $220,000 as its
share in the first drillings in Lake Maracaibo, Venezuela, in the
partnership it maintained with Phillips and others—a second well
came in as a producer. At Catlettsburg, the bottom of a large
asphalt tank fell out, wasting $167,000 worth of product but
fortunately without injuring any workmen. The *National Petroleum News* carried an article on how the Little Inch pipeline, extending from Texas to Ohio, would affect the market position of
various companies in the Middle West, but the project was still
stalled in the courts.

By June 1958, Rex Blazer reported Allied sales were off 36 per
cent and profits down 73 per cent because the recession had reduced action in the steel industry by half. In June, Mr. Blazer
gave a speech at Transylvania College, oldest college west of the
Alleghenies and Lew Ware's alma mater. Mr. Blazer had, by this
time, moved beyond the problems of marketers, his subject on the
occasion of his first public speech years before. Now he was more
philosophic, and his observations more penetrating.

"You are," he told the students of the small college, "in this

ot to live comfortably, but usefully—not to receive, but
" Then he moved briskly into the present. "The concep-
rugged individualism appears to be no longer popular. The
influence of mass thinking and the surrender of personal responsibility are evidenced in the spread of group action by teenagers,
the almost universal acceptance of dictatorial leadership in the
trade unions, the preference for compensation based on standard-
ized jobs instead of on personal competence, the willingness to
give greater power to government at the expense of individual
freedom, and the widespread effort to obtain the implied security
usually associated with employment by a large corporation . . .

"Apparently there is no single explanation for this placing of
greater reliance on group action, this ever-increasing collectivism.
It seems to be associated with a growing inclination to attach importance to size, as such. It finds expression in our substitution
of mass thinking for individual appraisal and decision. Probably
one factor has been the development of better channels of communication by means of the radio, television, the wider circulation
of newspapers, and the tremendous influence of the news commentators and columnists. Mass propaganda has been the inevitable
result of mass communication. Many of us are unaware of the
amount of subtle propaganda with which we are bombarded
daily. I am sure we often fail to realize the extent to which we
are influenced away from individual opinion and toward group
thinking . . .

"At a recent dinner, I sat next to the president of a large university which has an outstanding engineering school. Although
this educator is an outstanding scientist and engineer, he expressed serious concern because of the undue importance being
attached to engineering and the related sciences. He was disturbed
by the answers to a questionnaire which had been filled out by
more than four hundred engineering seniors, showing that not a
single person intended to become a teacher, and only one expressed a desire to enter into business for himself. All the others
planned to obtain employment with some corporation . . .

"Of this country's half dozen largest corporations, all but one
are engaged principally in industries that were completely unknown to Transylvania graduates of less than a century ago.

These great industries have grown out of the invention of the telephone and other practical applications of electricity, from the development of the automobile and the discovery of oil. Because scientific progress and corporate growth appear to be so closely associated, there is every indication that corporations will continue to grow in size and number . . .

"Only a history of many volumes could accurately describe the social impact of this amazing corporate growth, with its accompanying public ownership of American business, which contributes to a broad distribution of wealth such as has never been known elsewhere . . . The country's number one corporation has more employees than the total population of any one of our four least populous states. It is not surprising that many people are disturbed by the concentration of wealth and economic power . . . but most fair-minded persons will agree that in practice this power has not been used unreasonably and that our large corporations have served the public well. Certainly it is an interesting situation and there must be a reason why our corporate system appears to be working out so satisfactorily . . .

"Generally speaking, the management of a corporation is self-perpetuating. The executives usually select their own successors. It is popularly believed, though, that when people have undisputed authority for long periods they will abuse their power and suffer loss of character. Why then are our large corporations headed almost invariably by men of outstanding character and competence? I believe the answer lies in the system by which they are trained and promoted over a period of years to important positions . . .

"Modern business is extremely complex. It is divided into many departments with successive layers of responsibility and authority. The top management has its staff members, some of whom act as coordinators between department heads who, in turn, have their staffs—and so on down the line to the hundreds and often thousands of supervisors . . .

"The process of evaluation and promotion continues over a long period. To reach the top in a large corporation usually requires many years . . . scores of people in the various levels of management will have reported in writing their impressions of the individual, and all these reports, together with pertinent additional information, will have been assembled in a personal folder to which reference is made hundreds of times over the period of that person's employment. The system is not perfect. It unduly favors certain types of people. It affords too little encouragement to original thinkers and to others who may be inclined to question long-established policies. It is more protective to the company than inspirational to the employee. It tends toward specialization and too often fails to develop the broad interest and training essential for leadership. Greater stimulation is needed . . . but it is obvious that any person who succeeds in becoming a chief executive is almost certain to have character and ability . . .

"Not everyone can stand the strain. The head of one of our largest steel companies tells the story that when asked how his company went about the choosing of a chief executive he replied, 'Well, we just look over our list of vice presidents and if we can find one who hasn't had a coronary thrombosis we elect him president.'

". . . that suggests that our corporations may be getting too large . . . under our system of competitive enterprise, that question will be decided in terms of competitive efficiency. Younger companies are always forging ahead while older companies may be losing ground. There are certain self-corrective features which tend to retard the growth of large companies . . . Probably the greatest difference between my point of view and that of you young people who may be entering the business world, is that I would have less awe of the efficiency of large companies. They have their internal weaknesses. They are . . . favorite targets for politicians and self-seeking labor leaders . . . Many of you would be happier if you were to assume some of the risks involved in small enterprise . . . every young person should weigh the advantages of freedom and the challenge afforded by a career based on individual achievement . . . You should have great faith in yourselves and the courage to try the things you want to do. You are far better equipped than any previous generation. Your horizons are broader. The frontiers are different, but they are just as challenging . . ."

It was a marvelously subtle speech designed to goad the young into doing better for the imperfect world into which they were maturing. Usually Mr. Blazer spoke from notes, extemporaneously. This was from a complete draft, prepared personally.

The Wall Street Journal, in June 1958, carried a lengthy article forecasting events in the Middle East, in which it stated that "the big question in the minds of many diplomats, oil men and local politicos is not who's winning the cold war; the edge is generally conceded to Arab nationalist forces led by Egypt's Gamal Abdel Nasser, and ultimately, to Russia. What worries most observers here is simply how long the West can hang on to its oil interests in the Middle East, which are vital now and are fully expected to become increasingly so as far ahead as most oil men and European economists can see."

Nasser had just returned from a three-week tour of Russia; the United States fleet was patrolling the Mediterranean; American oil investments were being increased in the area. On the surface all looked well; but beneath the surface unrest was increasing. Nonetheless, oil was flowing to the West again.

Aminol was making plans to open a refinery of its own north of the Neutral Zone; it would have a capacity of 30,000 barrels a day; could desulphurize its crude, and produce products for Europe across the sea.

In June 1958, the company also took advantage of a low-interest market to issue $10 million worth of ten-year debentures at 4½ per cent. The Continental Bank of Chicago, long a good friend of the company, wanted to handle the issue; so did the First National Bank of Chicago; Mr. Blazer, pleased that the company's account was considered so substantial, expressed no strong preference.

The Udex came on stream at Buffalo in July; Mr. Blazer, Sam Mosher and Paul Endacott of Phillips joined as a committee to search for a new president for Aminol; meanwhile, it was agreed that Ralph Davies would remain chairman. The recession continued to reduce industrial activity throughout the country

One Ashland division that was having an unusually hard year in 1958 was the Cleveland Tankers. Early in the season, they had experienced heavy ice and fierce storms. Later in the season, the water level in the Lakes fell; the Lakes are shallow anyway, and dredged only sufficiently to allow bare clearances. One result of the low levels was that the Cleveland tankers could not carry full cargoes; the *Taurus* punched a hole in her pump room by scraping ground; the *Meteor* broke a propeller; the *Mercury* touched ground (which meant it had to go into drydock to be checked over); the *Pleiades* rubbed bottom also; the national Maritime Union contract was up for renegotiation. Suddenly it becomes clear that corporate reports unintentionally hide the reality of men earning their livings in all sorts of areas and waters; out drilling in every kind of weather; peering from the wheelhouses and the forepeaks of ships on the river and of Lake tankers; aloft in company planes going to meetings and conferences; late at night in offices; at the refineries toiling around the clock; traveling; worrying; working. The thousands of persons who devote a large part of their lives to this—and other—great enterprises are apt, in the rain of statistics about net sales and earnings, to be unmentioned. But from time to time the semantic curtain parts, and we glimpse reality.

Rex Blazer, writing the directors, reported that George Sisler, the new advertising manager, had visited the various divisions. He and his assistants, Leonard Manley[6] and Teo Nutini,[7] had emerged with a proposed budget of $1.828 million for the company and its subsidiaries.

In June 1958, the economic tide turned. Business, Everett Wells reported, was up again; the Ohio Valley Improvement Association produced a dazzling, comprehensive booklet on the developments in the Ohio Valley, and it is obvious that these efforts had not slackened in the slightest.

[6] Leonard N. Manley, born 1927 in Ashland, Ky., attended the University of Kentucky, Eastern University, the Art Institute of Pittsburgh. A football player with a flair for art—an unusual combination—he is, today, Sales Promotion Manager for Ashland Oil.

[7] Teo Nutini, a Florentine artist, met a Kentucky girl while she was attending the University of Rome. They married and emigrated to Brazil, where they lived in Rio de Janeiro and São Paolo; eventually reached the U.S.A. and Ashland, Ky., where he has been, ever since, with Ashland Oil; is now advertising manager.

Political developments, in fact, interested the whole seventh floor; they were worried not only over the Ohio Valley, but, along with the other oil companies, were concerned about the direction of the voluntary oil import program.

Mr. Blazer, enjoying his role as the elder statesman of the company and hugely relishing his chats with some of the younger men between daily contacts with his long-time associates, wrote the directors, commenting favorably on the activities of Hull and Chamberlain on behalf of the waterways. He said, "We are interested in many projects affecting the development of the Ohio Valley, and especially those involving water conservation and the avoidance of floods. In fact, all such improvements contributed toward the growth of this great valley . . . one of the most significant economic developments of the entire country . . ."

Then he mentioned some of the activities of the men in the company that contributed toward the Ashland community. "I would estimate that there are no less than fifty honors and important recognitions extended every year to the personnel of our company . . . Recently Everett Wells was appointed by Governor Chandler as one of four members of the State's Conservation Water Resources Study Commission. This is an important new commission . . . Everett represents industry; the other three members represent agriculture, municipalities and recreation . . . Rex has been making an important contribution to Eastern Kentucky as a member of the Eastern Kentucky Regional Planning Commission . . . John Fred Williams occupies an important position as Chairman of the Governor's Citizens Advisory Highway Committee and also, as a member of the State Fair Board; he holds many positions of less importance, as do Everett, Rex, Alex, and others. Wilburn Caskey, of our Purchasing Department, is serving a term as Mayor of Ashland; numerous members of our organization have served from time to time as members of the State Legislature . . ."

In September, Mr. D. C. Dunaway, discovered by Messrs. Blazer, Mosher and Endacott, was elected president of Aminol; he had twenty overseas years with various affiliates of Standard of N. J.; Aminol was lifting 80,000 barrels a day, was also a part of an Iranian Consortium, and active in Mexico.

The same month, September 1958, Everett Wells wrote to Captain Carson, the Administrator of the Voluntary Oil Import Program, suggesting that these quotas should not be restricted to major companies . . . As usual, the company was busy in all directions.

The 1958 fiscal year's end reflected the recession, however: net sales had fallen back to $280 million, net profits to $10.3 million. The figures were the lowest since 1955.

The company was gratified by the discovery of oil in Green County, Kentucky. The company moved in fast; before many months they began building a pipeline from a point near Greensburg, Kentucky, to the Aetna plant in Louisville, with a connecting line to the Louisville Refining Company (J. Fred Miles' old firm). It was estimated that 10 million barrels of reserves were still under the surface in those fields, and that 8 million could be recovered. The lines would cost, when completed, some $2 million.

But by the fall of 1958, the management had become so displeased with the workings of the voluntary oil import program that a group consisting of Everett Wells, Bill Hull and Mr. Blazer descended upon the departments of State, Commerce and Interior. Senator John Sherman Cooper had arranged appointments with some top officials; the Ashland trio saw Robert Anderson, the Secretary of the Treasury; Thomas Mason, Assistant Secretary of State for Economic Affairs; Royce Hardy, Assistant Secretary of the Interior; Fred Mueller, Undersecretary of Commerce; and Cecil Milne, Assistant Secretary of Defense for Supply and Logistics.

In the mailroom of the firm, as though to illustrate the infinite diversity of interests a large company contains, a twenty-nine-year-old supervisor, Billy C. Clarke, had his third novel published (*The Mooneyed Hound*), and was holding an autograph session at a Catlettsburg bookstore.

The implications of the oil import situation to the company were so serious the management discussed the issue in the 1958 annual report. Having no "historic" position as an importer, but being faced with competition from refiners who had, Ashland was confronted with the need either to reduce its prices for domestic crude oil or to switch to the purchase of foreign crude oil itself.

Fortunately, it had its own transportation facilities through which to receive foreign crude oil. In order to avoid such a choice, with its subsequent disruption of long-established relations with domestic producers, Ashland was among those companies plumping for import quotas based on refining capacity; an ideal nobody in the company really expected to see realized.

Nationally, reassuring news was disclosed in November 1958, when the first full-range firing of a U.S. intercontinental ballistics missile (Atlas) took place from Cape Canaveral, Florida. The Administration had switched the U.S. first-line defense system to missiles from airplanes. By this time, however, international power plays and defense reactions had become subject to widespread public misunderstanding. In both England and France, domestic considerations began to take precedence over efforts to maintain world position, and in the U.S., disturbing rumors about American military capacity began to circulate.

January 1959, opened with a bang: there was an explosion and fire at one of the refineries, and $125,000 worth of damage was done; fortunately, no one was injured. Captain Carson of the voluntary import program suggested a program based on refinery throughputs and the majors, predictably, objected loudly; the program to allocate the imports on the basis of "historic" position was blocked as discriminatory, by the Department of Justice; the corridors of government and the offices of the oil industry alike were noisy with arguments. To Ashland, Captain Carson's program brought great cheer; if adopted, they and other refiners would be benefited.

At Ashland, heavy rains fell, the waters in the river rose; floods appeared in western Pennsylvania and one of the Ashland terminals was affected; a pumping station had to be shut down. Nature continued to furnish proof that there was more than simple economics to the subject of waterways improvements.

Ed Emrick, long since through his period of trial and steeled by the experience, was elevated to the post of treasurer, in place of Ned Seaton, the smiling man, who retired from the post but retained his position on the board of directors. Ned Seaton's son, Bill Seaton, was immersed in the intricacies of insurance for the company; he showed signs of having inherited his father's acumen and grasp of detail, plus some gifts of his own. He and Orin Atkins, whose paths crossed at the intersection where insurance and law converge, worked particularly well together.

In the legal department, a young man named Arloe Mayne[8] was making his mark; in research and development, still a loosely organized activity at Ashland, a group of men was creating new scientific order where only empirical methods had once existed. These included Harold Houlton, Ollie Zandona, Tom Paulsen, Bill Gammon and Arnold Leas; their ranks were increased by a newcomer named John Hall.[9]

With Ed Emrick moving into the treasurer's post, it was necessary to obtain a new head of exploration and development; Raymond Althouse was hired. Althouse had been president of the Royalite Oil Company of Canada, and prior to that, assistant to the president of Cities Service. As usual the company had high hopes the new broom would sweep oil into existence; Rex explained all this in a letter to the directors. By now, these letters emanated from Rex Blazer, Everett Wells and Paul Blazer in

[8] Arloe W. Mayne, born 1921 in Gold Bug, Ky., a hamlet consisting of "a general store, two or three churches, a Post Office and a handful of homes." Gold Bug was swept out of existence to make way for a superhighway. Mayne's family, in Kentucky "since his great grandfather," came originally from England in the early days of the Republic, were teachers and farmers who worked in the coal mines when necessary. He attended Cumberland College and the Law School at the University of Kentucky, graduated in 1951, was interviewed and hired by Mac Burnam, who questioned him on a situation he had recently explored as part of preparation for an article in Law Journal: a stroke of luck that, he says, made him appear immensely knowledgeable. Once asked to draw the Ashland table of organization during a trial, he encountered great skepticism when he said the firm had none. He was being factual: it has not had, and never did have, a formal table of organization. Mayne is now head of the Ashland legal department and a vice president.

[9] John R. Hall, born 1932 in Dallas, Texas, graduated summa cum laude from Vanderbilt University where he was captain of the football team; served as a 2nd Lieutenant in the Army in 1956; worked a year for Esso Standard Oil at their Baltimore, Md., refinery; was hired by Ashland in 1957, worked as assistant to the coordinator of R&D—a title whose vagueness does not suggest the quality of the research team at this period. Mr. Hall will reappear in these pages.

heavy volume; some directors complained their reading took considerable time, but none complained of lack of information.

With oil flowing copiously from Green County, Kentucky, it was decided to reactivate the Aetna refinery; the indefatigable John Fred Williams accepted the head post in the Ashland Heart Drive, and the city of Ashland informed Mr. Blazer it was going to construct a new high school, and call it the Paul G. Blazer. "Their motives are not unmixed," he said, smiling, but he was enormously pleased.

In March 1959, the government established a mandatory oil import program, and licenses were issued, valid for a 112-day period to run from March to June. The licenses included a quota for both crude and unfinished oil for Ashland—for 11,300 barrels a day. The company was highly pleased.

The resolution of the import situation was based on a sliding scale of percentages. During the initial period, quotas were cut back more than 20 per cent below levels operative during the voluntary period; importation of finished products was restricted.

In general, the industry received the program with relief, and considered it, on balance, fair. Critics, enamored of the free trade concept but largely unaware of the precariousness of international oil movements, sought to alter the program from the inception.

Shortly after, in July 1959, Roland Whealy, who had taken a leave of absence in December 1957, to become a refinery technologist in the Office of Oil & Gas (his appointment was significant enough to warrant an announcement by Fred A. Seaton, Secretary of the Interior), rejoined the company.

Washington had been an elevating experience for Whealy; his associates there found him both skillful and personable. Mr. Blazer, who, of course, had kept well informed of Whealy's progress, suggested New York might be suitable headquarters for a vice president of Whealy's capacities. "A far cry," Whealy said later, "from my early days in Ashland, when—during the shortened work weeks of the Depression—I actually sat in the courthouse to watch petit cases for distraction."

His departure and return to the company, however, is a striking instance of the fact that it was becoming so large all its activities and personalities cannot be held in mind at once; from time to time one loses sight of whole sectors as well as persons that suddenly surface with fresh accomplishments. For instance, during this period Ashland Oil narrowly lost a competition to buy Aurora Oil, Michigan's largest independent distributor. The purchase price, paid by Ohio Oil, was $37 million—a sum well within Ashland Oil's purse.

Concurrently, the MV *Aetna-Louisville,* one of the newer Ashland Oil towboats, was the first vessel to pass through the newly completed Markland Dam. Guests aboard the vessel included Senator Allen J. Ellender of Louisiana and Mr. Paul Blazer, both smiling at the experience.

In the fall of 1959, Mr. Blazer attended an American Petroleum meeting in Chicago. During the traditional cocktail party at the Swedish Club, hosted by the First National Bank, he ran into J. Howard Marshall. Both men were heavy with resentments; each had heard remarks the other had made since their separation. When they met head-on, the spectators scattered and left them alone. Later, however, they wound up in the Ashland Oil hospitality suite in the Conrad Hilton Hotel, and there they argued and reminisced until dawn.

The following day, still without rest but in a state of exhilaration, Mr. Blazer descended from the plane in Ashland. Lucile Blazer, there to greet her husband Rex, thought Mr. Blazer looked remarkably elegant in his homburg. But once home, he collapsed.

"It was well worth it," he told the disapproving Dr. Winans, and reached again for the instrument that kept him in touch with the rest of the world: the telephone.

In August 1959, Ashland Oil received a trial order for 100,000 gallons of high energy fuel developed from virtual teacup efforts by Arnold Leas and his associates. With every passing week, the technical brain trust proved of greater value and the technological change in the industry, of which Mr. Blazer had warned Palmer Talbutt so many years before, was sweeping everyone before its path.

The sweep and momentum of the changes seemed especially clear in 1959, because it was the centennial year of the industry.

On August 27, 1859, Edwin Laurentine Drake, a spurious colonel and a real retired railroad conductor, struck oil in Titusville, Pennsylvania. Like most births, the first oil well came into the world hard: Drake's shaft was 69½ feet long, and achieved with the aid of tools made by Uncle Billy Smith of Tarentum, a local blacksmith. All told, the tools weighed less than a hundred pounds, and cost $76.50. When oil was found, Drake attached a common pitcher pump to his pipe, and brought between eight and ten barrels of oil to the surface daily.

Drake died a pensioner of the Commonwealth of Pennsylvania, but one hundred years later, the industry he primed pumped out 7 million barrels of crude oil a day in the U.S. alone; the nation consumed more than 9 million barrels a day.

In Titusville, Pennsylvania, where Drake had labored and found his minor miracle,[10] the Centennial celebrations lasted a week and attracted notables and attention from all over the country. The Post Office issued a special stamp; the *Today* show featured a well especially drilled for the occasion (it came in dry); featured speakers included the Secretary of the Interior Fred Seaton, M. J. Rathbone, president of the Standard Oil of New Jersey and Robert Dunlop, president of the Sun Oil Company.

The Centennial celebrations, as such events often do, managed to throw light on prevailing attitudes and thoughts about the future of the industry. The Bureau of Mines, casting a governmental glance at the clouds of the future, announced that twenty-five years hence the nation would need twice as much oil and gas as in 1959; wisely remained silent on the large subject of where this additional resource would be found.

And in 1959 the wheel turned round to repeat, with variations, a pattern from the past. Ashland purchased the Louisville Refining Co., and its subsidiary, the Producers Pipeline Company, for close to $5 million. This was J. Fred Miles' old company; he had resigned from the Swiss Oil Company to take charge of the operation.

In the years since, it had gone through several incarnations.

---

[10] He drilled, it was later discovered, on the only site in the region where an oil pool existed that close to the surface. All the later wells in the field had to be drilled much deeper.

By the time Ashland made the purchase, the firm owned 250 miles of pipeline in western Kentucky, and a refinery at Louisville with a processing capacity of 8,000 barrels of crude a day.

Among the pipelines was a section that ran from the oil fields of western Kentucky to Beattyville: It was the line that young Paul Blazer and Eric Shatford had created. Regaining this first child of his efforts in the oil industry must have given Mr. Blazer an unusual satisfaction.

The negotiation had been, like many of Ashland's, rapid, after Mr. Blazer, Orin Atkins and the other members of the acquisition team had concluded their end. Ollie Zandona and his team knocked at the Louisville refinery door early one morning. They swept in to begin their evaluation and de-bottlenecking to the astonishment of the men in the plant, who learned in this abrupt fashion that they had new owners. Presumably the old owners were still drafting the announcement.

In September 1959, the *Louisville Courier-Journal* magazine section carried an article on Ashland Oil and Paul Blazer. Mr. Blazer was intrigued, and explored the company's contribution to the state. He discovered that Ashland officially spent $100 million a year in Kentucky. Rex Blazer, who had Willis Winter, the executive assistant to Frank Colegrove at Allied Oil, transferred to Ashland in 1958 to be assistant credit manager under Ned Seaton, judged the time now right to elevate him to manager: the multi-faceted company was rolling along.

Several press articles appeared about Mr. Vandeveer. He endowed a chair at Southern Illinois University, and discreet questioning had elicited the information that he had been quietly supporting a number of worthy projects and causes. Both Messrs. Vandeveer and Newman, in fact, disproved the adage that money does not bring happiness; both were happy millionaires with many interests and philanthropies.

At the end of September 1959, Jack Dalton died: he was 90 years old and considered wealthy. He and John Kelly had owned the Great Eastern Refining Company, from whom the Swiss Oil Company had bought the tiny Catlettsburg refinery in 1924. In

1959, it all seemed a very long time ago, indeed. But Jack Dalton, of whom most of the great world has never heard, was a famous man in the region: he had started as a coal miner in 1889. By World War I his wealth was estimated at $28 million; he lost this—and more—wildcatting for oil. He lost twenty-seven gasoline stations in the 1937 flood; altogether made and lost more fortunes than most people did jobs. When Death called, it found him negotiating for a ninety-nine-year lease on a coal mine.

Mr. Blazer said, ". . . he had a friendly personality, was a shrewd trader, got along well with people, but was financially irresponsible. He had remarkable vision and usually operated his business profitably, but almost as fast as he made money, he spent it on ventures in which he was inexperienced. Jack Dalton never learned to write, but he "drew" his signature. He read understandingly. Occasionally, during the last fifteen or twenty years I had heard from him indirectly, but it probably has been twenty years since I last saw him."

It is an interesting sidelight; but wonder arises that it is part of an ordinary—for Ashland—communication to the board of directors.

The end of the fiscal year in 1959 found Ashland net sales back to the $300 million level, and net earnings up to $14.3 million—second highest in the company's history to date.

In October a signal honor came to Rex Blazer when he was elected president of the National Petroleum Association, the industry's trade association. This post, and his membership on the API board, brought Rex into closer association with Robert G. Dunlop of Sun Oil. Years earlier, young Dunlop had been impressed by Paul Blazer during his Washington days; now he was to find the nephew of Mr. Blazer interesting and congenial. In the years since he had first watched Mr. Blazer, Dunlop had progressed up the ladder at Sun Oil; had become the first president of the company that was not a member of the Pew family. His first major speech as Sun Oil president was made at Atlantic City at the NPA annual meeting.

In October 1959, the time was also judged opportune to reveal a sequence of events that had begun earlier when Tom Paulsen appeared one day in Harold Houlton's office with a beaker and said smiling, "Guess what this is."

"What?" Houlton answered obediently.

"Naphthalene," Paulsen answered. He had, through a shortcut the textbooks had ruled out of reason, found a way to make it from petroleum. Important in the manufacture of resins, plasticizers and insecticides, naphthalene was in very short supply in 1959. A number of oil companies were feverishly searching for ways to manufacture it from petroleum and it was rumored that Sun Oil had broken through. But Paulsen had actually succeeded and was to prove to be the first.

Paulsen obtained four patents[11] as a result of his work, but of course the whole team was involved in the various aspects of the project. Mr. Blazer was persuaded, cajoled and argued with; Bob Yancey was knee-deep in its possibilities; Hal Houlton as research and development director had ideas, as did Arnold Leas; John Hall proved to be a demon at economic analysis and his slide rule was assiduously employed; a small pilot plant was constructed to prove the process, and it did.

Finally, Bob Yancey negotiated a deal with Universal Oil Products Company—a firm well advanced in selling new processes to the industry—on a fifty-fifty licensing basis, with the two companies splitting the royalties. The process was named Hydeal.

At the same time, numerous conversations were held with chemical companies; plans were underway to construct such a plant at (Mr. Blazer's choice) Buffalo, where the economics appeared soundest. The plant might cost $2 million, Mr. Blazer told the directors, and would produce 25 million pounds of naphthalene and 4 million gallons of benzene.

Mr. Blazer put this move in perspective in describing it to the directors: he related how Yancey and Paulsen had gone around with the lawyers, negotiating; how Chub Moffitt and Bill Humphreys were directing a sales effort to line up contracts for the proposed plant; and how Everett Wells was keeping atop the situa-

[11] Thermal Cracking of Cycle Oil; Cyclohexane Manufacture; Dealkylation for Benzene; Dealkylation for Phenol; Dealkylation for Naphthalene; U.S. Patents Nos. 2,819,203; 2,934,575; 2,951,886; 3,055,956.

tion for the seventh floor aerie on Winchester Avenue in Ashland. But it seems obvious the free-flowing creativity in the atmosphere within the technical brain trust had something to do with it, too.

To shade these sunny possibilities and genuine contribution to the industry's state of the art, a denigrating item appeared in Drew Pearson's column under the byline of Jack Anderson. It said:

> HOW TO STRIKE OIL—Roland Whealy has just returned to the Ashland Oil & Refining Co. after a two-year leave of absence with the Oil Import Administration which sets oil import quotas. He served as Administrator Matt Carson's right bower. Among the new companies suddenly authorized to import oil this year was Ashland Oil & Refining whose allocation was double that of any new importer in its district. When Carson later announced a 6 per cent reduction in individual allocations, Ashland's quota went down only 3.8 per cent. A grateful company promoted Whealy to vice president on his return.

Immediately after this item appeared, the Secretary of the Interior's office issued a statement:

> REPORT ON OIL ALLOCATION
> SYSTEM CORRECTED
> A published report that a former employee of the Oil Import Administration could have participated in allocations to the oil firm from which he was on leave of absence is untrue, Elmer F. Bennett, Undersecretary of the Interior, said today.
>
> Company allocations under the mandatory oil import program are made under a formula recommended by a cabinet-level interagency committee composed of the State, Treasury, Defense, Interior, Commerce and Labor Departments; and subsequently incorporated in the appropriate regulations of the Interior Department. The formula operates automatically and is not subject to interpretation or amendment by employees of the Oil Import Administration, Mr. Bennett said.

Roland A. Whealy, referred to in a columnist's account, was appointed Refining Specialist, Office of Oil and Gas, on or about February 1, 1958. On or about the first of March 1958, he was assigned additional duty as a technical assistant to Captain M. V. Carson, Jr., Administrator of the OIA. He resigned to return to Ashland Oil Company on July 31, 1959.

While serving under Captain Carson, Mr. Whealy did not handle or process any correspondence or applications from the Ashland Oil Company, his former employer.

In reference to Ashland Oil Company, the regulations governing the issuance of oil import allocations were strictly followed, and Ashland's initial allocation and later reductions reflected the identical treatment given to the other oil companies in Ashland's category.

Mr. Blazer, who passed both clippings along to the directors, said, "I doubt that the article will seriously injure Ashland Oil & Refining Company, but such publicity tends to discredit the Government's import program and, obviously, Roland Whealy has been grievously maligned."

Another man thought so, too—and he was the Secretary of Commerce, Frederick H. Mueller. He wrote, on September 14, 1959,

Dear Roland:
I just want you to know that all of your associates when you were here in government are fully cognizant of your integrity and take no heed of the insinuations in the Drew Pearson column of September 10th, 1959 . . .

The Pearson column item was remarkable mainly because it was the first critical comment in the national press the company had ever received: a remarkable record for any enterprise, let alone one that had so many interests in so many places, and employed so many persons. But even as a tempest in a teacup, it made barely a slop.

An entirely different sort of behind-the-scenes story that was not publicized, however, was recalled within the company when Tom Lumly was reported in the trade press to have suffered a heart attack and to be retiring. In 1939, Mr. Lumly was offered a job as Ashland's general refinery superintendent by Mr. Blazer. Lumly declined, with thanks, preferring to go into business for himself. But his first contract as a refinery engineering contractor was given him by Mr. Blazer; Ashland financed Lumly's payroll until the contract was completed, and in effect, helped him get off the ground. With his own energies and talents from there on, however, Mr. Lumly built his Refinery Engineering Company into one of the industry's best-known organizations.

But the import quota program itself, without personalities, provided plenty of press copy. *The New York Times* ran two separate articles at this period, detailing the workings of the program, and some of its effects, and repeated—without attribution—a number of criticisms. With so many entities and conflicting interests, all the comments about the program were, obviously, not without inspiration.

On the world stage, 1959 was a year to tax credulity. For the first time, a Soviet chief of state visited the U.S.; amazement resulted on both sides. In Nikita Khrushchev, the American public saw a personage of overwhelming vulgarity and crudity; Mr. Khrushchev had difficulty in containing his own incredulity at the sight of America's abundance.

But the Russia that Mr. Khrushchev governed was still able to send chills along the spines of the reflective: in September it sent aloft Lunik II and hit the moon. In October, it catapulted Lunik III. This vehicle circled the moon and radioed back photographs of its dark side, about whose aspect man had speculated since his beginnings on earth.

In contrast to these startling achievements, the launching of the world's first nuclear submarine bearing ballistics missiles, by the U.S., seemed undramatic.

At Ashland, where hard work and pressing immediacies naturally dominated attention, further shifts were made in the titles of top management, reflecting new situations. Both Bob Yancey and Orin Atkins became administrative vice presidents: Yancey to head the technical side and Atkins the corporate. Both would continue to report to Everett Wells and Rex Blazer, but in practice this meant consultation. The line-up of the top team had finally taken form: two senior and two younger men.

Early in 1960 the company issued a second employee stock option list. The first, in 1956, had contained a little over 70 names; the second had 208. Only 18 names were repeated. An initial assumption that this lack of overlap means great changes in the key employee line-up is not unwarranted, but it does not mean that many men had left. Actually, it meant that there were more key employees than before, thanks to growth and acquisitions; also, that the intent of the management was not to heavily reward a few, but to give an opportunity to participate to as many as possible.

In looking over the list, it is noticeable that the salaries, by and large, were modest in comparison to the usual large company or by metropolitan standards; the theory that men are in business for purely economic reasons dies hard: we are surprised.

Early in February 1960, Everett Wells, Ray Althouse and Bob Gordon Jr. were busy in Shreveport, Louisiana, negotiating offshore oil leases as part of a group that included Sohio, Skelly Oil, United Gas, United Carbon, Hope Natural Gas, Mississippi Gas. The Ashland share in this venture amounted to $3.5 million; the company was already buying 20,000 barrels a day of Louisiana crudes.

But refinery margins were shrinking again. The *Alice Through the Looking Glass* nature of modern industry, in which the company must run to keep up with a moving landscape, again was at work. First, industry improves its technology and widens its profit margins temporarily; then inflation slowly forces materials and labor costs up, the market resists further product price increases, and then, again, industry improves its technology. As far as society is concerned, this system is the closest thing to perpetual motion—and perpetual progress—the world has ever seen, but man, ever-resistant to change, emits loud outcries at every step of this magic ladder.

At Ashland, the condition of the industry compelled more refinery improvements; it was decided to spend another $1 million at Catlettsburg for a new vacuum unit; by the time this was completed and the work at Buffalo finished, the company's refineries would have a capacity to process 145,000 barrels a day.

The pinch was really on, though. Industry statistics in early 1960 reflected a 35 per cent drop in refining profits, while the profits for crude producers had dropped 4 per cent and the profits of integrated companies had dropped 12 per cent. By lucky happenstance, the *New York Herald Tribune* chose that moment to emerge with full-page listing of the companies on the Big Board who had paid dividends every year without fail for the preceding twenty years; Ashland Oil & Refining was, by alphabetical position and its record, prominent among them.

Even though these industry statistics did not change the financial community's views of independents, analysts nevertheless began to take notice of the firm. John S. Herald, Incorporated, issued an analysis in which it described the company as ". . . a 12-state operator, comparable to Pure Oil or Continental. Its refinery properties have a capacity of 162,000 barrels of crude processing and are worth $85 million; its transportation facilities include boats, pipelines and tankers that are rated at $20 million; its marketing properties at $30 million."

In the middle of March 1960, Mr. Blazer heard a squishing noise. "It sounded," he said later, "familiar—like the noise a pump makes when the line it supplies develops an orifice. It was quite regular." He got up and walked around, and the noise traveled with him. It matched, in fact, the rhythm of his heart. He told Mrs. Blazer about it, and she put her head near his and listened, but the sound of their breathing prevented her from hearing it.

They were in Phoenix at this time, and Mr. Blazer planned a trip on a commercial airline to Tulsa. He called the American Airlines for reservations, and asked if he could bring his oxygen tank—and a number of other questions—all of which alarmed the ticket agent on the other end of the phone. Finally, the ticket agent said the airline wouldn't sell him a ticket at all, unless a physician cleared him for travel. Mr. Blazer then called Dr. Bullington, and arranged for an appointment.

The examination proceeded without incident. Mr. and Mrs. Blazer were on the verge of departure, when he recalled the strange sound in his neck. "Oh, by the way," he said to the doctor, and Bullington reached again for his stethoscope.

After listening, he told Mrs. Blazer to place her head against Mr. Blazer's neck and listen while they both held their breaths. With the sound of their breathing removed, she could distinctly hear a sinister and regular squish.

After that, events moved quickly. A company plane rushed Mr. Blazer to Houston, Texas, where he entered the Methodist Hospital. There, a fellow Tulane alumnus and friend of Dr. Bullington's, Dr. Michael deBakey, confirmed the diagnosis. Mr. Blazer was immediately prepared for surgery.

The difficulty was a blockage in the right carotid artery—one of the two arteries that supplies blood to the brain. It was extremely serious—even critical—because a clot was forming. Although the examination had contained painful moments, the operation itself proceeded quickly. Mr. Blazer was conscious—and fascinated—throughout. Skipping details, the operation resulted in a clearing of the carotid, and the placement of a nylon patch.[12]

In all recorded medical history, only one other person had heard that sinister squishing sound, and called attention to it in time to have his life saved—and he was a physician.

In 1960, while Mr. Blazer was undergoing his operation in Houston, an event in Russia astonished the world. Francis Gary Powers, an American pilot, bailed out of his U-2 reconnaissance plane over the land of mystery, was captured and put on public exhibition. Until then, the general public had never heard of these soaring vehicles that were sent to hover over the USSR and photograph its activities. The connection with Ashland Oil was not obvious except to experts: the refinery at Catlettsburg supplied the fuel for these advanced planes; Arnold Leas and the technical brain trust had developed it. But while the newspaper headlines shrieked, Ashland Oil's men remained mute.

12 Dr. deBakey's bill impressed Mr. Blazer as too modest, but the doctor said it was standard. Consequently, Mr. Blazer donated a considerable sum to Tulane Medical School, deBakey's alma mater.

Business during 1960 improved both for the company and throughout the nation. Ashland Oil reduced its price on crude oil and its crude oil suppliers automatically emitted fierce outcries. Partly as a result of the reduced crude oil prices, however, sales began to improve, refinery throughput increased—and the company began to buy more crude oil. By August 1960, refinery throughput reached 158,000 barrels of crude oil a day, and refinery profits improved.

Mr. Blazer, tireless in his role as corporate diarist for the board of directors and well recovered from his operation, resumed his discursive letters. The list of men who received copies of these letters extended to more than thirty, in addition to the board itself.

"I am sure everyone who receives a copy knows the contents are confidential," he said serenely.

By the end of September 1960, the accountants plunged into the task of adding the score. They emerged within 28 days—a very brief period considering the scope of the task—with the results: $303 million in net sales, and $14.9 million in net profits.

Within the nation, great sweeping changes had begun to emerge. The presidential election campaign featured, for the first time, television debates between the candidates. From this time forward, the medium would dominate the scene, in terms of influence. For the first time since the early days of civilization, appearance and rhetorical ability would again move masses of men, as immediately and intimately as when the Forum was the stage.

The campaign issues revolved around the missile gap and Cuba. Implicit, but largely unstated in the debate, was the menace of Russia and the state of U.S. readiness to meet its challenge.

In early November 1960, when the votes were tallied, they proved excruciatingly close. Mr. Kennedy had an edge of only 118,550 votes out of more than 68 million cast: a plurality of less than 1 per cent.

Section Nine—The Soaring Sixties

1961–1966

In early 1961, the air was heavy with imminent change. Shortly before he entered the White House, while still President-elect, John Kennedy was photographed while on vacation. Wearing a casual shirt, his hair tousled, squinting against the sun, he was sitting at the wheel of a small open automobile. The photographer had obviously taken no pains; had violated the usual rules, in fact. Sunlight slanting through leafy overhead trees cast a dappled pattern on the subject. But the result was of a very youthful-looking man; incredibly youthful in appearance to be President of this superpower. Its publication coincided with a general rush of upward feeling throughout the country.

From this year forward, whoever wrote about matters economic in the United States had to change his pace; put on seven league boots and race in them to keep abreast of events. The nation, straining toward the infinite year after year, began suddenly to move on economic levels beyond the dreams of mankind. It has since dipped, but never yet to the levels of the past.

Ashland Oil entered 1961 with the praises of the *Value Line* report ringing in its ears, with respectful notice from *Petroleum Week,* and with a gratifying amount of attention from *The Wall Street Journal,* for its annual report figures. These figures were issued—as usual—in the middle of December, although they represented business up to the close of the previous September.

November 1960 had been the greatest sales month in the Ashland history, but profit margins in refining continued to narrow. In the past, this situation had always led the refiners to technological change; pending the nature of this change, management had no other recourse than to economize. Ashland was economizing, to a large extent, by waterflooding its Kentucky oil-producing properties. These secondary recoveries, although they cost money, nevertheless did not cost as much as searching and drilling for new oil: such costs were continually rising.

What the firm needed was new horizons; the technical brain trust was confident of the direction of the future, and as a result of its persuasions, petrochemicals dominated everyone's thoughts. The new economies in refinery operations were made rigorous.

With more than 40,000 shareholders and 5,000 employees; with the refineries processing over 150,000 barrels of crude oil daily; with 5,000 miles of pipelines in its possession; with 26 terminals in 11 states and 3,400 service stations in operation, the firm seemed well situated. But its efforts had been Herculean for a very long time. Between 1946 and 1960, the company had increased by a factor of 15; it had enlarged from sales of $20.4 million to $303 million; its income had risen from $1.3 million to $14.9 million.

Nevertheless, it retained a strong regional flavor. Dr. Joseph Massie's book, entitled *Blazer and Ashland Oil,* appeared in late January 1961, printed by the University of Kentucky Press, and was widely reviewed—in Kentucky. The *Louisville Courier-Journal* praised the Blazer family and the Ashland Oil & Refining Company.

In fact, honors seemed to pour upon the Blazers at this point. Paul Blazer Jr., for eight years a member of the executive committee of the University of Kentucky Alumni Association, was elected a director of the Kentucky Medical Foundation; the new Paul G. Blazer High School in Ashland, as yet unbuilt, won an AIA design award. When completed, the new school would consist of seven buildings, some of them cantilevered over the hillside to create a modern campus setting.

As usual, the company was moving ahead of its reputation; while Kentucky was awakening to its growth and momentum, Everett Wells, Roland Whealy and Bob Yancey were in Washington, D.C., pursuing conversations with the Department of the

Interior in an effort to obtain government permission to build a spur pipeline connecting the Buffalo refinery with the Canadian Interprovincial line. The firm had several good reasons.

One reason was that the rate of exchange between Canada and the U.S. had switched: where the advantage was formerly 5 cents in favor of the Canadian dollar, it had moved to 4 cents in favor of the U.S. dollar. This was a very potent reason, because the 9-cent change could be translated into a 25-cent reduction in the cost of each barrel of Canadian oil Ashland could obtain.

Another reason was that the Buckeye Pipeline, which delivered oil to Buffalo for Ashland (among other customers), commingled its crude oil. This meant that the oil the refinery received was not ideal for the Buffalo processes—especially since the Udex installation. Canadian oil was excellent for these purposes.

The Interprovincial line, on the other hand, agreed—if a spur line were built—to batch the oil it delivered. And because Buffalo was to be the first Ashland petrochemical unit, it was important to the company that it arrange the best possible procedure.

The Department of the Interior, however, viewed this with a distinctly chilly eye: not that the Department objected to Ashland Oil improving its position, of course—but because importations of Canadian crude were restricted. It viewed the proposition for a spur line as a camel's nose underneath a very large tent: it feared a whole troop of camels would march in the same direction.

Ashland, already receiving 8,000 barrels of crude oil daily from Canada via Bay City, Michigan—whence it was transported, by Cleveland Tankers, to Buffalo—wanted permission to bring in 10,000 barrels a day through its new spur.

With the dexterity of men experienced in dealing with the importunities of businesses, the officials at the Department of the Interior skillfully created a number of straw men to blunt the first fine fervor of Ashland's enthusiasm. They asked for assurances that Ashland had no plan to introduce lower-priced crude oil into Buffalo and thus upset the market there for local producers and then for more assurances that no local marketing arrangements had already been reached, and so on.

Within a few months it was realized by both sides that the discussion would become a campaign. Mr. Blazer, Ashland's heavy gun, moved onto the scene firing broad rationalizations. Suppose, he argued, that a national emergency arose? Did not existing marketing arrangements prior to World War II prevent pipelines from developing? Would not a spur line from Interprovincial to Buffalo actually contribute to national defense, by being an insurance against similar disrupted markets during another emergency in the future? It is hard not to believe that both sides did not enjoy some elements of these encounters.

But the stakes were serious, just the same. That February, seven months after ground had first been broken, naphthalene began to be produced at Catlettsburg at the rate of 40 million pounds a year; soon another reformer would be added to the refinery equipment to produce benzene as well.

Sales contracts for the Ashland naphthalene had been made with Allied Chemical, American Cyanamid, Monsanto, Reichhold Chemicals, and others; plans were well along to install a Udex unit into Catlettsburg as well. Throughout the U.S., eleven Hydeal units were licensed; Ashland could look forward to receiving royalties from these in the future.

To the young researchers and engineers engaged in these efforts, it meant that Ashland Oil had finally broken into the exciting ambient of chemicals; looking around corners, they could see great vistas.

This was not the only avenue that beckoned. Orin Atkins and Mr. Blazer had, by this time, achieved a close partnership on financial matters that began on their first visit to New York City together some years before. On that visit, when the two men arrived in their hotel suite, Orin Atkins had been astounded when Mr. Blazer sank, the picture of exhaustion, into an easy chair, and asked Orin if he had any ideas as to what to do, whom they should see, and how to go about it. Atkins, thinking Mr. Blazer was completely lost in the big city, bestirred himself, alarm bells ringing through his system. He began to make phone calls and line up appointments with various financial firms and banks. By the time they left New York, both men had good reason to feel satisfied. Mr. Blazer was subtle.

One result was that by the spring of 1961, not only Mr. Blazer but also Orin Atkins had a number of friends in the New York financial community. As a fallout of these contacts, analysts were regularly finding their way to Ashland itself to probe the company's activities after a period of relative inactivity, and Ashland stock began to move slowly upward on the Big Board.

One of the friends Atkins made was Ken Hill.[1] In the spring of 1961, sitting in his office at Eastman Dillon, Union Securities & Co., in the Chase Manhattan Plaza, Hill began conversations that would eventually lead to an alteration of destinies at Ashland and elsewhere. The immediate subject was the United Carbon Company, one of the world's largest manufacturers of carbon black (an ingredient highly important to rubber), and owner of oil and gas properties in the southwest.

Hill was a member of the board of United Carbon, and Sylvan Coleman—chairman of the board of E. F. Hutton & Co.—with whom he was talking, was also chairman of United Carbon's board of directors.

That spring, Cities Service Company had purchased, for a large sum, the Columbian Carbon Co., one of United's strongest competitors. Both Hill and Coleman watched the transaction with great interest, and then began to add together their thoughts regarding United Carbon, its future and its management.

Then Bill Briggs, of the Bank of New York, asked Hill to draw up an estimate of the value of United Carbon in the event of a sale or merger. Hill drew up an estimate and shortly afterward, talks began with SunRayDX Oil.

In February 1961, Edward L. McDonald,[2] the brilliant title

[1] Kenneth E. Hill, born in California and currently a resident of Westfield, N. J., graduated from the University of California in 1938; three years later earned an M.S. at the same school while working as an instructor, spent 1942 with the Conservation Commission of Los Angeles, entered the U.S. Naval Air Corps as a second lieutenant and served until 1946. Emerging from the service, he became a petroleum engineer for the Chase Manhattan Bank in New York City, and attended N.Y.U. School of Business Administration from 1946–1948; became a vice president at Chase; left the bank in June 1958 to become partner in charge of petroleum and natural gas activities at Eastman Dillon, Union Securities & Co., in New York, a post he still occupies.

[2] E. L. McDonald, born 1871 in Louisville, Ky., was the son of a Confederate major named Edward Hitchcock McDonald, and one of nine

lawyer who had attracted and assisted J. Fred Miles, and who was a member of the Swiss Board and, later, Ashland's until 1954, died in his ninety-first year.

Mr. McDonald, one of the founders of Swiss Oil, served on its board until 1936; he was also secretary and a director for Ashland Oil & Refining, the successor company, until 1954. Then, at the age of 83, he decided it was time to retire; turned his reins over to his son Angus W. McDonald, who remains a director and secretary for Ashland.

In the late 1950s, Dr. Joseph Massie interviewed the elder McDonald. The tape reveals a speaker with a soft southern accent, witty and articulate. J. Fred Miles always considered McDonald the most brilliant man in the Swiss organization; the records show he was a skillful and valuable chief counsel; he led the companies successfully through many a tangled legal thicket.

Mr. Blazer attended the funeral, at which he was an honorary pallbearer, together with Ned Seaton, Everett Wells, Rex Blazer, and director Charles S. Evans.

---

children. He went to Rugby School in Louisville and received a degree from the University of Virginia Law School in 1890. After receiving his degree, E. L. returned to Louisville to practice law; became chief counsel for the Louisville Title Company, and was in this post when J. Fred Miles persuaded him to join the Swiss Oil venture. In 1918, when Swiss was formed, E. L. McDonald became a director and general counsel, and moved to Lexington, Ky., where he remained the balance of his life.

E. L. McDonald resigned as secretary of Ashland Oil & Refining in 1953 and Angus McDonald, his son, who had been assistant secretary of the firm, became secretary; E. L. also retired as a director and his place was assumed by Angus.

Angus McDonald, born in Louisville in 1912, graduated from the University of Virginia Law School in 1935; joined his father in the practice of general law in Lexington the same year. Today the firm is known as McDonald, Alford & Rozell.

E. L. McDonald went to work every day until a few weeks before his death in 1961. A soft-spoken, pleasant and eminently sensible man, he was more interested in law than in business; for a number of years considered the litigous situation of the fledgling Swiss Oil Company one of the most interesting of situations; was later amazed that this venture, out of the dozens formed in Eastern Kentucky at the time, should prove to be the sole, exceptional survivor.

E. L. McDonald, secretary and a director of the
Ashland Oil & Refining Company.

Within the company, sales fell off somewhat, but the Hydeal
unit was profitable; plans were underway to manufacture cyclohexane, a material useful in making nylon; to enter jet fuels on
a larger scale via a new aliphatic unit; despite an economy drive,
costs kept rising.

The fact was that the company, like the country, had begun its
move upward—although at the moment all that seemed evident
was an increase in the cost of doing business.

It was not until April 1961 that the economy began to turn upward, and that was a month of such lurid events internationally
that these attracted almost everyone's attention. The first such
happening was Russia's feat of sending a man, Major Yuri Gagarin,

aloft and into orbit in a space vehicle that traveled around the earth once and was then safely returned; the second, at the end of the month, was the failure of a small invasion force of Cuban exiles to achieve a successful landing on their homeland. This effort, sponsored by the U.S., was so far below the standards of the fabled American efficiency as to shock the public. Outcries against the CIA began to appear in the press, and the entire discussion of Communist inroads in Latin America became subject to confused, and confusing, debate.

During the first week of July 1961, Mr. Blazer wrote the board that he, Rex Blazer and Everett Wells attended the funeral of Armstrong A. Stambaugh, ex-chairman of the board of the Standard Oil Company of Ohio. Mr. Stambaugh had been a friendly competitor for years. But especially after they became neighbors in Scottsdale, a city near Phoenix, highly favored by oil industry

The Hydeal unit.

men, the Stambaughs and the Paul Blazers became close personal friends.

Although retired from the post of chairman at Sohio, Mr. Stambaugh remained influential in the firm; had an employment contract similar to that between Mr. Blazer and Ashland Oil. He was 76 when he died—five years older than Mr. Blazer—but he had the same outlook (he was known as a strong marketing man), was of the same generation, and his death was a serious personal loss.[3]

What with funerals and the apparent plateau Ashland Oil seemed to have reached in 1961, there seemed reason to believe the company's great period of growth was over. *Fortune's 500* list of top U.S. manufacturing concerns showed Ashland Oil 154th in sales, 170th in assets, 212th in ratio of earnings against sales; 157th in profits in relation to invested capital; 20th in domestic sales among oil companies (just behind Ohio Oil), and 5th in return on invested capital among oil companies.

In July 1961, we read with a sense of wonder that Hydeal earnings accounted for 20 per cent of the profits at the Catlettsburg refinery. The Blazer refinery genius seemed to have waned, and the younger generation to have taken over. In September, the end of the fiscal year, the figures reveal net sales of $312 million, and net profits of $15.2 million.

During the fall, the Ashland accountants usually totaled their yearly figures and made forecasts. As a rule, it took at least a

[3] Armstrong A. Stambaugh, born 1885 in New Germantown, Pa., was educated at Ohio Northern University at Ada where he received a B.A. in 1910, and Harvard Law School, where he received an LL.B. in 1913. He worked for Holliday, Grossman & McAfee, counsel for Sohio, from 1913–1928; became a director and vice president of Sohio in 1933, senior vice president and chairman in 1950.

Mr. and Mrs. Blazer were visiting the Stambaughs in Scottsdale, when they realized the dry air of the Southwest was better for Mr. Blazer's health than the moist humidity of Florida. "Stam" took Mr. Blazer to see Mountain Shadows, a new development, and Mr. Blazer decided to build there. Through the years the couples became extremely close; according to Mrs. Blazer, Mr. Stambaugh and Mr. Blazer never tired of conversing.

THE SOARING SIXTIES: 1961–1966

month to compile these figures upon which management based much of its strategy.

Mr. Blazer, living in his own form of retirement, was free to devote his attention to whatever interested him. Because of his tenuous grasp upon life, he lived intensely in the present, as intensely as any man who expected each minute might be his last. Nevertheless, the extent and particularity of his interests were surprising. Jim Breuil, bothered by pains in the back of his neck, had tried various remedies; from his description of the symptoms, Mr. Blazer suspected an arterial difficulty: he suggested deBakey, and the doctor confirmed his guess. One matter of great interest, therefore, was the course of Mr. Breuil's operation in Houston; another—as usual—was the editorial and pictorial content of the Ashland annual report.

Bud Perry was creator of the *Ashland Dealer* and *Ashland News,* and also editor of a corporate quarterly called the *Ashland Log.* Perry had elevated the *Log* to a slick magazine, and did yeoman's work on a variety of allied matters. He worked in an office next to Mr. Blazer's and enjoyed every moment of it. But the preparation of the Annual Report was an ordeal for Perry, for this document aroused all Mr. Blazer's perfectionism.

Many men worked on the report and as a result revisions were extensive. Perry and Teo Nutini were charged in some measure with the illustrations and layouts. These required many agonizing reappraisals.

On one occasion, driven beyond endurance, Perry burst in on John Fred Williams, vice president and personnel director, and shouted at him for an hour. John Fred, a man of considerable calm, arose only once, and that was to close the door; spent the rest of the hour rocking in his chair and grunting occasionally to show that he followed and appreciated the tirade. When Perry had exhausted himself, John Fred fed him some honeyed words and helped him out.

Mr. Breuil's operation that fall turned out to be a success; he was to feel forever after that Mr. Blazer had saved his life as much as did Dr. deBakey; the annual report, despite Perry's hurt feelings and Mr. Blazer's conviction that it could have been improved, appeared as usual. Behind the scenes, Mr. Blazer, Orin Atkins,

Everett Wells, Bob Yancey and Rex Blazer were really watching another, larger target very closely.

1962

In January, they were all rudely shaken by the fact that President Kennedy, who had spoken against river tolls during his campaign speech in Kentucky (while Mr. Nixon had implied he would ask for their imposition), asked for a 2-cent-per-gallon excise tax on fuel oil transported on the inland waterways. Mr. Blazer, who was chairman of the National Waterways Conference, found himself the only member of this group who was not for instant warfare. He had decided, some time before, that in the long run the government would not be able to restrain itself from taxing, tolling and using the inland waterways as a means of raising revenue—despite the long-range consequences. (Mr. Blazer's pessimism regarding the trend of government was deep, although seldom stated.)

Being of this opinion, he thought perhaps the region could buy a little time by not fighting the 2-cent tax, but the region was up in arms.

There was also another bill to contend against that went farther than the President's recommendation. Representative Van Zandt of Pennsylvania and Senator Beall of Maryland had jointly proposed a commission be established to set tolls based on the ton-miles of transport on the inland waterways; they plumped also for licenses to transport, and for registration fees.

President Kennedy's toll was part of an overall plan regarding transportation matters in general; it seemed to Mr. Blazer that once the company was drawn into an argument between competitive forms of transportation, it would be in trouble. The railroads were important to Ashland as a means of transportation, and also as customers of diesel fuel. Mr. Blazer did not believe the issue was a transportation matter; he felt it was a matter of regional development, and thought the region would decline—which would hurt the railroads too—if user taxes and tolls were imposed on the waterways.

Nevertheless, he spurred himself into a number of public appearances; attended a meeting in Washington; wrote the Mississippi Valley Association regarding the tax. To Mr. Blazer, the choice was between bucking a young Administration, or being saddled with the Van Zandt proposal, which would add as much as "one or two mills per ton mile—as much as 50 times the fuel tax." Ever realistic, he preferred the lesser evil; he was not so sanguine as to believe in no evil. Still, he was shocked at the difference between the course of action stated by Kennedy, the candidate, and the action taken by Kennedy, the President

Of course his view favoring compromise was confined within the Waterways Conference itself; Mr. Blazer had no intention of abandoning the fight prematurely, but his colleagues in the Conference thought he was deserting. In fact, he and a group consisting of Congressman Frank Smith (himself once on Kennedy's Natural Resources Advisory Committee), and Wade H. Hollowell, a banker from Greenville, Mississippi, made a trip to the White House and talked to two of the President's personal assistants: Mike Feldman, a figure close to the President, and Robert Turner, an economist from the Bureau of the Budget.

Mr. Turner was of the view that users of the waterways should be progressively taxed, to pay for the costs of government improvements of the waterways; Mr. Feldman was less didactic, and said simply he did not believe the 2-cent tax was onerous. Mr. Feldman also assured the group the Van Zandt bill did not have the Administration's backing, and that was a relief.

The railroads, in the interim, put together a four-car promotion they called the Free Enterprise Special, and sent it out to whip up sentiment for a national transportation system that would equalize charges on rails, roads, air, and waterways. Altogether, the brouhaha over President Kennedy's proposals on transportation would startle the most phlegmatic.

To the men of Wall Street, the summer of 1962 had not been altogether pleasant; the market fell off in April and May and that was not good. The price of United Carbon, for instance, fell from 70 to 50, and the merger talks with SunRayDX fell apart.

To Ken Hill of Eastman Dillon, and Sylvan Coleman of E. F. Hutton, the situation at United Carbon did not improve; they bided their time until a new deal seemed possible. At this juncture, Orin Atkins and Mr. Blazer arrived in New York on one of their trips. This time the Ashland men wanted to discuss a $25-million sinking fund debenture, due in 1987—twenty-five years hence.

Hill welcomed the visit, and Eastman Dillon joined A. G. Becker in the venture. The issue appeared in early fall and sold well, despite slightly depressed conditions.

Financial deals of this magnitude involve myriad details and a great deal of work; these consumed much of Atkins' time. But during his frequent visits to Eastman Dillon, both he and Mr. Blazer exuded a desire to expand Ashland, and Hill regarded them speculatively.

One day in the fall of 1962, Hill mentioned United Carbon, and both Atkins and Mr. Blazer visibly came to attention. The men began to discuss the possibilities and to tick off the details: oil, gas, research and development, properties, men, sales. Finally, Hill picked up the phone and called Sylvan Coleman at E. F. Hutton. Coleman, to whom negotiations are the staff of life, gave the traditional response, "the company is not for sale." But he agreed to meet the men.

From 4:30 until 6:00, Hill, Atkins and Mr. Blazer went over the ground and the more they looked at it, the more enticing it became. Ashland had no strong ties to Akron, the heart of the tire industry; there was little doubt that both the Federal Trade Commission and Anti-Trust would approve Ashland's purchase of United Carbon, where they might disapprove the purchase of United Carbon by a larger oil company.

The men saw Coleman, who called Dick French, the president of United Carbon. He was, understandably, reluctant. But Hill contacted Frank Lindeman, the United Carbon head of production, and Lindeman quoted United Carbon's production and reserve figures. They were impressive. Orin Atkins and Mr. Blazer, joined by Everett Wells, knowing they were in a deal—the largest in Ashland's history—checked into the Hotel Pierre, and a round of non-stop meetings began.

"Mr. Blazer," said Sylvan Coleman later, "complained of his hearing. But it was my fate, no matter which side of him I chose, to always face his good ear. He could hear my faintest whispers to my assistants, and would answer them. What amazed me was his alertness. He was in his early seventies, and obviously not strong. But his mental alertness was phenomenal. From time to time he would say he was tired, and of course we were all tired; these sessions are grueling; the principals have to wear out lawyers, tax experts, insurance men; all the specialists. But when Mr. Blazer felt tired, he would excuse himself and go lie down and take oxygen, and perhaps nap for ten minutes or so. Then he would return transformed; invigorated. Each time, I felt I was confronting a fresh new opponent and I was tiring myself."

Mr. Coleman, whose soft lack of emphasis in conversation is cumulatively impressive, paused in his recollection, and then said, "It is very hard to get an idea at 3 or 4 o'clock in the morning, but after a rest, Mr. Blazer had many.

"The purpose of the continuous conference is to maintain secrecy. Negotiations involving many millions of dollars and the livelihood of thousands of persons cannot drag out for months— word leaks out; executives begin to worry about their futures. This leads to unrest and, of course, speculations. Make it quick!" Mr. Coleman said.

Nevertheless, word usually does leak out. There are eyes in the lampposts in Wall Street; and evidence that someone has discovered that negotiations are underway is usually, if not always, supplied by action in the stock.

"I suppose," said Mr. Coleman, "this is because a large negotiation, of necessity, involves so many men; lawyers, CPA's, estimators, engineers. Then there is need for tax rulings."

In this negotiation, of course, Mr. Coleman was the seller, and Mr. Blazer and Orin Atkins were in the buyer's chair.

To illustrate his philosophy as a seller, Mr. Coleman recalled a story he once heard about a man who made glasses and who was fitting them on a client. The client, finding his sight improved, smiled with satisfaction and asked, "How much?"

"Fifteen dollars," said the optician, watching the client closely. Seeing the man's smile remained broad, he then added quickly, "For the frames."

The client's smile contracted slightly, and the optician then said, "The lens is $10," and as the client looked up at him, said, "Each."

In this fashion, Mr. Coleman watched Mr. Blazer closely as each detail of the transaction unfolded. He also found himself watching Orin Atkins.

"Atkins was amazing," Mr. Coleman said. "He was obviously only in his late thirties, but he displayed the experienced mind of a man in his fifties. He was a lawyer, and yet he had a fine grasp of the financial elements. Furthermore, I discovered that he was knowledgeable regarding pensions, options, taxes and many other matters."

Mr. Coleman paused, and added, "He had, of course, a splendid teacher in Mr. Blazer. But I guessed he had actually few contacts, and had not only learned from his teacher, but also did a lot of reading. In all, I would say Atkins showed a remarkable amount of self-development, and exhibited the knowledge of a much older man."

But it was Mr. Blazer who held the center stage of Coleman's attention; and as the negotiations extended, he saw with wonder that the older man took no notes. "He seemed able to keep all details in mind," Coleman said, "while retaining the essence of the situation." (An observer said Mr. Coleman himself took no notes.)

While Mr. Blazer, Orin Atkins and others of the Ashland team were engrossed in various aspects of the United Carbon negotiations, the majority of the company's men were continuing daily business. A large enterprise consists of many activities, few of which can be allowed at any time to slacken. In general terms, the petroleum marketplace was going through a change of pace in the early 1960s. Gasoline, as a result of the shifts of population and the general flight to the suburbs, was caught in the retail revolution. For years, the struggle had been brand against price; the majors had spent billions making the public conscious of their brand names. Mr. Blazer was always scornful of this approach; he would discuss the length of time it took to regain the capital investment a new station location entailed; once he sent Palmer Talbutt out to take a survey. Palmer reported that the motorists in many a community bought gasoline from the man they knew; not the brand. In the early 1960s it briefly looked as though Mr. Blazer's side of the argument might win; motorists suddenly seemed to lose their belief in brands and were buying gasoline by price.

This led, inevitably, to regional price wars and conditions in the gasoline market became fierce. At the same time, profits from refining became more narrow, in terms of percentages, than Mr. Blazer said he could recall in forty-five years—an exaggeration, probably, if one bears in mind the early 1930s, but it tells the situation.

The situation in the round, however, was both larger and more complex than the problems of selling gasoline. Every product presented a whole series of problems, from manufacturing through marketing. Each had its group of specialists; each had competitors and advertising; prices and regulations; transportation and trends; supervisors and orientation. As the years passed, more and more of these had been gathered into the hands of Rex Blazer; the tall, portly, smiling figure, padding as surely as any hunter on his rounds; working until midnight in his office night after night, almost hidden behind great mounds of material to read, to answer, to absorb. He seemed able to quicken and increase sales in all directions.

It is no great surprise to discover that he had started holding great seminars at Ashland; the first of these included Frank Colegrave of Allied and his fuel oil salesmen; Palmer Talbutt's refinery sales group; Hugh Jenks and his asphalt specialists; the R. J. Brown Company men under Chub Moffitt and Mr. Metcalf. At its conclusion, the younger Blazer discussed the scope of the company, its growth over the years from a tiny group in three offices in the bank building at Ashland: he ascribed it to work and integrity. Suddenly it dawns that thirty-three years have passed since Rex came to Ashland looking for a job, and that a lot of water had gone over the dam: tons of it.

While Rex was speaking to the salesmen and their chiefs in Ashland, the exploration and development department was engrossed in its waterflooding operations in Kentucky; the great tows were toiling up the Father of Waters; drilling crews were out in the fields of Oklahoma and a dozen other states; pipeline crews were working; the Lake steamers were plowing their way to port; the entire company was straining.

Shortly after noon on September 4, 1962, Ashland Oil's chief pilot A. Blaine (Berky) Berkstresser, 49, and co-pilot Ron Roberts, 30, took off from the Boyd County Airport in a company Lockheed Lodestar for Cleveland and Buffalo.

The plane was one of the two Lodestars the firm owned, in addition to three Cessna 310's. Company planes, like chauffered automobiles, are apt to receive a great deal of attention.

On this occasion, the pilots were to pick up men from Allied and Frontier oil divisions and bring them to Ashland for a meeting. The trip north was without incident; Berky and Roberts greeted the manager of fuel oil sales, the manager of home heating sales, a district sales manager and the executive assistant to the management of Allied Oil in Cleveland. The six men then flew in the Lockheed to Buffalo, where the plane was boarded by Clayton Maxwell, a vice president of Frontier Oil, his assistant and the Frontier manager of transportation. On this occasion, two men from the corporate home office in Ashland were with Mr. Maxwell; one was an administrative assistant to the Ashland Oil marketing division and the other an analyst in the management engineering department.

The plane left Buffalo at 8 o'clock in the evening with the two pilots and eleven passengers aboard. A little less than an hour later, the pilots reported to ground stations that they were 8,000 feet over Youngstown, Ohio, and exactly on course. The weather was fine; there were no problems; the report was routine. Nine minutes later the plane crashed and exploded near Lake Milton, a resort area 17 miles west of Youngstown. The impact was so violent the propeller hubs were driven more than seven feet into the earth, and the plane disintegrated when it landed. There were no survivors.

It was the worst private plane crash in the history of the country, and no explanation—although, of course, many theories—of the crash was ever reached.

All the various agencies and experts who investigated Ashland Oil's practices regarding the care and handling of its small airplane fleet agreed these were excellent. The firm was extremely safety-conscious in every respect, was loaded with awards and proud of its record in this respect whether the subject was re-fineries, boats, trucks, plants, pipelines or planes.

Nevertheless, the accident happened, and thirteen men died. Mr. Blazer was particularly and personally affected because Berky had originally told him about the importance of oxygen, and had introduced him to the practice of carrying small portable tanks of oxygen around with him. Had he not had such a portable tank in his apartment when he had his massive heart attack in La Jolla in 1950, the doctors were convinced he would not have lived. Berky had indirectly saved his life, and Mr. Blazer was not a man to ever forget such a debt.[4]

Berkstresser had been an unusually cautious pilot; his attention to safety was well known through the company . . . His death in a mysterious crash was highly unlikely; but there it was.

Violent death is not at all unknown in the oil industry: it is an industry where danger waits at numerous points. The men who toil in the industry take many precautions; they are as careful as possible. But man has no protection against sudden and unfore-seeable malfunction of mechanical appliances. The experts, comb-ing through the wreckage of the Lodestar, decided that the plane had mechanically locked into a dive, and that the pilots could not extricate it. Within Ashland Oil—a very close-knit organization, the mourning was personal, but there was no blame to be attached to anyone.

After the first round of conversations, all held either in the Hotel Pierre or the Chase Manhattan Plaza in New York City (both Eastman Dillon and E. F. Hutton have offices in the same build-ing), both parties adjourned to prepare their organizations and calculations.

In October 1962, it was decided to move the negotiations to Houston, Texas, where United Carbon has its headquarters.

Ken Hill, who had meanwhile resigned from the United Carbon

[4] Rex Blazer, whom the men were journeying to meet in Ashland, boarded the company's remaining Lodestar, visited all the widows and families of the deceaseds; attended all the funerals.

board of directors, reserved first-class plane seats for himself and several lawyers; Eastman Dillon was to represent Ashland Oil. To Hill's astonishment, Mr. & Mrs. Blazer and Everett Wells entered the plane also, but proceeded to the tourist section.

The size of the negotiation was in the neighborhood of $150 million. One complex factor was in the method of calculating part of the payment of this enormous sum through production of oil from the United Carbon estimated reserves. In order to have this method succeed, the reserves had to be realistically esti-mated—and that area was one in which both Ken Hill and Frank Lindeman, the oil production vice president of United Carbon, excelled.

Mr. Coleman, on the other hand, was very conscious of his obligation to the board, employees and stockholders of United Carbon, a firm that had employed him as a consultant in 1933, and had since elevated him to the post of chairman of the board.

United Carbon had, actually, been the creation of a remarkable man named Oscar Nelson, who put together a group of small carbon black manufacturers in the 1920s, and built it in a fashion very similar to that of Mr. Blazer at Ashland Oil, into one of the top three carbon black companies in the world.

When Mr. Nelson died in 1953, two of his longtime associates managed the company for three and a half years, but a young president was clearly needed. Mr. Coleman, to whom the company turned, enlisted the aid of Ken Hill, and the two of them set-tled on Richard French, a vice president of Standard Oil of Ohio.

Once installed as president, French worked hard. Aware that he had experience mainly in one area, he studied corporate manage-ment privately and in special seminars; surrounded himself with men of similar, somewhat academic, bent. He found oil and gas, sparked ambitious research and development efforts in carbon black, located plants overseas, and on the surface moved rapidly.

"Directors cannot always tell how a company is performing," Ken Hill says, "until time has passed—enough time, at least, to compare promise with performance. By 1961, we were apprehen-sive."

By 1961, they had reason for their apprehension: United Carbon had slipped to a poor third in its industry; Cabot and Columbian Carbon seemed to be moving faster. Both Hill and Coleman felt the negotiations with Ashland to be well timed.

At the time of the discussions, French wanted a new five-year contract, had just constructed a new research and development building, had established headquarters in Houston, Texas (from Charleston, W. Va.). But some of the United Carbon operations were not profitable—notably its synthetic rubber plant in Texas—and although French kept saying this problem would be solved, it continued to drain earnings.

"We began to think," said Hill, "that French's oil and gas operations were supporting the synthetic rubber effort, and also masking weaknesses in the carbon black action."

"Many companies wanted to buy United Carbon," said Mr. Coleman later, "but almost all wanted to do so on the basis of a stock exchange. United's stock had held up well, but Ashland came with cash. In my view, their offer was excellent. I had a study made, and discovered the majority of United's shareholders had bought their stock at a price that would give them, if the Ashland offer was accepted, a profit of 100%."

Mr. Coleman paused, and said quietly, "It was my *obligation* to inform these shareholders of this opportunity."

The atmosphere of the final negotiations in late October 1962, therefore, was very propitious. Nevertheless, the negotiation was very large and Mr. Blazer wondered if it might not be *too* large.

Meanwhile the skies were darkening over the great world, and there was a stillness of imminent doom. A year before, in 1961, in the midst of their euphoria over their spectacular accomplishments in space, the men in the Kremlin suddenly became aware they were not as far ahead of the Americans as they had thought. In fact, they were behind. The U.S. had quietly slid sixteen submarines into the oceans, each armed with Polaris missiles equipped with nuclear warheads, capable of reaching and destroying Russia. Intermediate missile bases ringed the USSR; at these bases U.S. technicians were maintained by agreement of the host countries. Overhead U-2 planes flew, soaring at heights the Russians could not equal; they photographed every surface move the Russians made. Russia was both vulnerable and exposed.

One consequence of this realization was that the Soviet Union abruptly broke its pledged word and the moratorium on nuclear testing; clumsily set off, in the autumn of 1961, a monster 50-megaton thermonuclear device that fouled the world's atmosphere. Khrushchev, in a frenzy of exacerbated bitterness, declared no other nation had weapons so large.

But the real source of Khrushchev's rage was Russia's inability to directly menace the U.S., for at the time Russia had no intercontinental missiles that could reach our shores. It possessed only intermediate missiles.

Russia's solution was Cuba. During September 1962 (and perhaps earlier), the USSR began shipping missile technicians and parts for its IRBM's into the Red redoubt, where Fidel Castro, cocky since the exiles' abortive invasion, strutted and fulminated against the U.S. But the U-2's flew daily over Cuba, and the movement of men and their canvassed cargo soon attracted attention.

In various U.S. Government laboratories the U-2 photographs were enlarged and examined, and their meaning was unmistakable. Informed, the President reacted immediately.

On October 22, 1962, President Kennedy informed the nation that it confronted a nuclear gun, aimed at its temple, and the people held their breath.

To Ken Hill, in the middle of the negotiations underway between Ashland Oil and United Carbon, the experience was unforgettable. "We would negotiate and then listen to the radio," he recalled. He marveled at Mr. Blazer, whose calm was indestructible. "If war occurs," he remembers Mr. Blazer saying "then there is nothing we can do. But if it does not occur, and we do not conclude the business at hand, we will have wasted our time. Therefore we should apply ourselves."

So the negotiations in Houston continued and finally the weary men reached the largest point: Ashland would pay $150 million for United Carbon. Ninety-five million dollars would be paid in the form of oil production over a period of time, the balance was cash.

In order to raise this huge sum, Ashland planned to issue new debentures; it settled on a figure of $60 million. Five million dollars would be applied to settle some United Carbon debts.

At the very last moment, it was discovered that the sale would make United Carbon liable for substantial state taxes; Mr. Coleman thought first that Ashland should assume the whole liability, and then softened only slightly—not half way.

Mr. Blazer stuck. Half way or not at all. After several days of suspense, Mr. Coleman suggested that Eastman Dillon reduce its fee as its contribution to resolving the impasse. This succeeded in shifting the agony to a new quarter. The brokers joylessly agreed to this suggestion, however, and another point was passed.

Afterward, Mr. Blazer said of Mr. Coleman, "It was a pleasure to struggle with him."

And Mr. Coleman observed, "Mr. Blazer was a man of amazing resiliency; he was a hard and resourceful bargainer. Furthermore, he had trained his men to act in the same decisive school; to act with dispatch."

For both Orin Atkins and Ken Hill, the negotiation was one of the peaks of their lives. Hill had landed a coup for Eastman Dillon, Union Securities & Co. Within Ashland Oil, Atkins had arrived; he had played an integral role in the largest and probably most complex deal in the history of the company.

Both young men congratulated one another. Hill said, "It was obvious that Orin could sense a situation and move fast, and that he was being groomed."

SCALING THE MOUNTAIN

The importance of the negotiations regarding United Carbon was many-faceted: in addition to being the largest acquisition Ashland had made, it carried the company beyond the confines of its traditional activities; the rubber industry, through carbon black, loomed directly ahead.

While the United Carbon talks progressed, the management at Ashland had also been busy in the campaign against tolls, and in a search for alternatives in the event the campaign fell through.

The results of its search for alternatives emerged in early November 1962, almost simultaneously with the United Carbon issue, when the board was informed of the imminent purchase of the Central Louisiana pipeline system of Humble Oil & Refining. This system, which included a number of gathering lines, purchased most of the oil produced in that area, and could deliver 50,000 barrels of crude a day. Ashland would be able, with this line in its possession, to bring 40,000 barrels of Louisiana crude into its refineries, with the exception of oil for Catlettsburg, which could be put on the river barges at Cincinnati; from there to Catlettsburg even the suggested user charges would not make the transportation too expensive to be practical.

A glance at the map alone will not reveal the ramifications of the company's solution: it included various tie-ins with other pipeline systems operated by other oil companies at various places; the company could also build large river terminals in the event the tax threat abated.

For the time being, the new acquisition—which included the position of posting price for crude oil in the Louisiana region the line served—effectively removed both the refinery at Catlettsburg and the company from their former position of vulnerability to a crude oil shortage, and also reduced the critical nature of a waterways toll threat.

At this juncture, a final flare-up in negotiations between Ashland and Mr. Coleman occurred: this time over the fact that the United Carbon reserves were slightly lower than original estimates. According to the formula in the letter of agreement, Mr. Coleman's side would absorb that difference. He demurred, and offered to split the difference, and Mr. Blazer began to scramble out of the deal. He went so far, in fact, as to ask the Standard Oil of Ohio if it wanted to come in as a partner on the purchase, but that company, after putting the matter through the labyrinth of its organization, turned it down.

The entire Ashland top team, including Orin Atkins, Rex Blazer, Everett Wells, Bob Yancey and Mr. Blazer, reserved one of the small dining rooms in the company office for lunch and discussion. The review was exhaustive and the men blew hot and cold for several hours. The deal was, after all, immense. Standard of Ohio had turned down an opportunity to participate. Mr. Coleman was hard to overcome. The shareholders might object, the United Carbon company might not have good potential. But in the end, the decision was unanimous. They would go ahead.

The amount of money at issue was a little less than $500,000, but apparently it was the last straw that Mr. Blazer would not accept; Mr. Coleman, realizing this, capitulated on the point. Ashland Oil made the deal alone. Pending a disapproval of the stockholders of the two companies, and that was unlikely under the circumstances, the United Carbon and Ashland Oil companies were bound.

Against this moving backdrop, Ashland's year-end statement and annual report for 1962, showing (as of the end of September) net sales of $318 million and net earnings of $15.3 million, shone brightly; everyone mentally added United Carbon to this total and was impressed.

Ordinary citizens who are awed by the paperwork involved in the purchase of a home would be stunned by the details of this negotiation: it created a schedule of activities as closely coordinated as a military battle plan, stretching from December 19 to April 1. Every week carried steps to be taken—from the filing of proxy material with the SEC to the submission of evidence of distribution by the Managing Underwriters; between these milestones were wedged meetings of directors and stockholders, registration statements, mailings, printings, memorandums, receipts, the filling and filing of forms, tax rulings, price meetings, the listing of debentures, the preparation and completion of documents, loans, mortgages, checks, and a host of other necessary matters. In this operation, Orin Atkins acted as field general, and Mr. Blazer served as head of the general staff. The costs of these efforts in time, telephone calls, trips, hotels, travail and trouble, ran into many thousands of dollars.

1963

While this large undertaking was launched, Everett Wells signed an agreement to buy Humble's Louisiana Ferriday pipeline system, a network extending 500 miles in that area, for $3.5 million; the

Lodestar was busy shuttling men back and forth to Houston, Texas, to Natchez, Mississippi, to New York; by mid-January (the usual Christmas parties passed in a blur for the management), the seventy-page Ashland proxy statement was prepared and printed (United Carbon's proxy statement ran sixty pages and was finished at the same time); the indentures covering $25 million in sinking funds due in 1988 and $35 million in sinking fund subordinated convertible debentures due in 1993—formidable documents running to one hundred pages—were also ready and mailed.

At the same time, plans long fallow began to bear fruit: a 67-mile Parish pipeline, laid in partnership with Placid Oil Co., went into service; the company obtained a 34-acre tract on the western outskirts of Lexington; the Ferriday purchase was slated to take effect on July 1; it had already been decided to start construction on a new $300,000 terminal for storage of crude oil near Natchez; the crude oil department, totaling its figures, estimated Ashland was now obligated to take 100,000 barrels of crude oil in excess of its needs, and at the moment, as if by black magic, a new field was discovered in western Kentucky producing more than 5,000 barrels a day.

Among the top management figures at United Carbon, Frank Lindeman seemed most impressive to Ashland. Mr. Lindeman was in charge of oil exploration and development, and Mr. Blazer, always searching for the man who could find oil for Ashland, was highly impressed; so was Everett Wells. They made plans to reorganize the Ashland oil and exploration department and put Lindeman in operating charge; they planned other steps while awaiting official word from Washington on whether or not the marriage could be consummated (they had already obtained informal approval).

Other questions arose: Who would go to Houston? The Ashland management was already as thin as a wafer, considering the size of the company; the need for basic changes was upon them.

Until the acquisition of United Carbon, virtually every company brought into the Ashland orbit was in practically the same business. It was relatively simple for the refinery experts to evaluate another refinery; for transportation to look over towboats and barges; for the oil and gas men to assess properties; for marketing to add another product and string of service stations, or customers, to their lists. But United Carbon was in carbon black—an industry the Ashland men knew only vaguely; its structure was highly organized; it had a number of high-salaried executives; it was a public corporation with many shareholders.

Mr. French was already known to the men of Ashland, but his vice presidents were not; Ashland invited them; they were widely introduced and observed. On the whole, they made excellent impressions.

Huddling together, the top five at Ashland agreed to shift all the Ashland sales to Rex Blazer's broad shoulders. That meant that henceforth Chub Moffitt and his R. J. Brown division, which included Bronoco, et al., would report to Rex; so would Palmer Talbutt and refinery sales. Only United Carbon would be held out; but Hugh Jenks and asphalt, Frank Colegrove and Allied Oil, Earl Weaver and branded marketing would be joined by the others under Rex.

Everett Wells would keep an eye on oil and gas matters—which in 1963 would account for two-thirds of the company's capital expenditures; Bob Yancey, who watched over refinery operations, would report to Everett.

Orin Atkins would work on finance, watch over matters legal and accounting, relations with the financial community, the government and related areas, and continue to work with Mr. Blazer on acquisitions.

And United Carbon would remain under Dick French, although the various departments in that organization could contact their counterparts in Ashland for help, advice and assistance.

On February 18, 1963, the government gave a favorable tax ruling on the United Carbon acquisition, and three days later the Ashland debentures were oversubscribed. From this moment, Ashland Oil & Refining was big business.

But this was not the final step. That could not be concluded till the stockholders of both companies were told and approved the specifics of the transaction; until proper documents had been prepared and copies filed with the SEC; until the proxies and the votes had been collected and tabulated; until the oil and gas reserves had been checked by an independent group; and many other matters resolved.

Mr. Blazer dictated a letter to the Ashland directors and made plans to go to Houston for a check-up; Orin Atkins, tireless, plunged into the details of the new debenture issue; Everett Wells and his oil experts pored over the details of the new properties and the caliber of men United Carbon might bring them

The press, of course, followed the course of the United Carbon acquisition avidly; so did the rest of the carbon black industry, and the business community of Houston, Texas, where Mr. French had become extremely well known.

The ink was hardly dry on all the agreements, however, when Ashland, like most new purchasers, began to notice irritating flaws that had seemed minor before. Phillips Petroleum had a suit against United Carbon. During negotiations this suit had not loomed large, but Ashland, on closer examination, took it more seriously than did the executives of United Carbon. Then there was the losing synthetic rubber operations. Mr. Blazer also came to the conclusion that the United Carbon management was extravagant—an attribute to which he was notoriously averse.

"We do not believe in using profits from one division to support losses in another," he wrote the directors; he suspected the United Carbon management of holding other views.

On April 2, 1963, as though to verify Mr. Blazer's private comments, Rex Blazer gave a speech before the first annual meeting of the National Petroleum Refiners Association[5] in San Antonio, Texas. Mr. & Mrs. Blazer, who had traveled for the purpose from Ashland, were in the audience.

Pointing out the paradox whereby refinery experts labored to save money that the industry often lost in gasoline wars, the

[5] The new association had been formed by a merger between the National Petroleum Association, of which Rex Blazer was president, and the Western Petroleum Refiners Association, in which he was a vice president. In this dual capacity, he had been instrumental in bringing the two groups together.

younger Blazer described the industry-wide awakening to its technical weaknesses in 1958, and said "Each branch of the industry thinks it is being denied its share of the profits."

He said that large oil companies use their profits from crude oil production to subsidize their refining and marketing operations, and warned this practice would lead to the elimination of the depletion allowance tax if continued.

The speech created quite a flap, because it paralleled the arguments of critics of the oil depletion allowance; it also served notice that Ashland, although a giant, still acted and thought as an independent. The oil industry press gave it unusual prominence; all the Blazers were pleased.

Walker Marx, refinery superintendent at Catlettsburg, was the first Ashland man transferred to United Carbon in Houston. The management wanted a production expert of its own to learn the specifics of manufacturing carbon black. Officially, Marx was to act as a staff assistant to United vice president McKenzie. The accounting operations of United Carbon were shifted to Ashland; Frank Lindeman toured the Ashland oil and gas organization as preparation for a reorganization. Meanwhile there was enough ongoing business at Ashland to keep everyone busy.

In April 1963, Ashland sales continued up to hit a new high of more than $30 million—the figures keep getting larger and larger —for the first time, were averaging $1 million a day.

When news of Ashland's acquisition of the Ferriday pipeline reached the press, it was accompanied by an Ashland price listing lowering the price of crude in that Louisiana district. The outraged cries of these producers reached all the way to the Governor's office, and an investigation was threatened.

And during these months, the analysts of Wall Street kept bringing out statements on Ashland Oil; the company was now prominent on their maps.

The balance of the spring and summer passed swimmingly: in July 1963, FDR Jr., Undersecretary of Commerce, visited the region and met Mr. Blazer and the other members of Ashland's management; was duly impressed with the awfulness of river tolls. That same month the first crude oil tow was loaded from the new

Natchez terminal; oil continued to flow copiously in western Kentucky, Mr. and Mrs. Blazer entertained C. C. Desai, head of an Indian group that would share in creating a carbon black plant in India; Bob Yancey met some executives from U.S. Rubber (now Uniroyal) and learned more about carbon black than he knew before. It was then decided that young John Hall would become Ashland's man in residence at Houston.

On August 2, 1963, Hall reported at French's office, ready to go to work, and Mr. French informed him that he had resigned that very morning. The resignation, embodied in a short note, had followed a board meeting at Ashland where many thorny problems involving United Carbon had been discussed; Mr. French, who had been made a vice president of Ashland and a member of its board, had not had an easy time.

"Dick French was never really comfortable in business," said Sylvan Coleman, of E. F. Hutton & Co. "He would visit me, and very often the discussion would take a philosophical turn."

For his part, when he was later asked his analysis of Mr. French's resignation, Mr. Blazer had similar views. "He operated," said Mr. Blazer, "out of a textbook; he was impressed by the Harvard School of Business and similar theories. Naturally, we regarded him as a good man and wanted to keep him. And we tried to make him happy; we did not succeed."

Mr. French, however, did not reflect any particular unhappiness in his note of resignation. He said simply that ". . . single leadership and lowest feasible expense now becomes essential for the best progress and profits of the company." Then he departed on a trip around the world, and on his return attended some special courses at the University of California. In his summing up, he said, "How much money is enough? One million, ten million, thirty million? I had enough money; my children were grown. I wanted to do more with my life, and I discovered that I liked and enjoyed young people."

He decided, finally, on teaching, and is now an assistant dean of business administration at Ohio State University; a happy man.

But young John Hall was left sitting in the president's chair at United Carbon with, said Mr. Blazer, "no authority whatever." Obviously the Ashland management had placed an observer on

Rexford S. Blazer (1965)

the scene; later, Hall was to say that the executives Mr. French had selected were not overly impressed with the observer's abilities. If that is so, it was an error, for beneath a somewhat boyish exterior[6] Hall had discerning eyes. He watched, listened and evaluated with an intelligence that penetrated the situation with great clarity.

It was not a happy one. Mr. French's executive group spent a great deal of their time in meetings, doted on memoranda and in creating systems of protocol. One result was that the operating men were blocked from a free exchange with the policymakers; the files bulged with recommendations that gathered dust.

Personal relationships in this Byzantine arrangement resembled those at any court: the atmosphere was charged with intrigue and suspicion.

[6] He was only 31.

Orin E. Atkins (1965)

The Ashland management, discerning this situation both through Hall's reports and its own observations, created opportunities for the policymakers of United Carbon to make lucrative[7] exits, and accepting John Hall's recommendations, allowed the operating men to put their long-pent recommendations into practice.

The effect was electric: the earnings of the carbon black section began to move upward, and the decline of the company was not only arrested, but altered to an upward trend. To assist in the new movement, Ashland also sent Bill Gammon, a top member of the technical brain trust, to Houston to head up research and development.

One of the side benefits of the United Carbon acquisition was the arrival of Morrison M. (Budge) Bump[8] on the Ashland scene. A tall, florid and versatile businessman, Bump had at one time been United Carbon's marketing director; his knowledge of the

[7] Most of the United Carbon management had generous stock options.

[8] Morrison M. Bump, born in New York City in 1919, graduated from Andover Academy in 1937 and attended Yale. Joined the Union Paste Company of Hyde Park, Mass., in 1940 and became president of the firm from 1957–1959; joined United Carbon as Director of Marketing and executive vice president of its marketing subsidiary from 1959 to 1962; joined Ashland Oil in 1963 and is today an executive assistant.

company, he thought, might be valuable to Ashland Oil. But both Orin Atkins and Mr. Blazer, assessing Bump's talents, thought he might be more valuable in initiating acquisitions, and this estimate proved correct.

Toward the end of August 1963, in the midst of the United Carbon developments, with business booming in all directions, word came from Louisville, Kentucky, that J. Fred Miles had died.

Mr. Miles had dropped from the records of the company after he left in 1928, but of course he had not disappeared; he had remained on the Kentucky scene, active and interested.

In Louisville he was known as General Miles; shortly after Happy Chandler was elected Governor of Kentucky, the institution of Kentucky Colonels, a graceful way of honoring outstanding citizens and celebrities, became popular again. Chandler summoned J. Fred Miles to his office and, in an elaborate ceremony, made him commanding general of this titular army; the General enjoyed the distinction immensely: Mr. Miles had an active sense of drama.

He had continued, after he left the Swiss Oil Company, to operate with the shrewdness with which Mr. Blazer always credited him; had built the Miles Park Racetrack (he was always fond of horses and had an excellent racing stable all through the years); operated the Lafitte Oil Company and found oil in Louisiana; died wealthy, respected and popular, at the age of seventy-nine.

Mr. Blazer attended the funeral. "We are indebted to him," he wrote the directors, "as one of the incorporators, and the person most active in the organization of our company."

The momentum of the company was such that it outpaced the analysts; they were persistently describing where it had been—the target itself was usually ahead of their estimates. For instance, during the early autumn of 1963 Ashland had become the largest gatherer (through its pipelines) and purchaser of crude oil in the states of Kentucky, Indiana and Ohio. In Illinois its purchases equalled Sohio's, and it may have refined more; although the majors dominated the situation as a whole in crude oil purchases in Louisiana, Ashland was dominant in the central area; in Mississippi Ashland bought 23,000 barrels of crude a day; it was an important purchaser in Oklahoma, Wyoming, Montana and Canada as well.

Exactly what it means to be a dominant purchaser of crude oil is illustrated by the fact that when Ashland posted lower crude oil prices in the Illinois Basin, the producers there talked about appealing to Washington: a reaction that does not indicate that Ashland was at their mercy. Mr. Blazer found the increasing tendency of crude oil producers to run to government agencies for help a particularly vexing and onerous development; he could not understand why, he said, producers felt the laws of supply and demand should be suspended in their favor, when no such protection (particularly against falling prices) was offered the manufacturer of finished petroleum products. At first, this reaction strikes as flinty, but a recollection of the long record reminds one that Ashland itself had a record of continuing its purchases no matter how low the product market fell, and itself never whimpered at market vicissitudes.

Because the company management found itself almost continually in motion, more airplanes were added: a new Twin Cessna and a DC-3 joined the fleet. More office space was rented in Ashland.

Permission having finally been granted, the Interprovincial Pipeline of Canada built its spur pipeline into the Buffalo plant, and Ashland was receiving 10,000 barrels a day through this conduit; Aminol had found a new field in the Neutral Zone, and—as though to repeat the ironies of the incessant dips and sways of business—there was some discussion between Ralph Davies and Mr. Blazer about Ashland Oil buying Mr. Davies' share of that international venture.

The fiscal year ended and the accountants dove into their baskets to count numbers. This process had been speeded somewhat by the additional equipment and experts brought into the firm by the United Carbon addition, and the results, swollen by the addition of United Carbon, reached large figures indeed: net sales of $490 million; net profits of $20.9 million. The company had taken a giant step forward.

But no chronicle, however tangential, can pass silently over the assassination on November 22, 1963 of President Kennedy while he rode in a motorcade in Dallas. The effects and impact of the tragedy were lifted from what might have been an impersonal into an intensely human and traumatic event by the presence of television—which translated its meaning into immediate terms for the entire nation.

The stability of the government and the economy of the nation has seldom, however, been better illustrated; President Johnson assumed office and retained much of the direction of his predecessor, and little immediate change took place otherwise.

In Houston the following month (December 1963), Frank Lindeman died of what Mr. Blazer, from his store of accumulated knowledge on the subject, thought was a coronary thrombosis. It was known that Mr. Lindeman had suffered from angina and had to take nitroglycerin tablets to relieve these pains; Mr. Blazer learned that Mr. Lindeman had taken three such tablets without experiencing relief, and remarked that he himself had standing orders to consider it an emergency if he took two without relief. All of the management men at Ashland had formed a high opinion of Mr. Lindeman, and they were devastated to lose a man they had hoped would propel their exploration and development efforts forward. A series of conversations and evaluations for a successor began at once.

They settled, finally, on Cramen Stanton Jr., the chief geologist for United Carbon. Mr. Stanton had his work cut out for him: fields in Morrow County, Ohio, were opening up; more than sixty rigs were operating, most belonging to independents, and Ashland planned to drill at least 25 wells almost immediately.

Two days before Christmas 1963, Mr. Blazer received a letter from old friend Joe Levin, of A. G. Becker. In his letter, Mr. Levin noted that it was exactly twenty years ago that he and Mr. Blazer had put forward the first Ashland Oil & Refining issue—a 4½ per cent convertible preferred stock. That year the Ashland net income was $771,939.

Since then, the net income had been at a compounded growth rate of 18 per cent a year. Stockholders equity had multiplied more than twenty times.

"This record," Mr. Levin wrote, "is a most impressive testi-
monial to the caliber of the management the company has enjoyed. From what I have observed, you have put together a management team and an organization that could well duplicate this
performance in the next twenty years. This is, perhaps, an even
greater achievement . . ."

And so the year ended.

1964

The new year entered to the sounds of an old-fashioned oil
boom in Morrow County; Ashland Oil was the largest company
to enter the area—having the advantage of a pipeline there—and
Mr. Blazer, whose interest in crude oil exploration and development deepened as the years passed, made himself very active in
the situation. As usual, the rest of the management of the company, seeing that he had busied himself in this area, worked with
him when he requested it, and for the rest, handled other ongoing
matters.

One interesting side development was that Mr. Blazer began
working with young Jim Vandeveer,[9] on a number of crude oil
ventures in Ohio and elsewhere.

[9] James Vandeveer, born 1925, spent the formative years of his childhood on a farm W. W. Vandeveer purchased in Ohio; graduated from
UCLA with a B.S., having majored in business with a science minor.
Tall as his father and even huskier, was in the Army during World War
II where he became middleweight champion of the Infantry. In 1940, he
put in a brief stint as a salesman at Allied Oil; met Paul Blazer for the
first time in 1946. In 1952, young Vandeveer left Cleveland to assume control of Vanson (an enterprise kept out of the Allied Oil merger) that
owned 5 oil and gas wells in Louisiana. Vanson was losing; had debts of
$2 million. W. W. Vandeveer turned over his 100,000 shares in Ashland
Oil to his son as capital. Young Vandeveer built the company into a
success; returned his father's stock and by agreement received 25 per cent
for his accomplishment. He then joined Jim Breuil to buy an Oklahoma
company that had wells and promising leases; found oil in Colorado
and Oklahoma; ventured as far afield as Australia; built a home in Dallas
and is now a neighbor of Jimmy Ling; has for years been close friends
with the Hunts.

When he succeeded with Vanson, Jim Vandeveer began to receive tele-

Young Vandeveer proved to be a born entrepreneur, and Mr. Blazer, increasingly wistful regarding this talent as the years passed, was moved to write the directors (again) about the difficulty of finding a man to join Ashland's payroll who would put this gift at the disposal of the company's exploration and production department. "The trouble is," he said, "that they can make so much money on their own." It was one of the rare times that he came close to a complaint, but under the circumstances he could hardly be blamed.

The Ashland joy at the Ohio oil discoveries was soon cooled, however, by an announcement from Washington that the Secretary of the Interior was "shocked at the uncontrolled practices in . . . Ohio." A great many people seemed shocked, in fact, and agitation arose—as though from the very ground—for a quota to be clapped onto the state.

At about the same time, President Johnson, in his budget speech to Congress, came out strongly for special river taxes that were even higher than those proposed by President Kennedy; the new President went on to say that he believed fees should be extended wherever government services provide special benefits: the threat of tolls, a perennial apparition, seemed to arise on every occasion.

Nearer home, the union local at Catlettsburg signed an agreement, and in an unexpected gesture, asked that Mr. Blazer personally attend the signing. It had been at least twenty years since he had personally negotiated, but his presence in the valley seemed, by this time, patriarchal; the contract was for three years.

Other persons throughout the state seemed similarly thoughtful of Mr. Blazer. Kentucky organized a Constitutional Convention, with the delegates limited to fifty persons; Mr. Blazer was one of those asked to serve. When it convened, he was called to the rostrum and was asked to be Temporary Chairman; the newspapers of the state showed him holding the gavel during what amounted to an impromptu ceremony; ex-Governor and U.S. Senator Earl Clements was elected permanent chairman.

Recurring efforts to update Kentucky's constitution had in-

---

phone calls from Mr. Blazer. He was at first astonished when Mr. Blazer said he wanted counsel; came to enjoy these conversations; has continued over the years to remain a director of Ashland.

volved Mr. Blazer in 1947, when he was head of the state campaign, and again in 1960 when the changes failed to obtain approval from the voters. In 1964 his eagerness and activity on the subject would amaze the younger men in the company.[10]

Meanwhile, a stream of analysts began to visit Ashland; the top four gave talks before the New York Security Analysts, a group of investment bankers in northern Ohio; Bob Yancey explained to the National Petroleum Refiners' Association how asphalt had grown from a relatively simple product into a multi-faceted specialty with many applications; Rex Blazer, considered the best speechmaker in the company, made many appearances. The nature of the company's public relations was undergoing a subtle shift. It was becoming less regional, and more blue chip.

It should not be forgotten that descriptions of motion are equal to descriptions of time; Palmer Talbutt, that brash young man who stopped young Jim Snyder at the refinery one day and said, "Do you know who I am? I'm *P.C.T.*", was 65 years old in 1964; one reads this with astonishment, and a host of anecdotes come flooding back to mind.

On one occasion, leaving with a group of men from Pittsburgh —with everyone heading in different directions—Talbutt (who of course knew the airline schedule perfectly) swung around to the girl at the ticket counter and said, "Give me a ticket on your next plane."

"Where do you want to go, sir?" she asked.

"Anywhere," Talbutt replied. *"I've got business everywhere."*

Retirement at Ashland was a sometime thing: obviously with younger men moving up—and moving fast—older men had to make way. Yet to lose their experience and contacts was more than the company could consider wise. Mr. Blazer solved his problem by continuing as an extra member of the top team, operating without any real authority, but nevertheless influentially—as long as his abilities were present.

A similar arrangement was made with Palmer Talbutt: he be-

[10] In particular, Arloe Mayne, who worked closely with him on this project. Mayne found the experience exhilarating.

came a full-time consultant, and Joe Davis moved into the top spot in refinery sales.

Other signs of change appeared. Bob Gordon, the doughty Chicago financier who had been on the board of directors longer than anyone except Mr. Blazer and Charles S. Evans, resigned from the board because of disability. Mr. Blazer, who had gone through the fires of the depression with Mr. Gordon, and who talked to him regularly several times a week over the phone, was fast losing his contemporaries.

In August 1964, the *National Petroleum News* placed Mr. Blazer in its Hall of Fame, together with Samuel M. Kier. The practice is to select two men at a time. Samuel Kier was the industry's first important refiner and marketer, who had been in business a hundred years earlier. Mr. Blazer, on receiving this honor, was one of the handful of the living to be so selected. The others were J. Paul Getty and J. Howard Pew.

Mr. Blazer was, of course, pleased. But the honor highlights the fact that the laurels he received from the world were, in comparison to his accomplishments, rather scant. They consisted in the main of honorary degrees from Marshall University, Centre College, Pikeville College in Kentucky, and Wilberforce College in Wilberforce, Ohio, and an LL.D. and the Sullivan Medallion (a high honor) from the University of Kentucky. When great industrialists of the United States were mentioned in the national press, his name was seldom included. He had the ironic distinction of being one of the nation's more important men, but of being known only to the extremely well informed.

An absence of effort to obtain credit had much to do with this: Mr. Blazer's name had virtually been dropped from the public print for years. Few persons—even within the company—knew the extent of his involvement with its activities.

But the corporation itself was receiving more credit daily, in the circles that mattered to its economic destinies. Politically, like most corporations, it was neutral; it neither endorsed nor opposed any candidates, and hoped that no candidates would arise whose platform included an attack against hard work—that being their major preoccupation.

Nevertheless, the company was beginning to move in larger circles. Rex Blazer described luncheon at the White House (in company with other oil industry executives) and the comments of the President and some members of his Cabinet; Ashland was far from its once-obscure position. Neither could the company really complain of a lack of attention from informed and discerning circles; practically every major business publication seemed to include the firm in its periodic examinations—a fairly remarkable phenomenon because the firm did not employ any public relations experts.

In corporate terms, its board of directors was mixed between insiders and outsiders: eight members were officers in the company and eight were not. But the outsiders were not all the way out, most of them being large stockholders.

The 1964 elections, with their Johnson landslide, coincided with the accountants' reports on the 1964 fiscal year results: net sales of $527 million, net earnings of $27 million. The firm was moving forward in seven-league boots.

In October 1964, Bill Gammon was made a vice president of United Carbon, and John Hall, his tasks completed in Houston, was brought back to Ashland and made an executive assistant to the corporation; Bill Seaton was brought to the seventh floor as an executive assistant to work primarily with Rex Blazer; younger faces and men were appearing on the seventh floor.

In *Fortune's 500* that fall—a list prepared mainly on the basis of performances a year earlier—Ashland Oil had moved up ten places to No. 153. In reality, conservative accounting kept the firm lower on the list than the realities of the competitive situation but the management was not concerned.

One indication of its actual strength, however, and one that was to open many eyes, was the Pure Oil situation. Pure Oil, a firm whose operations resembled Ashland's in a territory that stretched farther south, came onto the auction block that fall, and offers ranged from $700 million to $750 million. The first of these purchase offers—as far as the public knew—came from a group consisting of Allied Chemical, Consolidated Coal Company and

Carl M. Rhoades & Co. Later, this group withdrew, and their places as suitors were taken by Laird & Co., Crichton Oil Company and Francis I. DuPont & Company, whose offer went to $750 million.

Orin Atkins, Mr. Blazer and the other men of Ashland watched this minuet with absorbed attention; they had studied Pure Oil and had decided that its operations were weak in precisely the areas where they themselves were most expert; were sure they could revitalize the operation. They busied themselves in planning how they could approach a merger.

At this point, another of the long-time associates died: Mr. W. W. Vandeveer. A remarkable combination of brawn and charm, he suffered a heart attack at home. He had been on the verge of resigning from the board; he was replaced by his son, Jim Vandeveer, whose abilities had been clearly evidenced.

Shortly after this, Bill Gammon, who had moved rapidly and well in the reorganization and quickening of United Carbon, was made president of that important subsidiary. Gammon had disclosed an excellent grasp of business as well as science; the choice was universally approved. Arnold Leas ascended to the post of research and development director, assisted by Scotty Patrick and Harold Sullivan.

"Orin and I," Mr. Blazer wrote the directors, "are working on some new mergers."

On that familiar note, the year 1964 ended.

1965

After the annual meeting early in January 1965, therefore, the newly elected board returned to the director's room on the seventh floor at the Winchester Avenue building in Ashland,[11] and ratified the team's recommendations.

Bob Yancey moved up to become senior vice president, and Orin E. Atkins, 41 years old, became president.

[11] Where an oil painting of Mr. Blazer overlooks a long, shining, walnut table surrounded by green leather armchairs.

Everett Wells (1965)

Other changes, moving the escalator forward, were concurrent: Bill Seaton moved along the seventh floor from an office beside Rex Blazer's to one alongside Orin Atkins; Bob McCowan moved up a floor from refinery sales to take Seaton's old post; John Hall became executive assistant to Mr. Blazer.

The changes were approved by the members of the board, who knew all the protagonists well, and releases went out to the world. In many respects, they provided proof of the Ashland management's unique qualities: neither Everett Wells nor Rex Blazer had yet reached sixty; both Atkins and Yancey were in their early forties. The only adequate comparison might be an army in the field, as far as the mixture of age groups is concerned.

The new line-up, consisting as it did of a subtle blend of Mr. Blazer, Rex Blazer, Everett Wells, Orin Atkins and Bob Yancey —and a group of younger men standing on the stage beside them —resembled a very old-fashioned portrait, with three generations represented. It meant the continuity of the company was established (barring accident, of course), for many years to come—as many years, perhaps, as the life of the company to date. A highly unusual and farsighted arrangement.

The pace of operations continued brisk. By March 1965, United's carbon black production was three times larger than before while operating costs remained largely the same; a hasty look at the landscape reveals, that month, that Everett

Wells was on his way back to Ashland after a business trip to England, Europe and the Middle East; Rex Blazer in Washington; Chub Moffitt and his new vice president for Bronoco, Edward A. Von Doersten, in St. Louis; Buck Weaver readying a speech before the Ohio Oil & Gas Association. As usual, we learn that "interesting negotiations are underway." A glance out the porthole from the corporate vessel gives the traveler the impression that though the landscape and activities change, the vessel stays the same.

This is, of course, deceptive. Hearings were held in Washington on the oil import program; the Secretary of the Interior was concerned, as were many other persons, with the paradox of fading oil reserves in the U.S. while refining capacity and national needs grew. There were other entities with more immediate concerns; objections were raised to the practice of exchanging import quotas —a practice that Ashland followed—in favor of a tariff.

The curious position of Ashland Oil on the national scene was again highlighted when *Forbes* magazine published a list of twenty-one oil companies and how they had fared in the market over a period of eleven years; Ashland was not among those listed. Men inside the company copied the data, however, and inserted Ashland into its statistical position; based on an appreciation of its market advance, it ranked fourth; in return on equity capital, third. Obviously, some author had used the library more than his spyglass.

Robert E. Yancey (1965)

While Orin Atkins took the stump in favor of the tri-state air-port—a project badly needed in rail-locked Ashland, the *National Petroleum News* published a savage article calling the exchange of import quotas a $175-million oil industry featherbed. Mr. Blazer, who had, decades before, wondered aloud why the consumer should pay for elaborate transportation routes when companies could arrange exchanges and thus keep their prices down, merely sighed. "The trade press," he said in one of his letters, now growing less frequent, but still as chatty and discursive as ever, "has reflected the viewpoints of the major companies as long as I can remember."

A letter came in from a stockholder who had listened to an analyst describe the oil industry, and who wanted to know why Ashland was not more like other companies. In particular, he was concerned about the troubles ascribed publicly to Pure Oil. It was being widely bruited that Pure's difficulty stemmed from the fact that it did not produce its own crude oil. (Pure operated four refineries; its sales doubled in ten years, but according to some analysts, Pure had to buy half the crude oil it processed outside the company for $3 a barrel, when it could have processed its own crude for $1: to this single cause the analyst ascribed all its difficulties.)

Mr. Blazer, replying gravely, said this view was ". . . typical of those most security analysts held some years ago . . ." Today, he explained, the difficulties are in securing markets. Regarding crude oil, he went on, "there is a serious oversupply."

"Reserves of oil," he said, "are, in many cases, held for years before they can obtain a market." It was a buyer's market, he said, as far as crude oil was concerned, and he denied that there was much resemblance between Pure Oil's position and methods, and Ashland Oil. "We are more like Union Oil of California," he answered.

The exchange raises an interesting point. It is fairly obvious that the chances of two companies' operating in exactly the same way is as remote as individuals being able to do so. Yet the myth that such insane identicality exists in both men and companies is probably one of the more prevalent of fallacies.

Early in March 1965, it became generally known that Ashland Oil and the Hunt oil interests had made a joint offer to buy Pure Oil at a price that would work out to $70 a share. The news came as a further development in a gradually unfolding situation that had kept the business community, and particularly the oil community, in a state of absorbed attention for some months. According to *Fortune,* in its recapitulation of the situation, Pure had been entering the shadows since 1961, although only an examination of the differences between its reports to the Internal Revenue Service and the subsequent tax advantages it gained from the nature of its operations, made this progression clear.

As the news of its managerial difficulties became more widely known, however, offers to take the company over came from a variety of quarters. The first of these, sparked by Loeb, Rhoades & Company, amounted to some $600 million; the second, from another group, to about $65 a share, or $700 million. Union Oil of California offered about $67.50 a share, and Pure Oil recommended this deal to its stockholders. Not all the stockholders were pleased: a dissident group believed that better arrangements could be made, and Ashland Oil's offer seemed to fit this expectation.

Pure Oil's management found a variety of reasons for saying they preferred not to see the company sold to Ashland Oil and the Hunt interests—among the rationalizations they conjured was the spectre of government disapproval, although Ashland had already learned no such objections existed. The Ashland team, however, had studied the situation carefully. In their analysis, Pure's manufacturing costs were higher than Ashland's; its crude oil costs were higher; its general overhead higher; and Ashland felt confident it could manage these same operations more economically and hence more profitably. It was an attractive opportunity for the Ashland shareholders.

They saw the company trot off, hand in hand, to marry the corporation from the Golden West, Union Oil of California, with all the sensations of a disappointed suitor. When they removed their eyes from the vanished target of their desire, it was to realize that the business community was, for the first time, looking at

The Blazers—Georgia and Paul—and Palmer Talbutt; the Blazers were celebrating the 50th anniversary of their first meeting. (1966)

Ashland itself with new eyes. Any firm that could, so quickly, raise almost $1 billion deserved the attention.

Very few observers, apparently, had realized the extent of Ashland's growth; the knowledge that it could summon up the resources for such a deal—even without the Hunts (who withdrew before the offer was finally rejected, for reasons that had nothing to do with the negotiation), caused a type of implosion that altered the atmosphere.

That was in June 1965. At the same time, Ashland announced an increase in the price of benzene, and this move was followed by Shell and United States Steel. The company was awarded a contract by the government for 62 per cent of the United States requirements for the thermally stable jet fuel used in the soaring U-2's, the balance was divided between Shell and Humble (whose work in this material was more widely known); in *Fortune's 500*, Ashland ranked second in "increase in net profit" with 31.5 per cent; fifth in "return on invested profit" with 14.1 per cent; seventh in "increase in sales" with 7.7 per cent among petroleum companies.

In October 1965, Ashland announced that negotiations had been concluded to buy the Catalin Corporation of New Jersey, a manufacturer of antioxidants, phenolic, urea and acrylic resins, color concentrates and molding compounds, for an amount of stock announced at some $8 million. Although, as usual, many details remained to be concluded, including the complex minuet required by the SEC (Catalin was listed on the American Exchange), the core of the bargaining between the two managements took only four days. The purchase extended Ashland's interests deeper into chemicals; Rex Blazer and Orin Atkins, going through motions with which they were both very familiar, immediately flew to Catalin to address its employees and assure them that they had joined a decent vessel.

Mr. Blazer, meanwhile, declared in a letter to the directors that ". . . if I were some years younger, the most important thing I could do for the company would be to spend all my time in Washington organizing the political opposition to tolls on the waterways." That pressure, apparently as regular as the morning sun, seemed deathless. Neither logic nor persuasion seemed to conclude the debate whose requirements drew, time and again, on the energies of the defenders; they were cast in the role of Sisyphus.

Equally indefatigable, Mr. Blazer attended, with other men from the company, the seventieth annual meeting of the Ohio Valley Improvement Association where he greeted his friends warmly; he was one of those who rose to honor the efforts of Representative Mike Kirwan, a staunch advocate of free waterways.

The leaves of autumn turned scarlet as 1965 drew toward its close; the refineries averaged 166,000 barrels of crude daily; a new cyclohexane unit performed well; the five domestic plants of United Carbon operated at near capacity, others were being operated overseas; undeveloped acres for crude exploration extended to well over a million; asphalt sales went up another 21 per cent; the string of owned or controlled stations for branded products grew to 3,500; a new pipeline terminal began carrying products out of Atlanta; the company acquired Kyova Pipe Company which brought in two more plants for $3 million; the number of employees grew to 7,600; the number of new units, extensions and expansions seems endless.

Net sales for 1965 went up to $604.8 million; net earnings to over $35 million; with a start of surprise it is noted that the company had doubled in size since 1959—six short years.

By December 1965, Ashland was beginning to experience some of the pain, as well as the pleasures, of being a large public corporation whose every move was followed by a host of observers seeking some special advantage. The tight money market forced interest rates up. One consequence was that some institutions began to sell their Ashland convertible 3⅞ per cent debentures for more attractive holdings. The debentures were, in turn, snapped up by arbitragers, who converted them into Ashland common stock they then dumped on the market in large quantities, in short sales. This complex and highly professional maneuver put pressure on Ashland's common stock. The top team on the seventh floor watched this procedure and its effect with little pleasure, and began to consider ways and means to protect the company and the stock, as well as the average investor, from these profiteers.

A tight money market, however, has its bright as well as dark side. In years past, thanks to a conservative accounting system and a habit of husbanding its cash Ashland Oil was able to go bargain hunting during difficult market periods; those had constituted, as a result, some of the best years of the company's life. The year 1966 was to be no exception.

1966

For Mr. Blazer, the year started off miserably; he had developed an extreme allergy, and blisters broke out over half his body.

At first the doctors thought his incredible varieties of medicines had begun to war upon each other, but after a number of tests, it was determined he had developed a rare staphylococcic infection. The only medicine that would affect this was so powerful he could endure its side effects only at intervals. In the interim he suffered, literally, like Job.

In this extremity, the affairs of the company was the only subject that could cause him to forget himself, and cradling his telephone on the pillow, he engaged in talkathons with persons all over the country, very few of whom suspected that the light voice, speaking so rapidly into the phone, was accompanied by such dreadful difficulties.

While the attention of the top management of the company was divided between their heavy operating tasks and a number of interesting new acquisitions, Mr. Blazer's attention returned to the refineries: his first and most lasting love.

He began to call the night operators; they were amazed to hear from him after so many years, but in answer to his questions they began to tell him about conditions on their shift.

While Mr. Blazer was thus finding his own form of relief, Orin Atkins and Everett Wells appeared in Washington at oil import hearings, a subject of constant assessment.

Atkins' statement at these hearings is interesting, among other reasons, because it reveals how the company's private opinion of its area has extended over the years: it is now described as being "bounded by the Mississippi River, the Canadian Border, Tennessee and Virginia, and the East Coast. . . . we are currently refining 170,000 barrels of crude oil a day . . . producing approximately 20,000 barrels of crude oil and liquids a day . . . 8,000 barrels a day in Venezuela and Canada . . . own 14 per cent of Aminol . . ." Both the figures, and the area, have expanded remarkably.

In mid-March 1966, some other acquisition activities surfaced: Ashland announced the purchase of the O.K. Tire & Rubber Co. of Littleton, Colorado, for some $6.4 million. O.K. Tire, whose gross sales amounted to some $10 million, sold tires and retread rubber; did tire recapping and repair, serviced machinery and machined wheels for sports cars; had factories in Colorado, Alabama and the State of Washington, as well as franchised dealers across the nation.

Mr. Blazer, interested in everything, was impressed by the O.K. franchises. With astonishment it is noted that he actually stopped at Shank's Tire Service on 20th Street and 4th Avenue in Huntington, West Virginia, to see his old friend Joe Shank.

To his disappointment, Mr. Shank was not there, although his sons were, and Mr. Blazer chatted with them. On his return home, he dictated a letter to Mr. Shank. He had known Mr. Shank's father, and recalled that the older man at one time considered buying Swiss Oil stock.

At about the same time as the O.K. Tire acquisition, discussions were underway with Warren Brothers, of Cambridge, Massachusetts, one of the nation's largest paving contractors, engaged in the construction of asphalt highways, airports and similar ventures. This was a large transaction; Warren Brothers, with gross sales of almost $160 million, cost Ashland Oil over $37 million.

The Warren Brothers negotiation was extremely complex. News of the agreement leaked, and created a flurry of activity among stock market speculators. One result of this was the need to renegotiate; the fit between the two companies—although both are heavily involved in asphalt—was not, in terms of product, as close as surface observation might have indicated. On the Warren Brothers end, the advantages of Ashland seem to have been its larger resources and position; on the Ashland side, the management took a long view. There was an overlap area, but it was not in the places where casual analysis might indicate: it was in expertise.

Through years of manufacturing and supplying asphalt, Ashland had developed a considerable body of knowledge regarding contracting that did not involve its facilities, but certainly enhanced its perceptions.

It was able, therefore, to evaluate a business such as Warren Brothers with more than the average insight, and to appreciate its possibilities; expansion of a company follows lines of knowledge as well as product connections. Warren Brothers seemed an excellent proposition in its own right.

Sandwiched between these acquisitions fell a smaller one, Chemical Solvents, for a little more than $1 million; the firm's name describes its functions.

At the same time that these milestones were passed (each of which would have loomed as large as a mountain only a few years back), the company ordered some $3 million worth of barges and a new towboat for the waterways, tolls or no tolls.

Another corporate purchase, Southern Fiber Glass Products, Incorporated, also for a little more than $1 million, fitted into the jigsaw puzzle because the Ashland Oil petrochemical arms produced the necessary raw materials used by this pleasure boat builder. Mr. Blazer was intrigued by the boats themselves. It can be recalled how he once spent weeks in the offices of ship's architects and marine engineers; it left him with a permanent interest in boat building. The Cobia boats so impressed him he persuaded Don Brewer, president of O.K. Tire, against that gentleman's misgivings, to accept one for the Denver market and it reposed for a considerable period in the headquarters of O.K. Tire.

By the time Derby Day rolled around in May 1966, Ashland Oil had added four fairly large companies to its string and was showing no signs whatever of heavy breathing. The Derby is traditionally the scene of the company's most important, most highly valued event, to which it invites its most important and influential customers.

In the middle of June 1966, as though to remind that the world of Ashland consists of more than corporate maneuvers, Bobby Fry, a worker at the Catlettsburg refinery, opened a valve releasing sulfuric acid into an alkalinization unit where some liquid—probably water—had seeped. The result was an instant explosion and fire; worker Fry was killed—the refineries' first casualty in thirteen years.

Among other damages, the fire destroyed part of the plant electrical system; 300,000 barrels of crude oil were lost; a number of hours of production downtime; and damage to production equipment. As usual in such an emergency, the wonder lies in the fact that the fire was quickly subdued before it could spread, but it

underlined the fact that the oil business, in most of its ramifications, is neither for the careless nor the faint of heart.

Mr. Blazer, who had already begun his search into refinery
operations, persisted in questioning the men at the plant about
this accident until he was satisfied he had solved the eternal question as to what had happened. He wrote the directors several
letters about this occurrence; he also wrote Mrs. Fry, saying that
it was not due to her husband that the accident occurred. He also
chose this time to tell the directors that Bob Yancey had given him
the "green light" to see what he could do about effecting some
economies at the plant.

Among the men that Mr. Blazer enlisted in this newly awakened
interest of his in the refinery was old associate Ben Heath, who
was nearing retirement age, and young John Hall, now Mr.
Blazer's executive assistant.

Mr. Blazer decided the local refinery superintendents should be
given more responsibility. He gave explicit directions to the
various shift foremen and hung, absorbed, on the phone while
they reported back to him the results. Within a few weeks he had
increased the throughput at Catlettsburg conspicuously. Dissatisfied with the fact that some of the newer operators at the plant
could not answer his questions as intelligently as the oldtimers,
he sparked a company training program for refinery operators,
and by the end of June, Catlettsburg was processing 95,000 barrels
a day.

At the same time, the ominous pressure of river tolls—a blanket
over Mr. Blazer's spirits at the best of times—seemed to lift when
discussions began regarding Capline, a giant 42-inch pipeline
project to extend 670 miles from the Gulf Coast to the Midwest.
The project would cost $100 million if completed, and would
effectively remove Ashland's dependence on the rivers if the company could participate for a large enough share.

Orin Atkins and Mr. Blazer, in the midst of the negotiations
they had concluded, had become interested, as were the other
members of the team, in the possibilities of a merger with the
Amerada Petroleum Corporation.

Amerada, one of the nation's largest oil producing firms, had
long been directed by Alfred Jacobsen. Mr. Jacobsen was in his

seventies, and his health was failing; he and Mr. Blazer, through the years, had discussed a possible merger.

Now, through the subterranean channels of big business, where diplomacy plays as important a role as in the affairs of government, Orin Atkins, Mr. Blazer and Everett Wells began to approach Mr. Jacobsen with a view toward combining the two companies.

The other members of the team, apprised of these tentative contacts, were keenly interested; if successful, such a merger would probably be the largest in the petroleum industry in many decades.

On the surface, none of this appeared. Rex Blazer, Orin Atkins, Everett Wells and Bob Yancey flew in the company jet to New York where they described the company's operations to the New York Security Analysts; a few weeks later they made a pilgrimage to a similar group in Baltimore; in October they were due to appear before still another assemblage of analysts in Los Angeles.

By August 1966, Mr. Blazer had succeeded in spurring the Catlettsburg processing ability to 100,000 barrels of crude a day; overall the refineries' throughput had risen to 200,000 barrels a day. Young John Hall, whose mettle Mr. Blazer had been testing in his infinitely various ways, was promoted to general refinery superintendent.

In the fall of 1966, Mr. Blazer's old friend A. A. Stambaugh was posthumously elected to the *National Petroleum News* Hall of Fame, in company with Sam Mosher of Signal Oil & Gas.

In September, Mr. Blazer departed from Ashland accompanied by Bill Gammon, for his annual checkup in Houston. Just before he left, and largely as a result of Mr. Blazer's encomiums, John Hall, at thirty-three, had become the youngest vice president of the company.

In business terms, the company was at a peak that would once have seemed incredible to its leaders: fiscal year's end 1966, net sales had soared to $699 million, net profits to $42 million.

In late November 1966, Mr. Blazer, assisted by Arloe Mayne, composed a broadside on the proposed changes in the state constitution and handed it to two young men on the seventh floor, Ed Monk and John Baker, for distribution; talked to J. Robert Fisher, owner-operator of the Fisher Chemical Co. and Gamma Chemical Co., two firms the team planned to add to the Ashland chemical complex, and made plans to leave for Scottsdale, for a rest.

A few days later, Mr. Blazer was ensconced in Scottsdale and telephoning constantly. Rex Blazer and Bob Yancey, due to speak before the Phoenix Security Analysts, flew out November 29, and arrived at the Westward Ho early in the evening.

They called Mr. Blazer, and he agreed to come into town the following morning and attend the luncheon, and take part in the presentation.

"I was at a party last night," Mr. Blazer told the men on the phone. "I guess I can't take parties any more. But I'll see you tomorrow about 11."

The following morning Bob Yancey waited inside the entrance of the hotel, and eleven o'clock arrived and departed, with no sign of either Mr. Blazer or Charles Anderson, his man. Restless, Rex began to walk around, and saw an elderly man slumped on a bench in the corridor. It took him a few seconds to realize it was Mr. Blazer. Both he and Bob Yancey reached him together.

"Are you in trouble?" Rex asked, but Mr. Blazer was already straightening up. It was an angina pain; he had many every day.

At the luncheon, Mr. Blazer spoke first. He was among friends, and he reminisced, for the topic was his favorite: Ashland Oil and the fine young men of its management. He mentioned Orin Atkins and Everett Wells, who were not present, as well as Rex Blazer and Bob Yancey, who were at the long table. They noticed that at one point he paused and took a nitroglycerin pill; they guessed he had another angina pain.

After the luncheon, Mr. Blazer took Bob Yancey for a drive around Phoenix; the city was his second home. He pointed out its attractions with pride. The two men paused for a drink at the Paradise Valley Country Club, one of his favorite places. Then Charles Anderson drove them to the Blazer home in Scottsdale. Bob Yancey, after a time, left for the airport: he had to go to Houston on other business.

Later in the afternoon Rex Blazer arrived. As he entered, Mrs. Blazer, gracious as always, greeted him and said, "Paul is lying down taking oxygen, but he'll be right in."

By the time Mr. Blazer entered the living room, Rex Blazer's son Richard arrived. Rex was pleased to notice that Mr. Blazer was in excellent form; his conversation sparkled.

"You should be proud of your father," he said to young Dick Blazer. "He's a very hard working man, like all the Blazers."

"You've always worked hard yourself, Paul," Rex said in response.

"I often think," said Georgia Blazer, looking at them, "about the College Inn, where Paul and I ran into Eric Shatford. If it hadn't been for that chance meeting, we would never have known anything about the oil industry . . ."

She drew on her memory, and repeated the conversation. "Shatford said, 'What are you doing, Paul?' and Paul said, 'I sell printing.' And Shatford said, 'I'm in the oil business at Blue Island, in South Chicago. Why don't you come out and sell us some printing?'

"So Paul visited him at Blue Island," she continued, "and that led, after a while, to a job. I wonder," she added, "how many people had their lives changed by that chance meeting?"

That opened the gates of memory, and Paul reminisced. Some of the stories were known to Rex but they were all new to Dick. Altogether, Rex Blazer thought, it was all very pleasant and relaxed.

A few days later, Mr. Blazer felt depressed, and thought he might be catching a cold. He called Dr. Bullington, who said the hospital was crowded. "If you feel worse tomorrow, call me," he said.

The following day, December 7, 1966, Mr. Blazer stepped on the bathroom scales and saw he had gained seven pounds in two days. This meant his body was retaining liquids—for he had not eaten much—a clear sign of danger. Again he called Dr. Bullington, who told him to come to the hospital.

Mrs. Blazer had a lunch date that day that she had kept with some reluctance. An hour and a half later, she received a message to return home. She was only a block or two away, but she suddenly regretted she hadn't taken the car. Almost from the moment she left her friend's house, she found herself running. Finally she stopped a boy driving a little motorized cart, of the sort used to take guests and their luggage to the hotel. He carried her the rest of the way.

When she arrived at the house, Mr. Blazer was on the phone, talking to Mrs. Phyllis Geyer, his secretary in Ashland. Among other matters, he instructed her to help a young man in the company, who had written him a note saying his overtime had been reduced, and asking for help. Such notes—from persons far more eminent—were a regular part of Mr. Blazer's mail.

Finally, he made a call to Orin Atkins, in New York, to discuss the Amerada merger—a very large negotiation indeed—still highly secret and in its initial stages. The distance between the young mans' problem, and the Amerada matter—which involved a possible merger and creation of a truly giant corporation—epitomized Mr. Blazer's range of interest.

Just before they were finally ready to leave, the phone rang again. It was the Houston WATS operator, who was following her standing instruction to call Mr. Blazer every hour, to see if he wanted to use the leased line. "No," he told her. "You needn't call back for a while; I am going away for a few days."

Mrs. Blazer was anxious to get her husband into the hospital, and she suggested that he not take the time to dress, so they got in the car. He was still in his slippers and robe; it was the first time ever that he had failed to dress. Charles Anderson, who usually drove, sat in the back seat. Mrs. Blazer, too nervous to be a passenger, took the wheel. Mr. Blazer, seated beside her on the front seat, was cheerful and reassuring all the way to St. Joseph's Hospital.

That night Mrs. Blazer remained at the hospital: the doctors had told her it might be a critical time. When some of the staff tried to persuade her to leave, she resisted. She was experienced in such places and didn't want her presence to worry him, so she made excuses: it was a long drive, it was late at night . . .

"You can call Charles," Mr. Blazer said. "He'll come for you."

"Why bother him at this hour? I can just sit here in this chair and doze. You don't mind, do you? It won't worry you?"

"Of course not," he said from the bed. "I'd like to have you."

The Sisters sent in pillows, a blanket and a footstool, and she curled up in a chair beside the bed.

As the night lengthened, they talked; they talked about everything under the sun: about their children, about their estate, about the Ashland Oil Company and about the people in the company . . .

He reminded her it was Pearl Harbor Day, and that on the same date, sixteen years before, she was beside him when he was placed under an oxygen tent. Together, they marveled at the wheel of time. At one point he put his hand out for hers, and said, "I am so grateful for my life; for the opportunities I have had . . . so grateful to so many people—and that includes you." She caught his hand and they sat there that way.

Later, Georgia Blazer said it was one of the most beautiful nights she had ever lived.

The next afternoon, a call came from their daughter Doris. She had checked and discovered she could get a reservation and reach Phoenix by midnight. Mrs. Blazer went out to the nurses' desk to answer the call, and noticed, vaguely as one does, a cardiograph flickering away that was connected to Mr. Blazer.

She told Doris that Mr. Blazer seemed to be holding his own, and suggested he might be able to enjoy her visit better a few days later, but the nurse interrupted. *"Let her come, Mrs. Blazer,"* she said. *"I think you need her."*

Doris arrived shortly after midnight and her father regarded her without surprise. He squeezed her hand feebly, and said softly, "I'm glad you're here."

The hours passed and the room was very quiet; after a time the nurse and some Sisters came in and the women stood there watching him. As they watched, the cardiograph in the hall flickered irregularly; the spaces grew long. To the watchers in the room, no change was apparent, but in the hall, the needle stopped.

In Pittsburgh, shortly after ten o'clock in the morning of December 9, 1966, Rex Blazer and Orin Atkins were in a business meeting when a call came through from Johnnie Daniels, Rex's secretary. She told the men that Mr. Blazer had died in Phoenix at 7:30. Then Everett Wells came on the phone. Everett said he would inform the directors, and the men went back to their conference.

When it concluded, they took the Sabrejet back to Kentucky. They arrived in the rain to find Ed Monk and John Baker waiting with cars. They drove back to the office; there were many details to handle. As they drove, they could see that the town had put up its Christmas decorations.

A couple of hours later, Paul Blazer Jr. and Rex Blazer took the jet to Phoenix; there the family sat up and discussed arrangements.

While these discussions were underway, the doctors at St. Joseph recorded all the essential details. Mr. Blazer had, they discovered, suffered further damage to his heart some months before his death; a minor blow had further weakened him. But there was no specific cause of death—just a general debilitation of the system. Then, in the night, the body was moved from the St. Joseph Mortuary to the Whitney & Murphy Funeral Home in Phoenix. From there it was transported to the airport and flown, via Eastern Airlines, first to Bakersfield and thence to Cincinnati. There, a United Ambulance hearse, long and shining, was waiting. The driver and an attendant drove it to Ashland, Kentucky and the Steen Funeral Home. That was on Saturday, December 10, 1966. Mrs. Blazer, arriving at Ashland in the jet at 6:30 the same evening, saw the ceiling lift just before her plane landed, and felt relieved to be safely home.

Meanwhile, the wire service stringer placed his story in Phoenix and newspapers around the country picked it up. It was brief, and referred to Mr. Blazer as a retired executive; gave only outlines of his career. *The New York Times* did not, apparently, have him in their files of the illustrious; their coverage was respectable but exceeded by local deaths; the great weekly news magazines did not mention him at all.

On the seventh floor in Ashland Oil's headquarters, Bob McCowan was commanding general of arrangements from the company end. He sent out telegrams according to lists prepared; made telephone calls to get extra automobiles. John Baker and Ed Monk, serving as his adjutants, contacted dozens of persons; all that night and the next day people came flying into town. The

Governor of Kentucky, Edward T. Breathitt, arrived; the president C. E. Spahr and three other officers from the Standard Oil Company of Ohio; Erling Lunde from Chicago, who had sponsored Mr. Blazer into the Chicago Chapter of the ATO, arrived; Joe Levin of A. G. Becker came down from Chicago; the widows of W. W. Vandeveer and A. A. Stambaugh came; Herschel Blazer and his wife and daughter arrived; Bill Freeman flew up from Florida; Earle Craig came from Pennsylvania; the list goes on and on; the names are familiar.

Saturday evening, only the family and Phyllis Geyer were admitted to Steen's, but on Sunday, December 11, visitors streamed through all day and on into the night.

Monday was very cold; it can grow cold in Ashland beside the river. Sixteenth Street was blocked off between Winchester and Carter; between 75 and 100 automobiles were parked, three abreast, to accommodate the persons who were invited to the funeral. It was by invitation only, because the First Presbyterian Church in Ashland is small. Inside the church, shaped like a sloping fan toward the pulpit, every pew was solid with people; there was great stillness. Not even a rustle was heard as the casket was wheeled in and placed before the pulpit. Then Charlie Evans, 88 years old and still a director of the company, walked down the aisle and stood before it for a moment, saluted silently, and returned to his seat. The Blazer family entered and sat in the pews reserved for them.

The Reverend Heinrich Eiler spoke the eulogy; it was brief. He was a young minister; he had not, like his predecessors, known Mr. Blazer long. He mentioned, briefly, the skeptical spirit of the age, and then, reading from the Old Testament, he discussed the meaning of a good life; a useful life; the life of faith.

The casket was wheeled from the church; the family filed out and people saw just a glimpse of Georgia Blazer's profile; her face marble and her head high.

Finally, the people left the church and entered their automobiles; there were policemen to direct them toward the cemetery and to hold back intrusive traffic; the long, long cortege traveled around the winding roads and up the hills. At the summit, they stood on the little hillocks made by other graves among the headstones, while under a canopy the family and their minister grouped; he spoke his words aloud and they said theirs silently to his spirit, and then the workmen lowered the casket into its final resting place. After all those years, all that work, that bright, quick mind, Paul Garrett Blazer, was gone.

Section Ten—Epilogue

1967

By late 1966, the corporate vessel known as Ashland Oil & Refining Company, after traveling the river for decades, found itself at last in the open sea.

The horizon revealed great new shapes and forms. The crew contained specialists and newcomers of all descriptions. Computers hummed to provide the statistics of navigation. Unknown and uncharted lands lay ahead.

Like the United States itself, the company left all previous experience. From here on, it will help to chart new pathways.

The figures at the end of 1966 were indicators: $723 million in net sales; $44.9 million in net profits.

While the conversations with the executives of Amerada were still underway, Ashland—moving with the speed and assurance of long experience—purchased the Archer Daniels Midland Chemical Company for $65 million.

Conversations with Amerada continued, but after exhaustive studies the merger could not be justified from the financial point of view of the Ashland shareholders and negotiations were terminated.

No man can tell where oil ends and chemicals begin. One third of all chemicals are made from oil. Technologically the two industries intermingle, but there is a great difference in the atmospheres of their separate markets. Oilmen are gregarious, open, competitive but fraternal, adventurous and concerned with improvements in processes. Chemical men concentrate on test tubes and laboratories; are introverts and inventors. Chemicals are products of leapfrogging innovations; their markets shift and sway with every passing day. The two industries today grapple in a no-man's-land where oil seeks to integrate forward and chemicals backward.

With the purchase of ADM Chemicals, Ashland Oil's top men began to coordinate their chemical ventures; formed the Ashland Chemical Company and put Bob Yancey in charge.

At the same time they moved onto the international stage; sought concessions in offshore Java and in Libya—both successfully. When the conversations with Amerada were broken off, the huge ship did not even sway, but sailed on—smoothly and inexorably.

By the end of the fiscal year in September 1967, the net sales were over $800 million, and net profits over $44 million.

The men on the vessel appear in their true guises as master mariners on the business seas. Bill Seaton, Bob Gordon Jr., Bob McCowan, Buck Weaver, John Hall, Bill Gammon, J. D. Hughes and Arloe Mayne are all new vice presidents. They join the men we have followed for so many years, on the quarterdeck.

Histories are not written about the present. But the present stands on the shoulders of the past. Today, Ashland Oil & Refining stands on these shoulders, and views—as do we all—a horizon whose dimensions no man has explored.

Bibliography

1. *Blazer and Ashland Oil,* Joseph L. Massie, University of Kentucky Press, 1960.

2. *Our Times,* Mark Sullivan Vol. 1, 1926; Vol. 2, 1927; Vol. 3, 1930; Vol. 4, 1932; Vol. 5, 1933; Vol. 6, 1935; Charles Scribner's Sons, N.Y.

3. *Speak To The Earth,* Max Miller, Appleton-Century-Crofts, Inc., New York, 1955.

4. *The Growth of Integrated Oil Companies,* John G. McLean & Robert W. Haigh, Harvard University Graduate School of Business Administration, Boston, 1954.

5. *The Chronological History of the Petroleum and Natural Gas Industries,* by James A. Clark with C. A. Warner and H. E. Walton, Clark Book Co., Houston, Texas, 1963.

6. *Oil for Victory,* the Editors of *Look,* McGraw-Hill Book Company, 1946.

7. *Only Yesterday,* Harper & Brothers, 1931; *Since Yesterday,* 1940; *The Big Change,* Harper & Row, 1952—all by Frederick Lewis Allen.

8. *A Man's Reach, the Autobiography of Glenn Clark,* Harper & Brothers, 1949.

9. *Tragedy and Hope, A History of the World in Our Time,* Carroll Quigley, MacMillan Company, 1966.

10. *The Iron Orchard,* Tom Pendleton, McGraw-Hill Book Company, 1966.

11. *Fightin' Oil,* Harold L. Ickes, Alfred A. Knopf, 1943.

(Continued)

Bibliography (continued)

12. *The Politics of Upheaval*, Arthur M. Schlesinger Jr., Houghton Mifflin Company, 1960.

13. *The Vandeveers of North Carolina, Kentucky and Indiana*, Whittet & Shepperson, Richmond, Va., 1960.

14. *My Life and Fortunes*, J. Paul Getty, Duell, Sloan, and Pearce, N.Y., 1963.

15. *Human Behavior in Industry, Industrial Organization and Management Series*, C. L. Morrow, McGraw-Hill, 1955.

16. *The American Petroleum Industry; The Age of Illumination*, Harold F. Williamson and Arnold R. Daum; Northwest University Press, 1959.

17. *The American Petroleum Industry, The Age of Energy;* Harold F. Williamson, Ralph L. Andreano, Arnold R. Daum, Gilbert C. Klose, Northwestern University Press, 1963.

18. *The Little Giant of Signal Hill*, Walker A. Tompkins, Prentice-Hall, 1964.

19. *Wall Street: Men & Money*, Martin Mayer; Harper & Brothers, 1955.

20. *Oil & Gas Journal*, Centennial and other editions.

21. *The 76 Bonanza*, Earl M. Welty and Frank J. Taylor, Lane Magazine & Book Company, 1966.

Index